Housework: Craft Production and Domestic Economy in Ancient Mesoamerica

Kenneth G. Hirth, Editor

Contributions by

Andrew Balkansky
Frances Berdan
Elizabeth Brumfiel
Ronald Castanzo
Michelle Croissier
Veronique Darras
Jason De León
Kenneth Hirth
Jesus Carlos Lascanco Arce
Blanca Maldonado
Deborah Nichols
Christopher Pool
Erick Rochette
Jeffrey Sahagún
Mari Carmen Serra Puche
Edward Stark
Carl Wendt
Randolf Widmer

2009
Archeological Papers of the
American Anthropological Association, Number 19

Housework: Craft Production and Domestic Economy in Ancient Mesoamerica

Kenneth G. Hirth, Editor

SECTION IV: CONCLUSIONS

Housework and Domestic Craft Production: An Introduction

Kenneth Hirth
Penn State University

Households are, without question, the most important social units in human society. They are interactive social units whose primary concern is the day-to-day well being of their kith and kin. Households reproduce themselves and provide their members with the economic, psychological, and social resources necessary to live their lives. Although households vary enormously in size and organization, they are the fundamental social settings in which families are defined and cultural values are transmitted through a range of domestic activities and rituals. Despite their many functions, it is the range and productivity of their economic activities that determine the success, survival and well being of their members. Households are the primary production and consumption units in society and provide the vehicle through which resources are pooled, stored, and distributed to their members. Survival and reproduction is their business and the work they do determines their success.

This volume is about prehispanic households and the diversity of work that their members engaged in both for themselves and the household as a whole. It focuses on one of archaeology's most visible dimensions of housework, how craft production was incorporated into the work regimes of ancient Mesoamerican households. Our interest in this subject stems from the strong disjuncture that exists between ethnographic and archaeological research on households. While archaeologists have a long-standing interest in the household and household archaeology (Ashmore 1981; Blanton 1994; Lohse and Valdez 2004; Sheets 1992; Tourtellot 1988; Webster and Gonlin 1988; Wilk and Ashmore 1988), households are often treated as stable and unchanging domestic entities because of the way we are

forced to study them methodologically. Nothing, of course, could be further from the truth.

Recent ethnographic research has demonstrated that households are highly dynamic and plastic social units that can change their composition and work regimes quickly (Wilk 1984; Wilk and Netting 1984). Robert Netting (1989, 1993) has shown that households are flexible, motivated, and innovative social units that can intensify production on their own initiative when economic conditions permit or require them to do so. While archaeologists recognize that households were important social institutions, they usually are not seen as a source of innovation or long term social change (but see Lohse and Valdez 2004). Archaeologists often turn to models of political economy to explain economic innovation and change (Brumfiel and Earle 1987; D'Altroy and Earle 1985; Earle 1997; Freidel et al. 2002; Rathje 1972, 2002). Archaeology as a discipline has been slow to recognize the dynamic nature of household production for two reasons. The first is the long recognized inability to study households in short-term temporal segments that can be correlated with meaningful episodes within the domestic life cycle (Haviland 1988; Hirth 1993). Without the ability to see the household in "short time" (Smith 1992) it is hard to evaluate how households respond to new conditions as flexible adaptive units. The second is the absence of a dynamic theoretical model of domestic economy and household behavior that archaeologists can use to interpret material remains. It is this second issue that this volume seeks to address.

The dimension of domestic economy examined here is the role of craft production in household work strategies.

ARCHEOLOGICAL PAPERS OF THE AMERICAN ANTHROPOLOGICAL ASSOCIATION, Vol. 19, Issue 1, pp. 1–12, ISSN 1551-823X,
online ISSN 1551-8248. DOI: 10.1111/j.1551-8248.2009.01009.x.

Domestic production in its simplest form is the production of goods for self consumption. This type of *ad hoc* domestic production is **not** the focus of this volume. Instead, we are interested in the production of craft goods intended for exchange and consumption outside of the households where they were produced. This form of activity is often referred to as *specialized* craft production (Clark 1995; Flad and Hruby 2007; Rice 1981; Wailes 1996). It is specialized in the sense that craft goods were produced for a specific purpose beyond the household ranging from exchange and gift giving, to meeting broader social, political or ritual needs. While craft production can occur in a range of domestic, public, and special purpose contexts it is only the former that supplies information about the household economy. In general, archaeologists identify specialized craft production in domestic contexts when production residues from the goods produced exceed what would be expected for auto-consumption and internal use (Clark 1995:279; Clark and Parry 1990:297; Costin 1991, 2001; Inomata 2001:322; Schortman and Urban 2004). This micro-view is a useful and practical way of identifying the production of craft goods in domestic settings that are intended for export.

It is important to consider the broader behavioral dimensions of domestic craft production. What does craft production reflect about the internal economic strategies of households and the wider patterns of household interdependence? A working assumption of this volume is that much of the specialized domestic craft production found in Mesoamerica provided important economic contributions to household subsistence budgets. While craft production may also have provided social status and meaning for individual craftsmen (e.g. Helms 1993), that is not the dimension of craft production explored here. The *raison d'être* of this volume is to bring this economic dimension into sharper focus and explore how craft production for exchange contributed to, and was incorporated into, normal household subsistence activities.

The production of craft goods for exchange was an important and specialized activity within the households where it was practiced. Nevertheless, few of the authors in this volume use the terms specialized or specialization to describe it. The reasons for this are varied, but in the ecological and evolutionary literature specialization is often used to describe the focused exploitation of a narrow suite of resources and/or the intensification of economic activities. While domestic craft production certainly reflects the intensification of work it does *not* represent a narrowing of economic activities from the perspective of individual producers. In Mesoamerica, craft production was often added to domestic work regimes *without* changing its other subsistence activities. As a result its appearance often reflects

an intensification, amplification and diversification of domestic work schedules rather than a narrowing of economic activities within the household.

In a recent publication on craft specialization Flad and Hruby (2002) distinguish between what they call the producer and product views of specialization and this dichotomy is especially appropriate here. If domestic crafting for use outside the household is examined from the *producer view*, then its place as a specialized activity remains murky since it is often only one of several economic activities used to support the household. However, if it is viewed from the *product perspective* then its role as a specialized activity is clear. The product perspective is concerned with where goods are produced and how they circulated throughout society. The presence of a few households producing and supplying craft goods for the society as a whole certainly qualifies as a specialized activity from the perspective of commodity circulation. It reflects a level of economic interdependence between households that Durkheim (1933) characterized as organic solidarity.

Conceptual issues aside, what is examined here is the intensification of domestic crafting for purposes of exchange and its effect on the economic wellbeing of the individuals and households that practiced it. It is a specialized activity for the products produced, but in most cases was only one of a suite of economic activities contributing to the household's overall economic wellbeing.

The Volume Goals

The contributions in this volume all focus on Mesoamerica (Figure 1). That is a practical matter because it is an area with excellent information on domestic craft production. Domestic craft production appears in some areas of Mesoamerica coincident with sedentary agricultural communities (Boksenbaum et al. 1987; Clark 1987; Balkansky et al. this volume) and continues as the main mode of production through the development of ranked and state level society. While the analysis of craft production employs examples from Mesoamerica, the discussion of the domestic economy is applicable to most ancient sedentary societies in both the New and Old Worlds. Small scale domestic craft production for exchange is one of the hallmarks the Mesoamerican economy (Feinman 1999). This is because a range of surplus production including craft goods was bought and sold in marketplaces across many areas of Mesoamerica. This gave households a ready outlet to sell small quantities of craft goods and other resources to consumers at the regional level. Even though households are fully capable of distributing craft goods through trade networks outside the

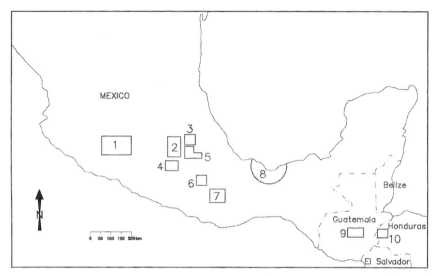

Figure 1. Regions in Mesoamerica discussed in this volume. 1) Tarascan region, 2) Basin of Mexico, 3) Tlaxcala, 4) Morelos, 5) Valley of Puebla, 6) Mixteca Alta, 7) Valley of Oaxaca, 8) Gulf Coast Region, 9) Motagua Valley, 10) Copan region

marketplace (Longacre and Stark 1992; Stark 1992), the marketplace concentrated demand and made it easier for producers to reach potential buyers. While a number of researchers have associated the development of craft production with the appearance of cities and urban markets (Braudel 1986; Childe 1950; Pirenne 1974), craft production in Mesoamerica occurred in both urban and rural areas (Brumfiel 1986, 1987; Hicks 1982). Certainly the marketplace was an important factor in stimulating the expansion of craft production at the regional level, but it does not by itself explain why the locus of production remained in the household.

The goal of this volume is to generate a better understanding of the prehistoric domestic economy and how craft production functioned within it. The central focus of the volume revolves around three primary questions or themes. First, how did crafting fit within the production goals and objectives of prehispanic households and their members? Second, was the production of wealth goods controlled by elites in Mesoamerican societies or were these goods also produced and distributed by non-elite households through independent commercial networks? Finally, are there better ways to conceptualize and model domestic craft production than the traditional approaches currently in use in archaeology? The contributors of this volume address these questions in different ways as they explore the role of craft production in the prehispanic domestic economy.

The first question is concerned with developing a conceptual model of domestic economy that archaeologists can

use to study households using archaeological techniques. This is a fundamental question not just for Mesoamerica, but everywhere where domestic craft production is found in the pre-industrial world. The volume uses a case study approach to examine the range and scale of domestic craft activity and what it tells us about levels of specialization in Mesoamerica. As mentioned above, the marketplace provided opportunities for households to engage in a diverse array of production activities. But domestic craft production developed long before the earliest suspected appearance of marketplaces in Mesoamerica (Blanton 1983; Feinman et al. 1984). While markets certainly increased the opportunity for households to produce and sell craft goods, similar forms of craft diversification also existed in early non-market economies.

The second issue examined here is how domestic craft specialists were integrated into Mesoamerica's broader political economy. Were non-elite artisans involved in fundamental ways or was the political economy a separate sector of the economy as it apparently was in the Andean region (D'Altroy and Earle 1985)? A considerable amount has been written about wealth goods in Mesoamerica and how important they were for elite to control (Aoyama 1999; Ball 1993; Brumfiel and Earle 1987; Demarest 1992; Fash 1991; Inomata 2001; LeCount 1999; Masson and Freidel 2002; Rathje 1972; Reents-Budet 1998). Despite years of research and focused excavations on elite structures in many areas of Mesoamerica, the actual empirical evidence for elite involvement in wealth good production remains meager. The available evidence is beginning to suggest that a significant percentage of wealth goods were produced in non-elite domestic contexts outside of the direct control of Mesoamerican elites. If this is true then the important question becomes how finished goods were concentrated in elite hands through mobilization, tribute, or commercial activities. Although a more comprehensive treatment is not possible here, several of the volume contributions suggest that independent, non-elite artisans were involved in the production of wealth goods both near the source of raw material (Rochette, chapter 13) and far away (Hirth et al., chapter 11). Considering how widespread this practice was and what it may imply about the organization of prehispanic political economy is a separate topic that needs more lengthy treatment than can be attempted here.

The third and final objective of this volume is to develop a better conceptual understanding of domestic economy and where craft production fits within it. Craft production would not be practiced if it did not contribute to the economic goals and/or the social obligations of the household. The primary objective of households is to reproduce themselves and they employ a variety of subsistence strategies in doing so. Minimizing risk and maintaining access to both subsistence and social resources is fundamental to household survival. Diversification of production strategies is one way this is accomplished (Halstead and O'Shea 1989; Messer 1989; Sahn 1989) and craft production provides a means to this end.

Archaeologists also need better concepts for describing and examining the structure of craft production in pre-industrial households. The current concepts of full- and part-time craft production are not useful in this regard and actually hinder, rather than help, our understanding of domestic craft production (Schortman and Urban 2004). The reason is that full- and part-time craft production are defined by the *amount of time* that artisans spend on their work. This says very little about the actual importance of craft production within the households that practice it. Using the same rationale it could be argued that a dedicated Iowa farmer with a 500 acre farm is only a part-time agricultural specialist because farming only takes place during a portion of the year. This of course, is not particularly helpful if we want to understand the structure of Iowa farming and the same is true of domestic craft production. Two alternative concepts, *intermittent crafting* (Hirth 2006) and *multicrafting* (Hirth 2006; Shimada 2007), are developed to describe the range and scale of craft production in domestic contexts. These concepts are evaluated by the contributions in this volume in terms of their utility in describing the structure and operation of different domestic craft industries.

The test of any approach is how well it explains the empirical data to which it is applied. The examination of

different types of domestic crafting within Mesoamerica provides a comparative framework for evaluating how the organization of production differed from activity to activity. Five utilitarian crafts (salt manufacture, bitumen processing, obsidian blade manufacture, ceramic production, and glue processing) are examined from different regions and different time periods alongside the production of four types of wealth goods (jade artifact manufacture, feather working, metallurgy, and generalized lapidary work). Although it is convenient to draw a distinction between utilitarian and wealth goods this is a false dichotomy because a number of these products (i.e. glue, pottery, bitumen, obsidian tools) can be considered to be either utilitarian or wealth goods depending on their use and/or the context where they occur. While glue and bitumen were simple mastics they also were used in the manufacture of high value feather or mosaic devices. No other volume that I know of attempts a regional comparison of different crafts like that attempted here. The reason is not a lack of interest by scholars in comparative research, but rather the difficulty of compiling information on multiple forms of craft production in the same area.

The archaeological data indicate that most types of craft production were carried out at the household level by independent, non-elite craft specialists who worked to support their families and to meet their respective social obligations. Empirical evidence is found for intermittent crafting and multicrafting for both utilitarian and wealth goods at the household level. The evidence for direct elite involvement in, or control over, the production of wealth goods remains limited. Elites certainly were involved in the production of wealth goods for their own use and employed both attached specialists (Widmer, this volume) and consigned production (Hirth et al., this volume) to obtain these goods. What is important is that elites do not seem to have exercised intentional, *restrictive* control over the production of wealth goods at the level of non-elite households. Instead, what appears to have existed was a system of relatively open access to resources (obsidian, jade, metal, etc) at the local level where they were transformed into different products by craftspersons at all levels of the social hierarchy (Rochette, this volume). The advantage of wealth good production by non-elites is that it creates large numbers of artisans at the domestic level with the knowledge and technology necessary to work valued resources. The issue for elites then becomes how to exploit this expertise and to accumulate valued goods through corvee and tribute production levies. This is a different view of wealth good production than has been proposed by scholars who favor a strong, top-down model of elite control over Mesoamerican economy (Chase and Chase 1996; Foias 2002; Manzanilla 1993; LeCount 1999; Santley 1983).

The Case Study Approach

The case study approach and the empirical information that it supplies provides the data to model social interaction and construct theories of cultural development. If conceptual and theoretical issues are not supported by empirical research then it is time to rethink them. This is the approach taken here. Contributors were selected who could evaluate the organization of domestic craft production from as many different perspectives as possible. The examination of different crafts (ceramic, lapidary, flaked stone tool production, etc) was based on the desire to avoid constructing a model of domestic craft production based on idiosyncratic features of only one craft industry. In this regard the distribution of ceramic goods and grinding stones are more constrained by weight and distance factors than are obsidian, textiles or salt.

Instead the case studies examine craft production for both utilitarian items and wealth goods. Even here, however, the examples were chosen selectively to interject as much diversity into the discussion as possible. The utilitarian crafts discussed include bitumen processing (Wendt), salt production (De León), ceramic manufacture (Balkansky et al., Castanzo and Vonarx, Pool), obsidian blade production (Darras, Hirth), and the fabrication of adhesives (Berdan et al.). As might be expected most of these crafts exploited local resources although one case is included where procurement networks were used to obtain raw material from outside the region (Hirth, chapter 6). The wealth crafts include jade carving (Hirth et al., Rochette), feather working as it relates to adhesive use (Berdan et al.), metallurgy (Maldonado), and shell working within the context of generalized lapidary and multicrafting (Widmer). These raw materials moved over greater distances from source to craftsmen than what is found for utilitarian crafts. The cases presented here run the gamut from the use of local materials (Rochette) to resources moving over both intermediate (Widmere, Maldonado) and long distances (Hirth et al.). Together these craft activities encompass a range of different mining techniques (obsidian, copper, clay), resource collection tasks (bitumen, shell, jade, orchids), and processing activities of both organic and inorganic substances.

It would have been nice to have widened the discussion by including additional craft activities like textile working (Halperin 2008; Hendon 2006), ground stone manufacture (Biskowski 2000), pulque making (Parsons and Parsons 1990; Taube 1996) or beekeeping (Dixon 1988). Unfortunately limitations of space did not permit additional cases but it is hoped that future studies will explore these and other examples. Nevertheless, the case studies selected illustrate the creative use of natural resources and technologies by Mesoamerican households to fabricate the items used by prehispanic populations. The widespread knowledge, skill, and ingenuity of prehispanic craftspersons is truly amazing especially when it is viewed in this collective way.

Technological studies indicate that craft production was dynamic and adapted to new situations. Technological adjustments were implemented as a response to changing resource levels or to make production processes faster and more efficient. Changes in the scheduling of production activities were a response to internal conditions within the household and external forces including changes in the level of demand, the organization of distribution networks, and the political and social conditions that affect economic interaction. While contributors to this volume approach this question from the perspective of their individual data, they all recognize the temporal and organizational boundaries in which they were framed. Between the Formative and Postclassic periods Mesoamerican societies were transformed from independent farming villages into ranked and state level societies. Changes in the demands of developing political and economic systems certainly affected the scale and organization of domestic craft production over time.

Following the same desire for breadth of coverage, papers in this volume are distributed widely over both space and time. This also was intentional since we did not want to discover patterns of household crafting that were only unique to the highlands or lowlands and not representative of Mesoamerica as a whole. Areal coverage includes contributions from Central Mexico (Berdan et al., Castanzo, De León, Hirth, Hirth et al.), West Mexico (Darras, Maldonado), the Gulf Coast (Pool, Wendt), the southeastern Maya region (Rochette, Widmer), the Mixteca Alta, and the Valley of Oaxaca (Balkansky et al.). The temporal span covered in these discussions is likewise broad, ranging from 1200 BC to AD 1521 and covering a range of both simple and complex societies. Although it would have been nice to have examples from Classic period settlements in the highlands to complement those from the southeastern Maya region (Rochette, Widmer), there was not enough space to include them.

One of the strengths of the volume is that most of the case studies with the exception of Xochicalco (Hirth) and Copan (Widmer) are examples of domestic crafting carried out in rural communities. This is a strength of the volume because most of the population in pre-Hispanic Mesoamerica lived in rural rather than urban settings. Archaeologists often focus explorations on urban settings because these settlements contain information about important political and religious institutions. Urban settlements, however, frequently are not typical of the society as a whole. Instead they create a range of new economic opportunities for households to adapt to. Urban populations, for example, create concentrated demand for goods and services that provide an opportunity for new crafting and service activities (Jacobs 1969) that may not be typical of the society as a whole. The presence of domestic craft production in rural sites indicates that it was a fundamental feature of Mesoamerican household economy that could be intensified in urban settings. One of the primary objectives of this volume is to more effectively model how craft production was carried out within domestic settings, and in so doing, expand our understanding of the overall household economy. While each of the papers differ in content, they all address in some way whether intermittent crafting and multicrafting provide useful frameworks for describing and modeling the organization of domestic craft production. This hopefully will advance the discussion of how domestic economies were organized in the pre-industrial societies that archaeologists commonly study.

The Volume Contents

The volume is organized into four sections based on the thematic focus of the individual contributions. The first section consists of this introduction and a single paper by Hirth (chapter 2) that examines the nature of the domestic economy and how researchers have addressed these issues in archaeological research. The second and third sections group the contributions into a discussion of utilitarian and wealth good production. The fourth section represents useful critical commentary on the volume's goals and accomplishments by Elizabeth Brumfiel and Deborah Nichols.

The main objective of Chapter two is to expand our theoretical and conceptual understanding of the household economy and the place of domestic craft production within it. It does four related things. It begins by discussing the approaches that archaeologists have used to investigate domestic craft production. The discussion then examines the traditional views of the household and why these fail to help archaeologists in their analysis of domestic crafting. This is followed by the presentation of a more dynamic view of domestic economy and how craft production fits within a diversified household subsistence strategy. The chapter concludes by defining the concepts of intermittent crafting and multicrafting and discusses why they are useful to the discussion of craft activity. These concepts are then evaluated by other authors in the volume as they examine the structure of different domestic craft activities.

The second section of the volume contains seven papers that examine the production of utilitarian goods within domestic contexts. The first paper is by Carl Wendt (chapter 3)

who discusses the evidence for domestic bitumen processing during the Early Formative period in the Gulf Coast region near the Olmec site of San Lorenzo (Figure 1). Bitumen is a natural petroleum product that was collected from seepages in the Gulf Coast and processed into small cakes suitable for use or trade. Bitumen production is difficult to classify in a conventional sense because it has both utilitarian and ritual usages; it can be used as a sealant, mastic, or even as an aromatic incense (Ortíz Ceballos and del Carmen Rodríguez 1994). Bitumen was used and traded throughout Mesoamerica and the evidence from Wendt's research indicates that it was collected and processed on a regular basis by nonelite households who traveled the waterways where natural seepages occur.

The next paper by Jason De León (chapter 4) reexamines salt production in the Basin of Mexico at the time of the Spanish Conquest (Figure 1). The technique used to manufacture salt involved leaching saline soils along the margins of Lake Texcoco and processing the resulting brine into salt. The author questions whether salt production was a full-time craft activity and feels it was probably practiced on an intermittent basis by households that also engaged in the intensive collection of wild resources from the lake. This production used a low quality ceramic type called Texcoco Fabric Marked as evaporator pans and shipping containers for processing and transporting salt during the Postclassic period. Texcoco Fabric Marked was a consumable within the context of salt production and De León suggests it was produced by the same craft individuals who manufactured salt. Since salt production was probably only practiced during the dry season it is an interesting example of intermittent multicrafting where ceramic production is a contingent craft for the salt manufacture.

Research by Andrew Balkansky and Michelle Crossier in chapter 5 examines the evidence for multicrafting in domestic contexts at the Tayata site in the Mixteca Alta around 1000 BC. The evidence indicates that shell, pottery, and flaked stone tools were occasionally manufactured in small amounts in the same residence. While the scale of production remains to be resolved this is an interesting case because it demonstrates that multicrafting is an old rather than a recent pattern in Mesoamerica. They broaden this discussion by examining other examples of intermittent crafting and multicrafting in the Valley of Oaxaca. The results suggest that a wide range of both utilitarian and wealth goods were produced in this way throughout both the Mixteca Alta and the Valley of Oaxaca (Figure 1).

Veronique Darras (chapter 6) examines the social conditions for the adoption and spread of obsidian blade technology into the Tarascan region of West Mexico between 1200–1450 AD (Figure 1). Blade technology was adopted relatively late in West Mexico and is important for our discussions here because it was introduced into the region through rural crafting households without elite sponsorship or supervision. The two rural communities of El Durazno and Las Iglesias are examined, both of which have clear evidence for agricultural terracing associated with households engaged in obsidian craft production. This provides a convincing case that craft production was part of a diversified household subsistence strategy that included normal maize agriculture with the production of obsidian blades. Craft production in this context was intermittent crafting. Households were located relatively close to obsidian deposits and produced blades for export to large urban sites elsewhere in the region. The fact that they introduced a new technology into the region underscores the creativity and resourcefulness of independent artisans and what they could accomplish without elite assistance.

Excavation of four domestic craft production workshops at the site of Xochicalco, Mexico is discussed by Kenneth Hirth in chapter 7. Xochicalco was an urban center with a population of 10–15,000 people that flourished during the Epiclassic period in western Morelos from 650–900 AD (Figure 1). Four domestic workshops were explored where obsidian prismatic blades were produced for distribution within the city and throughout its surrounding region. Excellent conditions of preservation and the identification of *in situ* production deposits permitted a detailed analysis of craft activity inside these households. Evidence for multicrafting was found with indications that 5–7 economic activities were practiced in all four households. These households combined obsidian blade production (all households) with agriculture (all households), obsidian lapidary work (all workshops), chert biface production (1 workshop), itinerant crafting (1 workshop) stucco manufacture (1 workshop), and the importation, finishing and commercial resale of performed obsidian bifaces (all workshops). This evidence underscores the importance of diversification as a primary feature of the normal domestic economy.

The contribution by Christopher Pool in chapter 8 shifts the discussion to ceramic craft production at the sites of Matacapan, Bezuapan, and Tres Zapotes in the Gulf Coast region (Figure 1). Pool's research makes several important observations. First, he demonstrates that most ceramic production occurred as intermittent production in non-elite households during the agricultural dry season. Ceramic production was a seasonal activity that helped diversify the subsistence activities of normal households. Second, evidence for multicrafting is also found that the author associates with periods of increased agricultural risk. Finally, indications of ceramic production are presented for an elite context at Tres Zapotes

that seems oriented toward auto-consumption rather than the production of high status ceramic goods.

Research by Ronald Castanzo in chapter 9 shifts attention from the site to the regional level. The author examines an exceptional situation where 89 ceramic and lime kilns were identified by survey and excavation in a three sq km area in the eastern Valley of Puebla (Figure 1). Ceramic and radiocarbon analyses date most of these features to the Early-Late Formative periods between 1000–150 BC. The size of these kilns reflect small scale production by individual households oriented to meet both local consumer and tribute demands. Although many kilns are concentrated in a small area, this appears to be the result of regional specialization and use over a long term period of time rather than a function of high output production. None of these kilns are at a scale to suggest anything other than intermittent ceramic production at the household level.

The third section this volume contains five papers that examine the production of wealth goods in Mesoamerica. The first of these is a contribution by Frances Berdan, Edward Stark and Jeffrey Sahagún that examines the production and sale of adhesives in the Basin of Mexico (Figure 1) at the time of the Spanish Conquest. Adhesives were manufactured from wild orchids collected from upland forest regions of the Basin of Mexico. They probably were manufactured on an intermittent basis by individuals in Aztec households who either sold them to consumers or to venders who worked in the marketplace. While orchid glues are in one sense a utilitarian commodity, they were also used by Aztec feather workers to make an array of important wealth goods that the authors discuss using data drawn from ethnohistoric documentation, museum research, and archaeological experimentation. These adhesives connect rural agrarian households, who foraged on an intermittent basis in forest environments, with urban artisans who produced the elaborate feather devices so important in Aztec ritual and political life. It is an example of how a simple product like orchid glue can link domestic artisans involved in very different forms of craft production.

This is followed by a paper by Kenneth Hirth, Mari Carmen Serra, Carlos Lascanco, and Jason De León (chapter 11) that examines the nature of lapidary production at Nativitas, Tlaxcala during the Late Formative period (500–100 BC) (Figure 1). Excavations at Terrace 5 identified a small rural household where jade beads were produced from raw material originating from sources along the Rio Motagua more than 1100 km away. Nativitas was a dispersed rural settlement, and although it is located only three km east of the large center of Cerro Xochitecatl, there is no indication that production in this household was directly or indirectly linked to Xochitecatl's influential elites. The available evidence suggests that the household combined small scale intermittent crafting with normal agriculture to create a diversified subsistence base. The use of jade from such a distance source is an intriguing and provocative anomaly and suggests that these independent craftspersons may have received some of their raw material as consigned production from Xochitecatl elite.

The contribution by Randolph Widmer in chapter 12 is one of the best examples of attached craft production ever excavated in Mesoamerica. This research discusses the evidence for craft production recovered from elite structure 9N-8 at Copan, Honduras (Figure 1). Excavations here uncovered evidence for a multicrafting workshop in Patio H that dated to the end of the Late Classic period. This craft activity involved the production of socially and ritually charged wealth objects. It included shell working, lapidary work in jade and other semi-precious materials, obsidian tool production, textile manufacture, and possible feather working. Most of this activity appears to have been aimed at the production of wealth items used by elite members inside the household. While providing a good example of attached production, it challenges our notion that specialized domestic craft production is best measured by concentrations of production debris that exceed auto-consumption and internal use (Clark and Parry 1990:297). Although this research was conducted over two decades ago, it is the first lengthy presentation of the information in English.

The subsequent discussion by Eric Rochette in chapter 13 examines the manufacture of jade beads in the middle Motagua Valley in east-central Guatemala (Figure 1). The Motagua valley was the primary source area for jade and jadeite found in Mesoamerica. Survey and excavation by Rochette have identified two important features about domestic craft production in this region. First, evidence for the manufacture of jade objects can be found in every site within the region. Second, there is no evidence that jade was only worked in elite contexts; jade objects were regularly produced in *all* domestic contexts. While we know that jade was a highly valued material throughout Mesoamerica, it was not a controlled substance in the Motagua valley. Rather, intermittent production appears to have been the norm in this region with most, if not all households engaging in some level of lapidary production. Stratigraphic testing at the site of Guayatan also identified one instance of multicrafting where both obsidian blades and jade beads were manufactured in the same context. What this work convincingly demonstrates is that even jade, Mesoamerica's most precious wealth good, was not controlled at the source. Instead it was worked in all domestic settings throughout the region resulting in high levels of wealth good production.

The last case study in this volume is presented by Blanca Maldonado in chapter 14 who examines the nature of Tarascan metallurgy. The Tarascans were the foremost metallurgists in ancient Mesoamerica and produced an array of wealth goods in copper-bronze alloys. Maldonado explores the ethnohistoric and archaeological evidence from her research on copper-bronze metallurgy in the Tarascan region (Figure 1). This evidence suggests that most copper was mobilized either through the tribute system or some form of direct elite exploitation. Mining, however, appears to have been an intermittent activity for households who cultivated during the rainy season and engaged in mining during the dry season.

The fourth and final section of this volume contains critical commentary and conclusions provided by Elizabeth Brumfiel and Deborah Nichols. This discussion examines the contributions this volume makes to the study of domestic craft production both in Mesoamerica and other areas of the ancient world. The household was the locale where most specialized craft production took place in Mesoamerica. The next chapter examines how the domestic economy was organized and the role that craft production could play within it.

References

Aoyama, Kazuo
1999 Ancient Maya State, Urbanism, Exchange, and Craft Specialization: Chipped Stone Evidence of the Copan Valley and the La Entrada Region, Honduras. Memoirs in Latin American Archaeology, 12. Pittsburgh: University of Pittsburgh Press.

Ashmore, Wendy
1981 Lowland Maya Settlement Patterns. Albuquerque: University of New Mexico Press.

Ball, Joseph
1993 Pottery, Potters, Palaces, and Politics: Some Socioeconomic and Political Implications of Late Classic Maya Ceramic Industries. *In* Lowland Maya Civilization in the Eighth Century A.D. Jeremy Sabloff and John Henderson, eds. Pp 243–272. Washington D.C.: Dumbarton Oaks Research Library and Collection.

Biskowski, Martin
2000 Maize Preparation and the Aztec Subsistence Economy. Ancient Mesoamerica 11:293–306.

Blanton, Richard
  1983 Factors Underlying the Origin and Evolution of Market Systems. *In* Economic Anthropology. Sudi Ortiz, ed. Pp. 51–66. Greenwich: JAI Press.
  1994 Houses and Households: A Comparative Study. Plenum Publishing, New York.

Boksenbaum, Martin, Paul Tolstoy, Garman Harbottle, Jerome Kimberlin, and Mary Nivens
  1987 Obsidian Industries and Cultural Evolution in the Basin of Mexico before 500 B.C. Journal of Field Archaeology 14:65–75.

Braudel, Fernand
  1986 The Wheels of Commerce. New York: Harper and Row.

Brumfiel, Elizabeth
  1986 The Division of Labor at Xico: The Chipped Stone Industry. *In* Research in Economic Anthropology, Supplement No. 2. Economic Aspects of Prehispanic Highland Mexico. Barry Isaac, ed. Pp. 245–279. Greenwich: JAI Press.
  1987 Elite and Utilitarian Crafts in the Aztec State. *In* Specialization, Exchange, and Complex Societies. Elizabeth Brumfiel and Timoth Earle, eds. Pp. 102–118. Cambridge: Cambridge University Press.

Brumfield, Elizabeth, and Timothy Earle
  1987 Specialization, Exchange, and Complex Societies: An Introduction. *In* Specialization, Exchange, and Complex Societies. Elizabeth Brumfiel and Timothy Earle, eds. Pp 1–9. Cambridge: Cambridge University Press.

Chase, Arlen, and Diane Chase
  1996 More than Kin and King: Centralized Political Organization among the Late Classic Maya. Current Anthropology 37:803–810.

Childe, Gordon
  1950 The Urban Revolution. Town Planning Review 21:3–17.

Clark, John
  1987 Politics, Prismatic Blades, and Mesoamerican Civilization. *In* The Organization of Core Technology. J. Johnson and C. Morrow, eds, pp. 259–285. Boulder: Westview Press.

  1995 Craft Specialization as an Archaeological Category. Research in Economic Anthropology 16:267–294.

Costin, Cathy
  1991 Craft Specialization: Issues in Defining, Documenting, and Explaining the Organization of Production. *In* Archaeological Method and Theory. Michael Schiffer, ed.. Pp 1–56. Tucson: University of Arizona Press.
  2001 Craft Production Systems. *In* Archaeology at the Millenium: A Sourcebook. Gary Feinman and T. Douglas Price. eds. Pp 273–327. New York: Kluwer Academic/Plenum.

D'Altroy, Terrence, and Timothy Earle
  1985 Staple Finance, Wealth Finance, and Storage in the Inca Political Economy. Current Anthropology 26:187–206.

Demarest, Arthur
  1992 Ideology in Ancient Maya Cultural Evolution: The Dynamics of Galactic Polities. *In* Ideology and Pre-Columbian Civilizations. Arthur Demarest and Geoffrey Conrad, eds. Pp. 135–158. Seattle: University of Washington Press.

Dixon, Clifton
  1988 Beekeeping in Traditional Agroecosystems in Southern Mexico. College Station: Texas A and M University, Department of Anthropology, Ph.D. Dissertation.

Durkheim, Emile
  1933 The Division of Labor in Society. New York: The Free Press.

Earle, Timothy
  1997 How Chiefs come to Power: The Political Economy in Prehistory. Stanford: Stanford University Press.

Fash, William
  1991 Scribes, Warriors and Kings. London: Thames and Hudson.

Feinman, Gary
  1999 Rethinking our Assumptions: Economic Specialization at the Household Scale in Ancient Ejutla, Oaxaca, Mexico. *In* Pottey and People. James Skibo and Gary Feinman, eds.

Pp. 81–98. Salt Lake City: University of Utah Press.

Feinman, Gary, Richard Blanton, and Stephen Kowalewski
1984 Market System Development in the Prehispanic Valley of Oaxaca, Mexico. *In* Trade and Exchange in Early Mesoamerica. Kenneth Hirth, ed. Pp. 157–178. Albuquerque: University of New Mexico Press.

Flad, Rowan, and Zachary Hruby
2007 "Specialized" Production in Archaeological Contexts: Rethinking Specialization, the Social Value of Products, and the Practice of Production. *In* Rethinking Craft Specializatin in Complex Societies: Archaeological Analysis of the Social Meaning of Production. Zachary Hruby and Rowan Flad, eds. Pp. 1–19. Arlington: Archaeological Papers of the American Anthropological Association, Number 17.

Foias, Antonia
2002 At the Crossroads: The Economic Basis of Political Power in the Petexbatun Region. *In* Ancient Maya Political Economies. Marilyn Masson and David Freidel, eds. Pp. 223–248. Walnut Creek: Alta Mira Press.

Freidel, David, Kathryn Reese-Taylor, and David Mora-Marín
2002 The Origins of Maya Civilization: The Old Shell Game, Commodity, Treasure, and Kingship. *In* Ancient Maya Political Economies. Marilyn Masson and David Freidel, eds. Pp. 41–86. Walnut Creek: Alta Mira Press.

Halperin, Christina
2008 Classic Maya Textile Production: Insights from Motul de San José, Peten, Guatelama. Ancient Mesoamerica 19:111–125.

Halstead, Paul, and John O'Shea
1989 Bad Year Economics. Cambridge: Cambridge University Press.

Haviland, William
1988 Musical Hammocks at Tikal: Problems with Reconstructing Household Composition. *In* Household and Community in the Mesoamerican Past. Richard Wilk and Wendy Ashmore eds.

Pp. 121–134. Albuquerque: University of New Mexico Press.

Hicks, Frederic
1982 Tetzcoco in the Early 16th Century: The State, the City, and the Calpolli. American Ethnologist 9:230–249.

Hendon, Julia
2006 Textile Production as Craft in Mesoamerica: Time, Labor and Knowledge. Journal of Social Archaeology 6:354–378.

Hirth, Kenneth
1993 The Household as an Analytical Unit: Problems in Method and Theory. *In* Prehispanic Domestic Units in Western Mesoamerica. Robert Santley and Kenneth Hirth, eds. Pp. 21–36. Boca Raton: CRC Press.
2006 Modeling Domestic Craft Production at Xochicalco. *In* Obsidian Craft Production in Ancient Central Mexico. Kenneth Hirth ed. Pp. 275–286. Salt Lake City: The University of Utah Press.

Inomata, Takeshi
2001 The Power and Ideology of Artistic Creation: Elite Craft Specialists in Classic Maya Society. Current Anthropology 42:321–349.

Jacobs, Jane
1969 The Economy of Cities. New York: Random House.

LeCount, Lisa
1999 Polychrome Pottery and Political Strategies in Late and Terminal Classic Lowland Maya Society. Latin American Antiquity 10:239–258.

Lohse, John, and Fred Valdez
2004 Ancient Maya Commoners. Austin: University of Texas Press.

Longacre, William and Miriam Stark
1992 Ceramics, Kinship, Space: A Kalinga Example. Journal of Anthropological Archaeology 11:125–136.

Manzanilla, Linda
1993 The Economic Organization of the Teotihuacan Priesthood: Hypotheses and Considerations.

In Art, Ideology and the City of Teotihuacan. Janet Berlo, ed. Pp. 223–240. Washington D.C.: Dumbarton Oaks Research Library and Collections.

Masson, Marilyn, and David Freidel
2002 Ancient Maya Political Economies. New York: AltaMira Press.

Messer, Ellen
1989 Seasonality in Food Systems: An Anthropological Perspective on Household Food Security. *In* Seasonal Variability in Third World Agriculture. David Sahn, ed. Pp. 151–175. Baltimore: John Hopkins University Press.

Netting, Robert
1989 Smallholders, Householders, Freeholders: Why the Family Farm Works Well Worldwide. *In* The Household Economy. Reconsidering the Domestic Mode of Production. Richard Wilk ed. Pp. 221–244. Boulder: Westview Press.
1993 Smallholders, Households, Farm Families, and the Ecology of Intensive, Sustainable Agriculture. Stanford: Stanford University Press.

Ortíz Ceballos, Ponciano and Maria del Carmen Rodríguez
1994 Los Espacios Sagrados Olmecas: El Manati, un Caso Especial. *In* Los Olmecas en Mesoamerica. John Clark ed. Pp. 69–91. Mexico City: El Equilibrista and Citibank.

Parsons, Jeffrey and Mary Parsons
1990 Maguey Utilization in Highland Central Mexico. An Archaeological Ethnography. Ann Arbor: University of Michigan, Museum of Anthropology, Anthropological Papers No. 82.

Pirenne, Henri
1974 Medieval Cities. Their Origins and the Revival of Trade. Princeton: Princeton University Press.

Rathje, William
1972 Praise the Gods and Pass the Metates: A Hypothesis of the Development of Lowland Rainforest Civilizations in Mesoamerica. *In* Contemporary Archaeology. Mark Leone, ed. Pp. 29–36. Carbondale: Southern Illinois University Press.

2002 The Nouveau Elite Potlatch: One Scenario for the Monumental Rise of Early Civilizations. *In* Ancient Maya Political Economies. Marilyn Masson and David Freidel, eds. Pp. 31–40. Walnut Creek: Alta Mira Press.

Reents-Budet, Dorie
1998 Elite Maya Pottery and Artisans as Social Indicators. *In* Craft and Social Identity. Cathy Costin and Rita Wright, eds. Pp. 71–89. Anthropological Paper, 8. Washington D.C.: American Anthropological Association.

Rice, Prudence
1981 Evolution of Specialized Pottery Production: A Trial Model. Current Anthropology 22:219–240.

Santley, Robert
1983 Obsidian Trade and Teotihuacan Influence in Mesoamerica. *In* Highland-Lowland Interaction in Mesoamerica: Interdisciplinary Approaches. Mary Miller, ed. Pp 69–124. Washington D.C.: Dumbarton Oaks Research Library and Collection.

Schortman, Edward, and Patricia Urban
2004 Modeling the Roles of Craft Production in Ancient Political Economies. Journal of Archaeological Research 12:185–226.

Sheets, Payson
2002 The Ceren Site: A Prehistoric Village Buried by Volcanic Ash in Central America. Ft. Worth: Harcourt Brace College Publications.

Shimada, Izumi
2007 Craft Production in Complex Societies: Multicraft and Producer Perspectives. Salt Lake City: University of Utah Press.

Smith, Michael
1992 Braudel's Temporal Rhythms and Chronology Theory in Archaeology. *In* Archaeology, Annals, and Ethnohistory. A. Knapp, ed. Pp. 23–34. Cambridge: Cambridge University Press.

Stark, Miriam
1992 From Sibling to Suki: Social Relations and Spatial Proximity in Kalinga Pottery Exchange.

Journal of Anthropological Archaeology 11:137–151.

Taube, Karl
1996 Los Origines de Pulque. Arqueología Mexicana 4:71.

Tourtellot, Gair
1988 Developmental Cycles of Households and Houses at Seibal. *In* Household and Community in the Mesoamerican Past. Richard Wilk and Wendy Ashmore eds. Pp. 97–120. Albuquerque: University of New Mexico Press.

Wailes, Bernard, ed.
1996 Craft Specialization and Social Evolution: In Memory of Gordon Childe. Philadelphia: Museum of Archaeology and Anthropology, University of Pennsylvania.

Webster, David, and Nancy Gonlin
1988 Household Remains of the Humblest Maya. Journal of Field Archaeology 15:169–190.

Wilk, Richard
1991 Household Ecology. Economic Change and Domestic Life among the Kekchi Maya in Belize. Tucson: University of Arizona Press.

Wilk, Richard, and Wendy Ashmore
1988 Household and Community in the Mesoamerican Past. Albuquerque: University of New Mexico Press.

Wilk, Richard, and Robert Netting
1984 Households: Changing Forms and Functions. *In* Households. Robert Netting, Richard Wilk and Eric Arnould, eds. Pp. 1–28. Berkeley: University of California Press.

2

Craft Production, Household Diversification, and Domestic Economy in Prehispanic Mesoamerica

Kenneth Hirth
Penn State University

Households are the most important social units in human society. This was emphasized in the volume's introductory essay but is worth repeating here. Households are where a society's members are born, nurtured, fed, and most often educated; in premodern societies they were where most goods were produced, pooled, and consumed. The *domestic economy* refers to what households do and how they were organized to meet their physical and social needs. It involves what work was done and how goods were distributed to, and consumed by household members. The domestic economy always has been the backbone of society and the development of political complexity is largely a history of how household labor, and/or the resources produced in the domestic economy, were mobilized by other institutions and the elite who supervised them (Johnson and Earle 1987). Households were important and they engaged in a range of subsistence activities for the benefit of their members.

Archaeologists have had a long standing interest in both households and craft production. The interest in households is due to their utility as a unit of archaeological analysis. Houses are things that archaeologists can excavate, so it is natural that the household has become an important focus of study. The subject of craft production is also of interest to archaeologists because its appearance implies a level of economic interdependence between segments of society (Childe 1934; Durkheim 1933). Archaeologists often examine household organization and craft production separately rather than discussing them together as is done here (but see Feinman and Nicholas 2000; Sheets 2000). Most often it is when houses are excavated and contain evidence for craft production that the two topics are discussed together

(e.g. Arnold 2001; Flannery 1976; Santley 1993; Winter and Pires-Ferreira 1976)

The view adopted here is that small scale specialized craft production was an important component of most premodern domestic economies around the world. While not as important as the production of food, its significance for households grew in proportion to the economic institutions that supported inter-household exchange and resource exploitation. In Mesoamerica this culminated with the development of the marketplace which enabled a significant expansion in domestic craft production. Most craft production in the ancient world took place in domestic contexts and a critical question is whether current archaeological concepts are adequate for understanding why this was the case. I believe they are not. Current concepts of full- and part-time craft production do little to further our understanding of the function and structure of domestic craft production in either rural or urban settings. The analytical focus should not be on the amount of *time* spent on craft production, but rather on the economic *strategies* that domestic units employed, and how craft production was integrated into the domestic economy.

This essay has three goals. First, it examines how archaeologists typically characterize craft production and whether these approaches are useful for understanding production in domestic contexts. Theoretical assumptions and analytical categories often influence how archaeological data are interpreted; unfortunately current approaches impede rather than amplify our understanding of domestic craft production. Second, it examines the structure of the domestic economy and how craft production fits within it. The

ARCHEOLOGICAL PAPERS OF THE AMERICAN ANTHROPOLOGICAL ASSOCIATION, Vol. 19, Issue 1, pp. 13–32, ISSN 1551-823X,
online ISSN 1551-8248. DOI: 10.1111/j.1551-8248.2009.01010.x.

concern here is in identifying the economic strategies of domestic units, how they operate, and why craft production is compatible with them. Third, it develops several alternative conceptual categories to discuss domestic craft production. This discussion advocates thinking of domestic craft production in terms of *intermittent* and *multicrafting* activities because they provide a better framework for describing, evaluating, and understanding the role of craft activities in the domestic economy. These categories describe craft activity in more dynamic terms and are better informed by ethnographic data. The utility of these concepts is evaluated by contributors throughout the remainder of the volume.

Archaeological Characterizations of Domestic Craft Production

The current view of domestic craft production in archaeology is the result of two conditions: (1) an incomplete understanding of how households operate, and (2) a failure to develop economic concepts appropriate for positioning craft production within the domestic economy. Part of this problem is that archaeologists have used craft production more as a measure of cultural complexity than a topic worthy of separate study. Another part of the problem is the limited treatment of households in the ethnographic literature. Households, when they are discussed, are usually described empirically rather than analyzed comparatively for common forms of organization. The result is an incomplete view of the domestic economy and the strategies that households use to exploit their environments. In the process, archaeologists often characterize households as stable, small-scale and self-sufficient producers that depend on motivations from outside forces to initiate change.

Three common misconceptions are identified here that influence the way that archaeologists view domestic craft production. These include: (1) classifying craft production by the amount of time worked by the artisan and characterizing full-time production as a more specialized form of crafting than part-time production, (2) the assumption that domestic craft production has low productivity and returns to scale because of limited household labor, and (3) that elite controlled the production of wealth objects because of the role that these goods played in the operation of premodern political economies.

1) Full- and Part-time Craft Production

Full- and part-time production is the most common way that archaeologists characterize differences in production intensity (Costin 1991; Feinman and Nicholas 2000). Emile

Durkheim (1933) and Gordon Childe (1934) both argued that full-time specialization represented an increase in the organic solidarity and cultural complexity of a society. Their focus was on the amount of time the artisan spent on craft production. For Durkheim, the importance of craft production lay in the interdependence that it created between social segments for the goods and services that they consumed. For Childe, an important hallmark in the evolution of society was the appearance of full-time craftsmen who were supported by agricultural surplus. The point of comparison for both these scholars was the level of interdependence associated with full-time craft production in industrial society.

This view continues today with full-time craft production often interpreted as having a greater level of both skill and specialization. Part-time production, in contrast, is often associated with small scale societies and less developed economic systems (Costin 1999; Feinman and Nicholas 2000). In these contexts, domestic craft production is usually a part-time activity because of the discontinuous nature of work and a primary commitment of household members to the production of food. *Full-time craft production* has been characterized as specialized, skilled, able to employ economies of scale, and representative of developed economies (Childe 1934; Peacock 1982; Santley et al. 1989; Torrence 1986:45–6). Conversely, *part-time production* is frequently described as unspecialized, less skillful, organized at the domestic level, lacking economies of scale, and found in less developed economies. While it is true that domestic craft production is often a part-time enterprise, its characterization as being less skilled, unspecialized, and associated with lower levels of development is not correct (Clark and Parry 1990; Feinman and Nicholas 2000; Torrence 1986:45).

There are two fundamental problems with the full- and part-time production dichotomy. First, the amount of time artisans spend in their crafts is *not* an accurate or useful measure of the economic system in which they work. Mesoamerica had a developed market system at the time of the Spanish Conquest and the vast majority of craft goods that moved through it were produced in domestic contexts (Berdan 1982; Feinman 1999; Hicks 1987). Better measures of economic complexity are the quantity and diversity of goods produced and consumed at the household and institutional levels (Beinhocker 2006; Gonlin 1994). Economic consumption can be high even under conditions where *all* craft goods are produced in domestic contexts by part-time producers. Whether this is possible depends upon the number of households engaged in craft production and how widely and efficiently goods are distributed through regional market systems.

A second problem with the full- and part-time production dichotomy is that it does not focus on the important issue of how craft production fits into domestic contexts. Without question, part-time production is generally *more compatible* with the production goals and needs of practicing craftsmen than is full-time production. This has to do with business risk. Full-time production results in considerable *risk* to craftsmen because of the cyclical nature of demand and the ability of consumers to delay craft purchases. Under these conditions part-time production can predominate even if consumer demand is capable of supporting full-time specialists. When the risk to craftsmen is high, part-time production will be more stable and will provide more opportunities for economic growth and diversification than full-time specialization. Part-time craft production is more compatible with how the household economy is organized (Hagstrum 1999, 2001; see below). It was this compatibility that made domestic craft production the backbone of the ancient Mesoamerican economy (Feinman 1999).

2) The Low Productivity of Domestic Craft Production

One of the challenges that households face is how to mobilize sufficient labor to produce enough resources to meet both their physical needs as well as to maintain social relations. Chayanov (1966) recognized that large households were more productive than small ones. In addition large households are able to mobilize more adult labor which makes work more efficient, safer, and more rewarding for its members (Durrenberger 1984; Wilk 1991:183). Large households make it possible for women to share child rearing and cooking tasks and to engage in a broader array of both subsistence and craft activities within the household (Clark 1989; Wilk 1991). This is especially critical when household labor demands are inelastic and multiple subsistence tasks must be carried out simultaneously (Wilk 1991:182). Household labor demands often require large labor pools which, depending on the type of work involved, may promote the appearance of inter-household labor exchanges or communal work (Wilk 1991:187; Sahlins 1972). It is the limitation of domestic labor that led neoclassical scholars to suggest that households could not intensify production (but see Netting 1989, 1993). From this perspective it was only when labor was freed from subsistence agriculture that more efficient forms of industrial production become possible (Waters 2007:29).

The scale of craft production in domestic settings is directly related to the available labor. Crafting households benefit from having a large and efficient work force. In addition to craft work, households need to procure raw materials, make tools, market, and transport finished goods to the intended consumers. It is for this reason that households

involved in craft production often are larger than households in the same society that are engaged in agriculture (Loucky 1979; Medick 1976).

Important for this discussion is that research on contemporary craft production has often argued that the returns from domestic crafting are less productive than the returns from agriculture. Rice (1987:172) has observed that artisans engaged in pottery production are often at the bottom of the socio-economic ladder and are less well off than households engaged in traditional farming. Among the Fulani, the hallmark of a successful potter is to have made enough money that they can buy land and give up manufacturing ceramics (David and Henning 1972)! The same is true of ethnic weavers in Otavalo, Ecuador who use the proceeds of domestic crafting to expand household agricultural holdings (Salomon 1973). Likewise, Arnold (1978:330, 1985) has argued that ceramic production is often found in areas where agricultural land is scarce, suggesting that craft production may operate as a failsafe activity that households can employ when agricultural land is in short supply or traditional agriculture is no longer possible. While this certainly was true in certain circumstances, it does not hold as a general principle. If it did we would expect to find that craft production: (1) was positively correlated with areas of high population density, (2) would not appear until after population densities had risen, and (3) occurred more frequently in poor agricultural areas or in areas under stress. To my knowledge the archaeological data do not support any of these three propositions.

While households *may* take up crafting as a response to stress, the archeological data indicate that this was *not* the primary cause behind the origins of craft production in Mesoamerica. Craft production occurs early in Mesoamerica, in many different environments and well before good agricultural land was in short supply. Well crafted, specialized ceramic vessels, figurines, and other items with social, ritual, and mortuary functions probably were produced by specialized craftsmen as early as the Early Formative period (ca 1000 BC) (Clark and Blake 1994; Di Castro Stringher 1997). Obsidian prismatic blades almost certainly were being produced by craft specialists in Central Mexico by 1000 BC (Boksenbaum et al. 1987). While few craft areas have been identified for the Early Formative period (but see Balkansky and Crossier, this volume; Castanzo, this volume; Wendt this volume), good evidence exists for obsidian workshops during the Middle Formative at Chalcatzingo, Morelos (Burton 1987; Hirth 2008) and possibly La Yerbabuena, Veracruz (Cobean 1997). The Mesoamerican data indicate that craft production developed hand-in-hand with sedentary village life, well before population pressure or shortages in agricultural land would have created resources stress.

3) *Elite involvement in craft production*

A number of scholars have argued that wealth goods played an important role in constructing socio-political relationships in emerging complex societies (Brumfiel and Earle 1987; Clark and Blake 1994; D'Altroy and Earle 1985; Frankenstein and Rowlands 1978; Hayden 2001). Elite used wealth goods for individual and corporate aggrandizement in feasts, ritual ceremonies, mortuary activities, building alliances, as well as in general social networking (Dalton 1977; Drucker and Heizer 1967; Hayden 2001). In tribal and chiefdom societies the mobilization of wealth goods was a fundamental feature of the political economy. Available ethnographic information indicates that emerging leaders used their entrepreneurial skills to procure wealth goods either by producing them, obtaining them through trade, or mobilizing them through individual social networks (Hayden 2001; Malinowski 1922; Pospisil 1963; Strathern 2007).

Wealth goods, whether in the form of beads, necklaces, blankets, decorative apparel, feather arrays or other symbolic forms, are all craft goods. In individual-centered political networks (Blanton et al. 1996) there is no such thing as too many valuables since all wealth goods can be strategically used and kept in circulation through the endless cycle of public feasting, social prestations, and individual network building. One way that elite could obtain wealth items was by sponsoring craft specialists who produced goods exclusively for them (see Widmer, this volume). They could do this by contracting their manufacture with existing specialists or by producing them inside their own households (Clark and Parry 1990; Lass 1998; Lloyd 1953:40–41; Malinowski 1922; Peregrine 1991). Archaeologists often refer to the production of craft goods within elite households as attached production (Ames 1995; Clark 1987; Costin 1991, 2001; Earle 1981; Lass 1998; Spielman 1998). The advantage is that it provides the elite with direct control over the supply of wealth goods.

Attached production certainly was an important component of Mesoamerican economy at least in the later state economies of Mesoamerica. Examples include Montezuma's sponsorship of Aztec feather workers (Katz 1966:53; Sahagún 1959:91), the manufacture of trade goods for Aztec pochteca (Sahagún 1959; Nichols 1994:186), and elite crafting among the Maya at Copan (Widmer, this volume), Aguateca, (Inomata 2001; Emery and Aoyama 2007), Motul de San Jose (Foias 2002), and possibly other sites (Ball 1993; Reents-Budet 1998). While elite were always interested in wealth and power, we must *not* credit them with too much involvement in the economy before we understand how production and distribution systems were organized in general terms. In other words, we must remember that inde-

pendent craft specialists were equally, if not more important in these societies and we must not overestimate the role of elite in directing economic activity (cf McAnany 1989; Potter and King 1995; West 2002). The questions that need to be answered are: (1) how important was attached versus independent production in the society's political economy, and (2) how closely did it conform to organizational strategies used by *all* households to intensify production?

We know that elite were large scale consumers and stimulated the production of both utilitarian and wealth goods when the distribution of these goods reinforced their social position (Clark 1987; D'Altroy and Earle 1985; Janusek 1999). One way that elite could obtain specialized goods was through periodic consignments with craft specialists (Clark and Parry 1990). While some may construe consigned production to be a form of attached specialization (Ames 1995:175; Clark and Parry 1990), I do not for the same reason that I do not consider my plumber, the neighbor boy who mows lawns, or a part-time, retired handyman to be attached to my household simply because I occasionally use their services. Consigned elite production is important because it underscores the existence of *independent* artisans who have the expertise to produce elite goods. It is not the temporary linkage of artisans to elite households through production consignments that is important, but rather that independent specialists existed in these communities as a precondition for their involvement in production for the elite.

The challenge for archaeologists is to explain the emergence of craft production and craft specialists in Mesoamerica. The presence of well made ceramic goods used in feasting, mortuary offerings, and long distances trade (Blomster et al. 2005; Clark and Blake 1984; Clark and Gosser 1995; Neff et al. 2006), suggests that craft production was already present by the Early and Middle Formative periods, long before agricultural land was in short supply. Craft production was a domestic activity, and at this stage finished products almost certainly moved through non-market forms of exchange. Given these conditions the key question is how did craft production fit within normal domestic production.

Households and Crafting: The Traditional View

While archaeologists have long recognized the importance of the household as a unit of study, cultural anthropologists have not. The reason for this is twofold. First, early ethnographers believed that larger kin groups (e.g. the lineage, clan, phratry) were the basis for social organization in early societies and that households only emerged with the breakup of these systems (cf. Morgan 1877; Engels 1972;

Smith et al. 1984). Second, the household was viewed as a transitory group whose form was dependent on larger patterns of descent, marriage, and residence rules found in society (Netting et al. 1984:xi). Cultural Anthropology viewed households more as a dependent variable and a residual category of other processes rather than as a topic worthy of separate study. It was not until the 1980s that households were "rediscovered" in cultural anthropology and a significant body of theoretical literature emerged to reshape our thinking about this fundamental human institution (Arcury 1982; Netting et al. 1984; Wilk 1989b, 1991). The feedback with archaeology was immediate and helped to spawn the current interest in household archaeology (Wilk and Rathje 1982; MacEachern et al. 1989; Santley and Hirth 1993; Wilk and Ashmore 1988).

This delayed interest in the household has produced a deficiency in both empirical and theoretical literature on how households operate (Wilk 1989a) and adapt to outside opportunities (Wilk 1991). The topics of family and household are generally omitted from traditional ethnographies or are so sketchily presented that they misrepresent their structure and operation. What this has created is a caricature of the household as a passive and powerless institution. This misrepresentation has developed slowly over time, more as a result of benign neglect rather than malicious intent. While unintentional, the traditional view of the household nevertheless colors the way archaeologists conceptualize and treat households in their analyses.

The traditional view of the household rests on five faulty assumptions about their function and operation. The first of these is that households are conservative, stable, and non-adaptive social units. One only needs to examine how households have been radically transformed over the past fifty years to recognize that this was never the case. Households are highly plastic and adapt quickly to new social and economic opportunities. The problem of defining the household in concrete terms (Hammel 1984; Clark 1989; Wilk 1991) is a function of the diversity produced by household adaptation.

Second is the assumption that households are self-sufficient economic units that orient their production to internal consumption rather than external exchange. The basis for this view is the Marxian contrast of production for use in traditional society, with production for exchange in capitalist economies (Sahlins 1972:83–85). As most archaeologists know, there never was a completely self-sufficient household; while self-sufficiency was an ideal goal, no household ever achieved it. In fact, to achieve self-sufficiency would have deprived households of many basic resources and raised their level of risk to the point of jeopardizing their very survival.[1] Similarly as we know from many ex-

amples, households regularly produce goods to meet social obligations outside the household.

A third erroneous assumption is that traditional households lack the ability to intensify production and require institutional assistance to do so. This was the perspective of much neo-evolutionary theory up through the 1970s which favored centralized political authority as the engine behind culture change (Carneiro 1970, 1974; Wittfogel 1957). We now know that this view is incorrect and that households are capable of sustainable intensification. This is the essence of the smallholder adaptation and the ability of households to intensify production under conditions of limited agricultural land (Netting 1990, 1993; Stone 1986).

The fourth fatal assumption is that households frequently do not produce a surplus (Harris 1959). This is linked to three factors: the concept of self-sufficiency, the idea that households are unable to intensify production, and the fact that some households may knowingly produce below required subsistence levels (Sahlins 1972). Although household production levels may vary, many regularly produce surpluses to meet social needs and to protect themselves from subsistence risk (Allan 1965; Hayden 2001; Oshea 1989).

The fifth and final misrepresentation of households is that they actively seek to minimize individual and group work. This belief is based on Chayanov's valuable research on household size and work (Durrenberger 1984) and Sahlin's (1972) characterization of the original affluent society. Chayanov was correct that large families reduce the consumer/worker ratio and lower the amount of work required per member. But that does not mean that large households work less. In fact large households may work more since they can deal more efficiently with multiple simultaneous (inelastic) labor demands within the annual work cycle (Wilk 1991:182–3). Gender studies have shown that shared child care enables women to expand the scope of household work by engaging in trade, craft activity, and work in different service areas (Clark 1989).

These five faulty views of the household are a product of not looking inside the household to model the actual activities that its members engage in. These problems are amplified when the focus shifts to the organization of craft production at the household level.

Frequent Misrepresentations of Craft Production

The traditional view of the household as a passive and inefficient unit of production has led to several misrepresentations about the structure of domestic craft production. There are four general crafting fallacies, and although several were mentioned above because they pertain to the household, they bear repeating because of the way they have jointly affected the direction of archaeological research.

The first and most fundamental of these crafting fallacies is that domestic craft production is a part-time, low volume affair that is symptomatic of an underdeveloped economy. This characterization comes to us from Childe (1934, 1962) and Durkheim (1933), who were more concerned with developing an evolutionary measure of cultural progress than they were in understanding the structure of domestic craft production per se. It is true that much domestic craft production occurs on a part-time basis and has a lower total output than industrial forms of production. But that does not mean that domestic craft production is symptomatic of an underdeveloped economy. Domestic craft production was the foundation of all the ancient civilizations from China to Rome to Mesoamerica (Berdan 1982; Lee-fang Chien 2004:71, 173; Peacock 1982; Trigger 2003; Wright 1998). It was also the foundation for complex market systems developed throughout antiquity. Volume of production is a function of the availability of raw materials, the demand for the craft goods, and how production is organized within society. Even sporadic, low volume craft production can meet the needs of a large consumer base if the number of producing units is large. Domestic craft production does not by itself indicate an underdeveloped economy.

A second misconception is that domestic craft production was focused on the manufacture of utilitarian goods, the majority of which were used by non-elite households. This view is based on the idea that domestic craft production was a natural extension of household self-sufficiency. From this perspective the origin of craft production lies with a few talented artisans who expanded production beyond their own consumption needs to produce goods for gifts and limited exchange (Tosi 1984). Whether this view is accurate is less important than the implication that domestic craft production would be confined to the production of only utilitarian goods. There is nothing to keep non-elite households from making wealth goods if the resources are available to do so. In fact, wealth goods are regularly made by non-elite members of society in tribal and chiefdom societies (Ames 1995; Malinowski 1922; Pospisil 1963). That non-elite households should be confined only to the production of utilitarian goods is an artifact of neo-evolutionary thinking rather than ethnographic fact.

The third and fourth assumptions are causally linked. The third assumption is that domestic craft production has a low marginal productivity. The fourth assumption is that because of low productivity, craft production is only adopted when more productive subsistence options cannot be practiced. The example mentioned above is that ceramic crafting is only adopted when agricultural land is in limited supply and farming is not available as a subsistence alternative (Arnold 1985). It is true that the productivity of domestic craft production is often low in both absolute and marginal terms. But that does not mean that it is not important to the domestic budgets of households that practice it. Furthermore, the notion that craft production is a default option for households under stress fails to recognize the entrepreneurial initiative of crafting households who forego agricultural opportunities and enter craft production in response to expanding demand or marketing opportunities (Stolmaker 1996; Cohen 1998; Meisch 2002). There are multiple reasons why craft production may be adopted including the flexibility it offers for work (Hagstrum 2001), the pivotal role craft goods play in gift economies (Dalton 1977; Lee 1993), and the personal fulfillment that crafting can supply the artisan (Helms 1993). The incentives for crafting are multiple and may just as often originate within the household as in external conditions.

Households and the Domestic Economy: A Dynamic View

The traditional view of the household does not expand our understanding of how domestic economies were organized, much less why domestic groups engaged in small scale craft production. The traditional view often characterizes household activities including craft production as a *secondary* result of other processes. What is often overlooked is that households frequently intensify production on their own, for internal reasons and without external pressure (Netting 1989, 1991). To understand the role of domestic craft production in Mesoamerica and elsewhere we need to identify the five common features of all household economic strategies.

The first of these is the most obvious: households, however structured, are the basic units of demographic reproduction and subsistence within society (Wilk and Netting 1984; Wilk and Rathje 1982). Survival and reproduction is their business and households actively utilize the resources around them to ensure their success. To this end, household labor is deployed to produce or procure needed resources. The primary economic goal of households is to enhance their economic well being, which results in healthier and larger households with more labor to reinvest in production activities (Wood 1998).

Second, households are not passive in their subsistence pursuits. Instead they are highly motivated to meet resource needs and grow because failure to do so threatens their very survival. There are few social safety nets in pre-industrial societies and as a result households are careful to ensure that adequate resources are available for household members. They anticipate their needs and produce to meet them. Despite the presence of underproduction in some households (Sahlins 1972), most households gear production to meet subsistence needs during years of economic shortfall. The result during normal years is the production of surplus available for normal consumption, intra-community sharing, and inter-group feasting (Allan 1965:38; Halstead 1989). Households intensify production to improve individual economic well being as well as to improve their social status within the community (Hayden 2001). They expand household labor through natural reproduction, recruitment, or the formation of reciprocal labor networks as desired or needed (Wilk 1991). In pre-industrial societies most work is planned, organized, and implemented within the framework of the household.

Third, self-sufficiency is an important principle of the domestic economy (Gudeman 2001:43), but it would be incorrect to assume that households are actually self-sufficient or that it is advantageous for them to be so. Self-sufficiency is the normal goal of households. They regularly consume food that they produce and normally do not rely on other households or the market for much of the food they need to survive. Nevertheless, household members optimize production and know how to meet their needs even if this involves exchanging a portion of their normal production for goods that they do not, or cannot produce. Household survival is enhanced by the development of multiple resource strategies and cross-cutting provisioning networks with other households. These networks provide a means by which households hope to mobilize resources during times of shortage (O'Shea 1989), even when they involve the periodic exchange of similar commodities (Gregory 1981).

Fourth, household have their own *internal stresses* to intensify production that are part of the normal household life cycle. Chayanov (1966) demonstrated that newly formed households with young children are under considerably more stress than older households with adolescents or unmarried adults (see Durrenberger 1984). The reason is that young children consume more resources from the household resource pool than they contribute, requiring the adult members to work harder than if they were just producing for themselves. One way to reduce this stress is to reside in larger multi-generational households that have a higher ratio of producers to consumers. This reduces the need to maximize the returns from each unit of labor since the consumption of young dependents is offset by more working adults.

While a great deal of variation can be found in the size of households in every society, large households always have a clear labor advantage over small households (Bernbeck 1995; Hajnal 1982). Large households have a higher marginal return per household member than small households which improves their overall economic well being. Higher productivity helps to buffer households against food shortages and large families have more labor available for household maintenance, investment in agricultural improvements (e.g. fencing, manuring, terrace building, etc.), and involvement in alternative forms of production such as crafting. This labor advantage is an important reason why many households in agricultural societies have multi-generational structures (Hajnal 1982).

Fifth and finally, households are actively motivated to minimize subsistence risk. Research indicates that unpredictable resource shortfalls were a major threat to the welfare and survivability of prehispanic households (Halstead and O'Shea 1989). One of the primary ways that households buffered themselves against risk was by developing diversified production systems that offset cyclical and seasonal resource shortfalls (Davies 1996; Messer 1989). According to O'Shea (1989), it is the need to *minimize risk rather than maximize production* that is the most important variable in structuring domestic production systems. It is within this context that diversification can provide a more secure and predictable adaptive strategy than the potentially more productive, but riskier strategy of economic specialization (Cashdan 1990; Winterhalder et al. 1999). Of course, diversification and intensification are complementary economic strategies that households used together to ensure their long term economic well being.

Housework: Crafting in the Domestic Context

If households actively pursue the economic well being of their members, what is the role of craft production in the domestic economy? Households in many areas of Mesoamerica were linked to one another through an active market system that provided opportunities for the free and open exchange of goods and services. It was not a modern market economy as we think of it today (Hicks 1987:101), but it allowed households to convert the resources they produced into a range of alternative products. The marketplace furnished the nexus and opportunity for domestic craft production to develop in Mesoamerica. But this was only a matter of degree, and the processes giving rise to the appearance of domestic craft production were already in place by the Early and Middle Formative periods, well before there is any evidence for marketplaces in Mesoamerica.

Craft production afforded an opportunity for diversification in the domestic economy by producing goods with both social and economic value. Food and goods circulated regularly between individuals as gifts and exchanges from the earliest moments in human history. The production of goods for exchange (rather than just use) was always an avenue of human activity. Where craft production became relevant for the domestic economy was when goods began to move as reciprocal exchanges against food and other resources used by households for subsistence. It was at this point that craft production became an economic activity that could contribute to household provisioning in several important ways.

First, craft production could significantly raise household productivity because it can be incorporated into the annual work cycle without disrupting other subsistence activities. In Mesoamerica, seasonal rainfall agriculture was a fundamental way of life for many households. In many areas this involves a period of intense agricultural activity followed by months of inactivity.[2] In the Mexican highlands, the dry winter months are periods of down-time when household labor is available for alternative subsistence activities (Sanders et al. 1979:82). Under these conditions agricultural households have two options if they need to expand production: they can develop more intensive forms of double cropping where hydraulic conditions permit, or they can add alternative production activities like foraging, animal husbandry, labor service, and/or craft production to their seasonal work calendars. A good example of a dry season craft activity in both the highlands and lowlands is seasonal salt making (Andrews 1983:25; Good 1995; Parsons 2001:178).

Large families are able to expand their productivity through craft production because they have the labor to do so often without having to disrupt agricultural activities important for household subsistence. Seasonal crafting also provides small households with a means of increasing productivity and reducing the stress on their higher consumer/producer ratios. Furthermore, certain crafts like ceramic production, are, for technological reasons, best conducted during the dry season when there is no rainfall (Matson 1965; Pool, this volume; Rice 1987). Crafting during the non-agricultural cycle therefore has three advantages; it provides an opportunity of raising overall productivity, it diversifies household production, and it makes use of temporary labor surpluses.

A second reason why craft production is easily incorporated into household work regimes is because it expands diversification strategies that are vital for their survival. Risk is minimized when production strategies are diversified. In Mesoamerica, the marketplace provided the opportunity for

households to produce craft goods that could be exchanged for other resources on a regular basis. The addition of crafting to the domestic work cycle provided a means to obtain goods that they could not produce. Craft goods represent durable wealth. Unlike food that spoils, most craft goods are imperishable, have longer use lives, and maintain their value until they are sold.

A third advantage of domestic craft production is that it allows households to use small scale labor surpluses in creative ways. Hagstrum (1999, 2001) has discussed the tactics of household diversification in terms of how work can be scheduled to fit the tempo of domestic life. Hagstrum models domestic work in terms of the *complementary* and *intersecting* technologies that households have access to and can apply to alternative production activities. It is the application of a known technology, like pyrotechnics used in cooking, to a new medium such as baking or firing clay that leads to the development of ceramic crafting. This provides an opportunity for the seamless incorporation of craft activities into the domestic economy.

From this perspective, crafting provides a means for increasing productivity by creating punctuated work schedules involving a mix of different activities. While the seasonal scheduling of craft activities was discussed above, Hagstrum notes that households frequently micro-manage their labor, moving easily from one activity to another on a daily or even hourly basis. For example, the complementarity of different types of domestic crafting makes it efficient for households to shift from agriculture to craft work during the heat of the day when work in the fields is more difficult (Hagstrum 2001:49). Craft production may also allow households to employ the labor of women, the aged and the infirm that might be unable to participate in other forms of work. Of these, gender is especially critical both in the organization of work within households and because of the many ways that women lead or take an active role in domestic crafting.

The fourth and final benefit of domestic craft production is that it protects the artisan from the vicissitudes of craft good demand. The incorporation of craft production into a domestic cycle alongside agriculture, pastoralism or other subsistence practices provides the stability necessary for the maintenance and expansion of crafting and other commercial activity (Abruzzi 1987). Craft production can be a successful subsistence strategy when there is demand for the goods produced. Nevertheless, craft production is a *risky business* for households to engage in as a full-time, specialized economic activity (Hirth 2006). This risk is based on the different cycles of production and consumption that drive craft activity.

To support a household with craft production, artisans require a continuous and predictable level of demand (i.e.

sales) for their wares. The dilemma artisans face is that the demand of craft goods is usually discontinuous or cyclical in nature (Douglas and Ischerwood 1979).[3] Consumers in subsistence households frequently plan the purchase of durable goods in relation to cyclical social needs (e.g. birth, marriage, etc), festival needs, or the amplified purchasing power associated with agricultural harvests. Households often delay craft purchases until the most productive period of their subsistence cycle or suspend them entirely during times of famine or resource shortfall. While delayed purchases can be strategically advantageous to consuming households, it is a major impediment for artisans since it places craft producing households at considerable risk. Fluctuating consumer demand makes it advantageous for craft production to be incorporated into a diversified domestic economy that mixes craft production with other subsistence pursuits like agriculture. This makes *part-time* craft production both safer and more predictable than the fluctuating returns associated with *full-time* craft activity.

Modeling Craft Production: Intermittent and Multicrafting

The key to modeling domestic craft production is understanding how households use the resources and economic opportunities they have to work with. Unfortunately, this remains *terra incognita* for anthropologists and archaeologists alike since, until recently, little research has addressed the internal organization of domestic economies (Wilk 1989a). The first step for archaeologists is to forget the time-worn categories of full- and part-time specialization and reevaluate household work by examining the range of economic activities that households engage in. The way to do that is to evaluate craft production in terms how it contributed to the overall domestic economy, and not the amount of time that the artisan worked. Was craft production an intermittent or continuous activity within the household? Did it involve a single type of work such as spinning or knapping, or were a suite of crafts conducted simultaneously within the household? To answer these questions requires an activity-focused analytical format. I believe the categories of *intermittent crafting* and *multicrafting* better characterize the way that craft activity was structured in domestic contexts.

Intermittent Crafting

Intermittent crafting refers to discontinuous or periodic craft production that takes place within domestic contexts alongside other subsistence pursuits. It is part-time production only to the extent that the other subsistence activities

performed by the household (e.g. agriculture, foraging, etc) can also be considered to be part-time. It is a better term than part-time production because it shifts the emphasis away from the amount of time that artisans spends on crafting to the more important issue of how craft production compliments and diversifies the total household subsistence strategy. The amount of labor committed to craft activities certainly varies from household to household, as does the importance of its contribution to the domestic economy.

Intermittent crafting occurs in societies at all levels of cultural complexity. It is common in stateless societies where it can occur alongside, or be embedded within the agricultural, herding, hunting, or gathering activities that households engage in (Brumfiel 1998:146; Clark and Parry 1990; Herskovits 1952; Malinowski 1922; Rosen 2003; Sheets 2000; Sundström 1974; Wiessner 1982). The same is true in state societies where intermittent craft production may continue alongside agriculture (Feinman 1999; Peacock 1982:17–23). Recognition that domestic crafting is conducted intermittently does not diminish its economic importance to the society since it may be the foundation on which advanced market systems operate. How important domestic craft production was to the household has to be judged on an individual basis vis-a-vis its other subsistence activities.

The key to understanding intermittent crafting is to recognize that its primary concern is *not* with the nature and organization of domestic crafting. Its primary concern is the nature of the domestic economy and how crafting contributed to the overall household social and economic wellbeing. From this perspective intermittent crafting is only a means to that end. Stephen Gudeman (2001) has emphasized the importance that households and communities place on economic investment in their corporate cultural base. How this is done from household to household varies greatly over time and space. After all, a day's work in many traditional households can consist of many short shifts of different types of jobs. Among the Otavalo for instance, "rest" consists of exchanging one type of household work for another (Salomon 1973:467). Task diversity, therefore, is a key to household production both for auto-consumption and for exchange and once we understand this, craft production can be viewed and evaluated in light of all the subsistence activities employed in domestic maintenance.

Multicrafting

Multicrafting is the practice of engaging in multiple crafts within the same household (Costin 2001:312; Feinman 1999; Hirth 2006; Shimada 2007). It often represents

Table 1. Evidence for multicrafting in prehispanic Mesoamerica

Site	Date	Production Activities	Type of Data	Reference
Central Mexico				
Teotihuacan: Tlajinga 33	Classic	Ceramics, Lapidary	Excavation	Sheehy 1992; Widmer 1991
Teotihuacan: La Ventilla	Classic	Lapidary, Shell	Excavation	Cabrera and Gómez 2008
Xochicalco	Epiclassic	Obsidian, Lapidary, Plastering	Excavation	Hirth 2006, also this volume
Otumba	Late Postclassic	Lapidary, Figurine, Pottery, Obsidian	Overlapping Surface Concentrations	Nichols 1994; Otis Charlton 1993
Basin of Mexico	Late Postclassic	Salt, Fabric Marked Pottery	Survey	Parsons 1994
Tenochtitlan	Late Postclassic	Obsidian, Figurines	Excavation	García and Cassiano 1990
Oaxaca				
San Jose Mogote	Early Formative	Flaked Stone, shell, pottery, basketry	Excavation	Marcus and Flannery 1996
Ejutla	Classic	Shell, Ceramics, Lapidary	Excavation	Balkansky et al 1997; Feinman and Nicholas 1993, 2000
El Palmillo	Classic	Flaked Stone, Maguey fiber	Excavation	Haines et al. 2004
West Mexico				
Tzintzuntzan	Late Postclassic	Obsidian, Lapidary	Surface Lithic Workshops	Pollard 1977
Maya Region				
Aguateca	Late Classic	Bone, Shell	Excavation	Emery and Aoyama 2007
Copan	Late Classic	Lapidary, Textiles, Shell	Excavation	Widmer 1987, also this volume

an increase in the commitment to crafting as a component of the domestic economy. The crafts practiced can be independent of one another, or interrelated if they use the same technology or technological investments (kilns, drying pits). Likewise, different craft activities can be contingent or sequentially related to one another as part of a single commodity sequence. An example would be the production of ceramic evaporation bowls for use as a consumable in the production of salt (see De León, this volume). The in-house production of an artisan's tools would be another example of contingent production (see below).

What is especially important is that the risk minimization and diversification strategies that give rise to intermittent crafting also permit the intensification of craft production. Multicrafting is a form of intensive craft production that is very compatible with household diversification strategies. It can be combined with other subsistence activities to create a more diversified form of intermittent crafting. Multicrafting often develops as craft activities are added to household activities at the expense of agriculture or other food producing activities. Which crafts are added may depend on the intersecting technologies and skills that household members already possess (Hagstrum 2001). Multicrafting enables artisans to reduce risk by producing a repertoire of products with different value, demand, and consumer consumption cycles. It is when agriculture disappears from domestic activities that the multicrafting household can be thought of as being a full-time crafting household for the first time.

There is ample evidence from the archaeological record that multicrafting was a regular feature of Mesoamerican prehispanic economy. Table 1 summarizes the evidence for multicrafting from several different areas of Mesoamerica. Evidence for multicrafting has been reported from the Basin of Mexico, Morelos, West Mexico, the Valley of Oaxaca, and several areas in the Maya region. While the quality of data vary from region to region there is no question that multicrafting was practiced in many households under different circumstances. Furthermore, since most forms of craft production go unnoticed in archaeological research because of the perishability of the materials worked, multicrafting may well have been fairly widespread throughout Mesoamerica. Careful archaeological research using a combination of technological, use-wear, and micro-debitage analyses is necessary to evaluate how common multicrafting was as a form of domestic craft production.

Although intermittent crafting and multicrafting could be construed as different forms of crafting they are not mutually exclusive categories. Instead, they represent a continuum of craft activity that encompasses the periodicity of work and the number of activities crafting households may engage in. For example, an artisan can perform one craft activity and do it intermittently throughout the year, or engage in multicrafting and likewise do it intermittently throughout the year. To construct a uniform view for craft activity we need to dichotomize craft production into intermittent/continuous periods of work and single/multiple

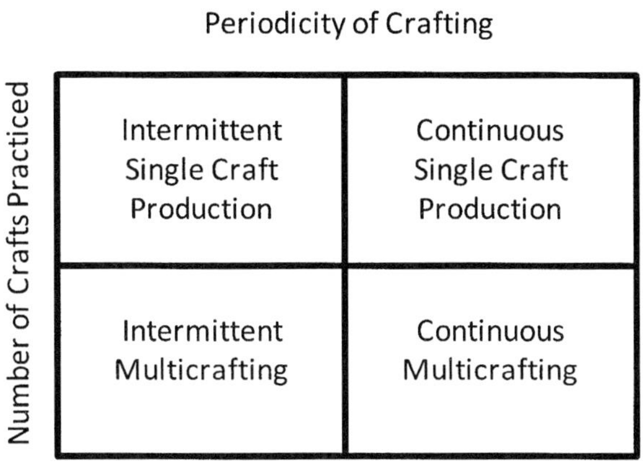

Periodicity of Crafting

Figure 1. Forms of craft production under different conditions of work periodicity and production diversity.

episodes of craft production (Figure 1). While typologies are useful for descriptive purposes, it is more productive to focus on the nature of the work and how it contributes to crafting endeavors within the household.

Two questions need to be answered for all forms of crafting. Are crafts contingent or independent work activities, and are the goods produced intended for internal consumption or distribution to consumers outside the producing household? *Contingent crafting* refers to the manufacture of finished goods that are needed by, and used in, the normal crafting process. An example would be the need for dyes in textile manufacture. Households can either purchase dyes or decide to produce them for themselves. When they do the latter we have contingent crafting.

Contingent crafting is often stimulated by the regular consumption of tools or finished products as part of the crafting process. Examples would be the production of ceramic vessels as evaporator pans in the manufacture of salt (see De León, this volume) or the manufacture of lithic tools for cutting or processing other types of goods (Anderson and Hirth 2009; Hirth, this volume; Hirth et al., this volume). Of course the question is does contingent production represent a form of multicrafting? The simple answer in my mind is yes for two reasons. First, contingent crafting often requires the craftsmen to acquire a different set of technological skills to make the tools needed for the production process. Second, possession of contingent crafting skills always provides households with the option to sell "contingently made" craft items if there is the opportunity and/or the desire to do so. In any event, the issue of craft consumption as opposed to production for exchange is always a question that must be addressed separately in archaeological research (Hirth and Castanzo 2006).

A question arising from this discussion is what conditions give rise to intermittent and multicrafting? The answer,

of course, is not easy to come by although I believe that it lies in the opportunities that household members pursue to expand their social networks, reduce subsistence risk, and otherwise increase their economic and social well being. After all, households practice diversified forms of production as part of their self-sufficient subsistence orientation. Multicrafting can be viewed as a continuation and amplification of diversified production systems for the purpose of exchange outside the household. The fact that craftspersons employ complementary and intersecting technologies (Hagstrum 2001) used for household maintenance in specialized domestic craft production demonstrates the compatibility of multicrafting with generalized features of the domestic economy.

Conclusions

We have a paradox in archaeology. There is widespread evidence for the practice of domestic craft production both in Mesoamerica and many other ancient societies around the world, but we lack a model that explains how or why this was the case. The model proposed here argues that craft production was an important part of the domestic economy that contributed to both the subsistence and social strategies of the household. The primary goal of the household is survival and successful reproduction. The key to success is developing a subsistence strategy that maximizes productivity while minimizing risk. It is this "mini-max" strategy that leads households to select a mix of subsistence activities to meet their needs.

Craft production allows households to employ labor in productive ways during times of the year when there are few work demands from other subsistence activities. The example mentioned here was seasonal rainfall agriculture where labor is available during the non-agricultural dry season (Costin 2001). Under these conditions craft production can increase household productivity and reduce its overall subsistence risk. Minimizing risk is important to the household's health and survival, and diversification of work is an important way to accomplish it. In this context, specialized domestic craft production is one component of the household's risk minimization and diversification strategy.

Much current research in archaeology employs the static concepts of full-time and part-time specialization that focus on the time that artisans work rather than the role of crafting within the domestic economy. Whether craftsmen were full- or part-time artisans is less important than how craft production was organized in ancient societies. Most craft production throughout prehistory took place within households and better models are needed to explain how and why this was the case. I believe that the desire to increase productivity and diversify risk were the twin motivations behind development of domestic craft production in Mesoamerica. If this is true, then full-time, single commodity craft production should be relatively rare in Mesoamerica except under conditions of institutional sponsorship.

Intermittent crafting and multicrafting were identified and illustrated in this paper as additional ways of conceptualizing and describing craft production. Intermittent crafting represents the addition of a crafting activity to the household's regular subsistence regime. Multicrafting represents the practice of multiple craft activities within the household. While multicrafting may reduce the amount of time spent on agriculture or other subsistence activities, it usually will not eliminate them. Both intermittent and multicrafting represent the continued diversification of the household economy through the addition of new forms of work that employ complementary and intersecting technologies in different ways.

Archaeologists often use the term specialization when discussing the appearance and development of craft activity. The concept of *specialization* cognitively stems from the idea that craft producers moved from part-time to full-time specialists in their chosen craft. This was *not* the case in Mesoamerica. More intensive forms of craft production in Mesoamerica are represented by multicrafting instead of full-time specialists. Because craftsmen regularly faced cycles of delayed demand for their goods, it was safer and more productive for craft production to remain in the household where it was buffered from risk by other subsistence activities. The contributions in this volume show that the path to intensification and increased craft production in Mesoamerica was through multicrafting which was a process of craft diversification rather than specialization.

Notes

1. By way of example we only need to consider how spouses were obtained in small scale societies. Complete self-sufficiency would deny households with the social networks needed to satisfy these and other economic and social needs.

2. Seasonal farming regimes are widespread throughout the world in both tropical and temperate environments, and provide an excellent opportunity for additional types of work including craft production during the non-agriculture period.

3. We see the cyclical nature of consumer goods in all levels of society. It is even evident in modern industrial

states before major festival days (e.g. Christmas, Easter, Valentine's Day, etc) and after tax returns.

References

Abruzzi, William
1987   Ecological Stability and Community Diversity during Mormon Colonization of the Little Colorado River Basin. Human Ecology 15:317–338.

Allan, William
1965   The African Husbandman. Edinburgh: Oliver and Boyd.

Ames, Kenneth
1995   Chiefly Power and Household Production on the Northwest Coast. *In* Foundations of Social inequality. Douglas Price and Gary Feinman, eds., pp. 155–187. New York: Plenum Press.

Anderson, J. Heath, and Kenneth Hirth
2009   Obsidian Blade Production for Craft Consumption at Kaminaljuyu. Ancient Mesoamerica 20:163–172.

Andrews, Anthony
1983   Maya Salt Production and trade.   Tucson: University of Arizona Press.

Arcury, Thomas
1984   Household Composition and Economic Change in a Rural Community, 1900–1980: Testing Two Models. American Ethnologist 11:677–698.

Arnold, Dean
1978   Ethnography of Pottery-making in the Valley of Guatemala. *In* The Ceramics of Kaminajuyú. R. Wetherington, ed. pp. 327–400. University Park: Penn State University Press.
1985   Ceramic Theory and Cultural Process. Cambridge: Cambridge University Press.

Arnold, Jeanne
2001   The Origins of a Pacific Coast Chiefdom: The Chumash of the Channel Islands. Salt Lake City: University of Utah Press.

Balkansky, Andrews, Gary Feinman, and Linda Nicholas
1997   Pottery Kilns of Ancient Ejutla, Oaxaca, Mexico. Journal of Field Archaeology 24:139–160.

Ball, Joseph

1993 Pottery, Potters, Palaces, and Politics: Some Socioeconomic and Political Implications of Late Classic Maya Ceramic Industries. *In* Lowland Maya Civilization in the Eighth Century A.D. Jeremy Sabloff and John Henderson, eds., pp. 243–272. Washington, D.C.: Dumbarton Oaks Research Library and Collection.

Beinhocker, Eric

2006 The Origin of Wealth. Boston: Harvard Business School Press.

Berdan, Frances

1982 The Aztecs of Central Mexico. An Imperial Society. New York: Holt, Rinehart and Winston.

Bernbeck, Reinhard

1995 Lasting Alliances and Emerging Competition: Economic Developments in Early Mesopotamia. Journal of Anthropological Archaeology 14:1–25.

Blanton, Richard, Gary Feinman, Stephen Kowalewski, and Peter Peregrine

1996 A Dual-Processual Theory for the Evolution of Mesoamerican Civilization. Current Anthropology 37:1–4 and 47–70.

Blomster, Jeffrey, Hector Neff, and Michael Glascock

2005 Olmec Pottery Production and Export in Ancient Mexico Determined through Elemental Analysis. Science 307:1068–1072.

Boksenbaum, Martin, Paul Tolstoy, Garman Harbottle, Jerome Kimberlin, and Mary Nivens

1987 Obsidian Industries and Cultural Evolution in the Basin of Mexico before 500 B.C. Journal of Field Archaeology 14:65–75.

Brumfiel, Elizabeth

1998 The Multiple Identities of Aztec Craft Specialists. *In* Craft and Social Identity. Cathy Costin and Rita Wright, eds., pp. 145–152. Archaeological Papers of the American Anthropological Association, 8. Arlington, Virginia: American Anthropological Association.

Brumfield, Elizabeth, and Timothy Earle

1987 Specialization, Exchange, and Complex Societies: An Introduction. *In* Specialization, Exchange, and Complex Societies. Elizabeth Brumfiel and Timothy Earle, eds., pp 1–9. Cambridge: Cambridge University Press.

Burton, Susan

1987 Obsidian Blade Manufacturing Debris on Terrace 37. *In* Ancient Chalcatzingo. David Grove, ed., pp. 321–328. Austin: University of Texas Press.

Cabrera Castro, Rubén, and Sergio Gómez Chávez

2008 La Ventilla: A Model for a Barrio in the Urban Structure of Teotihuacan. *In* Urbanism in Mesoamerica/El Urbanismo en Mesoamérica, vol II, Guadalupe Mastache, Robert Cobean, Angel García Cook and Kenneth Hirth, eds., pp. 37–83. Mexico City and University Park: INAH and Penn State University.

Carneiro, Robert

1970 A Theory of the Origin of the State. *Science* 169:733–738

1974 A Reappraisal of the Role of Technology and Organization in the Origin of Civilization. American Antiquity 39:179–186.

Cashdan, Elizabeth

1990 Risk and Uncertainty in Tribal and Peasant Economies. Boulder: Westview Press.

Chayanov, A. V.

1966 The Theory of Peasant Economy. D. Thorner, B. Kerblay, and R.E.F. Smith, eds., Homewood, Illinois: American Economic Association.

Childe, Gordon

1934 New Light on the Most Ancient Near East: The Oriental Prelude to European Prehistory. London: Kegan Paul.

1962 Man Makes Himself. New York: New American Library.

Clark, Gracia

1989 Separation between Trading and Home for Asante Women in Kumasi Central Market, Ghana. *In* The Household Economy. Reconsidering the Domestic Mode of Production. Richard Wilk, ed., pp. 91–118. Boulder: Westview Press.

Clark, John

1987 Politics, Prismatic Blades, and Mesoamerican Civilization. *In* The Organization of Core

Technology. J. Johnson and C. Morrow, eds, pp. 259–285. Boulder: Westview Press.

Clark, John, and Michael Blake
1994 The Power of Prestige: Competitive Generosity and the Emergence of Rank Societies in Lower Mesoamerica. *In* Factional Competition and Political Development in the New World. Elizabeth Brumfiel and John Fox, eds., pp. 17–30. Cambridge: Cambridge University Press.

Clark, John, and Dennis Gosser
1995 Reinventing Mesoamerica's First Pottery. *In* The Emergence of Pottery: Technology and Innovation in Ancient Societies. William Barnett and John Hoopes, eds., pp. 209–221. Washington: Smithsonian Institution.

Clark, John and William Parry
1990 Craft Specialization and Cultural Complexity. *In* Research in Economic Anthropology, Barry Isaac, ed. 12:289–346. Greenwich, Connecticut: JAI Press.

Cobean, Robert
1997 La Yerbabuena, Veracrua: Una Investigación de Rescate en la Región de Pico de Orizaba. Project Proposal. Mexico City: INAH.

Cohen, Jeffrey
1998 Craft Production and the Challenge of the Global Market: An Artisan's Cooperative in Oaxaca, Mexico. Human Organization 57:74–82.

Costin, Cathy
1991 Craft Specialization: Issues in Defining, Documenting, and Explaining the Organization of Production. *In* Archaeological Method and Theory. Michael Schiffer, ed., pp. 1–56. Tucson: University of Arizona Press.
2001 Craft Production Systems. *In* Archaeology at the Millennium: A Sourcebook. Gary Feinman and Douglas Price, eds., pp. 273–327. New York: Kluwer Academic/Plenum Publishers.

D'Altroy, Terrence, and Timothy Earle
1985 Staple Finance, Wealth Finance, and Storage in the Inca Political Economy. Current Anthropology 26:187–206.

Dalton, George
1977 Aboriginal Economies in Stateless Societies. *In* Exchange Systems in Prehistory. Timothy Earle and Jonathon Ericson, eds., pp. 191–212. New York: Academic Press.

David, N. and H. Henning
1972 The Ethnography of Pottery: A Fulani Case seen in Archaeological Perspective. Module 21. Reading, Massachusetts: Addison-Wesley.

Davies, Susanna
1996 Adaptable Livelihoods. New York: St. Martin's Press.

Di Castro Stringher, Anna
1997 Los Bloques de Ilmenita de San Lorenzo. *In* Población, Subsistencia, y Medio Ambiente en San Lorenzo Tenochtitlán. Ann Cyphers, ed., pp. 153–160. Mexico City: IIA-UNAM.

Douglas, Mary and Baron Ischerwood
1979 The World of Goods. London: W.W. Norton and Co.

Drucker, Philip, and Robert Heizer
1967 To Make My Name Good. Berkeley and Los Angeles: University of California Press,

Durkheim, Emile
1933 The Division of Labor in Society. New York: The Free Press.

Durrenberger, Paul
1984 Chayanov, Peasants and Economic Anthropology. New York: Academic Press.

Earl, Timothy
1981 Comment on Prudence Rice. Evolution of Specialized Pottery Production: A Trial Model. Current Anthropology 22:230–231.

Emery, Kitty, and Kazuo Aoyama
2007 Bone, Shell, and Lithic Evidence for Crafting in Elite Maya Households at Aguateca, Guatemala. Ancient Mesoamerica 18:69–89.

Engels, Friedrich
1972 The Origin of the Family, Private Property, and the State. Eleanor Leacock, ed. New York: International Publishers.

Feinman, Gary
1999 Rethinking our Assumptions: Economic Specialization at the Household Scale in Ancient Ejutla, Oaxaca, Mexico. *In* Pottey and People. James Skibo and Gary Feinman, eds., pp. 81–98. Salt Lake City: University of Utah Press.

Feinman, Gary, and Linda Nicholas
1993 Shell-Ornament Production in Ejutla: Implications for Highland-Coastal Interactions in Ancient Oaxaca. Ancient Mesoamerica 4:103–119.
2000 High-Intensity Household-Scale Production in Ancient Mesoamerica: A Perspective from Ejutla, Oaxaca. *In* Cultural Evolution: Contemporary Viewpoints. Gary Feinman and Linda Manzanilla, eds., pp. 119–142, New York: Kluwer Academic/Plenum Publishers.

Flannery, Kent
1976 The Early Mesoamerican village. New York: Academic Press,

Foias, Antonia
2002 At the Crossroads: the Economic Basis of Political Power in the Petexbatun Region. *In* Ancient Maya Political Economies. Marilyn Masson and Dave Freidel, eds., pp. 223–248. Walnut Creek, California: Alta Mira Press.

Frankenstein, Susan, and M. Rowlands
1978 The internal structure and regional context of early Iron Age society in south-western Germany. Bulletin of the Institute of Archaeology 15:73–112.

García Velázquez, Jorge, and Gianfranco Cassiano
1990 La Producción de Navajillas Prismáticas en el Postclásico Tardío: El Caso de la Plaza de la Banca Nacionalizada. *In* Etnoarqueología: Primer Coloquio Bosch-Gimpera. Yoko Sugiura and Mari Carmen Serra, eds., pp. 513–526. Mexico City: UNAM.

Gonlin, Nancy
1994 Rural Household Diversity in Late Classic Copan. *In* Archaeological Views of the Countryside. Glenn Schwartz and Steven Falconer, eds., pp. 177–197. Washington, D.C.: Smithsonian Institution Press.

Good, Catherine
1995 Salt Production and Commerce in Guerrero, Mexico: An Ethnographic Contribution to Historical Reconstruction. Ancient Mesoamerica 6:1–13.

Gregory, Clare
1981 A Conceptual Analysis of a Non-Capitalist Gift Economy. Cambridge Journal of Economics 5:119–135.

Gudeman, Stephen
2001 The Anthropology of Economy. Malden, Massachusetts: Blackwell Publishing.

Hagstrum, Melissa
1999 The Goals of Domestic Autonomy among Highland Peruvian Farmer-Potters in Peasant Craft Specialization: Home Economics of Rural Craft Specialists. Research in Economic Anthropology 20:265–298.
2001 Household Production in Chaco Canyon. American Antiquity 66:47–55.

Haines, Helen, Gary Feinman, and Linda Nicholas
2004 Household Economic Specialization and Social Differentiation: The Stone-Tool Assemblage at El Pamillo, Oaxaca. Ancient Mesoamerica 15:251–266.

Hajnal, John
1982 Two Kinds of Preindustrial Household Formation System. Population and Development Review 8:449–494.

Halstead, Paul
1989 The Economy has No Surplus: Economic Stability and Social Change among Early Farming Communities of Thessaly, Greece. *In* Bad Year Economics. Paul Halstead and John O'Shea, eds., pp. 68–80. Cambridge: Cambridge University Press.

Halstead, Paul, and John O'Shea
1989 Bad Year Economics. Cambridge: Cambridge University Press.

Hammel, E. A.
1984 On the *** of Studying Household Form and Function. *In* Households. Comparative and

Historic Studies of the Domestic Group. Robert Netting, Richard Wilk, and Eric Arnould, eds., pp. 29–43. Berkeley: University of California Press.

Harris, Marvin
1959 The Economy has No Surplus. American Anthropologist 61:385–99.

Hayden, Brian
2001 Richman, Poorman, Beggarman, Chief: The Dynamics of Social Inequality. *In* Archaeology at the Millennium: A Sourcebook. Gary Feinman and Douglas Price, eds., pp. 231–272. New York: Kluwer Academic Press.

Helms, Marry
1993 Craft and the Kingly Ideal. Austin: University of Texas Press.

Herskovits, Melville
1952 Economic Anthropology. New York: Knopf.

Hicks, Frederick
1987 First Steps Towards a Market-Integrated Economy in Aztec Mexico. *In* Early State Dynamics. Henri Claessen and Pieter van de Velde, eds., pp. 91–107. Leiden: E. J. Brill.

Hirth, Kenneth
2006 Modeling Domestic Craft Production at Xochicalco. *In* Obsidian Craft Production in Ancient Central Mexico. Kenneth Hirth, ed., pp. 275–286. Salt Lake City: The University of Utah Press.
2008 Unidad Doméstica, Comunidad y Artesanía en un Cacicazgo del Formativo Medio Revalorando la Importancia del Proyecto Chalcatzingo. *In* Ideología Política y Sociedad en el Periodo Formativo. Ann Cyphers and Kenneth Hirth, eds., pp. 93–125. Mexico City: UNAM.

Hirth, Kenneth, and Ronald Castanzo
2006 An Experimental Study of Use-Wear Striation on Obsidian Prismatic Blades. *In* Obsidian Craft Production in Ancient Central Mexico. Kenneth Hirth, ed., pp, 318–327. Salt Lake City: The University of Utah Press.

Inomata, Takeshi
2001 The Power and Ideology of Artistic Creation: Elite Craft Specialists in Classic Maya Society. Current Anthropology 42:321–349.

Janusek, John
1999 Craft and Local Power: Embedded Specialization in Tiwanaku Cities. Latin American Antiquity 10:107–131.

Johnson, Allen and Timothy Earle
1987 The Evolution of Human Societies. Stanford: Stanford University Press.

Katz, Friedrich
1966 Situación Social y Económica de los Aztecas durante los Siglos XV y XVI. Mexico City: Instituto de Investigaciones Históricas, UNAM.

Kovacevich, Brigitte
2007 Ritual, Crafting and Agency at the Classic Maya Kingdom of Cancuen. *In* Mesoamerican Ritual Economy. E. Christian Wells, and Karla Davis-Salazar, eds., pp. 67–114. Boulder: University of Colorado Press.

Lass, Barbara
1998 Crafts, Chiefs, and Commoners: Production and Control in Precontact Hawai'i. *In* Craft and Social Identity. Cathy Costin and Rita Wright, eds., pp. 19–30. Archaeological Papers of the American Anthropological Association, 8. American Anthropological Association.

Lee, Richard
1993 The Dobe Ju/'hoansi. Harcourt Brace, Fort Worth.

Lloyd, Peter
1953 Craft Organization in Yoruba towns. Africa 23:30–44.

Loucky, James
1979 Production and Patterning of Social Relations and Values in two Guatemalan villages. American Ethnologist 6:702–23.

MacEachern, Scott, David Archer, and Richard Garvin
1989 Households and Communities. Proceedings of the 21st Annual Chacmool Conference. The Archaeological Association of the University of Calgary.

Malinowski, Bronislaw
1922 Argonauts of the Western Pacific. London: Routledge and Kegan Paul.

Marcus, Joyce, and Kent Flannery
1996 Zapotec Civilization. New York: Thames and Hudson.

Mathien, Frances
2001 The Organization of Turquoise Production and Consumption by the Prehistoric Chacoans. American Antiquity 66:103–118.

Matson, Fred
1965 Ceramic Ecology: An Approach to the Study of the Early Cultures of the Near East. *In* Ceramics and Man. Fred Matson, ed., pp. 202–217. Chicago: Aldine.

McAnany, Patricia
1989 Economic Foundations of Prehistoric Maya Society: Paradigms and Concepts. Research in Economic Anthropology, Supplement 4:347–372. Greenwhich: JAI Press.

Medick, Hans
1976 The Proto-Industrial Family Economy: The Structural Function of the Household during the Transition from Peasant Society to Industrial Capitalism. Social History 3:291–315.

Meisch, Lynn
2002 Andean Entrepreneurs: Otavalo Merchants and Musicians in the Global Arena. Austin: University of Texas Press.

Messer, Ellen
1989 Seasonality in Food Systems: An Anthropological Perspective on Household Food Security. *In* Seasonal Variability in Third World Agriculture. David Sahn, ed., pp. 151–175. Baltimore: John Hopkins University Press.

Morgan, Lewis H.
1877 Ancient Society. Cleveland: World Publishing Company.

Neff, Hector, Jeffrey Blomster, Michael Glascock, Ronald Bishop, James Blackman, Michael Coe, George Cowgill, Richard Diehl, Stephen Houston, Arthur Joyce, Carl Lipo, Barbara Stark, and Marcus Winter
2006 Methodological Issues in the Provenance Investigation of Early Formative Mesoamerican Ceramics. Latin American Antiquity 17:54–76.

Netting, Robert
1989 Smallholders, Householders, Freeholders: Why the Family Farm Works Well Worldwide. *In* The Household Economy. Reconsidering the Domestic Mode of Production. Richard Wilk, ed., pp. 221–244. Boulder: Westview Press.
1993 Smallholders, Households, Farm Families, and the Ecology of Intensive, Sustainable Agriculture. Stanford: Stanford University Press.

Netting, Robert, Richard Wilk and Eric Arnould
1984 Introduction. *In* Households. Comparative and Historic Studies of the Domestic Group. Robert Netting, Richard Wilk, and Eric Arnould, eds., pp. xiv–xxxviii. Berkeley: University of California Press.

Nichols, Deborah
1994 The Organization of Provincial Craft Producton and the Aztec City-State of Otumba. *In* Economies and Polities in the Aztec Realm. Mary Hodge and Michael Smith, eds., pp. 175–193. Studies on Culture and Society, vol. 6, Institute for Mesoamerican Studies, Albany: State University of New York.

Otis Charlton, Cynthia
1993 Obsidian as Jewelry: Lapidary Production in Aztec Otumba, Mexico. Ancient Mesoamerica 4:231–243.

O'Shea, John
1989 The Role of Wild Resources in Small-Scale Agricultural Systems: Tales from the Lakes and the Plains. *In* Bad Year Economics. Paul Halstead and John O'Shea, eds., pp. 57–67. Cambridge: Cambridge University Press.

Parsons, Jeffrey
1994 Late Postclassic Salt Production and Consumption in the Basin of Mexico. Some Insights from Nexquipayac. *In* Economies and Polities in the Aztec Realm. Mary Hodge and Michael Smith, eds., pp. 257–290. Studies on Culture and Society, vol. 6, Institute for Mesoamerican Studies, Albany: State University of New York.
2001 The Last Saltmakers of Nexquipayac, Mexico. An Archaeological Ethnography. Anthropological Papers No. 92, Museum of Anthropology, Ann Arbor: University of Michigan.

Peacock, D
  1982 Pottery in the Roman world: An Ethnoarchaeological Approach. London: Longman.

Peregrine, Peter
  1991 Some Political Aspects of Craft Production. World Archaeology 23:1–11.

Pollard, Helen Perlstein
  1977 An Analysis of Urban Zoning and Planning at Prehispanic Tzintzuntzan. Proceedings of the American Philosophical Society 121:46–69.

Pospisil, Leopold
  1963 Kapauku Papuan Economy. Yale University Publications in Anthropology No. 67. New Haven: Yale University.

Potter, Daniel, and Eleanor King
  1995 A Heterarchical Approach to Lowland Maya Socioeconomics. *In* Heterarchy and the Analysis of Complex Societies. Robert Ehrenreich, Carole Crumley, and Janet Levy, eds., Archaeological Papers of the American Anthropological Association 6:17–32.

Reents-Budet, Dorie
  1998 Elite Maya Pottery and Artisans as Social Indicators. *In* Craft and Social Identity. Cathy Costin and Rita Wright, eds., pp. 71–89. Anthropological Paper No. 8. Washington, D.C.: American Anthropological Association.

Rice, Prudence
  1987 Pottery Analysis: A Sourcebook. Chicago: University of Chicago Press.

Rosen, Steven
  2003 Early Multi-Resource Nomadism: Excavations at the Camel Site in the Central Negev. pp. 750–761.

Sahagún, Fray Bernardino de
  1959 Florentine Codex. General History of the Things of New Spain, Book 9, The Merchants. Charles Dibble and Arthur Anderson, trans., Monographs of the School of American Research, No. 14, Part 10, Santa Fe.

Sahlins, Marshal
  1972 Stone Age Economics. Chicago: Aldine.

Sahn, David
  1989 Seasonal Variability in Third World Agriculture. Baltimore: John Hopkins University Press.

Salomon, Frank
  1973 Weavers of Otavalo. *In* Peoples and Cultures of Native South America. Daniel Gross, ed., pp. 463–494. Garden City: Doubleday/The Natural History Press.

Sanders, William, Jeffrey Parsons, and Robert Santley
  1979 The Basin of Mexico. Ecological Processes in the Evolution of a Civilization. New York: Academic Press.

Santley, Robert
  1993 Late Formative Period Society at Loma Torremote: A Consideration of the Redistribution vs. the Great Provider Models as a Basis for the Emergence of Complexity in the Basin of Mexico. *In* Prehispanic Domestic Units in Western Mesoamerica. Robert Santley and Kenneth Hirth, eds., pp. 67–86. Boca Raton: CRC Press.

Santley, Robert, Philip Arnold, and Christopher Pool
  1989 The Ceramics Production System at Matacapan, Veracruz, Mexico. Journal of Field Archaeology 16:107–132.

Santley, Robert, and Kenneth Hirth
  1993 Prehispanic Domestic Units in Western Mesoamerica: Studies of the Household. Boca Raton: CRC Press.

Sheehy, James
  1992 Ceramic Production in Ancient Teotihuacan, Mexico: A Case Study of Tlajinga 33. Ann Arbor: University Microfilms.

Sheets, Payson
  2000 Provisioning the Ceren Household: The Vertical Economy, Village Economy, and Household Economy in the Southeastern Maya Periphery. Ancient Mesoamerica 11:217–230.

Shimada, Izumi
  2007 Craft Production in Complex Societies: Multicraft and Producer Perspectives. Salt Lake City: University of Utah Press.

Smith, Joan, Immanuel Wallerstein, and H. Evers
1984 Households and the World Economy. Beverly Hills: Sage Press.

Spielmann, Katherine
1998 Ritual Craft Specialization in Middle Range Societies. *In* Craft and Social Identity. Cathy Costin and Rita Wright, eds., pp. 153–159. Archaeological Papers of the American Anthropological Association, 8. Arlington, Virginia: American Anthropological Association.

Stein, Gil
1996 Producers, Patrons, and Prestige: Craft Specialists and Emergent Elites in Mesopotamia from 5500–3100 BC. *In* Craft Specialization and Social Evolution. Bernard Wailes, ed., pp. 25–38. Philadelphia: University of Pennsylvania Museum, University Museum Monograph 93.

Stolmaker, Charelotte
1996 Cultural, Social and Economic Change in Santa María Atzompa in the Late 1960's. Vanderbilt University Publications in Anthropology No. 49. Nashville.

Stone, Glenn
1986 Settlement Ecology. The Social and Spatial Organization of Kofyar Agriculture. Tucson: University of Arizona Press.

Strathern, Andrew
2007 The Rope of Moka. Big-Men and Ceremonial Exchange in Mount Hagen, New Guinea. Cambridge: Cambridge University Press.

Sundström, Lars
1974 The Exchange Economy of Pre-Colonial Tropical Africa. New York: St Martins Press.

Tosi, Maurizio
1984 The Notion of Craft Specialization and its Representation in the Archaeological Record of Early State in the Turanian Basin. *In* Marxist Perspectives in Archaeology. Matthew Spriggs ed., pp. 22–42. Cambridge: University of Cambridge Press.

Torrence, Robin
1986 Production and Exchange of Stone Tools. Cambridge: Cambridge University Press.

Trigger, Bruce
2003 Understanding Early Civilizations. Cambridge: Cambridge University Press.

Waters, Tony
2007 The Persistence of Subsistence Agriculture. Lanham, Maryland: Rowman and Littlefield Publishers.

West, Georgia
2002 Ceramic Exchange in the Late Classic and Postclassic Maya Lowlands: A Diachronic Approach. *In* Ancient Maya Political Economies. Marilyn Masson and David Freidel, eds., pp. 140–196. Walnut Creek, California: Alta Mira Press.

Widmer, Randolph
1987 Excavaciones en el Conjunto 9N-8, Patio H (Operacion XXII). *In* Excavaciones en el Area Urbana de Copan, Tomo V. William Sanders, ed., pp. 155–318. Tegucigalpa: INAH.
1991 Lapidary Craft Specialization at Teotihuacan: Implications for Community Structure at 33:S3W1 and Economic Organization in the City. Ancient Mesoamerica 2:131–147.

Wiessner, Polly
1982 Risk, Reciprocity and Social Influences in !Kung San Economics. *In* Politics and History. Eleanor Leacock and Richard Lee, eds., pp. 61–84. Cambridge: Cambridge University Press.

Wilk, Richard
1989a Decision Making and Resource Flows within the Household: Beyond the Black Box. *In* The Household Economy. Reconsidering the Domestic Mode of Production. Richard Wilk, ed., pp. 23–52. Boulder: Westview Press.
1989b The Household Economy. Reconsidering the Domestic Mode of Production. Boulder: Westview Press.
1991 Household Ecology. Economic Change and Domestic Life among the Kekchi Maya in Belize. Tucson: University of Arizona Press.

Wilk, Richard, and Wendy Ashmore
1988 Household and Community in the Mesoamerican Past. Albuquerque: University of New Mexico Press.

Wilk, Richard, and Robert Netting
  1984 Households: Changing Forms and Functions. *In* Households. Robert Netting, Richard Wilk and Eric Arnould, eds., pp. 1–28. Berkeley: University of California Press.

Wilk, Richard, and William Rathje
  1982 Household Archaeology. American Behavioral Scientist 25:617–639.

Winter, Marcus, and Jane Pires-Ferreira
  1976 Distribution of Obsidian among Households in Two Oaxacan Villages. *In* The Early Mesoamerican Village. Kent Flannery, ed., pp. 306–311. New York: Academic Press.

Winterhalder, Bruce, Flora Lu, and Bram Tucker
  1999 Risk-Sensitive Adaptive Tactics: Models and Evidence for Subsistence Studies in Biology and Anthropology. Journal of Archaeological Research 7:301–348.

Wittfogel, Karl
  1957 Oriental Despotism: A Comparative Study of Total Power. New Haven: Yale University Press.

Wright, Rita
  1998 Crafting Social Identity in Ur III Southern Mesopotamia. *In* Craft and Social Identity. Cathy Costin and Rita Wright, eds., pp. 57–69. Archaeological Papers of the American Anthropological Association, 8. American Anthropological Association.

3

The Scale and Structure of Bitumen Processing in Early Formative Olmec Households

Carl J. Wendt
California State University Fullerton

The organization of domestic production activities has received little attention in Olmec studies. Most scholars who research Olmec (1400–400 BC) production have considered those items and activities that are most closely associated with the elite, for instance monument carving and ilmenite working (e.g., Cyphers 1997; Clark 1995; Drucker 1952). While it is important to study craft items and aspects of production that factored prominently in the political and economic lives of the elite, it is also critical to study domestic production activities in order to have a balanced understanding of the intricacies, variation, and breath of Olmec production organization. A better understanding of the organization of Olmec domestic production systems may also provide insights into how adaptive strategies shifted from the Archaic to the Early Formative. Most broadly, this approach will provide a means to evaluate how domestic production was integrated into Olmec political economy.

Bitumen processing among the Olmec (Figure 1) represents some of the earliest evidence for domestic craft specialization in Mesoamerica, and is the earliest documented evidence for non-elite domestic craft specialization in the southern Gulf lowlands (Wendt and Cyphers 2008). In this chapter, I use data on bitumen processing from the San Lorenzo Olmec rural levee sites of El Remolino and Paso los Ortices (Wendt and Cyphers 2008; Wendt 2005b) in the San Lorenzo region (Figure 2) to investigate domestic production organization, specialization, risk, and scheduling among the Early Formative Olmec (1400–1000 BC). In doing this I consider the ways bitumen processing activities were integrated with other domestic activities and how domestic craft producers were incorporated into the San Lorenzo Olmec

political economy. I also consider the important role that the innovation of bitumen processing technology played in the development of the San Lorenzo Olmec political economy. I argue that the intensification of Olmec domestic production occurred within a diversified household economy that was geared towards ensuring household survival, security, and well-being; as well as increasing household status and wealth.

Diversification and Innovation in Olmec Households

The Early Formative period was a time when Mesoamerican production systems were reorganized and intensified. This is also a time when local entrepreneurs would have been involved in innovating and modifying ways to build support and power networks in the development of institutionalized social inequalities (Clark and Blake 1994; Hayden 1995). How Early Formative households reorganized and intensified their production systems is important because it can provide information on how early innovations and adaptive systems were developed and structured, which in turn provide insight on the fundamental principals of production organization in later Mesoamerican societies.

Kenneth Hirth (2006; chapter 2, this volume) argues that production diversification strategies for buffering risk were important mechanisms that Mesoamerican households employed to ensure their survival and security during times of changing environments and economies. Drawing on a

ARCHEOLOGICAL PAPERS OF THE AMERICAN ANTHROPOLOGICAL ASSOCIATION, Vol. 19, Issue 1, pp. 33–44, ISSN 1551-823X, online ISSN 1551-8248. © 2009 by the American Anthropological Association. All rights reserved. DOI: 10.1111/j.1551-8248.2009.01011.x.

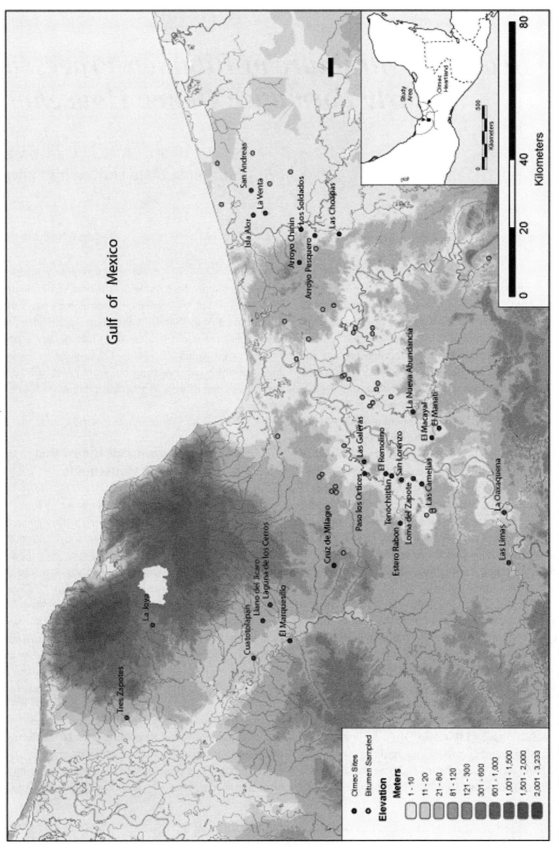

Figure 1. Olmec Heartland showing Olmec sites and the location of modern bitumen seepages.

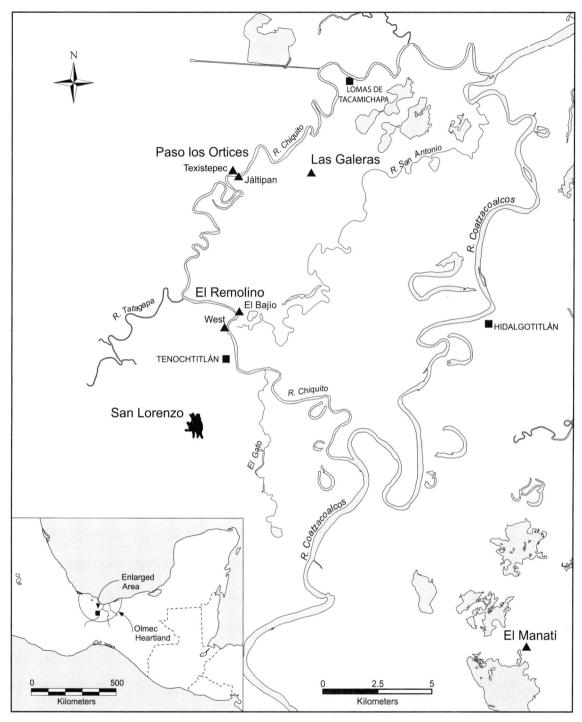

Figure 2. The San Lorenzo Olmec region.

growing body of literature on Mesoamerican domestic craft production (e.g., Feinman 1999), Hirth has modeled two different diversified domestic craft production strategies: 1) 'Intermittent Crafting' that involves periodic and part-time crafting, which complement other activities (subsistence) within households, and 2) 'Multicrafting' where multiple crafts are produced by specialists within the same household. Both intermittent and multicrafting complement subsistence production and are adaptive in that they increase household security and survival potential.

While Olmec households certainly were buffered against risk by diversification (and other risk minimizing strategies, e.g., storage and exchange), they did not diversify *only* as a response to changing environments or economies. Following Hirth (chapter 2, this volume), I argue that households represent the locus of economic change including changes in production strategies such as production intensification, specialization, innovation, and diversification. However, I contend that while Early Formative Olmec households were responding to outside factors and buffering against potential shortfall (adapting), they were also creating (innovating) new strategies to increase household security, stability, and perhaps status and wealth.

Early Formative household diversification strategies represent a continuation of successful Archaic period strategies. Researchers (e.g., Flannery 1986; MacNeish 1991) working in the highlands have documented subsistence risk buffering mechanisms, for example diversification and mobility, since the Archaic. I contend that during the Early Formative, as people became more sedentary and relied more on cultivated plants, diversification continued to be a successful risk buffering strategy even when other strategies such as storage and exchange increased in importance.

Along with diversification, Early Formative households also innovated new technologies (and techniques) to ensure their survival and increase their stability and wealth. One of the important Early Formative technological innovations was the cooking pot for food processing/preparation (Arnold 1999; Braun 1983; Lesure and Wake 2008; Hoopes and Barnett 1995). The innovation of pottery and direct-heat cooking was a technological breakthrough that made it possible to (1) prepare existing foods in a different way and (2) prepare a host of new foods not previously exploited (Lesure and Wake 2008). Thus this Early Formative period adaptation made it possible to increase both diet breadth (diversification) and food quantity (intensification) from the Archaic period on (Lesure and Wake 2008). In the Olmec region, the adoption of the cooking vessel not only made it possible to exploit a wider range of foods, but I argue that it also allowed the people to effectively process large amounts of bitumen and other materials (e.g., salt [Lesure and Wake 2008]). Processing of bitumen by indirect-heat cooking ('stone-boiling') would not have been efficient given the physical properties of bitumen (not to mention problematic due to the scarcity of hard stone in the San Lorenzo region).[1] However, with the development of the cooking pot and direct-heat cooking for food processing, lowland residents could now use this technology to effectively process the large quantities of bitumen that was required for watercraft manufacture and repair.

Finally, there is also little reason to argue that changes in domestic production organization from the Archaic to

the Early Formative period are necessarily attributable to a response to elite pressure or demand. Even in later, highly stratified Mesoamerican state-level societies there is little evidence for elites exerting pressure on households to intensify or specialize beyond that of tribute demands (Hirth 2006).

Bitumen Processing

Bitumen is a petroleum product composed of a mixture of complex natural hydrocarbons and oxidized products, and is what remains of crude oil upon the elimination of volatile components. In the Olmec region, many bitumen seepages are located in the central and eastern, low-lying areas (Fig. 1), and offshore in the Gulf of Mexico. In these areas, bitumen would have been available for collection from seepages and beaches where it washes ashore (Wendt and Lu 2006; Wendt and Cyphers 2008). No archaeological materials were found near any of the > 50 active seepages visited in the region (Wendt and Lu 2006). Indeed 3000 years of alluvial deposition and shoreline modification has obscured and destroyed Olmec settlement – some of which that might have been located near seeps active during Olmec times. However, the fact that not a single artifact was found during our survey of seepages suggests to me that most processing occurred away from seepages.

For bitumen to be effectively used it must be processed, which involves heating the natural bitumen and often mixing it with vegetal and/or mineral additives, such as sand, grass, straw, or leaves (Wendt and Cyphers 2008). Processed bitumen has the advantage of stiffening upon application and not melting in the sun (see Forbes 1936:42–45; Connan and Deschesne 1992). Tempering would also have had the advantage of increasing the volume of the final bitumen product, and would been a way to 'stretch' a given volume of raw bitumen. The Olmec used bitumen for decoration, waterproofing, and as an adhesive. Basalt aqueduct troughs from La Venta and San Lorenzo were joined together and bonded with bitumen (González Lauck, 1996:79; Wendt and Cyphers 2008), "knife" handles from El Manati were coated with bitumen (Ortíz Ceballos and Rodríguez 1994), and there is good reason to believe that bitumen was used to coat house floors and roofs, and to seal watercraft (Wendt and Cyphers 2008). Small 1–2 cm bitumen spheres have been discovered in many Olmec sites, and the Olmec occasionally decorated figurines with bitumen.

The distribution of bitumen artifacts at El Remolino and Paso los Ortices provides clues on how the San Lorenzo Olmec processed and used bitumen. Excavations in the Bajío area of El Remolino revealed abundant bitumen (Wendt

Figure 3. The pit feature containing slabs of bitumen from Paso los Ortices-Texistepec during field excavation

2005a; Wendt 2005b; Wendt and Cyphers 2008). The number of sherds with bitumen adherences (1852 of 75,345 or 2.46%), and their spatial patterning within the site suggests that some bitumen processing or preparation occurred within house-lots (Wendt 2005b; Wendt and Cyphers 2008).[2] Both El Remolino and Paso los Ortices have much higher densities of bitumen (lumps, slabs, and sherds with adherences) when compared to three habitation areas (B3–5, D5–9, D5–31) on the San Lorenzo plateau (Wendt 2003:514–518), suggesting that most bitumen was processed at levee sites for the manufacture and repair of watercraft. Bitumen was certainly used by the residents of San Lorenzo, but not to the degree it was in the levee sites.

Data from Paso los Ortices indicate that bitumen processing was sometimes organized as a specialized activity. The site is divided into a northern and a southern area by the Río Chiquito. In the southern (Jáltipan) portion, excavations revealed living surfaces and domestic areas and bitumen was nearly absent. Excavations in the northern (Texistepec) portion, however, produced abundant bitumen as well as a flat-bottomed, oval, and outslanting sided pit feature filled with about 250 kg of bitumen slabs (or cakes) arranged horizontally (Figures 3 and 4). The bitumen slabs were covered with a single layer of *tecomate* (a neckless jar form) sherds

with bitumen adherences. The bitumen slabs composing this feature have one flat, smooth side and distinct wood grain patterns on one or more of the other sides, together indicating that the slabs were formed when viscous bitumen was poured onto wood surfaces. Some of the rim sherds forming the top of the feature show clear asymmetrical stains suggesting that these sherds were part of vessels used to heat and process raw bitumen. There is no indication that bitumen was periodically added to the feature, but rather it appears to represents a single act of interment. This feature either represents the storage of bitumen slabs (1) processed for later trade, tribute, or local use, or (2) salvaged from some prior use and kept for future recycling (Wendt and Cyphers 2008). Bitumen processing experiments revealed that re-liquefying solid bitumen is possible, but requires higher temperatures and longer periods of time when compared to initial processing. Experiments also revealed that the more watery the seep bitumen, the longer it takes to process the substance into a usable, viscous state. Some watery bitumen took up to 160 hours of heating at 130° C to reach a usable, viscous state. This suggests that if households needed or wanted to conserve fuel they would have selected bitumen from seepages that contained viscous bitumen whenever available.

Sand and silt was discovered evenly mixed in the thin section samples of archaeological bitumen from El Remolino and Paso los Ortices. The inclusions indicate that these materials were either intentionally added during the heating or they represent material unintentionally incorporated into the amalgam. Impressions of decomposed vegetal matter were observed with the naked eye, a binocular microscope, and in thin sections. I suspect that the vegetal matter represents finely chopped grasses, leaves, palm fronds, and/or maize husks. As mentioned above, adding sand and vegetal matter to bitumen increases the material's viscosity and volume, and adds structure by forming chemical bonds.

Sherds from *tecomate* jars excavated at the sites often had residue of bitumen on their interiors and occasionally possessed drip marks on the exteriors of rims suggesting that the Olmec heated bitumen inside these multipurpose vessels. The shape of *tecomates* and the pattern of the drip marks (Wendt and Cyphers 2008) indicate that after processing, the amalgam was extracted with some sort of scooping tool that was probably made of wood. Besides pottery vessels, no other processing tools were discovered at the sites. Notably, like pottery production, bitumen processing is an additive technology that leaves very few production indicators of scale (Wendt and Cyphers 2008). Once processed, the bitumen amalgam would have been used immediately or fashioned into lumps, spheres, or slabs for later use. While processing bitumen in cooking pots renders them useless for

Figure 4. Half of the bitumen pit feature being excavated in the IIA-UNAM, Mapachapa laboratory.

food preparation, the vessels could still be used for storing, and their waterproof quality might even have been desired.

Bitumen Processing and Watercraft

Recent salvage operations along the Río Coatzacoalcos revealed the remains of two canoes tentatively dated to the Classic period (Delgado Calderón 2008). The canoes were identified from the 1–8 cm thick bitumen residue that coated their entire exterior hulls and took the shape of the watercraft. The shape and size of the bitumen outlines indicate that the canoes measured 5.1 m and 7.0 m long, and both were 75 cm wide (Delgado Calderón 2008). Although this find has not been adequately reported (Delgado Calderón 2008; Pringle 2008), it gives an indication of how the Olmec might have applied bitumen to watercraft, and it provides a basis for calculations of the amount of bitumen needed for canoe manufacture and repair. This in turn permits an estimate of the scale of Olmec canoe manufacture and aids in the interpretation of the bitumen pit feature from Paso los Ortices.

A canoe of the shape and size of the 5.1 m long Coatzacoalcos canoe (75 cm wide and 37.5 cm deep) would have roughly 64,500 sq cm of exterior surface area. A 4 cm layer of bitumen would take 258,000 cm^3 (258 liters or 68 gallons) of the substance. A 7.0 m long canoe with the same width, depth, and bitumen thickness would take 347,500 cm^3 (347.5 liters or 91 gallons) of bitumen. Interestingly, the bitumen pit feature from Paso los Ortices, which mea-

sured 1.9 m x 75 cm x 25 cm, is equal to 356,250 cm^3 (356.25 liters or 94 gallons) of bitumen – very close to the amount necessary to coat a 7.0 m long canoe with a 4 cm layer of bitumen.

Richard Lesure (1998:26) reports that during the Locona through Cherla phases (1700–1300 BC) plain-bodied *tecomates* from the site of Paso de la Amada in the Soconusco region have volumes ranging from 11–14 liters. Assuming that San Lorenzo phase *tecomates* have roughly the same volume, and since it is impossible to process a full vessel of bitumen due to material expansion during heating, I estimate that batches ranged from 9 to 11 liters (for the 11–14 liter *tecomates*) (Table 1). Under these assumptions, it would take 23–29 batches to coat a 5 m canoe with 4 cm of bitumen, 32–39 batches for the 7 m canoe, and 32–40 batches to make the Paso los Ortices pit feature. Table 2 provides an estimate of the amount of time needed to process one batch of bitumen. The calculation of 5–7 hours per batch is the estimated time to process only one batch from start (collecting of seep material) to finish (application). Time, of course, would be reduced if residents collected large qualities of seep material and mass processed them by running multiple batches at once. Also some of the processing activities could have been conducted concurrently, for instance the heating and grinding of vegetal additives. In addition, the amount of time to process a batch of bitumen would have depended heavily upon the consistency of the seep material used. As mentioned above, it took 160 hours of heating (processing) at 130° C to render watery bitumen (from the

Table 1. Estimations of the amount of bitumen required to coat canoes

		Thickness of bitumen layer		
		1 cm	**4 cm**	**8 cm**
5 m canoe*	cm^3	64,500	258,000	516,000
	liters	64.5	258	516
	11 liter vessel ***	7	**29**	57
	14 liter vessel****	6	**23**	47
7 m canoe**	cm^3	86,885	347,540	695,080
	liters	86.885	347.54	695.08
	11 liter vessel***	10	**39**	77
	14 liter vessel****	8	**32**	63
Bitumen Pit Feature	cm^3			356,250
	liters			356.25
	11 liter vessel***			**40**
	14 liter vessel****			**32**

*estimated exterior surface area of 64500 cm^2
**estimated exterior surface area of 86885 cm^2
***containing 9 liters of bitumen
****containing 11 liters of bitumen

Table 2. Estimate of time needed to process one batch of bitumen

	Hours
Collect bitumen and additives	1–2
Prepare additives (grinding, chopping, sorting)	1
Heating bitumen (and mixing in additives)	1–2
Cooling and applying to a surface	2
Total time	5–7

Table 3. Estimate of days required to process and coat a 5 m and 7 m canoe with a 4 cm layer of bitumen

	Batches	Hours (5–7 per batch)	5-hour days
5 meter canoe	23	115–161	23–32
	29	145–203	29–41
7 meter canoe	32	160–224	32–45
	39	195–273	39–55

Jáltipan seepage) into a usable form. However, when we used more viscous seep material (from the PEMEX-2 seepage) it only took 1.5 hours of heating (and processing) to obtain a usable product. Table 3 is an estimation of the days required to process bitumen and apply it to a 5 m and a 7 m canoe. The estimates in Table 3 are probably high since it is likely that multiple batches were processed at one time. And since the heating of bitumen would not require one's undivided attention, other tasks such as food preparation, looking after children, or the production of some craft items could be done concurrently. Nonetheless, even the lowest figure of 23 days shows that the collecting and processing of bitumen took a substantial amount of time. Canoe repair and maintenance almost certainly would have been an ongoing task requiring bitumen processing and perhaps recycling (Wendt and Cyphers 2008).

Bitumen collection and processing were most likely dry season activities due to the availability of dry fuel and vegetal additives and the scheduling of subsistence pursuits (Wendt and Cyphers 2008). Nevertheless, the proposed sea-

sonal production reached a high level, which is evident by the amount of stored processed slabs of bitumen at Paso los Ortices-Texistepec. Although the Texistepec area was clearly a locus of specialized, 'household level' bitumen processing at the Paso los Ortices, household stability and survival would have been ultimately dependent upon successful subsistence activities. However, an ample supply of processed bitumen certainly was important for maintaining watercraft that played a key role in fishing, as well as intra-regional exchange and communication.

The data from Paso los Ortices and El Remolino suggest that bitumen processing at Olmec levee sites was organized differently, on multiple scales, and related to other activities in complex ways. The organization of Olmec bitumen processing supports Hirth's argument that full-time/part-time categories of production specialization act to hinder our understanding of the structure of prehispanic domestic craft production. The northern Texistepec area of Paso los Ortices appears to have been an area of bitumen processing specialization that fits well with Hirth's Intermittent Crafting model, while processing (or preparation) at El Remolino seems to have been organized as a non-specialized, household based activity. Processing, or more appropriately, preparation at El Remolino was likely conducted on a 'needs basis'. At Paso los Ortices bitumen processing would have been intensified during periods when residents were free from subsistence activities, but they could easily have been involved in other tasks (e.g., cooking) at the same time they were processing bitumen. Multiple households at Paso los Ortices could have contributed to the pit feature and/or been involved in processing activities at the site. Overall, bitumen processing was most likely conducted where and when there was a significant need, for instance when surfacing a structure or coating a canoe.

The Archaic to Formative Transition: Technological Developments and Adaptations

Ethnographic and archaeological data from the Olmec region (Coe and Diehl 1980a, 1980b; VanDerwarker 2006; Borstein 2001; Symonds et al. 2002; Lane Rodríguez et al. 1997) support a diversified and complex model of Olmec subsistence activities. Fishing, hunting, gathering, and agriculture were important activities that were undertaken during different times of the year. A diversified subsistence strategy would have been vital for those individuals residing in settlements around rivers, lakes, and other water sources where fishing would have been significant. Although fishing for particular species in the region's rivers and lakes is seasonal, overall fishing would have been a year-round pursuit with certain times of the year being more productive than others. Farming, hunting, and gathering would have complemented fishing. Ethnographic research (Coe and Diehl 1980b:69–72) shows that farming the levees around San Lorenzo is mainly undertaken during the dry season, while the largest yields from modern farming occur in the uplands during the rainy season (Wendt n.d.).

A complex and diversified subsistence system mandates an equally complex organization of craft production and scheduling. As Hirth's Intermittent Crafting model predicts, specialized production would have taken place during those windows of time throughout the year when individuals were freed from alternative subsistence activities. Production specialization is evident at Paso los Ortices-Texistepec from the high density of archaeological bitumen, the bitumen pit feature, and the absence of habitation features in the area. Although the Texistepec area was clearly a locus of specialized bitumen processing at the Paso los Ortices, household stability and survival ultimately would have depended upon successful subsistence activities. However, an ample supply of processed bitumen certainly was important for maintaining watercraft that played a key role in fishing, as well as intra-regional exchange and communication. Levee villagers would have been involved in a diverse set of activities thought the year including agriculture, fishing, and bitumen processing.

Why did Olmec households intensify the production of some items? One answer is that the intensification of craft production would have been a way to minimize subsistence risk and resource shortfalls (Hirth 2006). This explanation works well in societies that can experience economic gain by increasing the output of craft items. However, economic gain (or security) from intensified production is dependent on effective distribution systems and ample consumers (Hirth 2006). And while the Olmec certainly intensified production there is no evidence for Olmec markets and little evidence for other non-household based distribution networks that would have acted to effectively distribute items to consumers. Also, for intensified craft production to be a viable risk buffering strategy there must be a steady supply of consumers. And although there might have been sufficient customers for processed bitumen, at present we do not have sufficient data on patterns of regional bitumen consumption to be able to adequately evaluate this idea.

Though it is possible that bitumen processing was coordinated above local domestic production units (by elite), there is at present no evidence to support this idea (Wendt and Cyphers 2008). Elite members of Olmec society could have obtained processed bitumen through exchange, tribute, or by consignment (see Clark and Parry 1990), or they simply could have processed it themselves. Moreover, elite control of bitumen processing is unlikely since an examination of Early Formative Olmec political economy reveals that much of the leaders' political and economic power lay in the ideational realm rather than the economic domain (Wendt n.d., 2003). San Lorenzo elite were certainly involved in the long-distance exchange of portable prestige items and intra-regional transport of basalt for monuments, but they do not appear to have been involved in the production and distribution of utilitarian goods or stable products (Wendt n.d.; c.f. Symonds et al. 2002).

The most satisfying explanation of Olmec domestic production intensification is that it developed within a diversified household economy geared towards ensuring household survival, security, and well-being, and increasing household status and wealth. Minimization of risk is not sufficient to explain the development of intensified forms of craft production during the Early Formative. Rather I argue that successful Archaic period (8000–2000 BC) adaptive strategies of diversification continued into the Early Formative.

Archaeologists (e.g., Flannery 1986; MacNeish 1991) have documented Archaic period subsistence risk buffering mechanisms, including diversification and mobility in Mesoamerica's Central and Southern Highlands. I argue that during the Early Formative, as people became more sedentary, diversification continued to be a successful risk buffering strategy even when other adaptive strategies such as storage and exchange increased in importance. Thus, subsistence adaptive strategies of diversification and intensification would have been geared more towards buffering against risk, while intensification of crafting would have initially developed as a way to ensure household security and stability, but also to increase status and wealth. Through time, with the introduction of more effective distribution mechanisms, the intensification of crafting would have been an effective way for households to achieve more security and stability. With regard to bitumen, the development of an effective bitumen processing technology would have initially permitted local residents to intensify their riverine subsistence pursuits. One byproduct of this is the creation of a transportation and communication infrastructure that could be exploited by San Lorenzo's developing elite to expand their polity and to incorporate many human supporters. Thus while risk buffering mechanisms were developed to buffer against potential subsistence shortfall, they facilitated the creation of social/political institutions, which became embedded into, and transformed the society.

The Cooking Pot and Direct Heating Technology

The incurved rimmed *tecomate* vessel was surely developed in the context of food preparation and was also used to process and prepare other products, such as salt (Santley 2004; Lesure and Wake 2008). I argue that the innovation of the ceramic cooking pot and the application of direct heating technology made it possible to process large quantities of bitumen, which was mainly used for sealing canoes – making these watercraft more effective, durable, and long lasting. The development of increasingly effective watercraft represents an adaptive response to the challenges posed and opportunities presented by a river-dominant environment (see Ortiz Pérez and Cyphers 1997). I contend that the incorporation of bitumen in the construction of durable and long-lasting watercraft contributed significantly to the development of the San Lorenzo river-based polity. This innovation was likely first developed as a local environmental adaptation for fishing and transporting people and goods, and only later became important in the transportation of hard stone (for monuments), tribute, and information, in the San Lorenzo polity (see Symonds et al. 2002).

Finally, it is important to mention that bitumen processing and ceramic production represent a good example of Hagstrum's (2001:50) 'intersecting technologies'. Both are additive pyrotechnologies that involve the selection of specific materials (seep bitumen or clay) and the selection, preparation, and addition of specific types, quantities, and mixtures of tempering agents. In fact, some thin sections of Early Formative bitumen artifacts and ceramic sherds from the San Lorenzo region revealed very similar tempering materials and techniques. This suggests that the technological knowledge of ceramic production certainly played an important part in the technological development of bitumen processing. It is also likely that bitumen processing was at least in part an activity undertaken by women. The processing of raw bitumen involves many of the same skills, tasks, and tools that often fall into women's domains (e.g., controlling fire temperatures for food preparation and pottery production, selection and combination of specific amounts of ingredients in food preparation and pottery production, 'ownership' of grinding tools).

Conclusion

Bitumen processing among the Olmec represents some of the earliest evidence for domestic craft activity in Mesoamerica, and is the earliest documented evidence for domestic craft production in the southern Gulf lowlands. Data on bitumen processing from Paso los Ortices support Hirth's Intermittent Crafting model of diversified domestic craft production. I argue that during the Early Formative domestic craft production developed within an extant and adaptive system of subsistence diversification as a way to ensure household security and stability, while at the same time providing a way to increase household status and wealth. The Olmec appear to have developed ways to minimize risk and maximize production within in the context of early the household – notably also where political and economic power surely developed.

By using the ceramic vessel as a tool (Braun 1983) to process bitumen, the Early Formative Olmec improved the efficiency and longevity of canoe travel within the region. This adaptation/innovation was later used and expanded upon by the San Lorenzo Olmec elite in developing their system of communication and transportation, which eventually contributed to the success of the San Lorenzo Olmec polity. The presence of natural seepages of bitumen and the development of a bitumen processing technology helped develop highly effective riverine transportation and communication systems that allowed the San Lorenzo Olmec to command a wider exploitative range (tribute, population control, natural resources) than other contemporaneous polities in the southern Gulf lowland region, and this helps explain why the San Lorenzo Olmec polity grew into one of the largest polities in Formative Mesoamerica.

The present study is important because the Early Formative period was a time when production systems in Mesoamerica were reorganized and intensified. Local entrepreneurs would have been involved in innovating and modifying adaptive systems to build support and power networks in the development of institutionalized social inequalities. How production systems were reorganized during the Early Formative provides insight on the fundamental principals of production organization in later Mesoamerican societies. Finally, this study highlights the importance of focusing on changes in production scale and scheduling when modeling early crafting systems.

Acknowledgements

I want to thank Ken Hirth for inviting me to participate in the 2007 SAA "Housework" symposium and this volume. Thanks to Edgar Huerta who assisted in the bitumen processing experiments at Cal State Fullerton. I thank the Consejo de Arqueología of the Instituto National de Antropologia e Historia for granting permission for sample export and for authorizing the Remolino and Paso los Ortices investigations. I also thank the municipal presidents of Texistepec, Jáltipan de Morelos, and Las Choapas for their support of the projects. Finally I thank the property owners who graciously allowed us to work on their lands and the archaeologists and fieldworkers who contributed to the success of the project. Funds for this research were provided by the National Science Foundation (BCS-0000354, BCS-0636107), the Foundation for the Advancement of Mesoamerican Studies, Inc. (#99068, #03059), and the National Geographic Society Committee for Research and Exploration (#6717-00).

Notes

1. Bitumen can be processed using a pit boiling technique, where a pit is excavated just back from a riverbank and a fire is set below. This heating technique has been described in the Near East (Ochsenschlager 1992), and while it is feasible in the Olmec region evidence for it is lacking.

2. The proportion of sherds with bitumen adherences to sherds without bitumen from the Bajío area of El Remolino seems high, however these types of data are seldom reported for sites within or outside the Olmec region (yet see Wendt 2003:table G.10) so my impression cannot be substantiated.

References

Arnold, Philip J. III
1999 *Tecomates*, Residential Mobility, and Early Formative Occupation in Coastal Lowland Mesoamerica. *In* Pottery and People: A Dynamic Interaction. James Skibo and Gary Feinman, eds. Pp. 159–170. Salt Lake City: The University of Utah Press.

Borstein, Joshua
2001 Tripping Over Colossal Heads: Settlement Patterns and Population Development in the Upland Olmec Heartland. Unpublished Ph.D. dissertation, Department of Anthropology, Pennsylvania State University.

Braun, David P.
1983 Pots as Tools. *In* Archaeological Hammers and Theories. J. Moore and A. Keene, eds. Pp. 108–134. New York: Academic Press.

Clark, John E.
1995 Craft Specialization as an Archaeological Category. Research in Economic Anthropology 16:267–294.

Clark, John E., and Michael Blake
1994 The Power of Prestige: Competitive Generosity and the Emergence of Rank Societies in Lowland Mesoamerica. *In* Factional Competition and Political Development in the New World. E. Brumfiel and J. Fox, eds. Pp. 17–30. Cambridge: Cambridge University Press.

Clark, John E., and William J. Parry
1990 Craft Specialization and Cultural Complexity. Research in Economic Archaeology 12: 289–346.

Coe, Michael D., and Richard A. Diehl
1980a In the Land of the Olmec, Vol. 1. The Archaeology of San Lorenzo Tenochtitlán. Austin: University of Texas Press.
1980b In the Land of the Olmec, Vol. 2. The People of the River. Austin: University of Texas Press.

Connan, Jacques, and Odile Deschesne
1992 Archaeological Bitumen: Identifications, Origins and Uses of an Ancient Near Eastern

Material. *In* Materials Research Society Symposium Proceedings, Vol. 267. Pittsburgh: Materials Research Society.

Cyphers, Ann, ed.
1997 Población, Subsistencia y Medio Ambiente en San Lorenzo Tenochtitlán. Mexico: Universidad Nacional Autónoma de Mexico, Instituto de Investigaciones Antropológicas.

Delgado Calderón, Alfredo
2008 El Túnel Sumergido de Coatzacoalcos. *In* Diario del Istmo, Janurary 12, 2008, accessed April 6, 2008, [http://www.diariodelistmo.com.mx/istmo_nivel3.php?id_noticia=85382].

Drucker, Philip
1952 La Venta, Tabasco: A Study of Olmec Ceramics and Art. Washington, DC: Smithsonian Institution, Bureau of American Ethnology, Bulletin 153.

Feinman, Gary M.
1999 Rethinking Our Assumptions: Economic Specialization at the Household Scale in Ancient Ejutla, Oaxaca, Mexico. *In* Pottery and People: A Dynamic Interaction. James Skibo and Gary Feinman, eds. Pp. 81–98. The University of Utah Press, Salt Lake City.

Flannery, Kent V., ed.
1986 Guilá Naquitz: Archaic Foraging and Early Agriculture in Oaxaca, Mexico. New York: Academic Press.

Forbes, R. J.
1936 Bitumen and Petroleum in Antiquity. Leiden: E. J. Brill.

González Lauck, Rebecca
1996 La Venta: An Olmec Capital. *In* Olmec Art of Ancient Mexico. Elizabeth P. Benson and B. de la Fuente, eds. Pp. 73–81. Washington: National Gallery of Art.

Hagstrum, Melissa
2001 Household Production in Chaco Canyon Society. American Antiquity 66:47–55.

Hayden, Brian
1995 Pathways to Power: Principles for Creating Socioeconomic Inequalities. *In* Foundations of Social Inequality. T. D. Price and G. Feinman, eds. Pp. 15–86. New York: Plenum Press.

Hirth, Kenneth G.
2006 Modeling Domestic Craft Production at Xochicalco. *In* Obsidian Craft Production in Ancient Central Mexico: Archaeological Research at Xochicalco. Kenneth G. Hirth, ed. Pp. 275–286. Salt Lake City: University of Utah Press.

Hoopes, John W., and William K. Barnett
1995 The Shape of Early Pottery Studies. *In* The Emergence of Pottery: Technology and Innovation in Ancient Societies. William K. Barnett and John W. Hoopes, eds. Pp. 1–7. Washington: Smithsonian Institution Press.

Lane Rodríguez, Marci, Rogelio Aguirre, and Javier González
1997 Producción Campesina del Maíz en San Lorenzo Tenochtitlán. *In* Población, Subsistencia y Medio Ambiente en San Lorenzo Tenochtitlán. Ann Cyphers, ed. Pp. 55–73. Mexico: Universidad Nacional Autónoma de Mexico, Instituto de Investigaciones Antropológicas.

Lesure, Richard G.
1998 Vessel Form and Function in an Early Formative Ceramic Assemblage from Coastal Mexico. Journal of Field Archaeology 25(1):19–36.

Lesure, Richard G., and Thomas A. Wake
2008 Adaptation, Organization, and the Transition from Archaic to Formative in Soconusco. Paper presented at the Sociopolitical Transformation in Early Mesoamerica: Archaic to Formative in the Soconusco Region conference, Los Angeles: Cotsen Institute of Archaeology, University of California.

MacNiesh, Richard S.
1991 The Origins of Agriculture and Settled Life. Norman: University of Oklahoma Press.

Ochsenschlager, Edward
1992 Ethnographic Evidence for Wood, Boats, Bitumen and Reeds in Southern Iraq: Ethnoarchaeology at al-Hiba. *In* Trees and Timber in Mesopotamia, Vol. 6. J. N. Postgate and Marvin A. Powell, eds. Pp. 47–78. Cambridge: Bulletin on Sumerian Agriculture.

Ortíz Ceballos, Ponciano, and María del Carmen Rodríguez
1994 Los Espacios Sagrados Olmecas: El Manatí, un Caso Especial. *In* Los Olmecas en Mesoamerica, John Clark, ed. Pp. 69–91. El Equilibrista and Citibank.

Ortiz Pérez, Mario Arturo, and Ann Cyphers
1997 La Geomorfología y las Evidencias Arqueológicas en la Région de San Lorenzo Tenochtitlán, Veracruz. *In* Población, Subsistencia y Medio Ambiente en San Lorenzo Tenochtitlán, Ann Cyphers, ed. Pp. 31–53. México, D.F.: Instituto de Investigaciones Antropológicas, Universidad Nacional Autónoma de Mexico.

Pringle, Heather
2008 Following an Asphalt Trail to Ancient Olmec Trade Routes. Science 320(5873):174.

Santley, Robert S.
2004 Prehistoric Salt Production at El Salado, Veracruz, Mexico. Latin American Antiquity 15:199–221.

Symonds, Stacey, Ann Cyphers, and Roberto Lunagómez
2002 Patron de Asentamiento en San Lorenzo Tenochtitlán. Mexico: Universidad Nacional Autónoma de Mexico, Instituto de Investigaciones Antropológicas.

VanDerwarker, Amber M.
2006 Farming, Hunting, and Fishing in the Olmec World. Austin: The University of Texas Press.

Wendt, Carl J.
2003 Early Formative Domestic Organization and Community Patterning in the San Lorenzo Tenochtitlán Region, Veracruz, Mexico. Unpublished Ph.D. dissertation, Pennsylvania State University.
2005a Excavations at El Remolino: Household Archaeology in the San Lorenzo Olmec Region. Journal of Field Archaeology 30:163–180.
2005b Using Refuse Disposal Patterns to Infer Olmec Site Structure in the San Lorenzo Region, Veracruz, Mexico. Latin American Antiquity 16(4):449–466.
n.d. Commoners and the San Lorenzo Olmec Political Economy. Manuscript in possession of the author.

Wendt, Carl J., and Ann Cyphers
2008 How the Olmec Used Bitumen in Ancient Mesoamerica. Journal of Anthropological Archaeology 27(2):175–191.

Wendt, Carl J., and Stan-Tan Lu
2006 Sourcing Archaeological Bitumen in the Olmec Region. Journal of Archaeological Science 33(1):89–97.

4

Rethinking the Organization of Aztec Salt Production: A Domestic Perspective

Jason P. De León
University of Washington

Despite the abundance of archaeological, ethnohistoric, and ethnographic data on Aztec salt production (see an excellent review in Parsons 2001), little has been said about the organization of salt production or the role it may have played in the domestic economy of the pre-Hispanic inhabitants of Lake Texcoco (Figure 1). This lack of research is surprising given that salt was a dietary necessity that the Aztecs produced, traded, and consumed on a large scale (Sahagún 1961; Gibson 1964; Parsons 2001). Moreover, the debris produced by salt production is easily identifiable and ubiquitous along the shoreline of Lake Texcoco, making it an ideal craft activity for archaeologists to study. Those who have discussed the organization of production suggest that it was year-round, large scale, and specialized (Charlton 1971:218; Parsons 1994: 277–8, 2001:300–1). In this chapter I reevaluate existing information regarding salt production within the context of a domestic economy. In so doing I attempt to answer two questions. First, how and why does salt production fit into a domestic economy model? Second, what types of activities would likely have been carried out in salt-producing households?

To model Aztec salt production, archaeological, ethnohistoric, and ethnographic data are employed. The archaeological data come primarily from surveys conducted on the shores of Lake Texcoco (Sanders et al. 1979; Parsons 1971) and excavations conducted at the salt production site of Xocotitlan (Figure 1) (Baños 1980; Sanchez 1989; Baños and Sanchez 1998). The ethnohistoric data come from colonial accounts of salt production written by Sahagún and various *conquistadores*. The ethnographic data come from Parsons' (2001) study of modern salt production in the Mexican town of Nexquipayac located on the northwest shore of Lake Texcoco. Additional ethnographic data from outside the Basin of Mexico are also discussed.

The results of this research indicate that Aztec salt production is best viewed as a highly skilled craft activity that was practiced intermittently along the lakeshores of Lake Texcoco. Salt production was a craft activity that households practiced alongside other subsistence activities such as farming, fishing, and harvesting of lake resources. Moreover, the data suggest that seasonal weather conditions and production constraints dictated that salt production be carried out in the dry season and away from residential structures. These findings not only force us to reevaluate some of the assumptions built into "part-time/full-time" craft production models, but also how we interpret isolated workshop activity areas and their relationship to nearby households.

Background: Salt Does the Body Good

Salt plays an important role in regulating the body's osmotic pressure and is crucial to hormonal and enzymatic processes (Lovejoy 1986:1). Because the body loses salt through the process of sweating and waste excretion,[1] it must be constantly replaced to sustain bodily functions. One way that salt levels can be maintained is through the consumption of naturally salt-rich foods, such as animal meat. Salt can be added to food as a flavoring or as a preservative. Diets that rely heavily on plant foods are more likely to be supplemented with salt than diets that primarily consist

ARCHEOLOGICAL PAPERS OF THE AMERICAN ANTHROPOLOGICAL ASSOCIATION, Vol. 19, Issue 1, pp. 45–57, ISSN 1551-823X, online ISSN 1551-8248. © 2009 by the American Anthropological Association. All rights reserved. DOI: 10.1111/j.1551-8248.2009.01012.x.

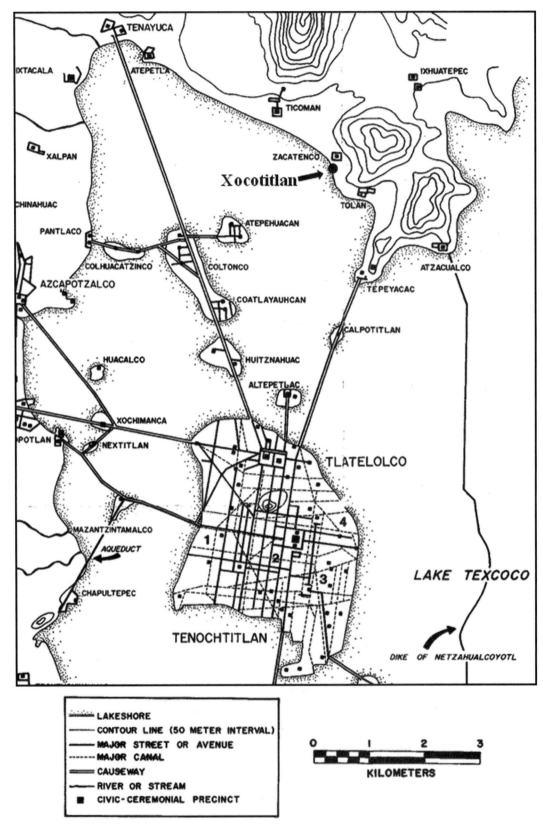

Figure 1. Map of showing location of the Postclassic salt production site Xocotitlan (based on Sanders et al. 1979 and Sanchez 1989).

of animal products (Lovejoy 1986). Vikør (1999:66) estimates that a strict vegetable diet of cereals or roots, which contain less than 20 mg of salt per 100 g, would require a minimum intake of 50 kg of vegetables a day to meet the human requirement of 10 g of salt. This indicates that individuals with meat-poor diets will require some type of salt supplement. In addition to diet, other factors such as body size, climate, and levels of physical activity determine an individual's necessary daily salt intake.

By the Postclassic period, it is estimated that the diet of the average person living in the Basin of Mexico may have been up to 80.0 percent reliant on maize (Sanders 1976:109) and less than 0.1 percent reliant on hunting (Sanders et al. 1979:286). Most Aztecs living in the Basin of Mexico probably needed an additional source of salt to meet daily body requirements. Apart from hunted terrestrial animal meat, salt may have been available through the consumption of insects, waterfowl, algae, and fish commonly found in and around the lakes of the Basin of Mexico (see Santley and Rose 1979; Parsons 2006, 2008). Although lacustrine derived foodstuffs were often harvested and commonly sold in the Aztec marketplace (Ortiz de Montellano 1990:115–8), the amount of salt that these foods contributed to the average person's diet is currently unknown.

In addition to being a biological necessity, the Aztecs (and other Postclassic people) produced salt for use in food preservation (Andrews 1983:10; Ewald 1985:9), tribute payments (Parsons 2001:153–4), as an important ingredient in rituals and medicines (Andrews 1983:10; Ewald 1985:9), as an ingredient in ceramic production (Ewald 1985:12), and as a mordant for dyeing textiles (Parsons 2001:245–7). In order to meet diet, tribute, and craft production needs of the Postclassic period, the Aztecs had to artificially produce salt.

Production Techniques

Salt production techniques in Mesoamerica typically involved one of two methods: 1) the reduction of brine through boiling or heating in ceramic vessels (Valdez et al. 1996; Parsons 2001; McKillop 2002) or 2) the solar evaporation of brine in basins (Andrews 1983; Williams 2002). Ethnographic data indicate that these methods are often mutually exclusive (Andrews 1983; Good 1995; McKillop 2002; Williams 2002). However, it is possible that prior to Spanish contact these methods were somehow combined. For example, solar evaporation could have been the first stage of brine reduction and boiling may have been the final stage. Excavations at the salt production site of Xocotitlan revealed a possible evaporation pan (Figure 2), which may have been

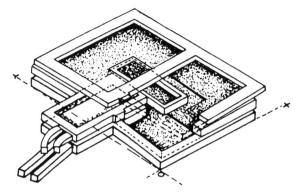

Figure 2. Possible solar evaporation pan from the site of Xocotitlan (redrawn from Sanchez 1989: Fig. 4).

used alongside some form of brine reduction using artificial heat (Baños 1980; Sanchez 1989; also see discussion of this possibility in Castellón Huerta [n.d.]). The brine used in salt production can be drawn directly from brackish pools of water (Good 1995; Williams 2002) or can be flushed from soils containing high levels of salt (Apenes 1944; Parsons 2001:18). Ancient salt producers along the shores of Lake Texcoco obtained brine by leaching out salts from saline rich soil (Sahagún 1961:84; Gibson 1964:338).

There were numerous production constraints on pre-Hispanic salt production that limited when and where this activity could be carried out. First, Aztec salt production required significant amounts of salt-rich soil (*salitre*), as well as water to flush those soils. Parsons (2001:137) found that modern Texcoco salt makers who used some methods similar to pre-Hispanic technology typically required 108–126 liters of water and 120–140 kg of *salitre* to produce 5 kg of dried salt. The acquisition and transport costs of these necessary raw materials limited where salt could be produced. While modern saltmakers were able to employ draft animals and motorized vehicles to assist in the transport process, Aztec salt makers would have faced high transportation costs, even when canoes were employed (Parsons 2001:137). In order to reduce these transportation costs, ancient salt production stations were located along the lakeshore zone in close proximity to water and *salitre* (Parsons 2001: 137).

Another factor that influenced ancient salt production was the seasonal fluctuations in rainfall and lakeshore levels. High-quality *salitre* is only available during the dry season, when lake levels recede and expose the preferred type of salt-rich soils (Gibson 1964:338; Parsons 2001:60). Given that over 100 kilograms of soil are needed to produce even a small batch of salt, it was unlikely that ancient producers stored the hundreds (if not thousands) of kilograms of *salitre* that would have been required to produce salt in the wet season. Moreover, rainfall would have prevented the outdoor

Figure 3. Texcoco Fabric-Marked Vessel (redrawn from Holmes 1885: Fig. 2).

boiling of brine or the use of solar evaporation methods. Dry season production would have not only enabled producers to exploit sunlight energy, they also would have had access to more dried vegetation for fuel. Gibson's (1964:338) research on the colonial period supports the proposition that both rainfall and lakeshore levels determined when salt could be produced.

Another aspect of salt production that was influenced by seasonality was the use of ceramics in the production process. Texcoco Fabric Marked (TFM) pottery is the most common artifact type associated with Postclassic salt production in the Basin of Mexico (Charlton 1969, 1971; Baños and Sanchez 1998; Parsons 2001:250) (Figure 3). The density of TFM sherds is often the basis for identifying production stations in the Basin of Mexico (see Parsons 1971). TFM pottery is highly porous, poorly fired, thin-walled, friable, and has textile impressions on its outer surface (Baños and Sanchez 1998:5; also see Tolstoy 1958:51; Charlton 1969; Parsons 2001:249–55). This pottery is typically monochrome and predominantly yellow, brown, red, or gray (Baños and Sanchez 1998:5). Prior to the firing of TFM pottery, a fiber cloth was wrapped around the vessel to increase the porosity of the receptacle.

Baños and Sanchez (1998:5) describe several types of TFM vessels from their excavations at the salt production site of Xocotitlan. This included circular vessels with flat bases that had average rim diameters of 18–20 cm and heights of 10–11 cm and 19 cm (see Parsons 2001: Table 7.5 for estimated sizes and volumes). Baños and Sanchez (1998:5) also report conical (flower-pot), rectangular (loaf-like), and oval shaped vessels. Parsons (2001: Table 7.5) calculates that these vessels had internal carrying volumes ranging from .40 to 4.50 liters. Despite the inextricable connection between TFM pottery and salt production, identifying the functions of these vessels has been problem-

atic. It is likely that these standardized vessels were used to dry (Baños 1980: 92–94), store, and transport different varieties of salt (Talavera 1979; see discussion in Parsons 2001:249–59). These vessels were probably manufactured by the saltmakers themselves (Baños and Sanchez 1998).

Some Mesoamerican archaeologists report brine boiling in thick-walled ceramic vessels (McKillop 2002). Given that TFM pottery is poorly fired and thin-walled, it is unclear if these vessels were ever used to boil brine over direct heat (although see Castellón Huerta [n.d.]).[2] This may indicate that the high-temperature boiling (using metal pans) that Parsons describes at the modern Nexquipayac workshops, is a recent development. Baños (1980:94) posits that TFM vessels were used to dry semi-solidified salt using indirect heat. This method is strikingly different from the direct boiling that was practiced in other parts of Mesoamerica (McKillop 2002), but similar to indirect heating methods reported from Puebla (Valdez et al. 1996). Castellón Huerta (n.d.) reports fabric marked pottery from Puebla that appears to have been directly heated using basal ceramic supports. The current evidence for the direct boiling of TFM pottery in the Basin of Mexico is ambiguous and requires further detailed examination.

Previous Discussions of the Organization of Salt Production

The few discussions of the organization of Aztec salt production characterize it as year-round, large scale, and specialized (Parsons 2001:300–1; Charlton 1971:218). These suppositions are based on the following: First, salt production was a localized activity that required expert knowledge and a suite of special tools. As previously mentioned, production was primarily restricted to the northern and western shores of Lake Texcoco to cut down transportation costs. Ethnographic studies indicate that the production of salt is a delicate and time-consuming process (Parsons 1994: 277; Parsons 2001:83–130) that requires some level of skill and knowledge. The fact that special ceramics were manufactured as a *contingent* craft used in the production process, signals some degree of specialization.

Second, salt production sites were physically detached from household structures. Most of the production sites identified in the Lake Texcoco survey had no house mounds associated with them (Parsons 1971). Because archaeologists often associate detached workshops with greater degrees of specialization (Costin 1991:25), the tendency may be to associate these isolated salt stations with more intensive production operating at a level above and beyond that of a domestic workshop (although see Muller [1984, 1986] for a

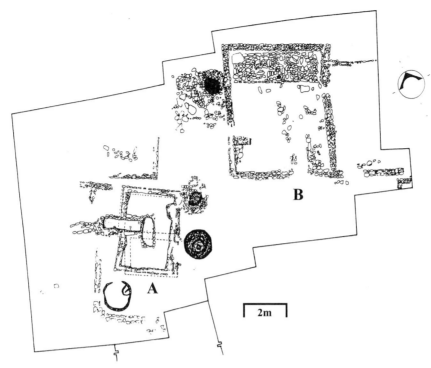

Figure 4. Floor plan of Xocotitlan (redrawn from Sanchez 1989: Fig. 3). A) Possible leaching or solar evaporation device. B) Structure possibly used for boiling brine and storage. Although salitre *could have been kept in this structure, it was likely too small to store the thousands of kilograms necessary to support a year-round operation.*

discussion of "limited activity" areas and their relationship to distant households).

Third, Sahagún describes "specialized" salt sellers in the marketplace:

> The seller of salt is a salt producer or a salt retailer. The salt producer gathers earth, hills it up, soaks it, wets it, distills, makes brine, makes ollas for salt, cooks it. The salt retailer displays the salt. He sets out on the road, travels with it, goes from market to market, makes use of markets, sells salt. He sells salt balls, salt bars, salt ollas [Sahagún 1961:84].

In this description, Sahagún describes traveling salt makers who manufacture special ceramics for their product and who produce different forms and types of salt. However, this description makes no mention of whether Aztec production was year-round or carried out on a large-scale. It is also unclear whether salt production was a domestic or non-domestic activity.

Finally, ethnographic data from Nexquipayac show that salt production there was a year-round activity that utilized direct boiling methods (Parsons 2001). Nexquipayac craftsmen overcame seasonal rains by using roofed enclosures to protect their boiling operations. *Salitre* soils were also stored in these structures to prevent rain damage. Moreover, salt producers used rubber tires as a primary source of fuel for their brine boiling operations. It has been assumed that Aztec salt producers were also able to overcome seasonal conditions in order to make their products year-round. In the following sections I argue that salt production is best viewed as a domestic craft activity that was but one of many resource strategies utilized by households along the shores of Lake Texcoco.

Domestic Salt Production

A major feature of domestic salt production was that many important manufacturing steps were carried out away from household structures. This was a characteristic of production for several reasons: First, given that salt production requires large quantities of saline-rich soil and water from the lakeshore, it was cost-efficient to locate production stations near those sources (Parsons 2001:137). In pre-Hispanic times, the lack of beasts of burden and the wheel meant that all soils would have had to be transported either on the backs of human porters or in canoes. To keep production and transport costs down, production sites were located near the best *salitre* sources (Parsons 2001:139).

Second, good quality *salitre* soils are usually only available during the dry season when receding lake levels expose salt rich soils (Gibson 1964:338; Parsons 2001:60). This explains why many of the salt production stations identified along the shores of Lake Texcoco appear to have been seasonal activity areas with no clear domestic architecture or remains. It would have been risky (or even impossible) to place permanent domestic structures in areas where lake levels changed significantly with the seasons. An analogy can be drawn with subsistence farmers whose fields, for various reasons, are often located away from their households and not associated with any domestic architecture.

Third, the special equipment used in salt making may have forced production to occur away from living quarters. Kilns for firing TFM pottery, large solar evaporation pans used to reduce brine (see Figure 2), and ovens for drying salt were all key components of the production process. This equipment might have been better placed away from the household where open workspace was available. It is possible though that small firing kilns used to produce TFM pottery may have been located in or near households (see Becker 2003), with finished ceramics being transported to detached production stations. However, if clay from lake soils were used for TFM vessels, if lake vegetation was used as fuel for firing, or if fuel was brought in by boat, these kilns may have been located closer to the water.

Fourth, the byproducts of salt production included broken ceramics, used *salitre* soils, and smoke from firing ceramics and boiling salt. These undesirable waste products would have been better kept outside of the home. The accumulation of soil alone would have necessitated a separate production facility. For example, we can estimate that approximately 120 kg of soil are needed to produce 5kg of salt (based on Parsons [2001]). Some households produced salt vessels that carried as much as 4.5 kg of salt each. Even if a household only produced five vessels that carried 4.5 kg of salt each, this would create approximately 600 kg of used *salitre*. The soil accumulation from just one season of salt production would have greatly polluted a living area.

The above four factors would have encouraged salt-producing households to use detached workshops. I argue that individual households ran production stations (lacking domestic structures) that some archaeologists have previously identified as "independent" workshops. Spatial separation between households and craft production work areas may sometimes create confusion when trying to discern domestic production from independent (detached) workshop production. Costin notes that:

> Explicit facilities, boundaries, and even force may be employed to protect valued resources and control production facilities. In contrast, the workshops of independent specialists will not be found in direct association with elite architecture or in restricted locations. Small-scale, independent production *is often* directly associated with commoner domestic architecture. As the scale of independent production increases, manufacturing *may be* moved to separate facilities [emphasis added] [Costin 1991:25].

Arnold and Santley (1993:238) suggest that as domestic production becomes intensified, work areas become more nucleated. In many instances these two propositions are supported. However, it is important to note that domestic production need not be small-scale (Feinman 1999; Feinman and Nicholas 2000) and more importantly, it may not be increases in scale or intensity of production that encourages the movement to separate or nucleated facilities.

I propose that it was environmental fluctuations in lake levels, the need to be located near raw materials, and the nature of salt production that necessitated that several key production steps *always* occurred away from the household in detached activity areas. Muller (1984) has identified a similar instance of part-time domestic salt production at some Mississippian sites that occurred away from households at what he terms "limited activity" sites. It is important to point out that the identification of limited activity areas for various Mesoamerican craft products is by no means a new idea (see Holmes 1900). Access to raw materials and pre-Hispanic transportation constraints no doubt limited where certain crafts could be produced. The point here is not so much the recognition of *where* salt could be produced in the Basin of Mexico, but rather delineating the multiple factors (e.g., environmental and technological) that impacted production and understanding how and why previously identified isolated workshops are best viewed as activity areas associated with nearby households.

Case for Detached Salt Workshops

I have argued that the initial production steps involved in making salt forced people to undertake this activity away from households in detached workshops. This creates the conundrum of identifying a household-based activity that is not associated with domestic structures or materials. In the following section I use several lines of evidence to support the contention that salt production was a household activity.

First, manufacturing constraints, not increases in the scale or intensity of production, encouraged the use of separate production facilities. *Salitre* was primarily available during the dry season and found in areas where water levels ebbed and flowed. Despite wanting to be near natural resources, it would have been impractical to build permanent living structures within the boundaries of a fluctuating lakeshore. The fact that during colonial times, urban areas located away from lakeshores were constantly subject to disastrous flooding indicates that changing water levels had serious effects on the lives of most residents of the Basin of Mexico (Gibson 1964:225, 236, 305). Given that Mesoamerican farmers were known to walk several kilometers to their fields, it is likely that the many domestic structures that Parsons (1971) identified along the lakeshore (but further inland) were associated with the salt production stations closer to the water (see Muller [1984:505] for a similar Mississippian example of this phenomenon). Additionally, because hundreds (if not thousands) of kilograms of soil were needed to sustain an individual workshop for one season, it would be more cost effective to move production facilities close to resources rather than use human labor to move soils to dry habitation zones. If lake reeds or rushes were used as fuel for heating or drying brine, this would have been as added incentive to placing production facilities near water. Finally, the high levels of noxious smoke, the thousands of broken ceramics, and the thousands of kilos of leached soils would have been best kept away from living quarters.

Second, the only well-known pre-Hispanic salt workshop structure (Xocotitlan) is small (Figure 4) and similar in size to the detached household workshops described by Parsons (2001) at Nexquipayac. Additionally, many of the salt production mounds surveyed by Parsons (1971:93–6) were single mounds (similar to isolated house mounds) (compare Tx-A4 and Tx-A5 in Parsons 1971:94) and seem to indicate that no more than a few people (perhaps one extended household unit) would have been able to occupy a single station.

Third, many Lake Texcoco house mounds show high levels of TFM pottery but are located away from the lakeshore. In his survey of the Texcoco region, Parsons (1971:93–116) describes seasonal salt production stations lacking domestic architecture as well as house mounds near the lakeshore with high frequencies of TFM pottery. The presence of TFM pottery in households away from salt production stations may indicate that (1) TFM vessels were produced in domestic contexts (away from lakeshore), (2) TFM vessels were used to store salt in the household, or (3) both TFM production and salt storage occurred in households located away from the water.

Fourth, recent archaeological studies of salt production in Puebla, Jalisco, and Oaxaca found that production sites often occurred away from households and typically close to water sources (Castellón Huerta n.d; Valdez et al. 1996; Hewitt et al. 1987). Valdez et al. (1996:183) interpret many of the isolated salt workshops identified in the Sayula Basin of Jalisco to represent "small family or domestic isolated work stations." Hewitt et al. (1987:806) posit that a few individuals or families at the Hierve el Agua site practiced intensive farming alongside relatively low-labor salt production using solar evaporation methods.

Based on current data, the most plausible scenario is that small temporary lakeshore production stations were run by nearby households. Although these detached workshops were physically separate from domestic structures, they were small and no bigger than necessary for an individual family to operate. Parsons (1971:93) even describes a house mound (Tx-A3) (located on a small island) connected by a causeway to a small seasonal production site (Tx-A1).

Full- Versus Part-Time Production

Although it was a complicated activity that produced for export, domestic salt production was probably a dry season (i.e., part-time) activity for several reasons. First, the best *salitre* soils for producing salt were only available during the dry season, when lake levels receded and exposed salt rich soils (Parsons 2001:60; Gibson 1964:338). Parsons (2001:137) estimates that to produce 5 kg of dried salt requires 130 kg of *salitre* and 110 kg (liters) of water. Although the leaching process can require up to 24 hours to produce brine (Parsons 2001:112), multiple batches of salt can be produced during the course of a work day (Parsons 2001: Table 2.2). If only one batch of salt is produced each day for 200 days a year, this creates 26,000 kg of *salitre* per year. Multiple production batches produced year-round would thus require thousands of kilograms of *salitre*, which would have been difficult and impractical to store during the rainy season. The possible storage area at Xocotitlan (Figure 4B) would have been too small to store enough *salitre* to maintain a year-round operation. The problem of storage in these workshop areas would have been exacerbated when rainy season precipitation caused nearby lake levels to rise.

Second, if solar evaporation was used in conjunction with some form of boiling or indirect heating, obtaining firewood would have been an additional production cost. Given the high population densities reached during the Postclassic period in the Basin of Mexico, fuel may have been difficult to procure, especially during the wet season (Parsons 2001:134). Dry maize stalks were likely an important fuel source for producing salt (as they were prior to the 1960's at Nexquipayac). These stalks would have been most abundant after the maize harvest during the dry season. Parson's informants at Nexquipayac used about 7500 kg of rubber scrap per year (Parsons 2001:131) to sustain one workshop. Rubber burns hotter and longer than traditional plant fuels, which indicates that even small salt production workshops would have required significantly more than 7,500 kg of maize stalks or wood to produce salt year round. If we assume that rubber burns twice as long as dried wood (which is probably a very low estimate), we can see that a year-round domestic workshop would have required 15,000 kg of organic fuel to sustain itself. These estimates are admittedly rough and require further refinement. The possibility of charcoal use in cooking would provide longer fuel burning time than fresh vegetation. Additionally, if lake reeds or rushes were used as fuel, they may have been available year round.

Third, minimal rainfall during the dry season allowed salt producers to use solar evaporation methods to reduce brine. The series of possible evaporation bins identified at Xocotitlan (Figures 2 and 4A) indicate that this activity may have been the primary means of reducing brine (Baños and Sanchez 1998:14). Solar evaporation would have been a more cost-effective, but slower way to reduce brine compared to reduction by fire. If firewood was scarce, this alternative method would have been attractive to households looking to diversify production activities without heavily investing in fuel procurement.

Fourth, if TFM ceramics were produced by saltmakers, this activity would have been better suited for the dry season when firing and drying activities were aided by lower levels of rainfall, humidity, and the availability of fuel (e.g., maize stalks). Archaeological and ethnographic evidence suggests that many kilns in Mesoamerica were open-air types that were constructed in outdoor areas (Arnold and Santley 1993; Becker 2003). The maintenance of an indoor kiln, especially during the rainy season, would have required significantly more labor than an outdoor seasonal kiln.

Fifth, if salt production was a dry season activity it may have complemented subsistence farming that was undertaken in the wet season. During the dry season, subsistence farmers would have had spare time (away from tending crops) to devote to other activities such as salt production. Full-time salt producing households would have had to rely on exchange relationships to obtain subsistence goods. Although salt was a biological necessity, the consumption rate of this material was low.[3] This fact combined with the cyclical nature of pre-industrial exchange relationships, full-time production at the expense of other subsistence activities would have been a risky household endeavor.[4]

Sixth, many ethnographic studies of Mesoamerican salt production indicate that it is a dry season activity because of the use of some form of solar evaporation (see Williams 2002:239; Andrews 1983:25, 35; Good 1995). The intensity of precipitation in the Basin of Mexico during the rainy season would make solar evaporation virtually impossible. As mentioned previously, the costs of maintaining a constant fire for brine reduction would have been costly for people relying on strictly organic materials.

Intermittent, Contingent, and Multi-Crafting

Given the diversity of available natural resources in Lake Texcoco, the fertile agricultural soils on the lakeshore plain zone, and the seasonal nature of salt production, it is likely that households in this region practiced a diverse range of craft and subsistence activities. Some of these activities were likely practiced intermittently and part of a *contingent* crafting tradition. In the following sections I discuss these craft and subsistence activities.

Craft Production

Salt production should be viewed as a craft activity that was carried out intermittently because it was most feasible during the dry season. The manufacture of Texcoco Fabric Marked ceramics was a contingent craft because it was used and consumed in the production of salt during drying and transportation. Both activities involved the manufacturing of different types of products. In the case of salt, this included products for human consumption (i.e., food additives or for meat salting) and for more industrial uses (e.g., textile production). Various standardized TFM vessels were likely produced to house different types of salt products (Baños 1980; Parsons 2001:255). Sahagún (1961:84) describes multiple types of salt being sold in the market place and ethnographic studies indicate that different types of salt are often produced within a single workshop (Parsons 2001:113, Good 1995).

The production of TFM vessels for drying, storing, and transporting salt should be viewed as a *contingent* craft directly related to salt production. However, it is also possible that households that produced TFM vessels also fired other types of ceramics for trade. If so, this would indicate that ceramic production in these households was not just a contingent activity related to salt production, but also a separate craft in itself.

Viewed outside of a domestic economy model, salt production and TFM pottery production could appear to be separate activities carried out by two different groups of people in separate localities. One could assume that households produced TFM pottery, while specialized detached workshops produced salt using traded for TFM vessels. When we examine these activities as embedded within a household economy model, however, we can see how these complimentary crafts were intimately linked. Identifying this linkage is also an important step towards understanding the relationship between isolated workshops and nearby domestic structures.

Complementary Subsistence Activities

Ethnographic studies have shown that some of the adaptive advantages of the household are that it is dynamic, adaptable, and capable of employing diverse economic strategies simultaneously (Netting et al. 1984; Wilk 1989). I have no doubt that those households that produced salt in the dry season also pursued a range of complementary subsistence activities in the wet season.[5] Below I briefly highlight some of the other possible subsistence pursuits that would have been available to seasonal salt producing households located along Lake Texcoco. The productivity and diversity of these additional activities strengthens the argument that salt production was but one of many lake-based subsistence activities that enterprising households would have undertaken to buffer against risk.

There is good evidence that the lake inhabitants harvested and consumed a variety of wild vegetation (see Table 3.2 in Parsons 2006) including the highly nutritious lake algae *tecuitlatl* (*Spirulina geitlerii*) (Ortiz de Montellano 1990:102–106). It is also likely that fishing was one of the most important subsistence pursuits for people living along the lakeshore. Parsons (2006: Table 3.3) has identified dozens of fish that were hunted and consumed at the time of Spanish contact. Gibson (1964:340) states that by the early 17th century over a million fish were being taken annually from the freshwater lakes of Chalco and Xochimilco by professional fishermen. Fishing industries were also reported from the salt producing communities of Texcoco, Tequiscistlan, and Xaltocan (Gibson 1964:340).

The hunting of water fowl was also an important activity carried out by lakeshore inhabitants (see Parsons 2006:116–121). Gibson (1964:342) remarks that some species of migratory ducks were intensively hunted seasonally, while other non-migratory birds were pursued year round. In addition to being important sources of protein, the feathers of these birds were often used in the production of ceremonial mantles (Gibson 1964:342).

When possible, the hunting of small land mammals was also source of protein for most people living in the Basin of Mexico (Ortiz de Montellano 1990:115). These animals ranged from larger deer and coyote to smaller rabbits, ar-

madillos, and weasels (Gibson 1964:343). In addition to being important food sources, wild animal hides from deer and ocelots were also traded in the marketplace (Gibson 1964:343).

Ethnohistoric and archaeological evidence indicate that maize farming did occur on the lakeshore plain zones and in nearby areas (Parsons 2006:71–2). The importance of this strategy no doubt depended on the availability of arable land and the size of the domestic labor force at the disposal of the household. Given that farming occurred during the rainy season, when possible this activity would have nicely complimented dry season salt production.

One of the most poorly understood components of the diet of Basin of Mexico peoples is the consumption of insects and their larvae. Ethnohistoric evidence indicates that dozens of species were consumed (Parsons 2006:59–63) and that they were a good source of calories and protein (Ortiz de Montellano 1990:115–119). The persistence of insect consumption among indigenous groups in Mexico suggests that the nutritional value of this food source cannot be underestimated (see Parsons 2008; Ramos-Elorduy et al. 1997).

Although I have listed the above activities under the rubric of *subsistence*, many of these resources were also sold in the marketplace during the 16th century (Sahagún 1961). Sahagún (1961:67–68) notes that salt was sold alongside "fowl...ducks, and other water birds" hinting that salt producing households may have also increased household wealth through the collection and trading of other lake resources (see descriptions in Parsons 2006:68–73). It is easy to envision households that had access to lakeshore products consuming a portion of those products and sending the rest to be traded in the marketplace.

Conclusion

Although the archaeological, ethnohistoric, and ethnographic evidence indicate that salt production has been an important activity along the shores of Lake Texcoco for several centuries, the nature of the organization of production has not always been clear. In this paper I have argued for a reevaluation of the organization of salt production and several key points are restated here. First, salt production is best viewed as a skilled domestic craft that produced for export and was practiced *intermittently* (i.e., seasonally) alongside a variety of other subsistence activities.

Second, it is often assumed that increases in the scale or intensity of production encouraged the use of physically detached workshops. In the case of salt production in the Basin of Mexico, however, it was production constraints and the seasonal nature of the craft that led to the use of detached domestic workshops. We should be cautious in how we interpret isolated salt production areas in this region. We can not assume that separate work areas automatically signal highly specialized (i.e., non-domestic) or elite-sponsored production.

Third, seasonality was the key factor in determining the length of time a household dedicated to salt production. This suggests that the "part-time/full-time" dichotomy often used by archaeologists is probably not useful for describing salt production in this region. Instead, salt production is better described as an *intermittent* craft activity that produced for export and required special tools, knowledge, and production steps. These are aspects of production that are too often only associated with "full-time" production. The data presented here call into question this assumption.

Fourth, TFM pottery production was a specialized and *contingent* activity for salt production. Although ceramic manufacture should be viewed as a component of salt production, households engaged in salt production should in fact be described as *multi-crafting* households. Two possible scenarios argue for a consideration of salt and ceramic production as separate crafts. It is possible that TFM vessels served some type of ritual or other special purpose(s), hence the multiple standardized forms. The ritual consumption of salt has been identified in ancient Mesopotamia (Potts 1984) and Mesoamerican (Andrews 1983:10; Ewald 1985:9). It is possible that certain vessel forms signaled a specific type of ritual or sacred salt variety. In this case, it would be the salt *and* the vessel that were important and distinct objects of production. The other possibility is that in addition to firing TFM vessels, other non-salt ceramics were made in the same kiln. These suppositions require further testing.

Fifth, the domestic economy model described here provides a better way of modeling the relationship between TFM pottery production and salt production. As many of the chapters in this book attest, a significant amount of evidence on domestic craft production in Mesoamerica is beginning to accumulate. Archaeologists need to recognize that individuals (and their households) make informed decisions about how best to provision themselves and to buffer against risk. Often, the addition of craft production to a household is used to complement and expand subsistence activities rather than to replace them. Only in the most dire (or elite sponsored) situations does craft production wholly usurp some form of farming, hunting, or gathering. The seasonal nature of salt production and the diversity and abundance of lake resources provided an optimal environment for households to develop multiple, not singular, resource procurement strategies.

Future excavations and analyses of salt production sites in the Basin of Mexico will need to focus on the production technology used by ancient peoples. Too much emphasis

has been placed on ethnographic analogies without adequate testing of our assumptions about pre-Hispanic salt production using archaeological data. For example, the issues of fuel costs, time-allocation, and workshop placement can be better understood by determining whether solar evaporation was used pre-Hispanically and also by understanding how much of a problem seasonal flooding was on the shores of Lake Texcoco. We also need to determine whether other types of ceramics were produced alongside TFM vessels. Finally, I would argue that future analyses of the domestic economy of Lake Texcoco households will need to address the role of gender. If I am correct in proposing that households along the lakeshore practiced a diverse and complementary range of craft and subsistence activities, then examining the role of gender in the division of household labor would likely be an important and much needed contribution to this line of research. For now, the combined ethnohistoric, ethnographic, and archaeological data on salt production suggest a much more complex and interesting situation than previously thought.

Acknowledgements

This research was originally written as a paper for a graduate seminar on the Aztec taught by William T. Sanders at Penn State in 2003. I would like to thank Dr. Sanders for encouraging me to explore salt production and moreover for teaching me the value of a cacao bean. We miss you.

Notes

1. A healthy person's urine alone contains an estimated 8 to 10 grams of salt per liter (Vikør 1999:65).

2. It is possible that brine was boiled in some other type of ceramic (non-TFM) vessels. This possibility remains to be tested.

3. Parsons (2001:5) uses an estimate of 2 g of salt per day per person for the Postclassic period. Still, it is difficult to estimate with any certainty how much salt was consumed during the Late Postclassic period. Several factors would have influenced consumption rates including the level of animal protein in the average person's diet, the level of consumption of other salt-rich foods (including lake shore products), and the intensity of craft production that involved industrial salt.

4. I am not eliminating the possibility that full-time elite sponsored production did not occur in some instances.

5. Here I am simplifying the discussion by drawing a false dichotomy between dry season salt production and wet season subsistence strategies. Many subsistence strategies

such as fishing and hunting probably occurred year round. Because salt production involved prolonged periods of waiting (i.e., for brine to evaporate, pots to dry, etc.), many other craft and/or subsistence activities were probably carried out simultaneously.

References

Andrews, Anthony P.
1983 Maya Salt Production and Trade. Tucson: University of Arizona Press.

Arnold, Philip J., and Robert S. Santley
1993 Household Ceramics Production at Middle Classic Period Matacapan. *In* Prehispanic Domestic Units in Western Mesoamerica. R. Santley and K. Hirth, eds. Pp. 227–248. Boca Raton: CRC Press.

Apenes, Ola
1944 The Primitive Salt Production of Lake Texcoco, Mexico. Ethnos 1:35–40.

Baños, Eneida
1980 La Industria Salinera en Xocotitlan Cuenca de Mexico. Tesis Profesional. INAH, Mexico City.

Baños, Eneida, and Ma. De Jesus Sanchez
1998 La Industria Salinera Prehispanica en la Cuenca de Mexico. INAH report.

Becker, Marshall Joseph
2003 A Classic-Period Barrio Producing Fine Polychrome Ceramics at Tikal, Guatemala: Notes on Ancient Maya Firing Technology. Ancient Mesoamerica 14:95–112.

Castellón Huerta, Blas
n.d. Procesos Technológicos y Especialización en la Producción de Panes de Sal en el Sur de Puebla. Manuscript.

Charlton, Thomas
1969 Texcoco Fabric-Marked Pottery, Tlateles, and Salt Making. American Antiquity 34:73–76.
1971 Texcoco Fabric-Marked Pottery and Salt Making: A Further Note. American Antiquity 36:217–18.

Costin, Cathy
1991 Craft Specialization: Issues in Defining, Documenting, and Explaining the Organization of Craft Production. Archaeological Method and Theory 3:1–56.

Ewald, Ursula
1985 The Mexican Salt Industry 1560–1980: A Study in Change. Stuttgart, Germany: Gustave Fischer Verlag.

Feinman, Gary M.
1999 Rethinking Our Assumptions: Economic Specialization at the Household Scale in Ancient Ejutla, Oaxaca, Mexico. *In* Pottery and People: Dynamic Interactions. James M. Skibo and Gary Feinman, eds. Pp. 81–98. Salt Lake City: University of Utah Press.

Feinman, Gary M., and Linda M. Nicholas
2000 High-Intensity Household-Scale Production in Ancient Mesoamerica: A Perspective from Ejutla, Oaxaca. *In* Cultural Evolution: Contemporary Viewpoints. G. M. Feinman and Linda Manzanilla, eds. Pp. 119–142. New York: Plenum Publishers.

Lovejoy, Paul E.
1986 Salt of the Desert Sun. Cambridge: Cambridge University Press.

Gibson, Charles
1964 The Aztecs Under Spanish Rule. Palo Alto: Stanford University Press.

Good, Catherine
1995 Salt Production and Commerce in Guerrero, Mexico: An Ethnographic Contribution to Historical Reconstruction. Ancient Mesoamerican 6:1–13.

Hewitt, William P., Marcus C. Winter, and David A. Peterson.
1987 Salt Production at Hierve El Agua, Oaxaca. American Antiquity 52(4):799–816.

Hirth, Kenneth G.
1993 The Household as an Analytical Unit: Problems in Method and Theory. *In* Prehispanic Domestic Units in Western Mesoamerica. R. Santley and K. Hirth, eds. Pp. 21–36. Boca Raton: CRC Press.
2006 Modeling a Prehistoric Economy: Mesoamerican Obsidian Systems and Craft Production at

Xochicalco. *In* Obsidian Craft Production in Ancient Mexico: Archaeological Research at Xochicalco. K. G. Hirth, ed. Pp. 287–300. Salt Lake City: University of Utah Press.

Holmes, W. H.
  1885 Evidence for the antiquity of man on the site of the City of Mexico. Transactions of the Anthropological Society of Washington 3:68–81. Washington, D.C.
  1900 The Obsidian Mines of Hidalgo, Mexico. American Anthropologist 2(3):405–416.

MacNeish, S., F. Peterson, and K. Flannery
  1970 The Prehistory of the Tehuacan Valley, Vol. 3: Ceramics. Austin: University of Texas Press.

McKillop, Heather
  2002 Salt: White Gold of the Ancient Maya. Gainesville: University Press of Florida.

Muller, Jon
  1984 Mississippian Specialization and Salt. American Antiquity 49(3):489–507.
  1986 Pans and a Grain of Salt: Mississippian Specialization Revisited. American Antiquity 51(2):405–409.

Netting, Robert, Richard Wilk, and Eric Arnould, eds.
  1984 Households. Berkeley: University of California Press.

Ortiz de Montellano, Bernard R.
  1990 Aztec Medicine, Health, and Nutrition. New Brunswick: Rutgers University Press.

Parsons, Jeffrey R.
  1971 Prehistoric Settlement Patterns in the Texcoco Region, Mexico. Memoirs of the Museum of Anthropology, Number 3. Ann Arbor: University of Michigan.
  1994 Late Postclassic Salt Production and Consumption in the Basin of Mexico: Some Insights from Nexquipayac. *In* Economies and Polities in the Aztec Realm. M. Hodge and M. Smith, eds. Pp. 257–290. Albany: State University of New York Institute for Mesoamerican Studies.
  2001 The Last Saltmakers of Nexquipayac, Mexico: An Archaeological Ethnography. Anthropological Papers. Museum of Anthropology, Number 92. Ann Arbor: University of Michigan Press.

  2006 The Last Pescadores of Chimalhuacan, Mexico. An Archaeological Ethnography. Anthropological Papers. Number 96. Ann Arbor: University of Michigan Press.
  2008 Beyond Santley and Rose (1979): The Role of Aquatic Resources in the Prehispanic Economy of the Basin of Mexico. Journal of Anthropological Research 64:351–366.

Ramos-Elorduy, Julieta, Jose Manuel Pino Moreno, Esteban Escamilla Prado, Manuel Alvarado Perez, Jaime Lagunez Otero, and Oralia Ladron de Guevara
  1997 Nutritional Value of Edible Insects from the State of Oaxaca, Mexico. Journal of Food Composition and Analysis 10(2):142–157.

Sahagún, Bernardino
  1961 Florentine Codex, General History of the Things of New Spain, Book 10: The People. Translated and edited by A. Anderson and C. Dibble. Monographs of the School of American Research and the Museum of New Mexico, No. 14. Santa Fe: The School of American Research and the University of Utah Press.

Sanchez, Ma. De Jesus
  1989 La Producción de Sal en un Sitio del Postclásico Tardío. Arqueología 2:81–88.

Sanders, William T.
  1976 The Population of the Central Mexico Symbiotic Region, The Basin of Mexico and the Teotihuacan Valley in the 16th Century. *In* The Native Population of the Americas in 1492. W. M. Denevan, ed. Pp. 85–155. Madison: University of Wisconsin Press.

Sanders, William T., Jeffrey R. Parsons, and Robert S. Santley
  1979 The Basin of Mexico: Ecological Processes in the Evolution of a Civilization. New York: Academic Press.

Santley, Robert S., and Eric K. Rose
  1979 Diet, Nutrition, and Population Dynamics in the Basin of Mexico. World Archaeology 11:185–207.

Talavera, E.
  1979 Las Salinas de la Cuenca de Mexico y la Ceramica de Impresión Textil. Tesis de Licentciatura.

Mexico City: Escuela Nacional de Antropología e Historía, Mexico.

Tolstoy, Paul
1958 Surface Survey in the Northern Valley of Mexico: The Classic and Postclassic Periods. Transactions of the American Philosophical Society 48(5).

Valdez, Francisco, Catherine Liot, Rosario Acosta, and Jen Pierre Emphoux
1996 The Sayula Basin: Lifeways and salt flats of Central Jalisco. Ancient Mesoamerica 7:171–186.

Vikør, Knut S.
1999 The Oasis of Salt: The History of Kawar, a Saharan Centre of Salt Production. Bergen studies on the Middle East and Africa; 3, Norway.

Wilk, Richard, ed.
1989 The Household economy: Reconsidering the Domestic Mode of Production. Boulder: Westview Press.

Williams, Eduardo
2002 Salt production in the Coastal Area of Michoacan, Mexico. Ancient Mesoamerica 13:237–253.

5

Multicrafting in Prehispanic Oaxaca

Andrew K. Balkansky
Southern Illinois University Carbondale
and
Michelle M. Croissier
Southern Illinois University Carbondale

In chapter two of this volume's introduction, Hirth high-lights the factual disconnect between observed household dynamics and the typical archaeological reconstruction: "archaeologists characterize households as stable, small-scale and self-sufficient producers that depend on outside forces to initiate change." This characterization runs counter to any number of ethnographic studies of household production (e.g. Netting 1993) and our own experiences working in rural Mexico. The gap between ethnography and archaeology is exacerbated by the lack of appropriate economic models for prehispanic Mesoamerica. Hirth suggests reconnecting archaeology with actual domestic behavior in a general model of household diversification that enhances economic well being and reduces risk.

Our evidence for diverse craft industries at the archaeological site of Tayata in the Mixteca Alta suggests an extension of the risk buffering strategy of Archaic foragers into early village times, a transition to sedentary lifeways that occurred by the mid 2nd millennium B.C. (Marcus and Flannery 1996:62–64). It was at Archaic macroband encampments like Gheo-Shih and Tlapacoya (a possible incipient village) that the archaeological record for craftwork begins (Marcus and Flannery 1996:59, 73–74; Niederberger 1979). The risk buffering framework also fits 16th century ethnohistorical patterns in the Mixteca Alta that suggest few if any full-time specializations outside of farming and a limited number of politico-religious roles (Spores 1984:72–74). This curious fact, despite the Mixtecos reputation as top-tier artisans (e.g. the Mixtec goldsmiths at Tenochtitlan; Saville [1920]) requires an explanation. Ethnohistorical patterns of diverse domestic economies that included part-time farming were true for a range of occupations, among them warriors, traders, curers and artisans. This same pattern is found ethnographically among contemporary Mixtecos, and not exclusively in rural areas (Murphy et al. 1997). An evolutionary pattern of risk buffering dating from the late Archaic period thus develops into an intermittent and multicrafting pattern in early Oaxacan villages and continues for the rest of the prehispanic era. Once established, the household-based risk buffering strategies were flexible and adaptable enough to survive transitions to urbanism, market economies and societal collapse.

We endorse the diversification/risk buffering model because it fits both an evolutionary trajectory coming out of the Archaic as well as the Mixteca Alta's ethnographic household economies. We emphasize, however, that Mesoamerican domestic craft production cannot be understood by imposing arbitrary boundaries over varied and dynamic productive regimes (e.g. Pool and Bey [2007], writing on ceramics; and see Costin's [2005] survey of the literature). This observation holds whether one is comparing chiefly societies similar to Tayata or the status gradients common among prehispanic Mesoamerican households (Feinman et al. 2006; Hirth 1993; Marcus and Flannery 1996:103). We should instead view each domain or variable continuously, rather than reducing our observations to dichotomies that "oversimplify what is more likely to be an axis of continuous variability by making its extremes into typological pigeonholes" (Drennan and Peterson 2006:3966). This approach seems a better fit for a prehistoric situation where full-time craft

ARCHEOLOGICAL PAPERS OF THE AMERICAN ANTHROPOLOGICAL ASSOCIATION, Vol. 19, Issue 1, pp. 58–74, ISSN 1551-823X, online ISSN 1551-8248. © 2009 by the American Anthropological Association. All rights reserved. DOI: 10.1111/j.1551-8248.2009.01013.x.

specialization was limited or absent, even in the most highly urbanized settings.

Our discussion of household craft production in Oaxaca emphasizes its earliest manifestations at the Formative period site of Tayata (our data pertain primarily to the late Early Formative and initial Middle Formative, ca. 11th to 9th centuries B.C. cal.). But to understand our results, we make comparisons with Tayata's contemporary at San José Mogote as well as the much later Classic period sites of Ejutla and El Palmillo to help generate expectations for Tayata. Each of these cases illustrates multicrafting at analytical levels of house, residential ward and settlement as defined in Feinman and Nicholas (2007), Hirth (chapter two, this volume) and Shimada (2007). We illustrate our approach with reference to diverse craft activities found among several of Tayata's excavated houses, as well as detailed compositional and technological analyses of pottery to reconstruct an ancient firing program in the absence of formal kilns. The comparative results show that the Oaxacan pattern of domestic multicrafting was established in early villages by 1000 B.C. and that similar though more intensive crafting regimes were ubiquitous in urbanized and market-based economies more than 1000 years later.

Classic Period Multicrafting

Oaxaca's craft industries, today as in the past, are situated domestically and belong to a diverse array of household economic strategies (e.g. Beals 1975; Cook and Diskin 1976; Shepard 1963). One key difference between past and present, however, is the tendency for modern craftworkers to concentrate their efforts on a single craft activity. In many instances, their home villages have become famous for a particular craft. Atzompa, for example, is known for green-glazed pottery; Teotitlán for geometric designs on woven rugs; Tilcajete for carved and brightly painted wooden animals; Xaagá and Mitla for cloth goods sold to tourists, and so forth—with this being a much abbreviated list of the dozens of Oaxaca Valley communities that continue to bring craft goods to market. Where we work, in the Mixteca Alta, Cuquila is linked to fire-clouded storage jars; Magdalena Peñasco to hand-made palm hats and baskets (now more commonly made of plastic); and even places once famous for crafts that are nearly extinct such as ironworking in Tlaxiaco. But these consolidated crafting strategies, although rooted in an earlier peasant marketing system (Warner 1976) are now the products of modern development and globalization (Thieme 2007). Household craft activity was organized differently in the past. Craftwork in prehispanic times, like today, was diverse (e.g. Blanton 1978; Flannery and Marcus

2005; Winter 1984), but multicrafting rather than the contemporary single-craft focus was the norm among households and communities (Feinman 1999). Thus the modern analogy only takes us so far and we must turn to archaeological evidence to understand prehispanic domestic craft production.

It is now 40 years since the inception of detailed archaeological studies of Oaxacan households (Flannery 1976). We know that craftwork, even production at levels meant for exchange, was done mostly or entirely in domestic settings on a part-time basis. This was true in all prehispanic periods since the advent of sedentism. We know that multicrafting began in Early Formative villages such as San José Mogote and its emergence was correlated with rising levels of inequality and political centralization (Flannery and Marcus 2005:468–469). We know that domestic multicrafting persisted through prehistoric transitions to urbanism and market economies. Historical sources (Spores 1984) suggest similar patterns for the Late Postclassic, although archaeological data on crafting and the late prehispanic economy remains limited.

Gary Feinman and Linda Nicholas' nearly 20 years of excavating Classic period sites in Ejutla and the eastern Oaxaca Valley offer further points of comparison (e.g. Feinman and Nicholas 2007). One of the fundamental lessons of their work is the extent of variation in the nature of craft production—in the choice of craft activity, their configurations within households, the technologies employed and in their intensities—even among contemporary sites. Ejutla was a Classic period, valley-floor site in which heavy densities of marine shell were found in one area of town (Feinman and Nicholas 2000). House excavations revealed craftwork that concentrated on marine shell and various kinds of pottery, but included lapidary, cloth and chipped stone. Shell was brought whole to the site, then cut, abraded, or perforated to produce plaques for mosaic inlay, beads, bracelets, necklaces and pendants. Shell by-products were tossed into middens near the house, along with animal bones and other domestic debris. Ejutla's shell workers did not consume their own goods since few finished pieces were found; instead, their efforts were directed toward high status consumers elsewhere, possibly including Monte Albán and Teotihuacan.

El Palmillo, another Classic period site, was located on a terraced hilltop where excavations showed numerous differences in household crafting compared to Ejutla (Feinman et al. 2002, 2006). In the El Palmillo excavations, shell was rare and pottery production limited in comparison with Ejutla; instead, chipped stone and maguey processing were paramount, although the intensities of production varied by terrace. Some of the chipped stone seemed destined for exchange beyond El Palmillo, and some for use in processing maguey fibers for weaving. Based on the sizes of spindle whorls used in weaving, residents of the uppermost terraces at El Palmillo made finer cotton cloth than weavers lower down the hillside who worked maguey fiber into coarser cloth. Pottery production, at lower intensities than Ejutla, was largely consumed within the site. Nevertheless, speciality fired-clay figurines and urns were consumed by higher-status residents of the upper terraces. Thus contemporary sites concentrated on differing kinds of craft production. Multicrafting was the norm, but craftwork varied in its form and intensity even within sites; and the items produced could be destined for consumption within the site or for consumers elsewhere in the region. We should, therefore, expect that craft production at Tayata would take varied forms and need not conform to patterns identified at its contemporary sites.

Revisiting a Firing Experiment

One further point of comparison offers still other kinds of expectations and interpretive contexts for our discoveries at Tayata. In the Ejutla case study, one surprise came from a series of enigmatic, debris-filled pits that were excavated near the house. These turned out to be pit kilns used in making fired-clay figurines; relatively commonplace to-rilla griddles, plates and bowls; and more specialized incense burners and urns (Balkansky et al. 1997; Feinman and Balkansky 1997; cf. Diehl et al. 1997). When evidence for pottery making turned up at the Tayata site (albeit without permanent kilns), it became necessary to revisit the prior study from Ejutla and look again at the implications of an experimental firing of a pit kiln.

Pit kilns are functional intermediates along the firing continuum from the open or bonfire method where pots and fuel are combined above ground, to updraft kilns where pots and fuel are in separate chambers (Miller 2007:121–128). Pit kilns would have been a less costly option than updraft kilns for intermittent potters making a limited number of vessels. In the experiment, clay pots were placed in a shallow earthen depression and covered in fuel, then straw to form a surface around the pots and fuel, and finally mud plaster to form the roof. After the pit kiln was ignited the mud plaster slowly hardened into a dome, protecting the pottery that might otherwise shift and break as the fuel is consumed; insulating the bonfire to conserve fuel and boost temperature; and allowing for better atmospheric control. This last point was especially important for understanding the reduction-fired gray ware pottery from Ejutla that could have been produced by cutting off the oxygen at a critical juncture (Rye

Table 1. Firing temperatures from experimental pit kiln. Thermocouples 1 and 2 were in the ground, below the kiln; thermocouples 3 and 4 were inside the firing chamber.

Time/hours	#1	#2	#3	#4
0.0	8° C	8° C	9° C	10° C
0.5	8° C	8° C	11° C	44° C
1.0	15° C	10° C	72° C	103° C
1.5	24° C	18° C	82° C	131° C
2.0	31° C	25° C	90° C	248° C
2.5	36° C	31° C	108° C	329° C
3.0	42° C	35° C	136° C	370° C
3.5	45° C	39° C	214° C	504° C
4.0	53° C	45° C	332° C	613° C
4.5	62° C	58° C	401° C	768° C
5.0	65° C	74° C	472° C	712° C
5.5	69° C	85° C	520° C	696° C
6.0	71° C	90° C	545° C	740° C
6.5	73° C	95° C	572° C	699° C
7.0	77° C	98° C	601° C	664° C
7.5	80° C	100° C	602° C	599° C
8.0	81° C	99° C	606° C	553° C
10.0	80° C	203° C	757° C	480° C
14.0	68° C	232° C	278° C	199° C

1981:98). Two thermocouples were placed within the firing chamber, two others in the ground below, with temperatures recorded over several hours (Table 1).

This experiment was limited in being run only once, but nonetheless offered independent data against which we could compare the production remains at Ejutla. One key result was seeing how the excavated experimental kiln section left few indications that pottery had been produced. The main indications were a thin layer of ash and charcoal, the baked and discolored earthen floor, a few broken vessels and clay concretions from the mud plaster dome (cf. Bordaz 1964). These kinds of ephemeral remains could easily be dismissed as "burned earth" or "ashy matrix with potsherds" and then forgotten.

Other results from the temperature data hold implications for understanding pot making at both Ejutla and Tayata (Table 1). First, the highest thermocouple reading in the experiment was 768° C (cf. Shimada et al. 1998). With more practice, a different mix of fuel, or a bigger bonfire, we could have boosted the temperature even higher; but it was nonetheless high enough to fire most pottery from prehispanic Mesoamerica. Second, temperatures needed to make a useful pot (above ~500° C) were sustained more than 5 hours. Maximum temperatures in pit versus open firing overlap, but it is much more difficult to sustain higher temperatures in the open or bonfire method. We comment further on firing temperatures when discussing the evidence for pottery production at Tayata in the next section of this paper.

The Formative Emergence of Multicrafting

These observations from Classic period Oaxaca provide expectations for our work at Early and Middle Formative Tayata, a chiefly center in the Mixteca Alta region where excavations and laboratory analyses have reinforced the Oaxacan pattern of household multicrafting, and intra- and intercommunity craft diversity (e.g. Balkansky et al. 2009). Multicrafting sites and houses were established in Oaxaca by ~1000 B.C. Although the productive intensity (always difficult to measure) appears to have been lower for most craft items than during the Classic and Postclassic periods (excepting certain items such as the non-obsidian chipped stone that might have reached its prehispanic apex in the Early Formative), it is clear that this activity was situated domestically. However, one notable difference from later periods with extensive market systems is the relative investment in crafting ritual paraphernalia and sumptuary goods, some of which were exchanged or gifted at great distances. This relationship between ritual, rank and craftwork is essential to understanding the origins of inequality and the growth of paramount chiefdoms (Flannery and Marcus 2005:468–469). By concentrating artisans close to home, village leaders could control production at least for some high-value goods, thereby increasing their prestige (cf. Hirth 1992).

Our best evidence for early craft activity in Oaxaca comes from Kent Flannery and Joyce Marcus' excavations at San José Mogote, and more generally the results of their *Human Ecology Project* (e.g. Drennan 1976; Flannery and Marcus 2005; Whalen 1981). House 16–17 at San José Mogote is a good place to start. This was a relatively high-status house with an adjacent lean-to where the occupants manufactured chert bifaces, shell ornaments, baskets, mold-made pottery and used tools possibly related to woodworking. There was more deer meat consumed, more foreign pottery and jade ornaments associated with this house than others at the site. Marcus and Flannery (1996:104) comment: "These houses, and others of the San José phase, suggest that the higher a family's status in the community, the more likely that family was to be involved in craft activities and have greater access to deer meat, marine shell, jade, and imported pottery."

Craftwork was also organized by residential ward. Area A at San José Mogote was inhabited by families making iron ore mirrors (ritually significant sumptuary goods traded with other chiefly centers) and shell ornaments, specialized production that lasted for three centuries. Some shell, incidentally, was made into iron-ore mirror holders (Joyce Marcus, personal communication 2008), indicating that inter-craft relationships were being exploited at an early date. The res-

idents of Area A were late arrivals to San José Mogote, and might have been drawn or compelled to relocate there by elite patrons. Flannery and Marcus (2005:469) argue that "craft specialization by residential ward was present as early as there were leaders to foment it." It seems that multicrafting at San José Mogote took place at levels of the house, residential ward and entire community, although not all houses or wards were working the same variety of crafts. These kinds of craft diversity might have had their origins in chiefly competition, but became widespread patterns in Mesoamerica (see discussion of Classic period; cf. Hirth 2000).

In the rest of this paper we address questions about domestic craft production at Tayata, linking our results to the broader themes of risk buffering and prehispanic multicrafting. We describe Tayata's multicraft industries and reconstruct the unknown firing technologies of ancient Mixtec potters with evidence from excavations, experimentation and laboratory analyses of pottery. This focus on pottery production is meant to answer extant questions about Mixtec pottery but also to illustrate the empirical requirements of an integrative approach. One of our fundamental premises is that Mesoamerican craft production—especially in periods prior to states and regional market systems—is not reducible to economic models derived from other civilizations or the modern world. That is why we refer to ethnohistorical information about Mixtec social structure, ethnographically-observed economic activity and regional survey data wherever possible. These frames of reference—built on a remarkable degree of cultural continuity in the Mixteca Alta—keep the analyst's interpretations within realistic boundaries.

Multicrafting at Tayata

The Tayata excavations are still ongoing, so this account is preliminary, although we appreciate the opportunity to situate our work in a comparative framework of craft production and household strategies. Our Early and Middle Formative craft-intensive houses were high-status, with all craft activities taking place within the domestic setting. Middens adjacent to these houses held a mix of craft and domestic debris (e.g. shell-working byproducts alongside discarded pottery and animal bones). We have thus far excavated six houses in their entirety, including the horizontal spaces surrounding them. This broad horizontal perspective is bringing into view the exact spatial relationships of various households, production areas, middens, storage pits, burials and public areas at a barrio or neighborhood level. Although not all of the houses were intact, the Tayata project nonetheless is the most significant dataset we have on pre-urban

Mixtec houses and domestic activities. Other excavation projects in the Mixteca Alta report the likelihood of finding pieces of early houses within test pits (Blomster 2004; Zárate 1987); but those studies, although important because so little is known about these early periods, simply do not have sufficient horizontal exposures to clearly identify structures or recognize domestic production. This is an important methodological point brought forth in Feinman and Nicholas' *Ejutla Shell Project,* in which craft production areas and refuse were often located outside the excavated house (e.g. Feinman 1999).

One of our best-preserved Tayata houses had evidence for multicrafting by the 11th-century B.C. (Excavation 2, House 1). We think that the occupants of this house were relatively high status people. The house was resurfaced and modified several times over a period of about 300 years. The occupants had access to a wide range of obsidian and other chipped stone. Burials contained fancy foreign pots as grave goods. Iron ore mirrors were found in the excavations, as was a nearly complete jade or greenstone ear spool.

House 1 middens and potential work areas revealed evidence for obsidian tool production (Kenneth G. Hirth, personal communication, 2007) that was much more intensive than we had anticipated. Although access to obsidian blades was common to many houses at Tayata (cf. Flannery and Marcus 2005:69), not all householders worked obsidian to the same degree. Production evidence includes many small percussion and pressure flakes oftentimes with retouch, shatter and other unidentified macro-debitage from middens and potential work areas adjacent to the residences. On the whole, the evidence for obsidian working at Tayata is similar to San José Mogote (Parry 1987), although regional surveys show that it is more abundant in the Mixteca Alta than the Oaxaca Valley (Kowalewski et al. 2009; Kowalewski et al. 1989). There is a similar divergence in the non-obsidian chipped stone. This regional pattern is borne out in the excavations at Tayata, where heavy midden debris from the reduction process included chert nodules, flake cores, hammerstones and heat-treated chert. The volume of the non-obsidian chipped stone from House 1 seems to have gone beyond expedient production.

Much of our evidence for pottery production, discussed in greater detail below, also comes from House 1. Firing features with layers of ash intermixed with gray body sherds that might have been wasters or kiln furniture pockmarked the surface outside the house. These firing features were dug into the ground and differed from the smaller surface-level burns that were probably kitchen fires. There were sheets of mica found within the house that could relate to pottery production; mica might have been used as temper (although it has other possible craft-related uses [Flannery

and Marcus 2005:87–88]). Tayata pots often had mica temper, as does most pottery sold in Mixteca Alta markets today. The mica came from the interior of the house, where based on ethnographic analogy one would expect the pots were formed and dried. These householders thus made pottery (especially gray wares, see below), chipped stone and obsidian tools (perhaps to work other more ephemeral materials) more or less concurrently (at least within the limits of our AMS dates).

In a second well-preserved Tayata house (Excavation 4, House 4), we found cremated human burials with shell-bead necklaces and fill containing decorated pottery, fired-clay figurines and shell-production debris (Duncan et al. 2008). These householders were relatively well off, and the act of cremation along with the burial goods were probable status markers. The house itself was located on a low rise near the center of the site, adjacent to areas later covered with public buildings. Middens and burials contained marine shell in greater abundance than elsewhere on the site. All identified shell species were from the Pacific Ocean. We found various kinds of chert perforators and blocks of raw material that likely related to intensive shell-ornament production (obsidian tools were also being made, but it is not clear that it related to the shell ornaments). There is good evidence that residents of this house either made shell ornaments or sponsored shell-ornament production; they also consumed at least some of their products as found in the cremated burials. House 4 also had evidence for pottery production (detailed below) with local tan wares and ash left on burned surfaces near the house. It is not clear if pottery production went beyond the needs of this house, so we may have just one craft done intensively (shell ornaments) and others (chert and obsidian reduction, pottery production) more expedient in nature. Still, it is clear that the shell workers had the capacity to expand the range of their productive activities should the need arise. It is also noteworthy that in both examples, it was high-status families that were performing the craftwork themselves.

Pottery Production at Tayata

When mapping sites in the Mixteca Alta, survey archaeologists routinely walk over infinities of potsherds but never see evidence of pottery production on the surface. The first author of this paper has surveyed many Mixtec sites, but has never seen wasters or other debris from production facilities such as kilns. This disconcerting fact is mirrored in the limited house excavations at Mixtec sites where pottery firing areas remain unknown. These negative results contrast with the Oaxaca Valley where surveyors found dozens of pottery production sites (Feinman 1982; cf. Stark and Garraty 2004) and excavations at Monte Albán uncovered formal updraft kilns (Winter and Payne [1976]; and more recently, Markens and Martínez López [2004]). Other excavated kilns and firing areas from the Oaxaca Valley and Ejutla are cited in Balkansky et al. (1997). So where are the kilns or other firing areas at Tayata? How might we reconstruct an ancient firing program, even in the absence of formal kilns? How were the Zapotec-style gray wares—assuming a local origin—produced?

Based on modern analogues and the excavations at Tayata, it appears that domestic-scale potters using a fairly basic firing technology were capable of high-intensity production (after Costin's [1991] distinction between scale and intensity). Present-day Mixteco potters generally use updraft kilns similar to those from Atzompa, although the potters of San Juan de las Huertas and San Juan Ñumí use an open-air or bonfire method and one family we know from Magdalena Peñasco uses a semi-subterranean firing method for their tortilla-griddles (Figure 1). In the Huertas, Ñumí, and Peñasco examples, potters work part-time on their craft as the agricultural cycle and other economic activities permit. It is likewise true that market demand for pottery has declined in recent years, and this has affected household divisions of labor and time-spent on pot-making. Men who used to be potters often work as day laborers and women then become more involved in pottery production and marketing. This modern view contrasts with the image of relatively undifferentiated, low-intensity, domestic-scale production that is default position in many archaeological models. Yet the modern Mixtec situation fits what is surmised from archaeological cases elsewhere in Oaxaca where potters producing for market exchange probably worked only part-time at their craft and firing technologies varied with productive intensity.

The Tayata excavations uncovered several open-air firing features that could have been used for pottery production and quartz pebbles that look like burnishing stones in houses and trash middens. One potential firing area dating from the 13th century B.C. (all dates calibrated), was a baked earthen surface with upright stone deflector; the deflector formed a break against the direction of prevailing winds and would have helped raise the temperature of the bonfire. Although no pottery or other direct evidence of production was found in this feature, the burned surface was much larger than other burned surfaces at the site that one presumes were used for cooking (although dual use for cooking and limited pottery firing could have occurred). In a second example, dating from the 11th-century B.C., an ash-filled depression near an excavated house contained large numbers of similar tan ware vessels (this ware is described in Spores [1972]; it

Figure 1.   Modern comal-making (tortilla griddles) at Magdalena Peñasco. The kiln is dug into the underlying tepetate (subsoil), the comals are balanced on a metal pipe and the fuel is burned below the comals. Photo: Katie South.

is the analog to *café* or dark-firing pastes in the Oaxaca Valley, Shepard [1967]). The excavated feature in many ways resembled the Ejutla pit kilns, although none of the clay concretions diagnostic of the mud plaster dome were found. Several other firing features, including the stone-lined pits with dense ash layers from Excavation 2, House 2 (Figure 2) might have been used to make pots. In all examples from Tayata, the firing features were located in door yards outside the house itself like modern Mixteco potters.

These features variously fit definitions of pit kilns as well the open firing or bonfire method (also above-ground firing) (Rye 1981; Velde and Druc 1999); these methods are the likely precursors of all later firing techniques and are similar to those used by San Marcos potters who market their tortilla griddles in the Oaxaca Valley (Flannery and Marcus 1994:21–24; Payne 1994). However firing technologies form a continuum, making descriptions based on operating principles more useful than formal criteria, especially in archaeological cases (Miller 2007:124). In open firings, pots are placed on the ground either above, inter-mixed with or covered in fuel. This ephemeral method is the least costly in terms of labor and building materials but carries very high fuel costs. Wood and charcoal sources, however, would have been abundant in the Formative Mixteca Alta, and charcoal production remains important in rural areas today. Dried maguey leaves, corn husks and cobs are other likely fuel sources, again based on modern analogies. Open-firing could have produced Oaxaca's early gray wares simply by covering the pots late in the firing sequence. Smothering the pots in dirt or ash would suffice to smudge the surface either gray or black (e.g. Rye 1981:98; Stolmaker 1973). The firing pits described above could have been used in much

Figure 2. (A) Multiple firing features outside Early Formative house; (B) close-up of one set of firing features; (C) excavation of typical firing feature showing burnt soil, charcoal, ash and line of stones dividing the firing chamber. Photos: Liz Farmer and Ismael G. Vicente Cruz.

It therefore seems likely that the ancient Mixtec used relatively impermanent or ephemeral firing features at the household-scale, making it difficult for archaeologists to identify production loci in the Mixteca Alta. The solution to this puzzle is consistent with the range of technologies and domestic organization in the modern Mixteca Alta, and reinforces the view that production intensities sufficient for supra-household exchange in pottery were viable by the Early Formative. We turn now to analyses of the pottery itself, to see what can be inferred indirectly about production technologies.

How the Mixtec made Gray Wares

We are reconstructing the production technologies used to manufacture Early and Middle Formative gray wares from the Mixteca Alta, comparing the Tayata pottery to contemporary types from San José Mogote and other sites in the Oaxaca Valley. Here, we present preliminary findings on the mineralogical composition and firing properties of a small sample of gray wares excavated at Tayata. Technological studies of the pottery are necessary for sites like Tayata, where direct evidence of production is limited given the relative invisibility of above-ground firing and other ambiguous firing features (Rice 1987:153–158). Our ultimate aim is to integrate a technological approach to pottery analysis with more traditional studies based on style (cf. Flannery and Marcus 1994), building on Spores' (1972) initial type descriptions. Among Oaxaca archaeologists, an explicit, technological perspective in pottery analysis is absent more often than not, but its presence is usually instructive (e.g. Feinman et al. 1989; Shepard 1967). In this brief, illustrative description, we discuss some of the techniques we are using, integrating results from X-ray diffractometry (XRD), refiring experiments and studies of surface-core profiles. The authors will expand this pilot study in the coming months, significantly increasing the sample size and integrating other experimental and analytical methods, including elemental analysis and microscopy. Our goal here is simply to provide a small window into the range of technological variation in Tayata's gray wares and to infer what we can about the techniques used in making them (i.e. their composition and the firing program).

Oaxaca's gray ware tradition is diagnostic of the Zapotec civilization; it began in the Early Formative and continues with the black ware pottery of Coyotepec (Caso et al. 1967; Flannery and Marcus 1994:21–24). The prehispanic Mixteca Alta nonetheless had its own gray ware tradition (Spores 1972) and there is considerable speculation going back many decades about the relationship of gray wares

the same way, although being somewhat more substantial could reflect a greater productive intensity or the functional requirements of the pots themselves (e.g. if the pit firing facilitated gray ware production [cf. Whalen 1981]).

in the Mixtec and Zapotec regions of Oaxaca (e.g. Bernal 1965; Paddock 1966). The school of thought that began with Ronald Spores in the 1960s assumes that most gray wares found in the Mixteca Alta were made locally, and that apart from linking events chronologically have only limited value in deducing ethnicity or political relationships among Mixtec and Zapotec regions (Balkansky 1999). It nonetheless remains an open question whether each of these assumptions is really true; whether the Mixteca Alta's gray wares were first imported from the Oaxaca Valley and then copied, or whether these were instead parallel, mutually influential traditions. To answer these questions, we need to discover how Early Formative Mixtec potters made their gray wares.

These are big questions that have vexed Oaxaca archaeologists for a long time; but we have preliminary results that complement our excavation data and the prior regional surveys. For the purposes of this study, we created a working typology of a sample of gray ware bowls. *Types 1, 2,* and *3* are varieties of Spores' (1972) Nochixtlán Valley gray wares. *Types 4* and *5* have carved exteriors and correspond stylistically with Delfina Fine Gray and Leandro Gray of the Oaxaca Valley (Flannery and Marcus 1994). *Type 5* also resembles and might instead be Calzadas Carved, if it came from the Olmec area (Coe and Diehl 1980). *Type 6* corresponds with the distinctive Coatepec White-rimmed Black, first defined in the Tehuacán Valley but with multiple potential production zones (Flannery and Marcus 1994; MacNeish et al. 1970). Thus far only a small sample of Tayata's Early and Middle Formative pottery that corresponds with this working typology has been analyzed via XRD (n = 35), refiring experiments (n = 15) including loss-on-ignition (LOI) and surface-core profile studies (n = 35). These complementary approaches allow us to deal with both pottery composition and firing in ways that are mutually informative. The analytical methods are described in Croissier (2008).

XRD mineralogy

Sample surfaces from sherds were removed using a diamond-tip drill bit, then sonicated in distilled water and dried in a furnace for 12 hours (sample size ranged from 1 to 4 grams—much more than is needed for XRD since we anticipate future chemical testing). The samples were then ground to powder fraction, prepared as slurry mounts and analyzed using PANanalytical X'Pert PRO Diffractometer and software. *Type 1* pastes contain calcite as the major component with quartz as a secondary component, minor amounts of feldspar (albite-anorthite) and trace amounts of montmorillonite. *Types 2* and *3* have quartz as a major component with calcite as a secondary component, minor amounts of feldspar and trace amounts of montmorillonite. *Type 4* pastes have quartz as a major component, minor

amounts of feldspar (albite) and possibly trace amounts of ankerite. *Type 5* is similar to *Types 2* and *3* but lacks montmorillonite. *Type 6* pastes have quartz as the major component with a minor amount of feldspar and possibly trace amounts of mica.

Table 2.   Munsell surface-core characteristic profiles at 100° C increments, where (–) equals no change or same as above.

	Surface	**Subsurface**	**Core**
Type 1	2.5Y6/1	2.5Y6/2	2.5Y4/1
400° C	–	–	–
500° C	2.5Y7/1	–	2.5Y5/1
600° C	10YR8/2	10YR7/2	2.5Y5/2
700° C	10YR8/3	7.5YR7/4	7.5YR7/4
800° C	–	–	–
900° C	10YR7/3	–	–
1000° C	–	–	–
Type 2	7.5YR2.5/1	7.5YR5/1	7.5YR3/1
400° C	–	7.5YR5/6	–
500° C	–	5YR5/8	5YR3/2
600° C	7.5YR4/4	–	5YR4/6
700° C	5YR4/6	5YR4/6	–
800° C	–	2.5YR4/6	2.5YR4/6
900° C	2.5YR7/8	–	–
1000° C	–	–	–
Type 3	10YR7/3	10YR6/2	10YR4/1
400° C	–	–	–
500° C	–	7.5YR6/4	10YR5/2
600° C	–	–	10YR5/3
700° C	7.5YR7/3	7.5YR6/6	7.5YR6/4
800° C	7.5YR8/4	7.5YR7/4	7.5YR7/4
900° C	–	2.5YR5/6	2.5YR5/6
1000° C	–	–	–
Type 4	GLEY17/10Y	GLEY17/10Y	GLEY17/10Y
400° C	–	–	–
500° C	–	–	–
600° C	–	–	–
700° C	10YR8/2	10YR7/2	10YR7/2
800° C	–	–	–
900° C	–	7.5YR7/4	7.5YR7/4
1000° C	10YR8/3	5YR7/6	5YR7/6
Type 5	2.5Y2.5/1	2.5Y2.5/1	2.5Y3/1
400° C	–	–	2.5Y3/2
500° C	–	10YR4/2	10YR4/2
600° C	10YR5/3	–	–
700° C	–	7.5YR5/4	7.5YR5/4
800° C	7.5YR5/4	–	–
900° C	5YR6/6	5YR4/6	5YR4/6
1000° C	–	–	–
Type 6	GLEY14/N	GLEY14/N	GLEY15/N
400° C	–	–	–
500° C	GLEY15/N	–	2.5Y4/1
600° C	10YR6/3	10YR5/1	10YR5/2
700° C	–	10YR5/2	10YR5/3
800° C	10YR7/3	7.5YR5/4	7.5YR5/4
900° C	10YR8/3	5YR6/6	5YR6/6
1000° C	–	2.5YR5/8	2.5YR5/8

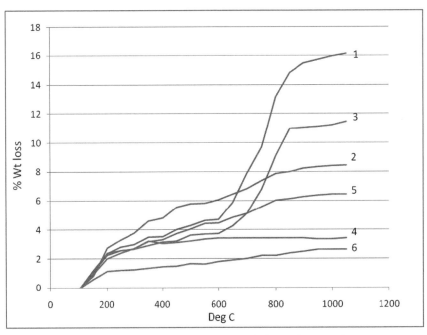

Figure 3. Loss on ignition results showing % weight loss relative to firing temperature for Tayata gray ware Types 1–6. Weight loss at 100–300° C reflects loss of interlayer water. Weight loss at higher temperatures, significant in Types 1 and 3, reflects (a) the combustion of organics at 300–600° C for pastes of low organic content and 300–1000° C for pastes of high organic content; (b) dehydoxylation and loss of crystalline water, which for montmorillonite starts at 300° C and is complete by 750° C; and (c) the breakdown of calcium carbonate ($CaCO_3$) to calcium oxide (CaO) at 700–900° C.

Refiring experiment

Samples were fired in 50° C step-increments for 15 minutes between 150° C and 1050° C under free access of air. The samples were allowed to cool for 30 minutes between firings; Munsell soil colors (Table 2) were determined; and the samples were weighed to calculate loss-on-ignition (LOI) and estimate total weight loss (Figure 3). Value and chroma changes began at 400–500° C for *Types 1, 2, 3, 5,* and *6,* but were not observed in *Type 4.* Changes in hue from Y or GLEY to R began at about 500–600° C for *Types 1, 2, 3,* and *5;* at 700° C for *Type 4;* and 600° C for *Type 6. Types 1* and *3* show the greatest weight loss (approximately 16% and 11%, respectively) from about 600–900° C. *Types 2* and *5* show a continuous decrease in weight (approximately 8 and 6%, respectively), culminating at around 900° C. Whereas *Types 4* and *6* exhibit little weight loss (about 3%), most of which occurs from 100–400° C for *Type 4* and 100–900° C for *Type 6.*

Surface-core profiles

Profile studies show variability within and among gray ware *Types 1, 2, 3* and *5* with sometimes diffuse, but more often sharp boundaries between surface and core (Figure 4). This is suggestive of a poorly controlled firing atmosphere in which maximum temperatures were sustained for short periods only (Rice 1987:153–158; Velde and Druc 1999:107, 170–172). Poor control over the firing atmosphere is evident in Munsell measurements (brownish grays), consistent with incomplete reduction and/or smudging (dark grays and blacks) at the end of the firing cycle (I to X in figure). In contrast, *Types 4* and *6* have uniform surface-core profiles (gray and dark gray, respectively) suggesting they were fired in a well-controlled atmosphere favorable to the formation of ferric oxide ($Fe_2O_3 \rightarrow FeO$) and thus the production of a "true" or completely reduced gray ware (XI and XII in figure). These results from the surface-core study are interesting when viewed alongside the firing temperatures recorded in the Ejutla pit kiln experiment (Table 1). Even in a relatively well-controlled firing experiment with an enclosed firing chamber, internal temperatures peaked and higher temperatures were sustained at different intervals. Poor atmospheric control is mirrored in the Tayata surface-core profiles, at least for those types presumed to be local.

Our preliminary analysis only approximates the paste recipes and firing practices that Tayata's Early and Middle

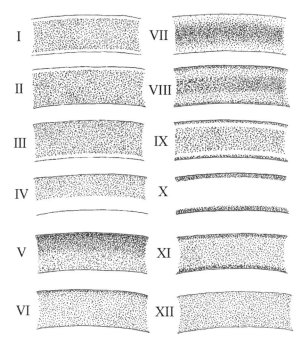

Figure 4. Surface-core profiles showing degree of reduction, where stipling represents reduced/smudged surfaces and an absence of stipling represents complete oxidation.

Formative potters used in making gray ware vessels. Provenance, of particular interest for questions about Tayata's relations to other regions, cannot be established definitively in the absence of chemical characterization (Mommsen 2001) but can be postulated based on mineralogical composition and other physical properties. We therefore propose, pending further chemical testing, that *Types 1, 2, 3,* and possibly *5,* owing to their calcite content were made locally, given the Mixteca Alta's extensive limestone deposits, calcareous clays and subsoils (Kirkby 1972). The presence of calcite and particularly montmorillonite (the breakdown of calcite is reversible but not montmorillonite) suggests that these types were fired at temperatures below 700–800° C since the clay structure is destroyed with the loss of crystalline water by 750° C and calcite decomposes to lime by 800–900° C (Deer et al. 1992; cf. Broekmans et al. 2008; Drebushchak et al. 2005; Shoval 2003).

We cannot at present determine if calcium carbonate was added to the paste as temper, was a constituent of the clay(s) or both. But for calcite to be an effective fusing agent it must be fired above 900° C to alter the structure and form CaO, a reactive oxide which combines with the silicates to form a melt (Velde and Druc 1999:25). It is unlikely that Tayata's gray wares—at least *Types 1, 2, 3* and possibly *5*—were fired at high enough temperatures for the calcite in these pastes to make an effective flux. However, according to Kornilov (2005), the organogenic origin of calcite in

calcareous clays contributes to the formation of a local reducing medium that affects the transition of Fe^{3+} to Fe^{2+}. The formation of FeO catalyzes the decomposition of calcium carbonate and facilitates the formation of new phases and the sintering of clays, thus improving the strength of the vessel at lower temperatures (see also Hausler 2004; Maniatis et al. 1981).

Weight loss at specific temperature ranges correlates with transformative processes in the creation of pottery (loss of surface water, loss of crystalline water, sintering and vitrification; see figure), but there is a great deal of overlap when one factors in time as a variable (Velde and Druc 1999:53–54, 126–129). Although it is possible to correlate LOI estimates with changes in Munsell relative to our working typology, we do not have a large enough sample size or comparative measures (e.g. Mössbauer patterns) to estimate maximum firing temperature or determine the firing cycle. In low-fired pottery reconstructing the firing program based on Munsell color changes is challenging and in our case (low-fired reduced pottery with a significant calcium carbonate component) it is complicated by the nature of reduction relative to composition and unreliable as the sole proxy (Drebushchak et al. 2005; Mitri and Davit 2004; Wagner et al. 1998). That said, *Types 1* and *3* show the greatest weight loss and changes in Munsell colors, followed by *Types 2* and *5.* Greater LOI and changes in Munsell colors of the above mentioned types (along with the presence of calcite and montmorillonite) suggests they were fired at lower temperatures or shorter firing cycles than *Types 4* and *6,* which show relatively little weight loss. The types with the greatest weight loss, *Types 1, 2, 3,* and *5,* show changes in chroma and value suggesting the loss of organics that were present in the paste. *Types 4* and *6* show only gradual changes in hue reflecting the increasingly higher oxidation state of iron, but no change in chroma and value, which confirms the relatively low organic component of these types. The clearest pattern we observed is that between 800 and 900° C samples within a given type shared the same Munsell color, which, along with the mineralogy, suggests that our working typology corresponds to real differences in paste.

The combined results of XRD, refiring experiments and surface-core profiles suggest that Tayata's gray wares (*Types 1, 2 3,* and possibly *5*) were made using local clay(s) and that pastes varied only in proportional amounts of non-plastics: calcite to quartz/feldspar. *Type 1* has more calcite than quartz/feldspar and *Types 2, 3* and *5* have more quartz/feldspar than calcite. These differences in clay preparation technique either reflect the addition of non-plastics as temper or, more likely, the removal of the clay's non-plastic inclusions. The absence of montmorillonite in *Type 5* (if indeed it is local) suggests it was fired at a higher temperature and/or with a longer firing cycle. *Type 1* vessels were fired high enough (close to 800° C), but not long enough, to decompose some of the calcite and produce their characteristic yellowish light gray surfaces and gray to brownish gray interiors. *Types 2, 3,* and *5,* in contrast, were sometimes smudged at the end of the firing cycle that probably fluctuated from oxidizing to reducing. This leaves us with *Types 4* and *6,* which are distinct in all measured respects. Although we cannot estimate the firing temperature based on the data at hand, both are completely reduced "true" gray wares which could not have been produced in open firing. Thus, either they were imported to the site (provenance unknown) or we have yet to discover some type of enclosed firing structure (e.g. Balkansky et al. 1997; Shimada et al. 1998). Such structures existed by the Late Formative in the Oaxaca Valley (Whalen 1981) whereas all examples of *Types 4* and *6* used in this study came from initial Middle Formative contexts. Although the pit features from Excavation 2, House 1 (Figure) appear analogous to Whalen's (1981:Figure 28) horizontal kilns, we are not yet convinced that this is what we have found.

We conclude from this study that Tayata's gray ware was above ground or open-pit fired at less than ~800° C in reducing atmospheres that were insufficient for complete reduction. These results are consistent with the varied internal temperatures in the Ejutla firing experiment (Table 1) and the variation in surface-core profiles from Tayata—even in potsherds from the same vessel. These results are also consistent with the archaeology of San José Mogote and William O. Payne's (1994:13) observations about modern open firings that would make the practice "archaeologically undetectable." However, the use of calcareous clay fabrics produced more stable and impermeable vessels, which came close to being "true" gray wares, even with the limitations of open or pit firing. Furthermore, most—but by no means all—gray wares from Tayata were produced locally. Finally, different technologies were used to make different kinds of pottery (which correspond nicely with our working typology) and this variation reflects the technological choices of ancient potters using distinct recipes and firing protocols. Future studies may allow us to determine the organization of production based on how these potting traditions (including other wares) correspond to different households or sectors of the site.

Conclusion

One of Tayata's more striking traits, evident from our first surveys and becoming more apparent as we excavate, are the organizational subsets within the site. Each sector of the site looks a little bit different than the others in layout and architecture; each sector is spatially discrete. In their craftwork, houses in each sector emphasized different clusters of craft activity. Marine shell ornaments, for example, seem to be made in only one part of the site. Chipped stone tool production, although ubiquitous, was more intense in certain areas, especially in obsidian. The production of gray (or smudged-ware pottery, following our discussion above) was prevalent in some parts of the site but not others. We have direct evidence for informal or ephemeral pottery firing in more than one area of the site, but some of these zones or sectors were making pottery more intensively than others. Multicrafting was the norm at Tayata, but not with the same emphases in all craft-working houses (cf. Flannery and Marcus 2005).

Tayata is a compelling demonstration of householders integrating craftwork with agriculture from an early date, establishing patterns that became broadly typical of prehispanic Mesoamerica. Tayata's multicraft arrangements were integrated with broader Mesoamerican exchange spheres, catalyzing the site's early growth and establishing a tradition of domestic multicrafting that lasted into the Colonial period. Risk reduction as a general strategy might be seen as a driver in producing mixed household economies; it might also help explain economic variation at levels of site and region. Regardless, given the overlapping spheres of craft activity in both intermittent and multicrafting, we think it best to describe variation in craft production as continuous, allowing for flexible and rapidly shifting productive patterns (e.g. Hagstrum 2001). We recognize this continuum in the Mexican ethnohistoric and ethnographic records. We should expect the same household dynamism in the prehispanic world. Viewing craft producers along a continuum of variation fits actual household strategies better than alternative dichotomies.

We suspect that supra-household organization was likely significant in production and exchange. This would include horizontal integration among households of similar stature but also more vertical forms of integration. It was at the supra-household level that rank first emerged, perhaps from among collections of householders seeking a further extension of the risk-reduction strategy—a strategy of pooled resources that would include cosmological as well as material realities (cf. Shimada 2001). We note that it was among relatively high-status houses where the most intensive craftwork was performed (although it is not clear whether it was elites themselves doing the work as Ames [1995] describes for the Northwest Coast or Inomata [2001] for the Classic Maya). By focusing on the link between the domestic production of ritual/sumptuary goods and emergent leaders (Flannery and Marcus 2005:468–469), we might now have the proper contexts to test Spores' (1983) ethnohistorically-based hypothesis that social stratification grew from the ritual realm. Regardless, we are surely seeing the beginnings of a household-based economic interdependence that various theorists view as fundamental to prehispanic complex societies (e.g. Drennan and Peterson 2006; Feinman 2006).

We know from ethnohistorical sources that these intermediate-level arrangements were important, but finding them archaeologically is another matter. This is why we think a broadly conjunctive approach to household production (e.g. Bayman 1999; Costin 2001; Shimada and Wagner 2007) better approximates actual links among houses at different scales of analysis (Marcus 2004). We are therefore looking at material and social processes in craft activities that run the gamut from performance characteristics to exchange systems and from social hierarchies to cultural values. But in broadening our criteria for a proper study of household production, it becomes even more difficult to draw broad generalizations from single classes of data or sites. This is a good thing. The point is not that every house, site or culture was different; but rather that significant patterning will emerge from a totality of evidence that exceeds one house or one site. Household archaeology must be about understanding specialized production at multiple spatial scales or we will miss one of the fundamentals of Mesoamerican life.

Acknowledgments

We thank Ken Hirth for organizing the *Housework* symposium and edited volume. This was a rare opportunity to get direct feedback from one of the best in the business. We also appreciate the expert advice from our SIUC colleague, Izumi Shimada. There is nothing like having Shimada across the hall ready to field questions about craft production. We are grateful to Peter Swart, Greta Mackenzie, Amel Saied and Corey Schroeder for making the world-class facilities of the Stable Isotope Laboratory at the University of Miami Rosenstiel School of Marine and Atmospheric Science available to us. They are remarkably tolerant of the lesser scientists in their midst. The Tayata excavations were funded by the National Geographic Society and the National Science Foundation (BCS-0229778, BCS-0640170). Officials of the Instituto Nacional de Antropología e Historia and the Centro INAH Oaxaca supported this research in various ways, with many thanks to Joaquín García Bárcena for his support of high resolution artifact analysis during his tenure as president of the Consejo de Arqueología.

References

Ames, Kenneth M.
1995 Chiefly Power and Household Production on the Northwest Coast. *In* Foundations of Social Inequality. T. Douglass Price and Gary M. Feinman, eds. Pp. 155–187. New York: Plenum Press.

Balkansky, Andrew K.
1999 Settlement Pattern Studies in the Mixteca Alta, Oaxaca, 1966–1996. *In* Settlement Pattern Studies in the Americas: Fifty Years Since Virú. Brian R. Billman and Gary M. Feinman, eds. Pp. 191–202. Washington, D.C.: Smithsonian Institution Press.

Balkansky, Andrew K., Gary M. Feinman, and Linda M. Nicholas
1997 Pottery Kilns of Ancient Ejutla, Oaxaca, Mexico. Journal of Field Archaeology 24:139–160.

Balkansky, Andrew K., Felipe de Jesús Nava Rivera, and María Teresa Palomares Rodríguez
2009 Los orígenes de la civilización Mixteca. Arqueología Iberoamericana 2:25–33.

Bayman, James N.
1999 Craft Economies in the North American Southwest. Journal of Archaeological Research 7:249–299.

Beals, Ralph L.
1975 The Peasant Marketing System of Oaxaca, Mexico. Berkeley: University of California Press.

Bernal, Ignacio
1965 Archaeological Synthesis of Oaxaca. *In* Handbook of Middle American Indians, vol. 3, part 2: The Archaeology of Southern Mesoamerica. Gordon R. Willey, ed. Pp. 788–813. Austin: University of Texas Press.

Blanton, Richard E.
1978 Monte Albán: Settlement Patterns at the Ancient Zapotec Capital. New York: Academic Press.

Blomster, Jeffrey P.
2004 Etlatongo: Social Complexity, Interaction, and Village Life in the Mixteca Alta of Oaxaca, Mexico. Belmont, California: Wadsworth.

Bordaz, Jacques
1964 Pre-Columbian Ceramic Kilns at Peñitas, a Post-Classic Site in Coastal Nayarit, Mexico. Ph.D. dissertation, Department of Anthropology, Columbia University.

Broekmans, T., A. Adriaens, and E. Pantos
2008 Insights into the Production Technology of North-Mesopotamian Bronze Age Pottery. Applied Physics A—Materials Science and Processing 90:35–42.

Caso, Alfonso, Ignacio Bernal, and Jorge R. Acosta
1967 La Cerámica de Monte Albán. Memorias del Instituto Nacional de Antropología e Historia, 13. México.

Coe, Michael D., and Richard A. Diehl
1980 The Land of the Olmec, vol. 1: The Archaeology of San Lorenzo Tenochtitlán. Austin: University of Texas Press.

Cook, Scott, and Martin Diskin, eds.
1976 Markets in Oaxaca. Austin: University of Texas Press.

Costin, Cathy L.
1991 Craft Specialization: Issues in Defining, Documenting, and Explaining the Organization of Production. *In* Archaeological Method and Theory, vol. 3. Michael B. Schiffer, ed. Pp. 1–56. Tucson: University of Arizona Press.
2001 Craft Production Systems. *In* Archaeology at the Millennium: A Sourcebook. Gary M. Feinman and T. Douglass Price, eds. Pp. 273–327. New York: Kluwer Academic/Plenum Publishers.
2005 Craft Production. In Handbook of Archaeological Methods: Volume II. Herbert D. G. Maschner and Christopher Chippindale, eds. Pp. 1034–1107. Lanham, MD: AltaMira Press.

Croissier, Michelle M.
N.d. Technological Analysis of Gray Ware Pottery from Tayata. Unpublished MS, Department of Anthropology, Southern Illinois University Carbondale.

Deer, W. A., R. A. Howie, and J. Zussma
1992 An Introduction to the Rock-Forming Minerals. 2nd edition. Essex, England: Longman Scientific & Technical.

Diehl, Richard A., Alfredo Vargas González, and Sergio Vásquez Zárate
1997 Proyecto arqueológico La Mojarra. *In* Memoria del Coloquio Arqueología del Centro y Sur de Veracruz. Sara Ladrón de Guevara González and Serio Vásquez Zárate, eds. Pp. 197–209. Xalapa: Universidad Veracruzana.

Drebushchak, V. A., L. N. Mylnikova, T. N. Drebushchak, and V. V. Boldyrev
2005 The Investigation of Ancient Pottery: Application of Thermal Analysis. Journal of Thermal Analysis and Calorimetry 82:617–626.

Drennan, Robert D.
1976 Fábrica San José and Middle Formative Society in the Valley of Oaxaca. Memoirs of the Museum of Anthropology, 8. Ann Arbor: University of Michigan.

Drennan, Robert D., and Christian E. Peterson
2006 Patterned Variation in Prehistoric Chiefdoms. Proceedings of the National Academy of Sciences 103:3960–3967.

Duncan, William N., Andrew K. Balkansky, Kimberly Crawford, Heather A. Lapham, and Nathan J. Meissner
2008 Human Cremation in Mexico 3000 Years Ago. Proceedings of the National Academy of Sciences 105:5315–5320.

Feinman, Gary M.
1982 Ceramic Production Sites. *In* Monte Albán's Hinterland, Part I: The Prehispanic Settlement Patterns of the Central and Southern Parts of the Valley of Oaxaca, Mexico. Richard E. Blanton, Stephen Kowalewski, Gary Feinman, and Jill Appel, eds. Pp. 389–396. Memoirs of the Museum of Anthropology, 15. Ann Arbor: University of Michigan.
1999 Rethinking Our Assumptions: Economic Specialization at the Household Scale in Ancient Ejutla, Oaxaca, Mexico. *In* Pottery and People: A Dynamic Interaction. James M. Skibo and Gary M. Feinman, eds. Pp. 81–98. Salt Lake City: University of Utah Press.
2006 The Economic Underpinnings of Prehispanic Zapotec Civilization: Small-Scale Production, Economic Interdependence, and Market Exchange. *In* Agricultural Strategies. Joyce Marcus

and Charles Stanish, eds. Pp. 255–280. University of California, Los Angeles: The Cotsen Institute of Archaeology.

Feinman, Gary M., and Andrew K. Balkansky
1997 Ceramic Firing in Ancient and Modern Oaxaca. *In* Ceramics and Civilization, vol. 7: Prehistory and History of Ceramic Kilns. Prudence M. Rice and W. David Kingery, eds. Pp. 129–147. Westerville, Ohio: American Ceramics Society.

Feinman, Gary M., Sherman Banker, Reid F. Cooper, Glen B. Cook, and Linda M. Nicholas
1989 A Technological Perspective on Changes in the Ancient Oaxacan Grayware Ceramic Tradition: Preliminary Results. Journal of Field Archaeology 16:331–344.

Feinman, Gary M., and Linda M. Nicholas
2000 High-Intensity Household-Scale Production in Ancient Mesoamerica: A Perspective from Ejutla, Oaxaca. *In* Cultural Evolution: Contemporary Viewpoints. Gary M. Feinman and Linda Manzanilla, eds. Pp. 119–142. New York: Kluwer Academic/Plenum Publishers.
2007 Craft Production in Classic Period Oaxaca: Implications for Monte Albán's Political Economy. *In* Craft Production in Complex Societies: Multicraft and Producer Perspectives. Izumi Shimada, ed. Pp. 97–119. Salt Lake City: University of Utah Press.

Feinman, Gary M., Linda M. Nicholas, and Helen R. Haines
2002 Houses on a Hill: Classic Period Life at El Palmillo, Oaxaca, Mexico. Latin American Antiquity 13:251–277.
2006 Socioeconomic Inequality and the Consumption of Chipped Stone at El Palmillo, Oaxaca, Mexico. Latin American Antiquity 17:151–175.

Flannery, Kent V., ed.
1976 The Early Mesoamerican Village. New York: Academic Press.

Flannery, Kent V., and Joyce Marcus
1994 Early Formative Pottery of the Valley of Oaxaca, Mexico. Memoirs of the Museum of Anthropology, 27. Ann Arbor: University of Michigan.
2005 Excavations at San José Mogote 1: The Household Archaeology. Memoirs of the Museum of

Anthropology, 40. Ann Arbor: University of Michigan.

Hagstrum, Melissa
2001 Household Production in Chaco Canyon Society. American Antiquity 66:47–55.

Häusler, W.
2004 Firing of Clays Studied by X-ray Diffraction and Mössbauer Spectroscopy. Hyperfine Interactions 154:121–141.

Hirth, Kenneth G.
1992 Interregional Exchange as Elite Behavior: An Evolutionary Perspective. *In* Mesoamerican Elites: An Archaeological Assessment. Diane Z. Chase and Arlen F. Chase, eds. Pp. 18–29. Norman: University of Oklahoma Press.
1993 Identifying Rank and Socioeconomic Status in Domestic Contexts: An Example from Central Mexico. *In* Prehispanic Domestic Units in Western Mesoamerica: Studies of the Household, Compound, and Residence. Robert S. Santley and Kenneth G. Hirth, eds. Pp. 121–146. Boca Raton, Florida: CRC Press.
2000 Archaeological Research at Xochicalco, vol. 1: Ancient Urbanism at Xochicalco: The Evolution and Organization of a Pre-Hispanic Society. Salt Lake City: University of Utah Press.

Inomata, Takeshi
2001 The Power and Ideology of Artistic Creation: Elite Craft Specialists in Classic Maya Society. Current Anthropology 42:321–350.

Kaiser, Timothy, and William Lucius
1989 Thermal Expansion Measurement and the Estimation of Prehistoric Pottery Firing Temperatures. *In* Pottery Technology: Ideas and Approaches. Gordon Bronitsky, ed. Pp. 83–100. Boulder, Colorado: Westview Press.

Kirkby, Michael
1972 The Physical Environment of the Nochixtlán Valley, Oaxaca. Vanderbilt University Publications in Anthropology, 2. Nashville: Vanderbilt University.

Kornilov, A. V.
2005 Reasons for the Different Effects of Calcareous Clays on Strength Properties of Ceramics. Glass and Ceramics 62:391–393.

Kowalewski, Stephen A., Andrew K. Balkansky, Laura R. Stiver Walsh, Thomas J. Pluckhahn, John F. Chamblee, Verónica Pérez Rodríguez, Verenice Y. Heredia, and Charlotte A. Smith
2009 Origins of the Ñuu: Archaeology in the Mixteca Alta, Mexico. Boulder: University Press of Colorado.

Kowalewski, Stephen A., Gary M. Feinman, Laura Finsten, Richard E. Blanton, and Linda M. Nicholas
1989 Monte Albán's Hinterland, Part II: The Prehispanic Settlement Patterns in Tlacolula, Etla, and Ocotlán, the Valley of Oaxaca, Mexico. Memoirs of the Museum of Anthropology, 23. Ann Arbor: University of Michigan.

MacNeish, Robert S., Frederick A. Peterson, and Kent V. Flannery
1970 The Prehistory of the Tehuacán Valley, vol. 3: Ceramics. Austin: University of Texas Press.

Maniatis, Y., A. Simopoulos, and A. Kostikas
1981 Mössbauer Study of the Effect of Calcium Content on Iron Oxide Transformations in Fired Clays. Journal of the American Ceramic Society 64:263–269.

Marcus, Joyce
2004 Maya Commoners: The Stereotype and the Reality. *In* Ancient Maya Commoners. Jon C. Lohse and Fred Valdez, Jr., eds. Pp. 255–283.

Marcus, Joyce, and Kent V. Flannery
1996 Zapotec Civilization: How Urban Society Evolved in Mexico's Oaxaca Valley. London: Thames & Hudson.

Markens, Robert, and Cira Martínez López
2004 La organización de producción cerámica en Monte Albán. *In* Cuarta Mesa Redonda de Monte Albán. Nelly M. Robles García and Ronald Spores, eds. Oaxaca: Centro INAH Oaxaca, in press.

Miller, Heather Margaret-Louise
2007 Archaeological Approaches to Technology. London: Academic Press/Elsevier.

Mommsen, H.
2001 Provenance Determination of Pottery by Trace Element Analysis: Problems, Solutions and Ap-plications. Journal of Radioanalytical and Nuclear Chemistry 247:657–662.

Murphy, Arthur D., Mary Winter, and Earl W. Morris
1997 Household Adaptations in a Regional Urban System: The Central Valleys of Oaxaca, Mexico. *In* Economic Analysis beyond the Local System. Richard E. Blanton, Peter M. Peregrine, Deborah Winslow, and Thomas D. Hall, eds. Pp. 235–254. Lanham, Maryland: University Press of America.

Neiderberger, Christine
1979 Early Sedentary Economy in the Basin of Mexico. Science 203:137.

Netting, Robert McC.
1993 Smallholders, Householders: Farm Families and the Ecology of Intensive, Sustainable Agriculture. Stanford: Stanford University Press.

Paddock, John
1966 Oaxaca in Ancient Mesoamerica. *In* Ancient Oaxaca: Discoveries in Mexican Archaeology and History. John Paddock, ed. Pp. 83–242. Stanford: Stanford University Press.

Parry, William J.
1987 Chipped Stone Tools in Formative Oaxaca, Mexico: Their Procurement, Production and Use. Memoirs of the Museum of Anthropology, 20. Ann Arbor: University of Michigan.

Payne, William O.
1994 The Raw Materials and Pottery-Making Techniques of Early Formative Oaxaca: An Introduction. *In* Early Formative Pottery of the Valley of Oaxaca, Mexico. Kent V. Flannery and Joyce Marcus, eds. Pp. 7–20. Memoirs of the Museum of Anthropology, 27. Ann Arbor: University of Michigan.

Pool, Christopher A., and George J. Bey III
2007 Conceptual Issues in Mesoamerican Pottery Economics. *In* Pottery Economics in Mesoamerica. Christopher A. Pool and George J. Bey III, eds. Pp. 1–38. Tucson: University of Arizona Press.

Rice, Prudence M.
1987 Pottery Analysis: A Sourcebook. Chicago: University of Chicago Press.

Rye, Owen S.
1981 Pottery Technology: Principles and Reconstruction. Manuals on Archaeology, 4. Washington, D.C.: Taraxacum.

Saville, Marshall H.
1920 The Goldsmith's Art in Ancient Mexico. Indian Notes and Monographs, 7. New York: Museum of the American Indian, Heye Foundation.

Shepard, Anna O.
1963 Beginnings of Ceramic Industrialization: An Example from the Oaxaca Valley. *In* Notes from a Ceramic Laboratory 2. Pp. 1–24. Washington, D.C.: Carnegie Institution.
1967 Preliminary Notes on the Paste Composition of Monte Albán Pottery. *In* La Cerámica de Monte Albán. Alfonso Caso, Ignacio Bernal, and Jorge R. Acosta, eds. Pp. 476–484. Memorias del Instituto Nacional de Antropología e Historia, 13. México.

Shimada, Izumi
2001 Late Moche Urban Craft Production: A First Approximation. *In* Moche Art and Archaeology in Ancient Peru. Joanne Pillsbury, ed. Pp. 177–205. Washington, D.C.: National Gallery of Art.
2007 Introduction. *In* Craft Production in Complex Societies: Multicraft and Producer Perspectives. Izumi Shimada, ed. Pp. 1–21. Salt Lake City: University of Utah Press.

Shimada, Izumi, Victor Chang, Ursel Wagner, Rupert Gebhard, Hector Neff, Michael Glascock, and David Killick
1998 Formative Ceramic Kilns and Production in Batán Grande, North Coast of Peru. *In* Andean Ceramics: Technology, Organization, and Approaches. Izumi Shimada, ed. Pp. 23–61. MASCA Research Papers in Science and Archaeology—Supplement to Vol. 15. Philadelphia: Museum Applied Science Center for Archaeology, University of Pennsylvania Museum for Archaeology and Anthropology.

Shimada, Izumi, and Ursel Wagner
2007 A Holistic Approach to Pre-Hispanic Craft Production. *In* Archaeological Anthropology: Perspectives on Method and Theory. James M. Skibo, Michael W. Graves, and Miriam T. Stark, eds. Pp. 163–197. Tucson: University of Arizona Press.

Shoval, S.
2003 Using FT-TR Spectroscopy for the Study of Calcareous Ancient Ceramics. Optical Materials 24:117–122.

Spores, Ronald
1972 An Archaeological Settlement Survey of the Nochixtlán Valley, Oaxaca. Vanderbilt University Publications in Anthropology, 1. Nashville.
1983 The Origin and Evolution of the Mixtec System of Social Stratification. *In* The Cloud People: Divergent Evolution of the Zapotec and Mixtec Civilizations. Kent V. Flannery and Joyce Marcus, eds. Pp. 227–238. New York: Academic Press.
1984 The Mixtecs in Ancient and Colonial Times. Norman: University of Oklahoma Press.

Stark, Barbara L., and Christopher P. Garraty
2004 Evaluation of Systematic Surface Evidence for Pottery Production in Veracruz, Mexico. Latin American Antiquity 15:123–143.

Stolmaker, Charlotte
1973 Cultural, Social and Economic Change in Santa María Atzompa. Ph.D. dissertation, University of California, Los Angeles.

Thieme, Mary S.
2007 Changes in the Style, Production and Distribution of Pottery in Santa María Atzompa, Oaxaca, Mexico during the 1990s. Museum Anthropology 30:125–140.

Velde, Bruce, and Isabelle C. Druc
1999 Archaeological Ceramic Materials: Origin and Utilization. Berlin: Springer-Verlag.

Wagner, Ursel, Rupert Gebhard, Enver Murad, Josef Riederer, Izumi Shimada, Corinna Ulbert, and Fritz E. Wagner
1998 Production of Formative Ceramics: Assessment by Physical Methods. *In* Andean Ceramics: Technology, Organization, and Approaches. Izumi Shimada, ed. Pp. 173–198. MASCA Research Papers in Science and Archaeology—Supplement to Vol. 15. Philadelphia: Museum Applied Science Center for Archaeology, University of Pennsylvania Museum for Archaeology and Anthropology.

Warner, John C.
1976 Survey of the Market System in the Nochixtlán Valley and the Mixteca Alta. *In* Markets in Oaxaca. Scott Cook and Martin Diskin, eds. Pp. 107–131. Austin: University of Texas Press.

Whalen, Michael E.
1981 Excavations at Santo Domingo Tomaltepec: Evolution of a Formative Community in the Valley of Oaxaca, Mexico. Memoirs of the Museum of Anthropology, 12. Ann Arbor: University of Michigan.

Winter, Marcus C.
1984 Exchange in Formative Highland Oaxaca. *In* Trade and Exchange in Early Mesoamerica. Kenneth G. Hirth, ed. Pp. 179–214. Albuquerque University of New Mexico Press.

Winter, Marcus C., and William O. Payne
1976 Hornos para cerámica hallados en Monte Albán. Boletín del Consejo de Arqueología 16:37–40. México: Instituto Nacional de Antropología e Historia.

Zárate Morán, Roberto
1987 Excavaciones de un sitio Preclásico en San Mateo Etlatongo, Nochixtlán, Oaxaca, México. BAR Internacional Series, 322. Oxford: British Archaeological Reports.

6

Intermittent Crafting and Multicrafting at Xochicalco

Kenneth Hirth
Penn State University

For a long time in the history of Anthropology scholars have argued that the appearance of urban centers was an important catalyst for the development of craft specialization and other complex economic institutions like the marketplace (Braudel 1986; Childe 1934; Durkheim 1933; Pirenne 1974; Sjoberg 1960; C. Smith 1976; Wittfogel 1957). While the historical circumstances behind urbanism vary, there are well documented empirical associations between the size of cities and the number, intensity, and diversity of craft and service activities found in urban centers (Berry 1961; Chorley and Haggett 1967; Jacobs 1969; Ullman 1941). Urban craft production is often organized to fulfill the dual needs of both its resident population and the surrounding hinterland (Appleby 1976; Jacobs 1969; Kurtz 1987; Trigger 1972). As a result urban centers are a good place to look for evidence of craft production because they often contain the greatest concentration of craft activities found in society.

This study examines the structure of obsidian craft production in the prehispanic urban center of Xochicalco, Mexico (Figure 1). Xochicalco was a mid-size center of 10–15,000 persons that grew to prominence during the Epiclassic period (650–900 AD). Archaeological investigations were initiated in 1992 and 1993 in twelve areas of the site to systematically explore the structure of Xochicalco's obsidian craft industry. In the process five areas with evidence for *in situ* production of obsidian tools were excavated to identify the scale and context of urban craft production. Excavations revealed that craft production of commodities in obsidian was organized as a domestic industry (Hirth 2006a; Hirth and Webb 2006). Four household workshops and a market work area were excavated to collect information on how craftsmen practiced their trade. Extremely good conditions of preservation caused by the rapid abandonment of Xochicalco made it possible to collect an array of information usually not available from archaeological sites. As a result it provides one of the most complete pictures of domestic craft production available from Mesoamerica (Hirth and Webb 2006).

Obsidian craft specialists were a basic feature of Central Mexican economies from the Middle Formative period onward (Boksenbaum et al. 1987; Burton 1987). Obsidian blades quickly became the cutting tool of choice in all Central Mexico households and a specialized craft industry developed to produce them. Although obsidian craft production was a highly specialized activity, none of the domestic workshops at Xochicalco produced blades on a full-time basis (see Hirth and Andrews 2006b). Instead multicrafting was the norm in all four crafting households. Craftsmen produced obsidian blades and applied the same percussion, pressure, and abrading technologies to working other materials. These linked technological applications included the production of potch opal bifaces from locally available materials, the importation and finishing of preformed obsidian bifaces, and some lapidary production. Together these craft activities illustrate the creative ways that households chose to diversify their internal activities to support their members. The evidence for specialized and diversified craft production is presented and discussed here in terms of what it contributes to an understanding of intermittent production and multicrafting in prehispanic Mesoamerica.

ARCHEOLOGICAL PAPERS OF THE AMERICAN ANTHROPOLOGICAL ASSOCIATION, Vol. 19, Issue 1, pp. 75–91, ISSN 1551-823X, online ISSN 1551-8248. © 2009 by the American Anthropological Association. All rights reserved. DOI: 10.1111/j.1551-8248.2009.01014.x.

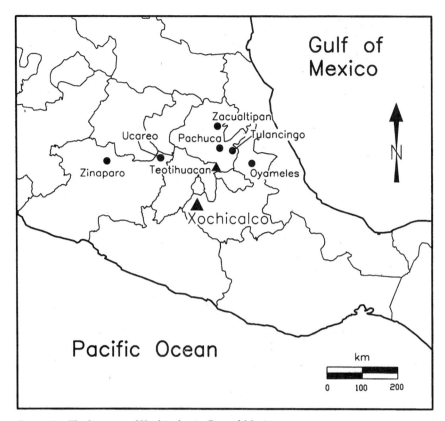

Figure 1. The location of Xochicalco in Central Mexico.

Xochicalco and its Obsidian Craft Industry

Xochicalco has long been recognized as an important prehispanic center in Central Mexico (Litvak 1971). The site rose rapidly to prominence as the capital of a regional political confederation that emerged in western Morelos during Teotihuacan's 7th century decline in power. It was an important urban center in Central Mexico throughout the Epiclassic period (AD 650–900) until it was conquered, burned, and abandoned around AD 850–900.

Xochicalco was one of several independent city-states that dominated Central Mexican prehistory during the Epiclassic period (Hirth 1989). Its large scale architecture and numerous monuments are a testimony to the site's importance as an influential political capital and religious center. In its heyday Xochicalco covered an area of just over four sq km and functioned as an important regional economic center. It had an active market that supplied the needs of both its resident population and rural residents throughout its hinterland. No other prehispanic site in Mesoamerica has better archaeological evidence for market activity than Xochicalco. Evidence for marketplaces can be found both in the architecture that defines the market area (Hirth 2000,

2009a) and the economic effects that market participation had on the material inventories of households that used the marketplace as a primary provisioning mechanism (Hirth 1998).

The marketplace was a fundamental economic institution for craftsmen since it provided a place to sell the goods that they produced. The market was also a work place where some craftsmen produced, finished, and modified goods to the specific needs or desires of consumers. Ethnohistoric sources indicate that obsidian craftsmen regularly produced blades and other items in the marketplace (Diaz del Castillo 1956:215–219; Sahagún 1977:3:148). At Xochicalco the excavation of plaza P27-A in what is referred to here as the South Market Complex confirmed that production also took place in the marketplace during the Epiclassic period (Figure 2). Concentrations of obsidian production debitage were trampled into the original earthen floor of the plaza that allowed the identification of work areas where obsidian craftsmen produced and sold obsidian blades and blade tools (Hirth 2006, 2009a).

In 1993 the Xochicalco Lithics Project excavated five areas to expose architectural features, to locate production residues, and to define the scale and organization of obsidian

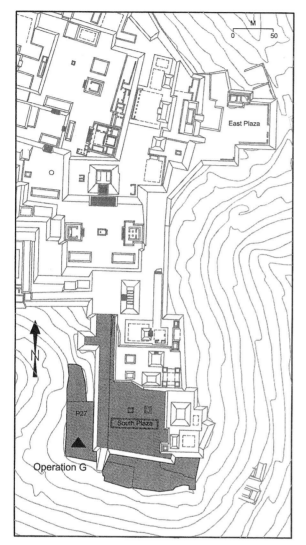

Figure 2. The location of plaza P27-A and Operation G in Xochicalco's South Market Complex.

craft production. These included four domestic workshops identified as Operations A, H, I and K and an obsidian work area (Operation G) located in the P27-A market plaza (Figure 3). Unusual conditions of deposition and preservation made these investigations very productive. Militarism was the basis for Xochicalco's rise to power and the cause for its abandonment when the site was dramatically destroyed by military conquest around AD 850–900 (Hirth 2000). Many residential structures were destroyed and burned during the attack on the site, trapping domestic assemblages on house floors when roofs collapsed. These materials included the remains of a wide range of domestic craft activities including the production of obsidian prismatic blades. The site was never completely reoccupied after its conquest and the creation of an archaeological zone at Xochicalco in

1929 protected the central residential core from modern destruction. The result was the recovery of *in situ* production data rarely encountered in archaeological contexts (Binford 1981; Schiffer 1985).

The discussion that follows focuses specifically on the evidence recovered from the four domestic craft areas. The reason for this is twofold. First, although craftsmen worked in the marketplace, it was not their permanent place of work (see Hirth 2006b for discussion). Rather craftsmen worked out of their homes and visited markets on a periodic basis to sell their goods. The household was the center for craft activity and provides the best information on how craft work was organized. Second, the evidence indicates that most of the craftsmen who worked in the marketplace were local artisans rather than itinerant craftsmen (but see Hirth 2006b, 2009a). Market work, therefore, was complementary to the activities that took place in the household.

The Organizational Structure of Crafting Households

The purpose of investigations was to examine the craft production of obsidian prismatic blades. Obsidian blades were used in each and every household at Xochicalco and it was felt that developing a thorough understanding of lithic production would foster a broader understanding of this important prehispanic craft. All four domestic households produced obsidian blades although this activity was not the only, or even the primary way that these households supported themselves. Although the research began by studying the structure of obsidian craft production, it finished by trying to model how craft production contributed to, and was incorporated into broader household subsistence strategies. In Mesoamerica most craft production began and ended in the household so it is important to understand how the households involved in obsidian crafting were organized at Xochicalco.

Three of the four domestic workshops (Operations H, I and K) had well preserved residential architecture; the fourth (Operation A) lay just outside the protected archaeological zone and was destroyed by deep tractor plowing just prior to the beginning of excavations (Figure 3). Investigations indicated that all four of these workshops were located in conjoint or multifamily residences. The three well preserved crafting households located on Cerro Xochicalco occupied residential structures between 210–348 sq. m. in size. The interior floor plans of these households are 210 sq. m. for Operation H (Figure 4), 348 sq. m. in Operation I (Figure 5), and 240 sq. m. for Operation K (Figure 6) (Hirth and Webb 2006). All of these households contained two or more

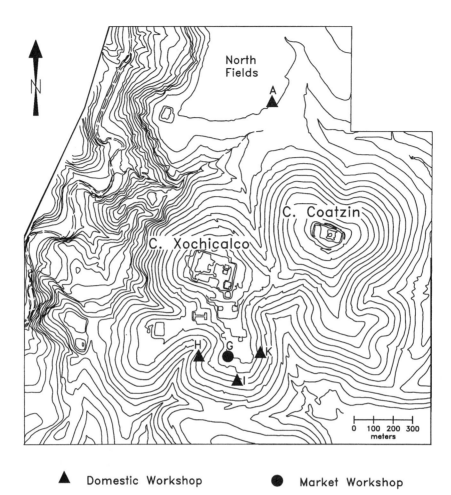

▲ **Domestic Workshop**   ● **Market Workshop**

Figure 3.   The location of the five intensively excavated obsidian workshops at Xochicalco.

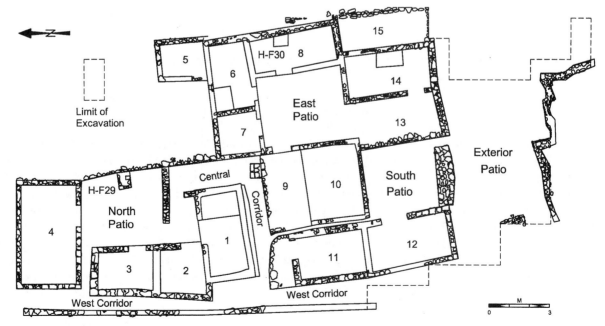

Figure 4.   The architectural floor plan of the Operation H household.

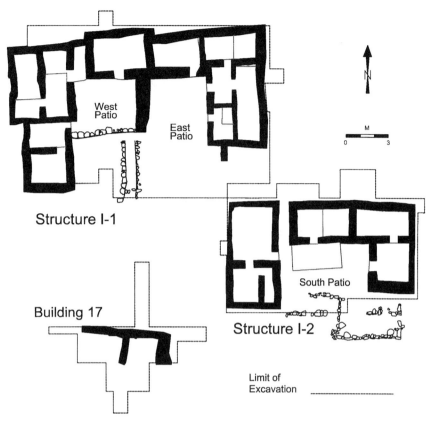

Figure 5. The architectural floor plan of the Operation I household.

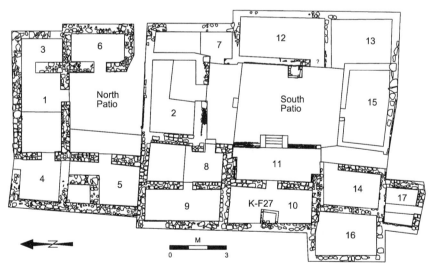

Figure 6. The architectural floor plan of the Operation K household.

nuclear families occupying adjacent patio groups within the residence.

The advantage of large households is that they can mobilize more labor for different craft and food production activities than small households (Bernbeck 1995; Hajnal 1982; Netting 1993; Wilk and Netting 1984). In crafting households this means that the different types of work including raw materials procurement, fabricating tasks, selling, and distributing finished goods, can be divided up among a greater number of individuals of both genders.

More labor also enables large households to more effectively combine craft production with normal food production without suffering labor shortages in key times of the year when several types of work must be carried out simultaneously.

The key to the effective use of domestic labor is a corporate household structure that binds the household together in terms of a unified set of economic goals (Wilk 1989a, 1989b, 1991). At Xochicalco, evidence for corporate structure at the domestic level is found in shared architectural space, resource sharing, the organization of work, and internal social differentiation that indicates the household was integrated under a single household head (Hirth 2006, 2009b). Corporate organization was evident in both the centralized food preparation and water pooling found in these households. Regarding the later, water was always in short supply at Xochicalco because the only permanent source was the Tembembe river, located 1–1.5 km west and 140–150 m below the main residential areas. To solve this problem household residents captured run off from their roofs and patios and stored it in subfloor cisterns (de Vega Nova 1993:Fig 2; González Crespo et al. 1995) or in large storage jars (*tinajas*). Stored water supplies were centrally located suggesting that water was used collectively by all members of the residence. Similarly, centralized food preparation was reconstructed from the distribution of whole ceramic vessels recovered from household floors. In all three households food preparation was confined primarily to one patio group and then distributed to all members of the household.

Corporate structure was also evident in the residential architecture suggesting internal social differentiation within the household. One room or cluster of rooms in each residence was more elaborately adorned than others. These rooms appear to have been sanctuaries occupied by the household head and used in important household rituals. One such area was Room 14 in Operation H which had ceramic and stone sculptures on its roof and contained a low bench or altar (Feature H-F30) on the back wall opposite the door (Figure 4). Operation K had a similar altar construction (Feature K-F27) in room 10 (Figure 6) and a stone sculpture of *huehueteotl* the old fire god sculpture located in the portico room 11 leading into this room (Hirth and Webb 2006:Fig 2.15). The patios where these sanctuary rooms are located contained the majority (72%) of the special ceramic vessels associated with high status or ritual activity at the household level (handled censers, figure incensarios, ceramic vases, miniature vessels). These patterns reinforce the view that Xochicalco households were integrated corporate groups with two or more nuclear families residing and working together under the authority of a single household head.

The Organization of Craft Work in Domestic Contexts

The same conditions that trapped domestic assemblages on residence floors did the same for production residues from craft activities. Figures 7–10 show the distribution of production debris and associated tools used in the manufacture of obsidian prismatic blades in Operations H, I and K. Two types of obsidian debitage concentrations were identified in the excavations: (1) primary activity deposits defined by discrete concentrations of macro and micro-debitage represented by labels H1, I1, K2, etc, and (2) smaller trace accumulations of micro-debitage represented by labels such as TH1, TI1, TK1, etc. Primary deposits were identified during excavation and represent materials that were laying on the floors of structures at the time they were abandoned. As such they represent activity areas where debris was allowed to accumulate on work surfaces. While not exactly contemporaneous, these deposits represent closely spaced production activities that occurred between major cleanings of floor surfaces (Hirth and Andrews 2006b:210–212 for a discussion of cleaning cycles). Trace accumulations represent slightly *earlier* activity deposits that were partially, but not completely, removed from floors during clean-up. They are small concentrations of micro-debitage under 1/8th inch in size identified either during excavation or from wet screening of soil samples taken from structure floors (Hirth 2006a).

These two classes of deposits provide the information for production tasks within domestic workshops. All of the lithic materials collected from work surfaces were plotted and false contour maps were created to look for patterning of production debitage within each workshop. Production tools were plotted alongside obsidian debitage concentrations that include hammerstones, pressure flakers, anvils, small pitted stone anvils, grinding palettes, and slurry bowls and slurry jars used in grinding operations. Together these distributions provide the basis for reconstructing the structure and tempo of craft activities within each residence.

One pattern evident in all three of the workshops is that crafting was carried out in multiple locations inside and outside the residence. This was an unanticipated finding since the manufacture of obsidian flaked stone tools creates an array of razor sharp hazardous waste that should be kept away from household residents (Santley and Kneebone 1993). This was not the case at Xochicalco. Work was not concentrated in one locale but was carried out in multiple, separate work areas in *each* household. The fact that all of the workshops were rapidly abandoned suggests that each production area may have been a locale where separate craftsman manufactured obsidian blades.

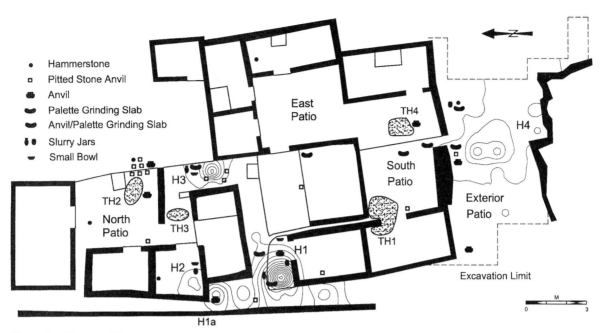

Figure 7. Obsidian debitage concentrations and crafting tools recovered from structure floors in Operation H.

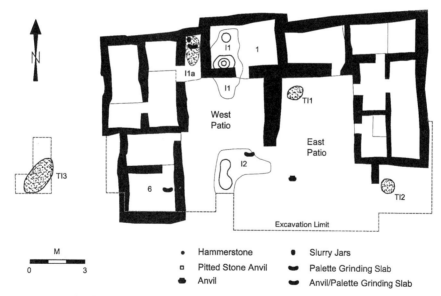

Figure 8. Obsidian debitage concentrations and crafting tools recovered from the floor of structure I-1 in Operation I.

In Mesoamerica it was common for sons to be trained in the professions of their fathers and this probably is how craftsmen were trained at Xochicalco. Depictions and descriptions of obsidian craftsmen from ethnohistoric sources in Mesoamerica identify them as men (Clark 1989) and it is likely that all the males within these households were trained in this craft. This was advantageous because it provided the household with a large pool of specialists who could change the tempo of work depending on internal needs. Whether craftsmen engaged in production on a regular or periodic basis depended upon a variety of factors including the level and periodicity of consumer demand, the availability of raw material, and whether the household also engaged in agriculture that required labor during the growing cycle (see below).

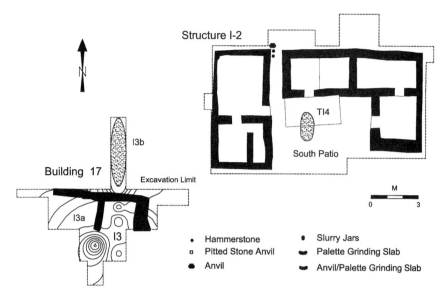

Figure 9. Obsidian debitage concentrations and crafting tools recovered from the floor of structure I-2 and Building 17 in Operation I.

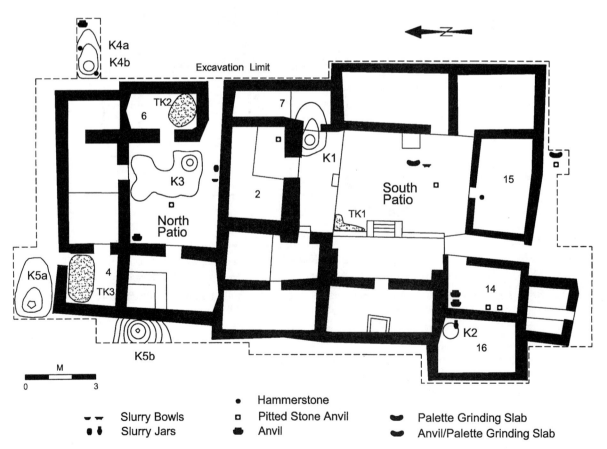

Figure 10. Obsidian debitage concentrations and crafting tools recovered from structure floors in Operation K.

Table 1. Comparison of output capacity of domestic workshops to actual core reduction rates in four domestic workshops. Core reduction information is based on experimental data from Hirth and Flenniken (2006:Table B3) where average core rejuvenation and blade reduction range from 1–1.5 hours per core for hand-held cores with an estimated 60 blades removed per core.

| | Calculated Monthly Core Reduction Rate | Output Capacity of Domestic Workshops | | |
		Craftsmen per Household	Monthly core reduction at 1 core/day	Monthly core reduction at 4 cores/day
Operation A	15–20	3–5	90–150	360–600
Operation H	45–50	3–5	90–150	360–600
Operation I	15–20	3–5	90–150	360–600
Operation K	15–20	3–5	90–150	360–600
Total	90–110	–	360–600	1,440–2,400

One question that needed to be answered was whether the multiple production areas identified on household floors were produced by different craftsmen or reflected an internal division of labor within the production process. Task specialization is recognized as an important way of increasing production efficiency and reducing work in the manufacturing process (Carrier 1992; Torrence 1986). At the domestic level this could consist of dividing and sequencing production activities (e.g. core rejuvenation, blade production, blade tool manufacture) within separate areas of the residence. Although special work areas were found in two workshops, the exterior patio in Operation H and Building 17 in Operation I (Figures 7 and 9), no evidence was found for internal division of labor *within* the workshops. No effort was made to streamline the production process and each activity area contains evidence for the same array of production tasks as any other. This suggests that each primary activity deposit was the work of a separate artisan. For a detailed discussion of the homogeneity of these work areas and the production debitage that they contain see Hirth (2006a:Tables 6.4–6.11) and Hirth and Andrews (2006a:260–262).

One aspect of production that is particularly noteworthy is that domestic workshops also obtained their raw materials independently of one another. Obtaining raw material was a significant challenge for Xochicalco craftsmen because obsidian does not outcrop in Morelos. Instead craftsmen obtained obsidian for blade production from three separate source areas: Ucareo, Michoacan; Zacualtipan, Hidalgo; and Pachuca, Hidalgo (Ferguson 2000; Hirth et al. 2006) (Figure 1). The straight line distance to any of these three sources is between 155–210 km, although the actual travel distance would be greater because of intervening mountainous terrain.

Combined INAA and technological analyses indicate that crafting households provisioned themselves with obsidian without the assistance of a centralized political institution or economic agency (Hirth 2008). Instead, households relied on itinerant craftsmen to supply them with obsidian in the form of used pressure cores (Hirth et al. 2006; Hirth 2008). All four domestic workshops were in operation at the moment of site abandonment, so the material from their activity surfaces reflect the procurement networks each household used at the time of the site's collapse. Source analysis indicates that each household developed its own supply network resulting in a significant amount of variation from household to household in the sources that they used. Operations A and I relied almost entirely on obsidian from Ucareo, Michoacan while Operation H used obsidian from Zacualtipan and Pachuca, Hidalgo, and lesser amounts of material from Ucareo, Michoacan. Operation K also relied on obsidian from the three sources of Zacualtipan, Ucareo, and Pachuca, but in notably different proportions from those found in Operation H (Hirth 2008:Table 2). The structure of these procurement networks underscores that craftsmen operated as *independent* craft specialists who were provisioned without the support of political institutions or elite patrons. Centralized assistance in procurement would have created more homogenous distributions of obsidian sources between households (Hirth et al. 2006; Hirth 2008). Likewise, support by elite patrons would have created source-specific concentrations of obsidian within the site; no evidence for this was found during intensive site mapping (Hirth 2000). Instead the evidence clearly indicates that Xochicalco's craftsmen were independent craft specialists.

All of the blades produced in the four workshops were intended for exchange outside the workshops rather than as a consumable used in another craft activity inside the household. Understanding the goal of production is fundamental for interpreting what the evidence for production means in organizational terms. This question was examined with use wear analysis since blades used for internal consumption in another craft would show systematic wear from use. The results of the use wear study revealed that all obsidian blades, except those used as preforms in the manufacture of blade tools, were intended for exchange outside the workshops (Hirth and Castanzo 2006). This indicates that production was intended to produce goods that could be sold to augment household subsistence. A discussion of the obsidian goods found in consumption contexts can be found in Hirth and Castanzo (2006).

Intermittent Production and the Issue of Specialization

How important was craft production to the households where it was practiced? Archaeologists have traditionally addressed this question by asking whether craft production was a full-time or part-time activity. This is an important question at Xochicalco because craft workshops were located in multi-family households capable of supporting high levels of production.

The amount of time that artisans worked on their crafts (full or part-time) is a difficult question to answer using archaeological data. It may not even be relevant for determining the importance of the craft to the overall economic well-being of the household since the return from part-time activities can range from very productive to providing the difference between hardship and above-the-minimum survival for the household (Costin 2007: 148–149). At Xochicalco this question was addressed as a resource flow model. Household productive capacity (measured in terms of a craftsman's ability to produce obsidian blades) was compared to output capacity (the total number of blades that could be produced if raw materials were available in unlimited supply). What the results indicate is that while productive capacity was high, output capacity was limited by the amount of obsidian that craftsmen had access to (Hirth and Andrews 2006b). Obsidian arrived at Xochicalco as already used pressure cores through infrequent contact with itinerant craftsmen. The cores craftsmen used were small and could produce an average of about 60 short blades.

Experimental work has confirmed that it was possible to rejuvenate and reduce the small cores coming into Xochicalco in a relatively short period of time. Even working slowly craftsmen could reduce 3–4 cores per day with moderate error corrections and one or two secondary core rejuvenations (Hirth and Flenniken 2006:Table B3). If it is assumed that artisans reduced only one core per day, the capacity to produce blades still far exceeds the amount of raw material entering the site. As mentioned above, all male household members probably were trained craftsmen. This together with the presence of multiple work areas in all three residences suggests that the 3–5 craftsmen were probably engaged in craft production at different points in time.

Table 1 summarizes the productive capacity of households and compares it to the actual number of cores estimated to have been reduced in all four domestic workshops. If each artisan reduced only one core per day, the productive capacity of household workshops is 4–5 times greater than the actual estimate for the number of cores reduced. If the higher estimate of 3–4 cores per day is used to calculate artisan productivity, the productive capacity soars to between 12–20 times the actual production rate! These figures suggest that there was not a full-time obsidian craftsman in *any* of the obsidian workshops at Xochicalco. There were too many capable artisans and too little raw material for households to engage in obsidian production on a continual basis. Only Operation H had enough total workshop output to have supported one full-time craftsmen. Even here, however, the presence of multiple work areas suggests that like other households, production was undertaken by a number of part-time specialists (Hirth 2006a).

The results suggest that the production of obsidian prismatic blades in domestic workshops was an intermittent rather than a continuous craft activity. What was particularly interesting is that none of the workshops *only* specialized in the production of blades. Instead they engaged in multicrafting and spread their crafting involvement over a range of different activities. Since this pattern is repeated in all four households it appears to be an intentional strategy that households used to enhance their economic well-being. This pattern of multicrafting is described below.

Specialization, Diversification and Multicrafting

Multicrafting as discussed in chapter two, refers to the practice of engaging in multiple crafts within the same household (Hirth 2006; Shimada 2007). The emphasis on craft *specialization* in archaeology has obscured our view of the range of work that artisans engage in. The concept of specialization implies a narrowing of production activities often to gain greater efficiency and/or increased scale of production (Carrier 1992). The way archaeologists often apply this concept is in terms of specific types of work or technological industries such as ceramic, lithic, metallurgy, or lapidary production. While logical from a modernist perspective it does not capture the way that prehispanic craftsmen actually worked. Consider Sahagún's description of the capable indigenous Mesoamerican craftsman,

> "el oficial de cualquier oficio mecánico primero es aprendiz y después es maestro de muchos oficios, y de tantos que de él se puede decir que él es omnis homo" (Katz 1966:51). The craftsmen of each mechanical craft first

Table 2. Diversified domestic production in four crafting households at Xochicalco.

Production Activity	Production Intensity
Operation A	
Obsidian Blade and Blade Tool Production	Primary Activity
Agriculture	Primary Activity
Obsidian Lapidary Production	Secondary Activity
Obsidian Biface Finishing	Secondary Activity
Itinerant Craftsmen	Possible Secondary Activity
Operation H	
Obsidian Blade and Blade Tool Production	Primary Activity
Poch Opal Biface Production	Secondary Activity
Obsidian Lapidary Production	Secondary Activity
Obsidian Biface Finishing	Secondary Activity
Stucco Processing	Secondary Activity
Agriculture	Likely Secondary Activity
Itinerant Craftsmen	Likely Secondary Activity
Operation I	
Obsidian Blade and Blade Tool Production	Primary Activity
Agriculture	Primary Activity
Obsidian Lapidary Production	Secondary Activity
Obsidian Biface Finishing	Secondary Activity
Itinerant Craftsmen	Possible Secondary Activity
Operation K	
Obsidian Blade and Blade Tool Production	Primary Activity
Agriculture	Primary Activity
Obsidian Lapidary Production	Secondary Activity
Obsidian Biface Finishing	Secondary Activity
Itinerant Craftsmen	Possible Secondary Activity

is an apprentice and later is a master of many crafts, and so many that it can be said that he is a man who knows them all (translation by author).

What Sahagún is describing is a very different view of prehispanic crafting than that held by most archaeologists. Instead of focusing on a narrow, specialized production activity, prehispanic craftsmen followed a broader, more diversified model of craft production. Craftsmen needed multiple skills to carry out their work and apparently applied them to a wide array of materials and activities. The reason for this was twofold. First, diversifying production activities insulated them from fluctuations in demand cycles for different types of goods (see chapter 2). Second, and equally important, becoming a master craftsman "who knows all the crafts" certainly would have increased the reputation and social prestige of the artisan (Helms 1993). From both these emic and etic perspectives, diversification of production activities, not specialization, was the key to crafting success both at the level of the individual artisan and the household in which he or she works.

The evidence from the four domestic obsidian workshops strongly supports the view that multicrafting and diversified craft production as discussed above were promi-

nent features of craft production at Xochicalco. While all workshops produced obsidian pressure blades, this was not their sole craft activity. Instead, Xochicalco craftsmen were involved in multicrafting in all four domestic workshops. Three or more craft activities were practiced in all of these households alongside agriculture (Hirth 2006a).

Table 2 summarizes the economic activities practiced in each of the four crafting households along with a subjective evaluation of their probable importance. Households at Operations A, I and K all show the same array of activity. Obsidian blade production and agriculture were the primary activities in all three households. The evidence for agriculture is indirect and is based largely on the fact that these households: (1) were large and had more labor than could be effectively absorbed by the craft activities that they practiced, and (2) do not differ in their artifactual assemblages from non-crafting, agricultural households at Xochicalco.

Also found in all of these households was evidence for lapidary production, obsidian blade tool production, and obsidian biface finishing. Lapidary work consisted primarily of manufacturing obsidian beads from exhausted blade cores, although other materials including a small amount of shell was also worked (Hirth and Flenniken 2006a: Photo 4.14). Lapidary work was a periodic, low volume activity,

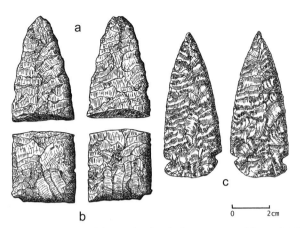

Figure 11. Imported large obsidian bifaces recovered from obsidian workshops at Xochicalco.

Figure 12. Bifaces manufactured from potch opal.

and while objects could have been produced for sale in the marketplace, the occurrence of obsidian beads in several offerings in the central elite center suggests that they could have produced as part of annual *tequitl* (service) obligations that all non-elite paid to their lord (Carrasco 1978). A range of obsidian tools in the form of small projectile points, eccentric blades, and notched blades also were produced from obsidian blades in these workshops (Hirth 2006a). The evidence for obsidian biface finishing comes from the large broken fragments and the diagnostic pressure and notching flakes recovered in obsidian workshops. What is interesting about these bifacial materials is that none of the workshops at Xochicalco had either the technical ability or access to enough raw material to make large bifaces (Figure 11). Instead, bifaces were obtained as already shaped preforms whose final pressure flaking and notching took place within the workshop prior to resale (Hirth and Flenniken 2006:97–99). This dimension of biface finishing adds an important dimension of *merchandising* to crafting households as they obtained preformed bifaces from obsidian suppliers that they finished prior to distribution.

The domestic workshop at Operation H differs from the other three by having an even greater array of crafting activities. Craftsmen here engaged in the same four craft activities as the other three crafting households (obsidian blade and blade tool manufacture, lapidary production, obsidian biface finishing) but at considerably greater intensity. Additional evidence was also found for two other economic activities, the manufacture of bifacial tools out of a local silaceous potch opal and the practice of stucco refinishing on a small scale. Potch opal is a porcellanite conglomerate with physical properties suitable for flaked stone tool manufacture. Two objects were manufactured from this material: bifaces used as spear and dart points, and small eccentrics used in personal adornment (Figures 12 and 13). Evidence

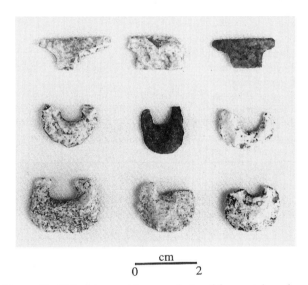

Figure 13. Bifacial eccentrics manufactured from potch opal.

for stucco processing was identified in the north patio of Operation H where plumb bobs, handled and unhandled stucco polishers, and a vessel partially filled with hardened stucco were recovered (Figure 14).

Operation H provides a picture of both more intensive and more diversified craft production. It had evidence for the highest levels of obsidian blade production and did more biface finishing (Hirth and Flenniken 2006a: Table 4.2) and lapidary work than any other workshop. Furthermore to sustain higher levels of blade production it also developed a more robust provisioning network to obtain raw material. Although it still depended on itinerant craftsmen to obtain obsidian cores, Operation H accessed obsidian from both the Zacualtipan and Pachuca sources that other workshops did not receive in large amounts. The picture is one of more intense levels of crafting at all levels.

Figure 14. Stucco finishing tools recovered from the north patio of Operation H.

Operation H had more than twice the level of obsidian blade production than other workshops and I believe that there is a strong possibility that some of its production was consumed by households in the surrounding region. Even though the obsidian sample from regional sites is very small, the neighboring Epiclassic site of Cerro Jumil has a very high proportion of blades manufactured from the Operation H workshop. Operation H was the only workshop at Xochicalco that had access to relatively large quantities of green obsidian from Pachuca, Hidalgo, many blades of which were found at Cerro Jumil. It is possible that one or more craftsmen from Operation H operated as itinerant craftsmen for sites like Cerro Jumil in Xochicalco's immediate hinterland. While this same possibility exists for all the workshops at Xochicalco, Operation H is the most likely candidate given its higher level of blade production and the type and quantity of obsidian used there (Hirth and Castanzo 2006:234–239 for discussion).

It was an unexpected surprise to identify multicrafting in all four domestic workshops. In retrospect it should not have been. We know, for example, that it was possible for a single obsidian craftsman to supply a large number of domestic households *if* they worked on a full-time basis. Sanders and Santley (1983) estimate that one full-time obsidian specialist could supply the needs of 5,600 adult consumers or 1800–2800 households per year. Our modeling indicates that the domestic obsidian workshops at Xochicalco, each with multiple craftsmen, represent a productive capacity well beyond the needs of Xochicalco's 10–15,000 residents. The obvious conclusion is that Xochicalco craftsmen were not full-time specialists. Likewise, if multicrafting was common among the Aztecs under conditions of high population densities and an active market system, then more intensive forms of production (e.g. full-time specialization)

should be rare earlier in time except under special circumstances. Given these conditions, an alternative to the full- and part-time models of craft production should have been apparent. That it was not is a reflection of how our theoretical templates structure the way we visualize and interpret archaeological data.

What is singularly most important is that none of the crafts were the full-time activity of a single craftsman. Instead, these households followed a diversified economic strategy of multicrafting combined with some agriculture. Multicrafting had two advantages. First, it allowed households to broaden their subsistence base by adding new types of remunerative work that they could engage in. Second, it was an economic strategy that provided the opportunity for full-time crafting to develop within a diverse mix of crafts. Operation H could be an example of a household that may have had a single full-time craft specialist engaged in an array of different craft activities. But even in multicrafting households the work of a full-time craftsmen still could be embedded in the broader subsistence activities of the entire household. From the perspective of subsistence risk, multicrafting and intermittent crafting are relatively safe economic strategies because they allow households to diversify their work regimes, take advantage of periodic labor surpluses, and expand total household income without exposing themselves to the dangerous cycles of fluctuating demand for the craft goods.

Conclusions

The obsidian craft industry at Xochicalco was based on domestic production. Craftsmen were part of large corporate households that integrated crafting into the domestic economy alongside agriculture and other subsistence pursuits. What is particularly significant is that none of the four domestic workshops at Xochicalco specialized in only one craft. Instead, all the workshops combined pressure blade and blade tool manufacture with lapidary work, the finishing and resale of obsidian bifaces, and other production activities including agriculture. These activities could be carried out simultaneously or intermittently over the course of the year as worked schedules permitted.

The important question, of course, is what significance do intermittent production and multicrafting hold for expanding our understanding of craft production in Mesoamerica? I believe there are several. The first is to recognize that intermittent craft production in domestic settings was the foundation for Mesoamerica's economy. In fact there is very little evidence for full-time production anywhere in Mesoamerica. The reason is that intermittent production provided households with a means to diversify work regimes and subsistence activities without engaging in a high risk activity like full-time craft production. Second, multicrafting was probably a common practice and pathway through which craft activity was intensified in Mesoamerica. Intensification of craft production may have occurred as new intermittent production activities were added to, and replaced other forms of work in the domestic economy. That multicrafting has been largely overlooked as an economic activity is a function of an overemphasis on specialization as a theme in archaeological research.

Researchers working in Mesoamerica need to shift their emphasis from craft production as a separate topic of research, to a more holistic perspective that places craft production within the context of the domestic economies in which they operated. At Xochicalco this pattern is beginning to emerge. Obsidian prismatic blades were staple necessities in every household both at Xochicalco and throughout its surrounding region. Ordinary households relied on and obtained their obsidian blades from craft producers like the ones described here. Even though households depended on craftsmen for all their obsidian blades, obsidian craft production was not a full-time activity at Xochicalco. It continued to be practiced as intermittent production within households committed to multicrafting and some level of agriculture. Craft production was firmly anchored in the diversified domestic economy where household members alternated between craftsmen, merchandiser, and farmer throughout the calendar year. Master craftsmen were not individuals who achieved a high degree of perfection in a single craft. Instead, they were as Sahagún tell us, "masters of many crafts" and we see this behavior in the multicrafting households at Xochicalco.

References

Alzate y Ramirez, Joseph Antonio
1791 Descripción de las Antiguedades de Xochicalco, dedicada a los señores de la Actual Expedición Maritima al Rededor del Orbe. Mexico City: Suplemento a la Gazeta de Literatura.

Appleby, Gordon
1976 The Role of Urban Food Needs in Regional Development, Puno, Pero. *In* Regional Analysis Volume 1 Economic Systems. Carol Smith, ed. Pp. 147–178. New York: Academic Press.

Bernbeck, Reinhard
1995 Lasting Alliances and Emerging Competition: Economic Developments in Early Mesopotamia. Journal of Anthropological Archaeology 14: 1–25.

Berry, Brian
1961 City Size Distributions and Economic Development. Economic Development and Culture Change 9:573–587.

Binford, Lewis
1981 Behavioral Archaeology and the "Pompeii Premise." Journal of Anthropological Research 37:195–208.

Boksenbaum, Martin, Paul Tolstoy, Garman Harbottle, Jerome Kimberlin, and Mary Nivens
1987 Obsidian Industries and Cultural Evolution in the Basin of Mexico before 500 B.C. Journal of Field Archaeology 14:65–75.

Braudel, Fernand
1986 The Wheels of Commerce. New York: Harper and Row.

Burton, Susan
1987 Obsidian Blade Manufacturing Debris on Terrace 37. *In* Ancient Chalcatzingo. David Grove, ed. Pp. 321–328. Austin: University of Texas Press.

Carrasco, Pedro
1978 La Economía del México Prehispánico. *In* Economía Política e Ideología en el México Prehispánico. Pedro Carrasco and Johanna Broda, eds. Pp. 13–74. México: Editorial Nueva Imagen.

Carrier, James
1992 Emerging Alienation in Production: A Maussian History. *Man* 27:539–558.

Childe, Gordon
1934 New Light on the Most Ancient Near East: The Oriental Prelude to European Prehistory. London: Kegan Paul.

Chorley, Richard, and Peter Haggett
1967 Models in Geography. London: Metheun.

Clark, John
1989 Obsidian: The Primary Mesoamerican Sources. *In* La obsidiana en Mesoamérica. Margarita Gaxiola and John Clark, eds. Pp. 299–319. Colección Científica 176. México: INAH.

Costin, Cathy
2007 Thinking about Production: Phenomenological Classification and Lexical Semantics. *In* Rethinking Craft Specialization in Complex Societies: Archaeological Analysis of the Social Meaning of Production. Zachary Hruby and Rowan Flad, eds. Pp. 143–162. Arlington: Archaeological Papers of the American Anthropological Association, Number 17.

de Vega Nova, Hortensia
1993 Interpretación de un conjunto habitacional en Xochicalco, Morelos. Cuadernos de Arquitectura Mesoamericana 24:19–28.

Diaz del Castillo, Bernal
1956 The Discovery and Conquest of Mexico 1517–1521. New York: Farrar, Straus and Cudahy.

Durkheim, Emile
1933 The Division of Labor in Society. New York: The Free Press.

Ferguson, Steve
2000 PIXE Analysis of Xochicalco Obsidians. *In* Ancient Urbanism at Xochicalco. The Evolution and Organization of a Prehispanic Society. Archaeological Research at Xochicalco Volume 1. Kenneth Hirth, ed. Pp. 284–290. Salt Lake City: University of Utah Press.

González Crespo, Norberto, and Silvia Garza Tarazona
1994 Xochicalco. Arqueología Mexicana 2:70–74.

Hajnal, John
1982 Two Kinds of Preindustrial Household Formation Systems. Population and Development Review 8:449–494.

Helms, Marry
1993 Craft and the Kingly Ideal. Austin: University of Texas Press.

Hirth, Kennth
1989 Militarism and Social Organization at Xochicalco, Morelos. *In* Mesoamerica after the Collapse of Teotihuacan A.D. 700–900. Richard Diehl and Janet Berlo, eds. Pp. 69–81. Washington: Dumbarton Oaks Research Library and Collections.
1995 The Investigation of Obsidian Craft Production at Xochicalco, Morelos. Ancient Mesoamerica 6:251–258.
1998 The Distributional Approach: A New Way to Identify Market Behavior using Archaeological Data. Current Anthropology 39:451–476 (with CA comment).
2000 Ancient Urbanism at Xochicalco. The Evolution and Organization of a Prehispanic Society. Archaeological Research at Xochicalco Volume 1. Salt Lake City: University of Utah Press
2006a Flaked Stone Craft Production in Domestic Contexts at Xochicalco. *In* Obsidian Craft Production in Ancient Central Mexico. Kenneth Hirth, ed. Pp. 137–178. Salt Lake City: University of Utah Press.
2006b Market Forces or State Control: The Organization of Obsidian Production in a Civic-Ceremonial Context. *In* Obsidian Craft Production in Ancient Central Mexico. Kenneth Hirth, ed. Pp. 179–201. Salt Lake City: University of Utah Press.
2008 The Economy of Supply: Modeling Obsidian Procurement and Craft Provisioning at a Central Mexican Urban Center. Latin American Antiquity 19: 435–457.
2009a Craft Production in the Mesoamerican Marketplace. Ancient Mesoamerica 20: 89–102.
2009b Household, Workshop, Guild, and Barrio: The Organization of Obsidian Craft Production in a Prehispanic Urban Center. *In* Domestic Life in Prehispanic Capitals. A Study of Specialization, Hierarchy, and Ethnicity. Linda Manzanilla and Claude Chapdelaine, eds. Pp 43–65. Ann Arbor: University of Michigan.

Hirth, Kenneth, and Bradford Andrews
2006a Craft Specialization and Craftman Skill. *In* Obsidian Craft Production in Ancient Central Mexico. Kenneth Hirth, ed. Pp. 258–274. Salt Lake City: University of Utah Press.
2006b Estimating Production Output in Domestic Craft Workshops. *In* Obsidian Craft Production in Ancient Central Mexico. Kenneth Hirth, ed. Pp. 202–217. Salt Lake City: University of Utah Press.

Hirth, Kenneth, Gregory Bondar, Michael Glascock, A. J. Vonarx, and Thierry Daubenspeck
2006 Supply Side Economics: An Analysis of Obsidian Procurement and the Organization of Workshop Provisioning. *In* Obsidian Craft Production in Ancient Central Mexico. Kenneth Hirth, ed. Pp. 115–136. Salt Lake City: University of Utah Press.

Hirth, Kenneth, and Ronald Castanzo
2006 An Experimental Study of Use-wear Striation on Obsidian Prismatic Blades. *In* Obsidian Craft Production in Ancient Central Mexico. Kenneth Hirth, ed. Pp. 318–327. Salt Lake City: University of Utah Press.

Hirth, Kenneth, and J. Jeffrey Flenniken
2006a More Interesting than You'd Think: The Percussion, Ground Stone and Lapidary Industries in Xochicalco Obsidian Workshops. *In* Obsidian Craft Production in Ancient Central Mexico. Kenneth Hirth, ed. Pp. 63–114. Salt Lake City: University of Utah Press.
2006b The Results of Experimental Studies in Obsidian Prismatic Blade Production. *In* Obsidian Craft Production in Ancient Central Mexico. Kenneth Hirth, ed. Pp. 315–317. Salt Lake City: University of Utah Press.

Hirth, Kenneth, and Ronald Webb
2006 Households and Plazas: The Contexts of Obsidian Craft Production at Xochicalco. *In* Obsidian Craft Production in Ancient Central Mexico. Kenneth Hirth, ed. Pp. 18–62, Salt Lake City: University of Utah Press.

Jacobs, Jane
1969 The Economy of Cities. New York: Random House.

Katz, Friedrich
1966 Situación Social y Económica de los Aztecas Durante los Siglos XV y XVI. Instituto de Investigaciones Históricas, Mexico City: UNAM.

Kurtz, Donald
1987 The Economics of Urbanization and State Formation at Teotihuacan. Current Anthropology 28:329–353.

Litvak King, Jaime
1971 Investigaciones en el Valle de Xochicalco: 1569–1870. Anales de Antropologia 8:102–124.

Netting, Robert, McC.
1993 Smallholders, Households, Farm Families, and the Ecology of Intensive, Sustainable Agriculture. Stanford: Stanford University Press.

Pirenne, Henri
1974 Medieval Cities. Their Origins and the Revival of Trade. Princeton: Princeton University Press.

Roque, J. Ceballos Novelo
1929 Ruinas Arqueológicas de Tepoztlan y Teopanzolco. *In* Guia para Visitar las Principales Ruinas Arqueológicas del Estado de Morelos. pp. 3–28. Mexico: SEP.

Sahagún, Fray Bernardino de
1977 Historia General de las Cosas de Nueva España. 4 volumes. Mexico City: Editorial Porrua.

Sanders, William, and Robert Santley
1983 A Tale of Three Cities: Energetics and Urbanization in Pre-hispanic Central Mexico. *In* Prehistoric Settlement Patterns. Evon Vogt and Richard Leventhal, eds. Pp. 243–291. Albuquerque and Cambridge: University of New Mexico Press and the Peabody Museum of Archaeology and Ethnology.

Santley, Robert, and Ronald Kneebone
1993 Craft Specialization, Refuse Disposal, and the Creation of Spatial Archaeological Records in Prehispanic Mesoamerica. *In* Prehispanic Domestic Units in Western Mesoamerica: Studies of the Household, Compound, and Residence.

Robert Santley and Kenneth Hirth, eds. Pp. 37–63. Boca Raton: CRC Press.

Schiffer, Michael
1985 Is there a "Pompeii Premise" in Archaeology? Journal of Anthropological Research 41:18–41.

Shimada, Izumi
2007 Craft Production in Complex Societies: Multicraft and Producer Perspectives. Salt Lake City: University of Utah Press.

Sjoberg, Gideon
1960 The Preindustrial City. New York: The Free Press.

Smith, Carol
1976 Exchange Systems and the Spatial Distribution of Elites: The Organization of Stratification in Agrarian Societies. *In* Regional Analysis, Volume II, Social Systems. Carol Smith, ed. Pp. 309–374. New York: Academic Press.

Torrence, Robin
1986 Production and Exchange of Stone Tools. Cambridge: Cambridge University Press.

Trigger, Bruce
1972 Determinants of Urban Growth in Pre-Industrial Societies. *In* Man, Settlement, and Urbanism. Peter Ucko, Ruth Tringham, and G. W. Dimbleby, eds. Pp. 575–599. Cambridge: Schenkman Publishing Company.

Ullman, Edward
1941 A Theory of the Location for Cities. The American Journal of Sociology 46:853–864.

Wilk, Richard
1989a Decision Making and Resource Flows within the Household: Beyond the Black Box. *In* The Household Economy. Reconsidering the Domestic Mode of Production. Richard Wilk, ed. Pp. 23–52. Boulder: Westview Press.
1989b The Household Economy. Reconsidering the Domestic Mode of Production. Boulder: Westview Press.
1991 Household Ecology. Economic Change and Domestic Life among the Kekchi Maya in Belize. Tucson: University of Arizona Press.

Wilk, Richard, and Robert Netting
1984 Households: Changing Forms and Functions. *In* Households. Robert Netting, Richard Wilk and Eric Arnould, eds. Pp. 1–28. Berkeley: University of California Press.

Wittfogel, Karl
1957 Oriental Despotism: A Comparative Study of Total Power. New Haven: Yale University Press.

7

Peasant Artisans: Household Prismatic Blade Production in the Zacapu Region, Michoacan (Milpillas Phase 1200–1450 AD)

Véronique Darras
CNRS Nanterre

The increasing interest in the archaeology of craft production has provided valuable information on the social and political economies of ancient societies. A number of scholars have discussed the nature of craft specialization, the social identity of craftsmen, and the factors involved in the organization of production and its related techno-cultural and social systems (Brumfiel and Earle 1987; Costin 1991, 2001, 2007; Costin and Hagstrum 1995; Costin and Wright 1998). In Mesoamerica, archaeological studies have examined the context and scale of production, the level of specialization, raw material provisioning, the distribution of finished products, and the identity of the artisans (Brumfiel 1987, 1998; Clark 1995, 1997; Clark and Bryant 1997; Clark and Parry 1990; Arnold and Santley 1993; Hirth 2006; Feinman 1999; Feinman and Nicholas 1993, 1995; Shimada 2007). Several of these studies explore the relationship between craft specialization, exchange, and power, emphasizing the sociopolitical role played by the elites in the management of specialized activities (see among others Clark and Parry 1990; Clark 1987, 1995; Santley et al., 1986; Spence 1981, 1984; Aoyama 1999, 2004; Inomata 2007).

Among these works, lithic production systems are fairly well documented, particularly obsidian blade and bifacial production. Several authors have raised the idea that prismatic blades were manufactured in non-domestic workshops by full-time craftsmen dependent on the elite (see among others Spence 1981, 1986, 1987; Clark 1987, 1995). Others have argued that most obsidian craft production occurred in domestic workshops by independent full- or part-time

artisans (Hirth and Andrews 2002; Hirth 2006). Although these studies demonstrate great diversity in the contexts of craft production, many authors now believe that *decentralized* and *independent* production were probably the norm in Mesoamerica (Feinman 1999; Hirth 2006).

It is within this framework that prismatic blade production in the Tarascan region of Zacapu (Figure 1) is discussed from thirteenth to fifteenth century AD. This region is important because it was where the Tarascan empire took form during Middle Postclassic period. Archaeological work indicates that this area underwent major spatial and social reorganisation around 1200 AD (Figure 2). These events reflect socio-political and ideological changes in Tarascan society brought about by the centralization of power. At the same time, deep transformations also occurred in the structure of obsidian production. Significant changes took place in raw material procurement strategies, production technology, and modes of distribution. Four main changes occurred at this time. They were: (1) the abandonment of mine workshops involved in earlier percussion industries at the Cerro Zinaparo and Cerro Varal obsidian deposits as well as contemporaneous hamlets in their general vicinity; (2) the appearance of small farming settlements that also engaged in specialized obsidian production 20–25 km south of these deposits; (3) the appearance of a new technology in the region involving the manufacture of prismatic pressure blades; and, (4) the utilization of a new and previously little used obsidian source at Penjamo (Guanajuato).

ARCHEOLOGICAL PAPERS OF THE AMERICAN ANTHROPOLOGICAL ASSOCIATION, Vol. 19, Issue 1, pp. 92–114, ISSN 1551-823X,
online ISSN 1551-8248. © 2009 by the American Anthropological Association. All rights reserved. DOI: 10.1111/j.1551-8248.2009.01015.x.

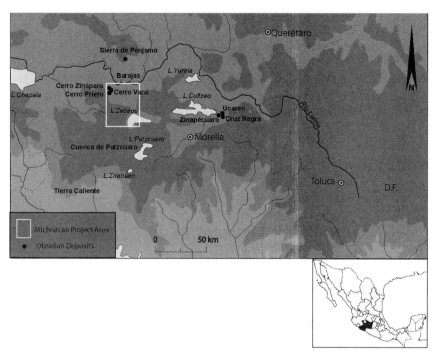

Figure 1. The north-central Michoacan region.

During the Late Postclassic period craft workshops could be found in both urban and rural settlements throughout the central highlands (Charlton *et al*. 1991). Despite variation in craft locations, most of the well-documented examples in Mesoamerica are from urban or civic-ceremonial contexts (see among others Spence, 1981, 1984, 1987; Hirth 1995, 2006; Aoyama 2006; Healan et al. 1983; Healan 1986). The prismatic blade workshops discussed here were located in very small rural settlements and their finished products were exported and consumed in neighbouring urban settlements.

Two rural sites are discussed in this paper: Iglesias del Cerro de la Cruz and El Durazno (Figure 2). The research conducted there provides a different perspective on both the location of production (at centralized, decentralized, domestic or non-domestic workshops), and the structure of production (in terms of intermittent crafting by independent or attached artisans). The information reflects a household production system administered by independent craftsmen who engaged in all stages of production from the acquisition of raw materials to the distribution of finished products in the nearby urban settlements. Likewise, the data suggest that the principal subsistence strategy at these two sites was farming, and that obsidian craftsmen who lived here engaged in the manufacture of prismatic blades on a part-time basis.

Geographical and Cultural Context of the Zacapu Region

The Zacapu region extends from the lake Zacapu basin and Tarascan volcanic mountain ranges on the south to the slope of the Vertiente Lerma to the north. This region contains important obsidian deposits at Cerro Varal, Cerro Zinaparo, and Cerro Prieto (Figure 2). Extensive archaeological research in the region was conducted between 1983 and late 1990s by the *Centro de Estudios Mexicanos y Centramericanos* (CEMCA, Mexico). This research focused on the reconstruction of population dynamics and cultural development from Late Preclassic (Loma Alta phase 1, 100 BC–BC 1) to the Spanish Conquest (Michelet 1992, 1998). Two main topics of this research were the study of major Tarascan settlements in the Malpaís of Zacapu (Migeon 1990, 1998; Michelet 1998) and prehispanic exploitation of the region's obsidian deposits (Darras 1991, 1999).

All three of the region's obsidian sources were exploited intensively during the Epiclassic (650–900 AD) and Early Postclassic periods (900–1100 AD), when obsidian percussion blades were produced and distributed for regional consumption (Darras 1999). However, around 1200 AD, the Lerma valley was largely abandoned along with the mine-workshops of Cerro Zinaparo and El Varal. At the same time significant population growth occurred in the Sierra of

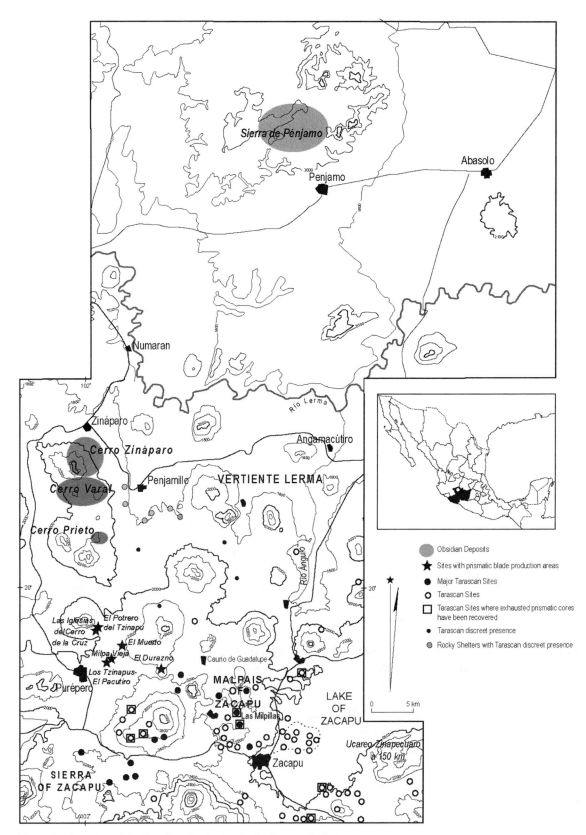

Figure 2. Location of the Late Postclassic sites in the Zacapu Region.

Zacapu (Migeon 1998; Michelet 1998, in press; Michelet, Pereira, Migeon 2005). During the Milpillas phase (1200–1450 AD), the number of settlements in the Sierra and Zacapu Basin grew to 61, of which 18 were concentrated in the Malpaís (Michelet 1992, 1998; Migeon 1990, 1998). These sites were occupied until around 1450 AD when they were rapidly and irrevocably abandoned and population probably moved toward the basin of Patzcuaro (Michelet 1989, 1998).

The Blade Production Sites

Fieldwork identified a number of small farming sites, seven of which had dense concentrations of obsidian refuse. All these sites are located halfway between the Malpaís of Zacapu and obsidian deposits of Zináparo and Cerro Varal (Figure 2). Evidence of prismatic blade production was identified in six residential sites that were also involved in agriculture (Table 1). Two of these sites had one or two mounds that appear to be civic-ceremonial structures. The degree of conservation at these sites is uneven so that four of these were studied using surface techniques while two (Las Iglesias del Cerro de la Cruz, El Durazno) were better preserved which permitted mapping and stratigraphic excavation. All these sites were occupied during the Milpillas phase and excavations at Las Iglesias demonstrate that the prismatic blade production first developed during this period.

Las Iglesias del Cerro de la Cruz (Mich 101) and El Potrero del Tzinapu (Mich 409)

Both of these sites are located on the slope of the volcano that overlooks the modern village of Villa Mendoza, near the town of Purepero. The site of Las Iglesias del Cerro de la Cruz consists of a terraced landscape covering approximately three hectares (Figure 3). A platform with one large civic-ceremonial mound was constructed on the highest part of the site. The remains of a rectangular stone structure 7.5 m × 6.5 m in size was also identified here that was interpreted as a great house. The slope below this platform contains an ample set of terraces covered with ceramic sherds and lithic materials. These terraces were constructed between natural andesite outcrops 10–20 meters apart that, unfortunately, have largely been destroyed by modern cultivation. Nevertheless, the presence of grinding stones, ceramic artifacts, obsidian, and andesite implements indicates that these were both residential and agricultural terraces.

Another sub-quadrangular structure approximately 8 m × 8 m in size was located at the extreme west end of the site along with two concentrations of obsidian. These concentrations cover 200–250 m² and are located between outcrops in rough terrain. A third isolated obsidian concentration covering 140 m² was located 1,000 meters to the northeast of this site. This concentration was identified as a separate site called El Potrero de los Tzinapus and contains high densities of obsidian refuse dispersed between andesite outcrops. No residential debris was located in this area and I suspect that the workshop was produced by residents of Las Iglesias del Cerro de la Cruz.

According to available data, Las Iglesias del Cerro de la Cruz represents a small village site. Although the number of residential structures cannot be accurately estimated, the presence of civic-ceremonial structures suggests the village was an integrated social group whose members were linked by family ties, common interests, and/or interpersonal bonds.

Archaeological investigations were conducted in the highest part of the site at structure 1 and in obsidian concentration 1. These excavations covered approximately 75 m² and uncovered several construction stages and a sequence of occupation that spans the Epiclassic to Late Postclassic periods. The archaeological evidence indicates that the great house was constructed during the Milpillas phase. An abundance of obsidian artifacts related to the pressure blade manufacture were recovered here which represents the first appearance of prismatic pressure blade technology in the region (Table 2). Earlier layers dating to the Epiclassic and Early Postclassic either did not contain prismatic blades, or did so, in very low quantities.

The ceramics recovered in structure 1 date to the Milpillas phase and reflect domestic activities. A flaked andesite industry, a mano fragment and evidence for a percussion flake industry, a bifacial industry and prismatic pressure blade industry all in obsidian (Tables 2 to 4). Finally, the obsidian recovered from concentration 1 (3 m × 4 m × 0.15 m in size) provide a good obsidian sample to reconstitute the pressure blade reduction sequence.

The Organization of Craft Production

The obsidian debris in the three workshop concentrations all pertain to pressure blade production. The debris recovered in these locales includes microdebitage reflecting *in situ* production and all stages of blade reduction. The collection from concentration 1 recovered 19 kg of obsidian debris containing 5,908 obsidian artifacts (Table 5).

Raw Material Procurement
Visual analysis (color criteria and general aspect) identified two varieties of obsidian, a translucent gray-banded black,

Table 1. Characteristics of the sites with blade production areas.

	El Durazno (Mich 100)	Las Iglesias del Cerro de la Cruz (Mich 101) El Potrero del Tzinapu (Mich 409)	Los Tzinapus-El Pacutiro (Mich 129) Milpas viejas (Mich 130)	El Durazno (Mich 407)
Surface	More than 1 ha	1,5 ha.	2500 m²	1 ha
Topography	Slope	Slope	Top of a hill	
State of conservation	Very destroyed	Milpa area but relatively well conserved	Very destroyed	Milpa area but good conservation
Civic-ceremonial structures	No	Platform with mound (*yacata*) and a "great house" associated with others stone structures;	Two mounds (*yacatas*)	No
Habitat	At least 20 structures	On the slope: residential and agricultural terraces.	Not identified	Two platforms with stone remains of structures.
Agricultarul terraces	Yes	On the slope: residential and agricultural terraces.	Yes	Yes
Ceramic materials	Yes	Yes	Yes, in the adjacent *milpas*	Yes
Basalt and Andesite Implements	–	Yes	Yes	Yes
Obsidian concentrations	Two small concentrations of 3 m².	Three concentrations: -Two concentrations of about 200 and 250 m² in the east part of the site. -An isolated concentration of 140 m² to 1000 m to the northeast.	Three concentrations: -100 m NW from *yacata* 1 of about 100 m². -a smaller concentration to the south of the yacata. -at 300 m from Mich 129, another concentration called Los Tzinapus (Mich.130) of about 100 m².	Four concentrations: On the Platform 1: - one adjacent to the structure 1, about 100 m² in extension. - another at the east side corner about 20 m² in extension. Between the platforms: - a small concentration about 20 m² in extension. -a concentration 75 m far the platforms about 250 m in extension.
Description	Obsidian debris from blade manufacture process	Obsidian debris from blade manufacture process.	Obsidian debris from blade manufacture process.	Obsidian debris from blade manufacture process.
Varieties of Obsidian	Translucent gray-banded black Translucent black-gray Green grayish. Visual Analysis: Cerro Varal, Penjamo	Translucent gray-banded black Opaque brilliant grey Visual and Physico-Quemical Analysis: Cerro Varal	Translucent gray-banded black Opaque brilliant grey Black Visual Analysis: Cerro Varal, Cerro Zináparo.	Translucent gray-banded black Translucent black-gray Green grayish Red Visual and Chemical Analysis: Cerro Varal, Cerro Zináparo, Penjamo
Others features	Sepultures			
Period	Late Postclassic	Epiclassic to Late Postclassic	Epiclassic to Late Postclassic	Late Postclassic

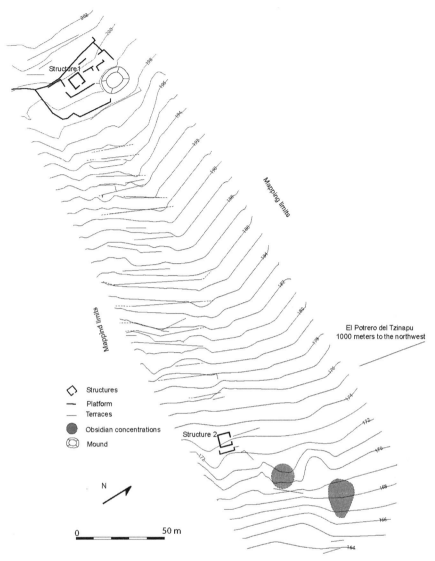

Figure 3. Map of Las Iglesias del Cerro de la Cruz.

Table 2. Las Iglesias del Cerro de la Cruz. Obsidian artifacts from the structure 1.

		Layer 1	**Layer 2**	**TOTAL**
Flake Industries	Cores	11	12	23
	Cortical flakes	9	1	10
	Flakes	227	146	373
	Implements	18	24	42
Biface Industries	Biface Reduction Flakes	22	11	33
	Projectile points	11		11
	Bifacial knives	5		5
Blade Industries	Cores	6	1	7
	Preparation products	23	1	24
	Pressure blades	203	74	277
	Rejuvenation flakes	6	3	9
	Microdebitage	169	109	278
	TOTAL	710	382	1092

Table 3. Las Iglesias del Cerro de la Cruz. Structure 1 – Categories of artifacts from blade industry.

Blade production/Mich 101	Layer 1	Layer 2	TOTAL
Crested blades C	1	–	1
Crested blades P	1	–	1
Multifaceted flakes	1	–	1
Percussion blades	6	1	7
1st Series blades – Complete	–	–	–
1st Series blades – Proximal	9	5	14
1st Series blades – Medial	24	6	30
1st Series blades – Distal	2	–	2
2nd Series blades – Proximal	23	7	30
2nd Series blades – Medial	76	28	104
2nd Series blades – Distal	7	3	10
3rd Series blades – Proximal	11	6	17
3rd Series blades – Medial	36	10	46
3rd Series blades – Distal	5	4	9
Rejuvenation flake	4	3	7
Rejuvenation platform flake	2	–	2
Fragmented prismatic cores	6	1	7
Implements on percussion blades	14	–	14
Implements on pressure blades (intentional modifications)	8	5	13
Projectile points	2	–	2
TOTAL	238	79	317

and an opaque gray/black. Optical sorting was validated by neutron activation analysis which indicates that only the Cerro Varal Source was exploited at this time, particularly the localities of Jaguey (Mich 150) and Las Navajas (Mich 117) located 20 km to the north. Fully 25.3% of obsidian artifacts many of which are percussion blades, are covered with cortex on half of the dorsal face. Fourteen exhausted cores were founded in this concentration that range between 10.2 cm × 2.6 cm × 2.1 cm and 11.5 cm × 3.2 cm × 2 cm in size. Several fragments indicate that some cores reached 13 cm in length. Technological analysis indicates that artisans made the blades from raw blocks of obsidian of moderate size and weight that could have been partially freed of cortex. In other work I propose that obsidian blocks weighed 2.0–3.0 kg, but the recent studies indicate a lower estimated average weight (1.5–2.0 kg). The use of a single source of obsidian and the selection of small unprepared blocks that were easy to transport, suggest that artisans procured raw material directly from the source and transported it back to the workshops areas where it was processed.

Reduction Sequence

As mentioned earlier, the workshops specialized in the production of prismatic blades using a reduction sequence that is described elsewhere (Darras et al. 2005; Table 5). Blocks were shaped with decortication flakes and brought to final polyhedral form after blade makers created a multifaceted platform that was subsequently pecked and ground. It is

Table 4. Las Iglesias del Cerro de la Cruz. Structure 1 – Andesite and Basalt Industry.

	Layer 1	Layer 2	TOTAL
Cores	–	1	1
Cortical flakes	20	18	38
Flakes	31	57	88
Implements (flakes)	1	1	2
Implements (slabs)	4	2	6
Ground implements	–	1	1
TOTAL	56	80	136

important to stress that a number of flakes and percussion blades also were identified with ground platforms (7.3%), indicating that grinding occurred early in the preparation sequence, and that the percussion reduction progressed using this ground platform. Blade makers usually took advantage of natural ridges to removed cortical flakes and blades; when these were absent, a crested ridge was created to remove crested blades (4.2%). Percussion and pressure blades were removed from a single face of the core leaving its opposite side in cortex or with multidirectional negative scars (Figure 4). The size of the exhausted cores and finished blades indicates that most blades ranged from 9–12.5 cm in length and 0.8–1.4 cm in width.

The Spatial Organization of Craft Production

The area of the residential and agricultural terracing covers a little more than two hectares within the site. More than

Table 5. Workshops Obsidian Materials from El Durazno and Las Iglesias del cerro de la Cruz.

CATEGORIES	Mich.101 Black-grey	Mich.407		TOTAL
		Green	Black-grey	
Percussion macroflakes	0		1	1
Percussion flakes – Unprepared platform	200	41	371	612
Flakes and percussion blades with ground platform	434	86	1177	1697
Percussion blades with unifacial or facetted platform	23	9	43	75
Flakes fragments	381	142	829	1352
Multifaceted flakes (platform preparation)	404	642	2177	3223
Crested blades	249	31	189	469
1st Series blades Complete	7	0	2	9
1st Series blades Proximal	218	64	302	584
1st Series blades Medial	320	63	274	657
1st Series blades Distal	161	27	209	397
2nd Series blades Complete	0	0	0	0
2nd Series blades Proximal	337	11	59	407
2nd Series blades Medial	748	9	25	782
2nd Series blades Distal	119	3	20	142
3rd Series blades Proximal	68	2	7	77
3rd Series blades Medial	157	5	25	187
3rd Series blades Distal	83	2	6	91
Rejuvenation flakes	188	8	130	326
Flakes from prismatic core	0	1	2	3
Plunging blades	1	0	1	2
Exhausted Prismatic cores – Complete	10	0	1	11
Exhausted Prismatic cores – Fragments	4			4
Implements on flakes	5	0	3	8
Flakes or blades with use-wear	198	0	36	234
Projectile points	1	0	1	2
Blade scraper	2	4	5	11
Undiagnostic percussion debitage	1590	330	2579	4499
TOTAL	5908	1480	8474	15862

twenty terraces were identified that were spaced 10–20 meters apart, creating areas large enough to accommodate both domestic units and *milpas*. The moderate density of surface material across these terraces suggests a low population density. The foundations of only two structures were identified that were 49 and 64 m² in size. This type of structure is referred to here as a great house following descriptions in the documentary sources that discuss "*casas de reunión, de consejo, o de velada*" (RM 1977:177). Archaeological investigations at Las Milpillas interpreted these structures as possible elite residences (1991 Migeon). The excavation of structure 1 provided few status markers except for two pipe fragments. The only evidence for special social status is the structure's size and the location adjacent to the civic-ceremonial mound. The excavation uncovered evidence for domestic activities reflecting food preparation, food storage, and the use of andesite and obsidian implements (Table 4). In addition to large quantities of prismatic blades, blade manufacturing byproducts and six fragmented and reused obsidian cores were recovered indicating the practice of blade

production inside the structure (Table 3). The second great house has not been excavated, although two areas of obsidian production were located within 40 and 60 meters of the structure.

Obsidian workshops 1 and 2 are located in the site's residential and farming sector, in an area with numerous andesite outcrops. In contrast, the workshop of El Potrero del Tzinapu is situated in an isolated area outside of the site. Workshops at Las Iglesias del Cerro de la Cruz appear to be located in proximity to one of the great houses, or in intentionally isolated areas away from residences.

There is no doubt that the occupants of Great House 1 had some connection with blade processing. If this structure was a residence, then its occupants were obsidian artisans who produced obsidian blades away from the household. If on the other hand, this structure was a communal building, then blade makers used it periodically. Either way, craftsmen at Las Iglesias del Cerro de la Cruz usually did not make obsidian blades in the place where they lived but moved to a special area outside the household for this purpose. The

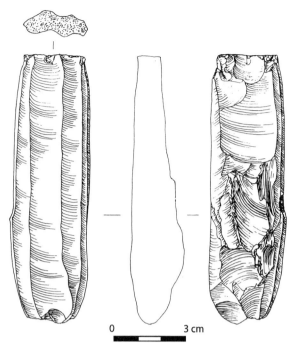

Figure 4. Exhausted Prismatic Core from Las Iglesias del Cerro de la Cruz.

location of obsidian workshops areas reveals a willingness to separate craft areas from residential space, very likely to protect household residents from the accumulation of obsidian debris. According to Hirth (2006:9), these obsidian workshops would represent *buffered workshops*.

Estimating Production Output

An attempt was made to estimate the quantity of raw materials brought to the site and the scale of production output following techniques used by other researchers (Clark 1997; Titmus and Clark 2003; Hirth and Andrews 2006). As expected, finished products were found in negligible quantities in workshop deposits. Estimates of blade output were based on the average number of blades produced per core. Clark (1997:197) estimates that as many as 230 blades could be removed from an average conical polyhedral core. Santley (1984: 64–65), however, uses a lower figure of 100–125 blades produced from a polyhedral core weighing 1–2 kg.

Titmus and Clark's replication experiments using the Mexica *itzcolotli* technique produced 161 blades from a core with a ground platform (Titmus and Clark 2003: 92). As the Mexica method was similar to that used by Tarascan blade makers, these estimates seem particularly relevant to this discussion. However, the exhausted cores recovered at both Las Iglesias del Cerro de la Cruz and El Durazno were not cylindrical cores. Instead, blades were removed from one face, a feature of core technology also noted by Parry (2002:

43) for blade production at Otumba. For this reason Zacapu cores could not have had the same 160 blade capacity as Mexica conical cores. Moreover, since Zacapu cores do not exceed 1 kg in weight, a lower output of only 100 blades per core is a more realistic estimate.

The central sector of this concentration covers roughly 100 m^2 and has an average depth of 20 cm representing a 20 m^3 deposit and 211 kg of obsidian waste. The remaining 150 m^2 of this deposit was estimated at 70% the central concentration which together produce an estimated weight of 432,6 kg for the entire workshop deposit (Table 7). Concentration 2 has a similar obsidian density, so the same estimates were applied to it.

An estimate of 100 blades per core and an average weight of 6 grams per blade (R = 4.5–7.5 grams) produced an estimate of 600 grams of blades per core. The 14 exhausted cores thus represent 8.4 kg of blades found in the excavated area. This produces an estimate of 4.7 kg of blades per cubic meter, or a total of 93.3 kg of blades for the 20 m^3 of the central concentration and 98 kg of blades for the remaining 150 m^2 (30 m^3).

This produces a low estimate of 191.3 kg of blades for all of concentration 1. This output is a low estimate of production output since the number of cores reduced in the locale may have been higher. This represents about one-third of the raw material brought into the site, which would have reached about 623.9 kg. Finally, when we add the average weight of exhausted and intact cores (97 grams) to these estimates we calculate that the averaged sized polyhedral core ready for pressure removal blades weighed 700–800 grams and was produced from a block of obsidian that averaged 2 kg in weight.

El Durazno (Mich. 407)

The site of El Durazno is located close to the modern village of Caurio de Guadalupe (Figure 2). It covers one hectare, lacks civic-ceremonial architecture, and appears to be a small hamlet. It contains two residential platforms with the associated remains of several structures, four obsidian concentrations, and several potential agricultural areas (Figure 5). The platforms are located on natural promontories called *mogotes* surrounded by level areas used for agriculture.

Residential platform 1 supports the wall lines of two structures, several unidentified stone alignments, and a line of large basalt blocks in one of the structures that delimit a concentration of obsidian debris, about 100 m^2 in size. The structure remains and obsidian concentrations are distributed in what appears to be a small central patio. Another

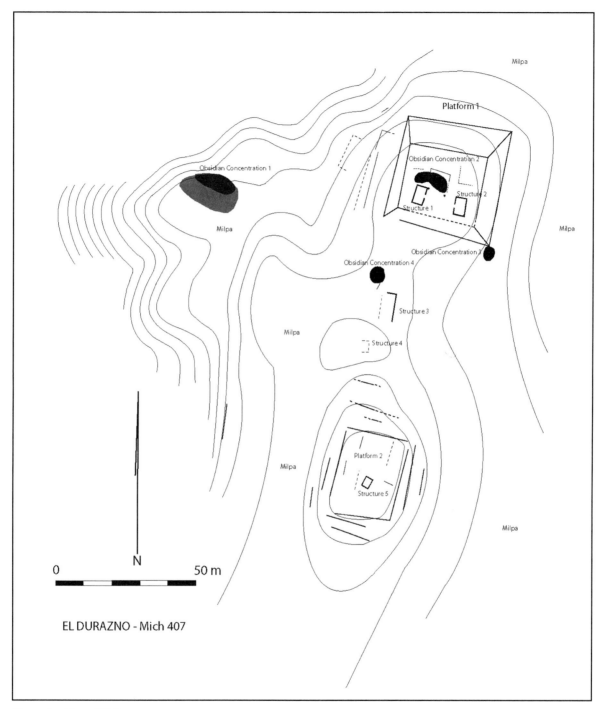

Figure 5. Map of El Durazno.

smaller obsidian concentration covering about 20 m² is located on the east side of the platform.

Residential platform 2 contains several structure walls but lacks any associated obsidian concentration. These two residential platforms are separated from one another by approximately 100 meters. Located between them are the re-

mains of two probable structures associated with a small obsidian concentration 20 m² in size. Finally, one other concentration of obsidian debris 250 m² in size was identified 75 meters to the northwest of both residential platforms. This obsidian refuse appears in the highest part of a *mogote*, scattered between basalt outcrops and into an adjacent field.

Small stratigraphic excavations were made in the residential area of platform 1 and in obsidian concentrations 1 and 2. Excavations in structure 1 recovered fragments of jars and bowls dated from the Milpillas phase, a mano fragment, and an obsidian scraper. In addition, significant amounts of refuse from obsidian pressure blade manufacture were recovered in the structure's occupation level (Table 5). Other domestic refuse was found outside of structure 1 including three grinding stone fragments, domestic sherds, and obsidian and basalt tools.

Systematic explorations in obsidian concentrations 1 and 2 recovered several kilos of obsidian reflecting specialized workshop production. Although collections are not available from other concentrations, field observations suggest that they were primary work places rather than trash deposits derived from workshops. Finally, collections across the site recovered clear evidence of domestic activities related to daily life and farming practices in areas surrounding the residential platforms.

The Organization of Craft Production

Excavations in both obsidian concentrations indicate that production was focused on the manufacture of obsidian blades. The debris was characterized by significant amounts of dust and microdebitage, as well as byproducts from the production of cores and blades. The assemblage recovered from concentration 2 (4 m² × 0.15 m), consisted of 31 kg of obsidian and 9,954 artifacts. The excavation in adjacent structure 1 recovered an additional 2.25 kg of obsidian and 651 core-blade artifacts.

Raw Material Procurement

Visual analysis identified four varieties of obsidian (translucent gray-banded black, translucent black-gray, green grayish and a rare red variety). These types came from three obsidian sources. The first two varieties represent 85% of the obsidian and came from the Cerro Varal source, in particular of the localities of Jaguey (Mich 150), El Varal (Mich 151) and Las Navajas (Mich 117). The red variety is from Cerro Zinaparo and represents only 0.1% of the collection. Finally, the greyish green variety represents 14.9% of the collection and derives from Penjamo located 75 km to the north. Unworked raw material, core preforms or polyhedral cores have not been found at El Durazno and the cores recovered are always exhausted. A high proportion of both the gray (14.5%) and green (23.3%) obsidians consist of decortication flakes. Generally, all the preparation products are small with more than 50% being less than, or equal to, 5 cm in length and 2.5 cm in width. All discarded cores are

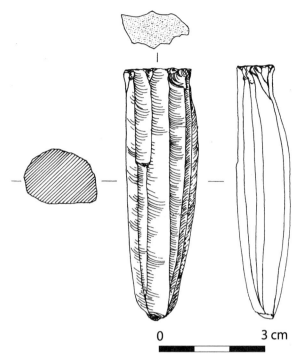

Figure 6. Exhausted Prismatic core from El Durazno.

also small, ranging from 6 cm × 3.4 cm × 1.7 cm to 9.2 cm × 2.6 cm × 1.7 cm in size (Figure 6).

The data indicate that the blade makers obtained most of their raw material from the closest obsidian source at Cerro Varal; smaller amounts of obsidian were procured from Penjamo. Morphological measurements indicate that all artifacts were produced from small blocks of obsidian. Craftsmen probably travelled directly to the sources and selected obsidian blocks of moderate size and weight that were easy to transport back to workshops. They generally selected unprepared angular blocks that weighed around 1.5 kg.

Reduction Sequence

The blade reduction sequence followed at El Durazno was similar to the one described for Las Iglesias with workshops engaged in the manufacture of prismatic cores and blades (Table 5). The high number of flakes and percussion blades with ground platforms (12.6%), indicates that the platform grinding occurred early in the core preparation sequence. As at Las Iglesias, percussion and pressure blades were removed from a single side of the core. In fact, the only difference observed between both sites is that pressure blades at El Durazno are smaller.

Table 6. El Durazno. Obsidian materials from Structure 1.

Mich.407 – CATEGORIES	Layer 1		Layer 2		TOTAL
	Green	Black-grey	Green	Black-grey	
Percussion flakes – Unprepared platform	13	68	1	4	86
Percussion flakes with ground platform	2	12			14
Crested blade with ground platform	4	4		1	9
Multifaceted flakes (platform preparation)	9	82	4	18	113
Percussion blades with Ground platform Complete		1			1
Percussion blades –with Ground platform Proximal		13			13
Percussion blades Medial		1	1	12	14
Percussion blades Distal		3			3
1st Series blades Complete	3	15			18
1st Series blades Proximal	2	19			21
1st Series blades Medial		5			5
1st Series blades Distal	3	13			16
2nd Series blades Complete		5	2		7
2nd Series blades Proximal		10	1		11
2nd Series blades Medial	2	6	6		14
2nd Series blades Distal	2	5	2		9
3rd Series blades Proximal	3	5			8
3rd Series blades Medial	2	7	1	7	17
3rd Series blades Distal	1	6	1	2	10
Prismatic exhausted core		1			1
Fragmented and reused prismatic exhausted core		1			1
Rejuvenation flakes	6	57	1	14	78
Debitage accidents				3	3
Blade Scraper		1	1		2
Burned Fragments		3		8	11
Natural fragments			2	10	12
Microdebitage	8	54	3	13	78
Undiagnostic percussion debitage	1	55		20	72
TOTAL	61	452	26	112	651

Spatial Organization of Craft Production

The obsidian concentrations revealed some variability in the behaviors associated with managing obsidian garbage within the site (Figure 5). Platform 1 contained two obsidian workshops with the main concentration located between two alignments of basalt blocks. The evidence suggests that this area was reserved for the manufacture of the prismatic blades. In addition to the presence of this specialized work area, artisans also made prismatic blades inside the structure (Table 6).

Concentration 3 located at the southeast corner of the platform 1 appears to be another smaller workshop associated with structure 2. Unfortunately, this area was not excavated so I cannot determine if this area was a workshop or a trash dump. In the case of the concentration 4, its spatial proximity with structures 3 and 4 suggests a functional link between them.

The situation on platform 2 is different and lacks the obsidian debris observed in the other areas of the site. The artifacts recovered here consist of ceramic sherds and lithic tools representative of domestic use. Likewise, no obsidian concentrations were identified in the area around the platform. In fact, the nearest concentration (1) is located 100 m away from the two residential platforms, in an isolated area marked by small outcrops.

Two strategies of production and waste management are evident in the data. First, the inhabitants of Platform 1 clearly were involved in the manufacture of prismatic blades. They carried out their activities in a specific and protected area, located adjacent to the residential structure. Except for a few ceramic sherds, the nearly exclusive presence of obsidian debris in this area indicates that it was a specialized place for working obsidian.

Second, the lack of evidence of blade manufacture on the Platform 2 suggests two alternatives. Either the structure's inhabitants were not engaged in obsidian craft production, or they opted to conduct it outside the residential platform to minimize the accumulation of dangerous obsidian refuse. In both cases, it is important to stress that basalt outcrops or blocks define the spaces used for the craft activity which served both to mark the area used for production and to contain the obsidian waste produced in it.

Estimating Production Output

Production at El Durazno involved two activities; the manufacture of obsidian blades and the production of cores that were taken to consumer sites where craftsmen produced blades. An estimate of the number of cores produced was calculated from the amount of refuse related to core preparation that was recovered in the El Durazno workshops. These estimates were then used to calculate the number of blades produced per core. The data needed to estimate the number of cores and the number of finished blades includes information on the size of the raw material to make the cores, the diameter of the polyhedral core, the number of errors and maintenance artifacts, and the width and thickness of finished blades (Hirth and Andrews 2006: 202). While data were available on the last two parameters, virtually nothing was known about the first two except that the blocks of obsidian probably weighed between 1.5–2 kg. Although Clark calculated core production and blade output at the site of Ojo de Agua in Chiapas with a high degree of precision (Clark 1997), it was difficult to apply his methodology to the El Durazno data. Instead data from the nearby site of Las Iglesias del Cerro de La Cruz was used since the production technology used to procure and produce obsidian blades was similar at both sites.

A 4 m² test pit was excavated in Concentration 2 which contained 26.7 kg of obsidian from Cerro Varal and 4.3 kg of obsidian from Penjamo. This concentration covered an area of 100 m² and represented a uniform deposit approximately 25 cm deep, for an overall volume of approximately 25 m³. The test excavation averaged 44.5 kg obsidian from Cerro Varal and 7.1 kg of Penjamo obsidian per m³; this represents a total of 1,112.5 kg Cerro Varal obsidian and 179.1 kg of Penjamo obsidian for the whole area.

Only one exhausted core weighing 71 grams was recovered from concentration 2. The excavation in Concentration 1 at Las Iglesias recovered 19 kg of obsidian, which included 14 exhausted cores weighing a total of 1033 grams (Table 7). To estimate the total number of cores from Concentration 2, we used 17.9 kg of waste as a representative base for the 14 cores recovered there, while recognizing that the initial number of reduced cores may have been higher. This calculation, however, includes all the debris produced during the whole core reduction process including waste produced during blade removal and core rejuvenation.

The obsidian artifacts recovered from Concentration 2 at El Durazno suggest that cores left the workshop as polyhedral cores after the removal of first and second series blades. While it is difficult to estimate the weight of waste produced during the last stage of production, rejuvenation products were minimal, representing less than 2% of the total debitage. In any case, the proportional calculation gives us 20 black obsidian cores and slightly more than 3 green obsidian cores for the excavated area (Table 7).

From this extrapolation, the number of blades can be estimated. Using the low figure of 100 blades per core and the average weight of 4.5 grams per blade and 71 grams per exhausted core, results in a total of 521 grams of obsidian; to this must be added the weight of waste produced during blade removal. However, it is likely that the cores produced in the workshop and transported to consumer sites did not exceed 600 grams in weight.

To calculate the total volume of obsidian for the whole concentration on the platform 1, we must be added to the initial sample of 31 kg, the weight estimated for the assumed cores (13.8 kg = 30.8%). When this density estimate is applied to the whole concentration on Platform 1, we get a total of 1,612.50 kg of Cerro Varal obsidian, and 254 kg of Penjamo green obsidian (Table 7). Of the nearly 1,867 kg of raw material brought into the concentration 2 workshop, approximately 575 kg left as shaped polyhedral cores (30.8%). Based on the estimate of 0.6 kg per core, we extrapolate that 958 cores were made in this workshop. At 100 blades per core, this represents a total output capacity of 95,825 prismatic blades produced by the artisans at this locale.

The Social Organization of Domestic Blade Production

The study of craft production typically examines several parameters that Costin identifies as constitution, context, concentration, and intensity of production (Costin 1991, 2001). As does Costin, I consider the constitution of production to refer to the size and structure of the group involved in craft activity.

At Las Iglesias del Cerro de la Cruz no spatial correspondence was found between the obsidian sectors and residential areas. It was suggested that the location of workshops outside of residential areas reflects a management strategy guided by a preoccupation to keep dangerous obsidian debris outside of household units. But this lack of spatial association also inhibits our ability to infer who initiated blade production, and whether production was organized at the household level. In fact, it is difficult to know whether each workshop was linked to a specific household unit, in which case we would have three domestic production units, or whether blade manufacture was carried out jointly using workers from different residential units.

Table 7. Calculations data for production output estimate.

	Las Iglesias del Cerro de La Cruz la Cruz	El Durazno
Obsidian Concentration	1	2
Largest Extension of the obsidian debris	250 m²	100 m²
Estimated Average depth	20 cm	25 cm
Excavation area	4 m × 3 m × 0.15 m	2 m × 2 m × 0.15 m
Average volume of whole obsidian area	50 m³	25 m³
Weight of black obsidian debris collected in the excavation	19 kg	26.7 kg
Weight of green obsidian debris collected in the excavation	–	4. 3 kg
Obsidian Density/m³	10.5 kg (heavy area)	51. 6 kg
Total obsidian waste estimated for the heavier area (100 m² × 0.20 m)	211 kg	–
Total obsidian waste estimated for the lower area (150 m² × 0.20 m) 70% of obsidian density for the heavier area.	232.05 kg.	–
Total black obsidian waste estimated for the whole obsidian concentration	432.6 kg	1,112.5 kg
Total green obsidian waste estimated for the whole obsidian concentration	–	179.1 kg
Number of exhausted cores in the excavated area	14	1
Average weight of the exhausted cores	97 grams	71 grams
Total of absolute weight of the exhausted cores (fragments and complete)	1.033 kg	–
Obsidian waste without cores (19 kg–1.033 kg)	17.9 kg	–
Waste estimate per core (obsidian waste without cores/number of cores)	1.3 kg	–
Number of black cores estimated for the 4 m² excavated area in El Durazno (26.7 kg/1.3 kg)	–	20
Number of green cores estimated for the 4 m² excavated area in El Durazno (4.3 kg/1.3 kg)	–	3
Lowest blade estimation per core	100	100
Average weight of second and third series blades	6 grams	4.5 grams
Blade average weight per core (second and third series)	0.600 kg	0.450 kg
Lower estimate of weight of black blades per m³	4.7 kg	64,5 kg
Lower estimate of weight of green blades per m³	–	10.2 kg
Lowest estimate of weight of black blades for the whole area	191.3 kg	370.8 kg
Lowest estimate of weight of green blades for the whole area	–	60.4 kg
Average weight of the pressure cores (blades + core + waste produced during removal of second and third blades)	0.700 kg	0.600 kg.
Weight of the assumed cores made in the excavated area in El Durazno (0.600 kg × 23)	–	13,8 kg
Total assumed weight of obsidian in the excavated area in El Durazno (31 kg + 13.8 kg)	–	44.8 kg
Estimate black raw material brought to the concentration	623.9 kg	1612.5 kg
Estimate green raw material brought to the concentration	–	254 kg

If the great houses were residences, then blade production would be the responsibility of their occupants. Furthermore, if these structures were occupied by the village rulers, this could mean that artisans were members of the local elite. In this regard, Great House 2 appears closest to the obsidian workshops, and, therefore, probably was involved in the blade manufacture. On the other hand, if great house 1 was involved in obsidian craft activity, why would its occupants locate their work area 350 meters to the east? The isolated workshop of El Potrero del Tzinapu raises the same question.

A second scenario is that the great houses were places dedicated to religious and social events that may have included craft activities. If this were true, then blade manufacture could have been realized at the community level in neutral and shared places outside of residential areas. While possible, I believe this scenario is highly unlikely because community production would have generated a heavier volume of obsidian refuse than is found at Las Iglesias. Whichever was the case, the great houses appear to have played an important role in organizing obsidian blade production. The most likely explanation is that obsidian blade production was probably organized at the household level.

In the case of El Durazno, the small size of the settlement, the contiguity of various household units, and their similarity to one another suggests that each one was occupied by a nuclear family, and that the hamlet was integrated through family ties. The archaeological work indicates that various households were involved in obsidian blade manufacture. Despite the presence of special areas for craft production, Structure 1 on the Platform 1 was also used occasionally as a locale to work obsidian. It is reasonable, therefore, to suggest that the occupants of Platform 2 were involved in blade manufacture, and carried out this activity in a separate locale outside the household. The data from El Durazno and Las Iglesias del Cerro de la Cruz suggest that blade manufacture in both sites was organized at the household level with workshops located in domestic contexts or in buffered workshops outside the residence.

The Obsidian Blade Craftsman: A Part-Time Producer

Another important parameter discussed by Costin is the intensity of production, or the time devoted to the craft activity (Costin and Hagstrum 1995: 620). The questions here are whether blade makers were full-or part-time artisans and did they engage in other subsistence activities in addition to craft production. Following this perspective, Hirth has proposed that certain indicators, such as the nature and volume of debris, their location, the way they were managed, and above all the coexistence of forms of multicrafting reveal different types of household activities (Hirth 2006). The number of obsidian refuse concentrations together with their internal composition, appears particularly important to evaluate the level of craft involvement.

Given the current state of information, it is difficult to determine with precision how much time the blade makers devoted to obsidian craft activity, and to estimate the rate of production per production unit. However, in both of the cases discussed here, there is clear evidence that craftsmen worked without intermediaries and production units were responsible for the entire production cycle, from resource procurement to the distribution of finished products. Consequently, to evaluate the amount of time artisans devoted to crafting, it is necessary to model three dimensions of craft activity: (1) the procurement of raw material (acquisition and transport); (2) the time devoted to blade manufacturing; and, (3) the final distribution of obsidian products (probably through marketplaces located in consumer sites). The hypothesis presented here is that household production units organized trips to obsidian deposits to procure raw material and then distributed finished goods to consumer sites, both of which required frequent movement and investment of time beyond simple blade production.

Raw Material Procurement

The morphological characteristics of obsidian debris at both sites suggest that raw material was acquired as angular blocks weighing no more than 2 kg. One important question is how much time did it take for artisans to procure their raw material? The nature of the cortex on the obsidian from Cerro Varal indicates that artisans did not use surface eroded nodules, but rather obtained angular blocks from mining activity. However, the numerous subterranean and open pit mines identified at the quarries date to the earlier Epiclassic and Early Postclassic periods when craftsmen engaged in the manufacture of percussion blades (Darras 1999). Quarry locations have not been located for the Milpillas phase (1200–1450 AD), nor is it possible to determine whether some of the quarries were used by artisans during the Late Postclassic period. However, two subterranean mines have been identified that may have been exploited by the Tarascan artisans from Zacapu, one in Cerro Varal, and another providing red nodules at Cerro Zináparo.

During earlier periods, obsidian extraction was guided by the concern to find angular blocks of good quality and large size that could serve to remove percussion macroblades and blades. While Tarascan artisans sought to obtain obsidian with few defects, above all they wanted small blocks. My hypothesis is that Milpillas phase artisans did not take the time to dig mines at Cerro Varal because they did not need to. Their ancestors had produced thousands of tons of debris, including many small blocks that were abandoned where they were extracted. For this reason it is likely that much of obsidian from Cerro Varal was obtained from surface collections of blocks exposed and discarded during Epiclassic and early Postclassic mining activities.

The green obsidian from Penjamo was probably collected on the surface. The cortex suggests that raw material was collected as exposed nodules. This conforms to the archaeological evidence at Penjamo where subterranean and open pit mines have not been identified. That craftsmen at both Las Iglesias del Cerro de la Cruz and El Durazno probably procured raw material from surface materials at the source collecting it in a relatively short period of time. That the artisans were the same ones that collected the raw material is likely because of the needed to select high quality obsidian for manufacture of blades.

Movement from Obsidian Deposits

The quantity of raw obsidian brought back to workshops reflects the frequency of resource movement, although it is difficult to identify the number of people involved in travel, how many kilos were moved per person, or how long people were engaged in craft activity. Despite these limitations it is still worth modeling the movement of obsidian to domestic workshops.

Studies on trade networks and itinerant merchants have focused on the average load that porters (*tlameme*) carried in the central highlands. The early descriptions of Diaz del Castillo indicate that porters, on average, carried a load of 23 kilos (two arrobas) over a distance of 21–28 km (Hassig 1985: 28–32). Subsequent research suggests greater variability in porter loads. Drennan, (1984: 105), for instance, proposed that a load of 30 kg was a reasonable cargo for a porter to transport over a distance of 36 km. In Michoacan, Warren (1968: 47–49) mentions that Tarascan porters often carried 32–72 kg of copper ingots over distances of 21–43 km (Pollard 1987:748–750). Lumholtz (1904: 358–360) discusses the *huacaleros*, or crate-carriers, who daily moved 68 kg of merchandise from the Sierra Tarasca to areas like Mexico City over distances of 48–64 km. This information indicates that porters daily carried loads above 30 kg over long distances. But is it reasonable to consider that it was the usual load of any adult male? The higher figures probably represent the load-carrying capacities of professional peddlers which was not the case of ordinary artisans. Based on the data from Michoacan, Warren's minimum weight of 32 kg is used as a reasonable cargo load for transporting obsidian.

It is estimated that a minimum of 1,866.5 kg of obsidian was brought into the workshop on the platform 1 at El Durazno, 1,612.5 kg from Cerro Varal and 254 kg from Pénjamo. Using a load weighing 32 kg per carrier, this represents 50.4 individual trips to Cerro Varal and eight trips to Pénjamo with each individual carrying 16 obsidian blocks weighing 2 kg each. The distances, however, differ between the two sources. Cerro Varal is located 25 km from El Durazno while Penjamo lies 65–75 km away depending on which outcrop artisans exploited. Taking into consideration the local topography (there is a natural corridor from the Sierra de Zacapu to the Vertiente Lerma), it is likely that the roundtrip from El Durazno to Cerro Varal could be made in one day since the walking trip to the source without a load only takes about 3.5 hours.

It is not known whether trips to obsidian deposits were made by one person or several. Trips, however, could have been organized at either the household or village level. In either case, even using a single porter, all the obsidian used in the workshop area on Platform 1 could have been acquired in about 50 trips to Cerro Varal, representing only 50 days of work. As noted above, the quantity of raw obsidian brought in to Las Iglesias was lower than El Durazno. Artisans there only obtained obsidian from Cerro Varal and

the 623.9 kg used could have been obtained in only 20 roundtrips.

Obtaining obsidian from Penjamo required more time. According to Pollard (1987:750), a distance of 10–12 leagues (75 km) was traveled in three days. This is a reasonable estimate for this trip because it is across relatively flat terrain and only involved crossing the Lerma river. Furthermore, the trip to the source without a load would be shorter, requiring 1–2 days producing a 4–5 day roundtrip journey. The eight trips from workshops to Penjamo would have only taken 32–40 days producing a total of 190.5 blocks of green obsidian weighing 1.5 kg apiece. This greater distance may explain why green obsidian is found in smaller proportions than black-grey obsidian. However, it is also possible that the lower quantities of green obsidian may reflect a lower level of regional demand if green blades were only used for ritual activities instead of daily tasks. Even if these estimates do not exactly reflect the frequency of journeys to obsidian deposits, it is clear that procurement of raw material procurement was a relatively insignificant part of the whole production cycle.

The Process of Blade Manufacture

The volume of obsidian debris recovered at workshops is a good indicator of the intensity of craft activity. It is clear that obsidian refuse at both Las Iglesias and El Durazno does not reflect intensive production of full-time specialists. Clark's replication experiments led him to propose that a craftsman could reduce 160 polyhedral cores in 50 days working 2–4 hours/day (1997:132). In that case, the 319 cores reduced in the workshop area 1 at Las Iglesias del Cerro de la Cruz would correspond to 99.7 days of work. Similarly the 958 cores estimated to have been manufactured at El Durazno represent 299.4 days of part-time work, the major part of which would have been in domestic workshops or at consumer sites.

Distribution to Consumer Sites

The Tarascan settlements throughout the Sierra-Malpaís of Zacapu consumed large numbers of prismatic blades, where they constitute almost 50% of the obsidian artifacts recovered in consumer sites (Darras *et al.* 2005). Nine of these sites contained a few exhausted blade cores and error products, suggesting blade removal on the spot. The presence of only such artifacts is not enough, however, to prove the existence of itinerant craftsmen (these artifacts may have been acquired to be recycled and used for other purposes). As mentioned earlier, blade makers probably distributed their products as itinerant craftsmen via the market network. It is likely that artisans distributed finished blades or made them in marketplaces. However, while the frequency of their movement is unknown it may have coincided with the calendar of the regional markets. In any case, the time invested in the distribution of finished products had to be proportional to the time invested in production within the workshops.

Production cycle data suggests that blade manufacture did not occupy a significant amount of time. To assess how much time was devoted to crafting requires determining the number of people involved in production and for how long. We have established that production took place at both sites during Milpillas phase (1200–1450 AD), but the precise timing of its beginning and end is unknown. While Las Iglesias del Cerro de la Cruz was occupied throughout the entire phase, El Durazno had a briefer occupation, being founded during middle of the thirteenth century. If this site was occupied for two centuries, which is likely, then the volume of obsidian waste recovered here is too small to represent a full-time activity. If blade manufacture at El Durazno was spread over two centuries all of the production refuse could be account for by 1.5 round trips to obsidian deposits every 10 years, and less than two days per year devoted to blade core reduction. The estimates for Las Iglesias del Cerro de la Cruz, are even lower. The 319 estimated cores reduced in Workshop Area 1 would only represent a little over 100 part-time days of work!

The amount of time spent in production would be higher if the duration of the craft activity was shorter, or if estimates of the amount of obsidian brought into workshops is too low. One thing, however, is absolutely certain: even if the duration of production is cut in half, or if estimates of worked raw material is doubled or quadrupled, estimates for the scale of blade production remains modest and continue to support the idea that craftsmen dedicated very little time to craft production.

Between Farming and Crafting

If blade making took relatively little time, then it is likely that the residents of these settlements invested most of their energy in other subsistence activities. Technological studies suggest that blade production was the only form of obsidian craft production practiced in these workshops. Although investigations were limited, no evidence was found for any other craft activities in these settlements. In contrast, there are good indications that agriculture was a main activity. Both sites have extensive agricultural terracing and the stone artifact assemblages recovered likewise suggest the

practice of agriculture. For the most part, the materials collected in the residential areas reveal domestic activities that include expedient percussion flaking, cooking, food storage, and hunting. The data indicate that these settlements provided for their basic needs; obsidian crafting was for all intents and purposes a secondary and complementary activity to farming which was the basis of the household economy (see Feinman 2003; Hirth 2006:276).

The El Durazno and Las Iglesias cases are good examples of what Hirth refers to as intermittent crafting (see chapter 2, this volume). Tarascan blade makers in the Zacapu basin were first and foremost peasant agriculturalists who engaged in craft activity during lulls in the cultivation cycle or during the dry season when agriculture was not possible.

Independent Peasants-Artisans

There is good evidence that the Zacapu blade makers were independent specialists operating without direct control by the elite. The sociopolitical context of production and the identity and social status of artisans in Tarascan society can be examined by looking at the geographic location, civic-ceremonial content, and variability of activities within and between sites.

The Geographic Location of Workshop Areas
During the Epiclassic and Early Postclassic periods obsidian artisans lived and worked at the Zinaparo and Cerro Varal obsidian deposits. This differs from the Late Postclassic period when blade makers resided and worked away from sources. During the Milpillas phase, craftsmen resided in intermediate locations 20 km south of the nearest source deposits and 5–15 km from large regional population centers. Las Iglesias del Cerro de la Cruz is located 5 km from the three craftsmen villages of El Muerto, Los Tzinapus-El Paticútiro and Viejas Milpas and 10 km from El Durazno (Figure 2). The clustering of these sites could reflect either their autonomy vis-à-vis the larger consumer communities of the Malpais, or just a desire to be located near one another.

Their location cannot be explained as a product of access to raw materials because all sites in the Zacapu region, including the large urban sites, are relatively close to obsidian deposits. In reality, the physical distance of workshop sites to the larger centers is one of the best arguments for independent craftsmen in these sites. Although it is more difficult to reconstruct corporate relationships, the proximity of sites could also be explained by craftsmen having familial bonds and/or sharing specific craft knowledge and common economic interests.

Presence of Cult Places

The presence of civic-ceremonial structures may reflect socio-political and religious independence as well as special social status (Hirth 2006: 282). Two of the six sites with evidence for obsidian craft production have civic-ceremonial structures: Las Iglesias del Cerro de la Cruz and Milpas Viejas (Figure 2). On the other hand, the sites of El Durazno and El Muerto do not have architecture with civic-ceremonial functions. As discussed earlier, the site of El Durazno probably contained three nuclear families linked by familial ties and depended on a larger site for ritual functions.

Intra- and Inter-site Variability Between Sites

Given the contemporaneity of both sites, further evidence for artisans as independent specialists comes from the differences found between the organization of production in these communities. For instance, craftsmen at the two sites did not work the same types of obsidian. The differences observed in procurement strategies could reflect idiosyncratic aspects of procurement or individual responses to commercial competitiveness. In spite of similar technological processes, the differences observed in the organization of production reflect decisions made at the level of individual workshops. In the same way, variation in the use of production space within and between sites indicates freedom in how crafting was organized within each production unit. The coexistence of buffered workshops and specialized domestic workshops reflects diversity in organization compatible with the entrepreneurial spirit of the independent craftsman.

Although these differences appear to indicate that production was carried out by independent craftsmen, the possibility exists that there are also chronological discrepancies between sites. Even if both sites were producing blades throughout the Milpillas phase, I suspect specialized production appeared earlier at the site of Las Iglesias del Cerro de la Cruz. Besides being closer to obsidian deposits, I think that the utilization of a single source may be indicative of the earliest Milpillas crafting sites in the region. The earlier occupation and the presence of civic-ceremonial structures, which reflects some importance, are other features that suggest that Las Iglesias may have been the first site engaged in this craft production. El Durazno, on the other hand, is not occupied until the middle of thirteenth century as a result of accelerated growth within the Malpaís of Zacapu.

According to this pattern, production systems would appear to have evolved quickly throughout the region over a period of about 100 years. El Durazno represents the last creation and probably the best example of professional independence. The decision to live closer to larger centers of consumption and the utilization of new sources illustrate this

independence. In the same way, combining domestic blade production with itinerant production in consumer sites reflect manufacturing decisions characteristic of independent craftsmen.

Paradoxically, this economic autonomy would have been accompanied by greater interregional socio-political dependencies. The lack of civic-ceremonial structures in hamlet communities indicates that they were incorporated into socio-political and religious networks dominated by one of the larger settlements of the Malpaís. Finally, there are no archaeological indications that blade makers had any special social status. On the contrary and above all for El Durazno, everything indicates that obsidian craftsmen were humble low status individuals.

Level of Integration in the Regional Political Economy

Political economy can be viewed as the group of rules governing the production, exchange, and mobilization of the material goods through the socio-political and power relations of society. Following Hirth (2006:281) Zacapu blade makers can be described as micro-entrepreneurs who were responsible for the whole production process without reliance on intermediaries.

One important question for understanding the structure of economic relationships is what degree of access was there to obsidian deposits. During the Late Postclassic, the obsidian deposits of Zináparo, Cerro Varal, and Penjamo were in depopulated areas bordering on territories occupied by groups of *Chichimecs*. The lack of Milpillas phase settlements at obsidian sources seems to indicate that obsidian was freely accessible to whoever wanted to supply himself, and that elites from the Zacapu region did not attempt to control access to, or exploitation of this resource.

The decision by blade makers to organize short trips to obtain raw material and not to shape polyhedral cores at the source may be explained by several factors: (1) the macroregional political context and the possible insecurity induced by the presence of the *Chichimecs*; (2) the geographic proximity of the obsidian deposits; and, (3) the part-time nature of obsidian craft production that required little investment in the raw material procurement.

Archaeological investigations by the CEMCA in the Malpaís provide valuable information on the distribution and consumption of obsidian blades (Migeon 1990; Michelet 1998). The Malpaís had 18 settlements during this period, several of urban character with large populations. The combined population estimate for these four sites which cover just under 4 km^2 is 16,000–20,000 persons (Michelet in press), which provide a good idea of the demographic density, and level of market consumption. According to available information, the craftsmen villages identified would have had to supply the region's total demand for obsidian blades. Analysis indicates that 48.2% of the obsidian assemblage recovered from the site of Milpillas, one of the largest Tarascan settlements in this region, consisted of prismatic blade segments. These blades were used as blanks for expedient tools, often used for cutting soft materials. The distribution of these materials does not reveal any quantitative and qualitative variation that might reflect differential access to resources.

The large quantities of items circulating and the contexts from which they were recovered indicate that prismatic blades were a common tool. During the Late Postclassic period, the prismatic blade became the most widespread artifact in the Tarascan peasant's tool kit. This contrasted strongly with the Epiclassic and Early Postclassic periods when pressure blades were rare products acquired through long distance networks (Darras 1998, 2005). Control of this resource by Tarascan authorities is not evident in the archaeological record, although it may have occurred through tribute payments.

In conclusion, the model that best explains the regional political economy rests on the idea of direct economic relations between the producing and consuming sectors, via independent craftsmen who distributed the merchandise that they produced. Tarascan sites in the Malpaís of Zacapu depended on these workshops for prismatic blades while utilizing other indirect networks to acquire obsidian for expedient domestic use. The commercial relations between producers and consumers were part of a flexible framework that lacked control of raw material, production, or the distribution of finished goods (Darras 2005).

Conclusions

Blade production in the Zacapu region during the Milpillas phase was a craft system managed by independent groups of peasants, living in rural zones in the vicinity of the Malpaís of Zacapu; they practiced craft production on an occasional basis as way to diversify and complement the procurement of household resources (see Hirth 2006, chapter 2, this volume).

The production of blades was organized at the household level, and work was carried out both in specific places within the residence area, as well as in buffered workshops. This system of organization corresponds to the type of production described as *independent decentralized production* (Hirth 2006:9). Craft production was conducted within a

very flexible framework and without direct control by the Tarascan elite. During the Milpillas phase obsidian and pressure blades were not strategic resources nor did they have a great economic value. The correspondingly low social status of these artisans was probably a result of the obsidian prismatic blade becoming an extremely common and cheap product in Tarascan society.

This model of craft organization described for the Zacapu region differs from the organizational system described in the basin of Patzcuaro by Pollard (2003; Pollard and Vogel 1994) and the Relación de Michoacan (1977). According to the Relación (1977: laminas XXVIII–XXIX) craftsmen were grouped by trade, and obsidian blade makers were represented in the Assembly of Uris under the direct control of the Cazonci. This information suggests that blade makers belonged to a professional corporation, or guild, under the authority of the Tarascan sovereign. Pollard (2003) described craft systems here as being dominated by the elite who would have controlled both access to the raw materials and the distribution of finished prismatic blades.

But the situation in Zacapu is very different. While the question of professional corporation organization is open for debate, the archaeological record shows that blade makers were part-time artisans who exercised their profession as autonomous, independent specialists. Why were there differences between Zacapu and Patzcuaro? It could be that the status of blade making in the Patzcuaro basin was the result of the consolidation by government in the middle of the fifteenth century. It is also possible that the organization of craft production in the Zacapu region reflects the situation prior to the more complex political unification and centralization of crafting within the Tarascan state. Archaeological studies have documented the absence of a strong hierarchy and accentuated socio-political disparities in the Malpais of Zacapu which may indicate that the region was organized by more equivalently ranked lineages (Michelet 1998). The organization of blade production in the Zacapu region would correspond to the period prior to the consolidation of Tarascan socio-political and economic control that prevailed until the Spanish conquest.

References

Aoyama, Kazuo
1999 Ancient Maya State, Urbanism, Exchange, and Craft Specialization: Chipped Stone Evidence from the Copan Valley and the La Entrada Region, Honduras. Memoirs in Latin American Archaeology, 12. Pittsburg: University of Pittsburg.

2004 Los artistas, Los artesanos, los guerreros y los escribanos en la corte Real maya del Clásico Tardío: evidencia de la lítica de los grupos domésticos en Aguateca, Guatemala. Los Investigadores de la Cultura Maya 12(1):106–119.

Arnold, Philip, and Robert Santley
1993 Household Ceramics Production at Middle Classic Period Matacapan. *In* Prehispanic Domestic Units in Western Mesoamerica: Studies of the Household, Compound, and Residence. Robert Santley, and Kenneth Hirth, eds. Pp. 227–248. Boca Raton, FL: CRC Press.

Brumfiel, Elizabeth M.
1987 Elite and utilitarian in the Aztec state. *In* Specialization, Exchange, and Complex Societies. Elizabeth Brumfiel and Timothy Earle, eds. Pp. 102–118, Cambridge University Press.
1998 The Multiple Identities of Aztec Craft Specialists. *In* Craft and Social Identity. Cathy Costin and Rita Wright, eds. Pp. 145–152. Archaeological Papers, 8. Washington, DC: American Anthropological Association.

Brumfiel, Elizabeth, and Timothy Earle, eds.
1987 Specialization, Exchange, and Complex Societies. Cambridge University Press.

Clark, John
1987 Politics, prismatic blades, and Mesoamerican civilization. *In* The organization of core technology. Jay Johnson and Carol Morrow, eds. Pp. 259–285. Westview Press.
1995 Craft Specialization as an Archaeological Category. Research in Economic Anthropology 14:267–294.
1997 Prismatic Blademaking, Craftsmanship, and Production: An Analysis of Obsidian Refuse from Ojo de Agua, Chiapas, Mexico. Ancient Mesoamerica 9:137–159.

Clark, John, and Douglas Bryant
1997 A Technological Typology of Prismatic Blades and Debitage from Ojo de Agua, Chiapas, Mexico. Ancient Mesoamerica 8:111–136.

Clark, John, and William Parry
1990 Craft Specialization and Cultural Complexity. Research in Economic Anthropology 12:289–346.

Costin, Cathy L.
1991 Craft Specialization: Issues in Defining, Documenting, and Explaining the Organization of Production. Archaeological Method and Theory, 1. Michael Schiffer, ed. Pp. 1–56. Tucson: University of Arizona Press.
2001 Craft Production Systems. *In* Archaeology at the Millenium: A Sourcebook. Gary Feinman and Douglas Price, eds. Pp. 273–327. New York: Kluwer Academic/Plenum Publishers.
2007 Thinking about Production: Phenomenological Classification and Lexical Semantics. *In* Archaeological papers of the American Anthropological Association 17(1):143–162.

Costin, Cathy, and Melissa Hagstrum
1995 Standardization, Labor Investment, Skill, and the Organization of Ceramic Production in Late Prehispanic Highland Peru. American Antiquity 60(4):619–639.

Costin, Cathy, and Rita Wright, eds.
1998 Craft and Social Identity. Archaeological Papers, 8. Washington, DC: American Anthropological Association.

Darras, Véronique
1991 Technologies préhispaniques de l'obsidienne: les centres de production de la région de Zinaparo-Prieto. Ph.D. dissertation, University of Paris I.
1994 Les mines-ateliers d'obsidienne de la région de Zináparo-Prieto, Michoacan, Mexique. Bulletin de la Société Préhistorique Française 91(4–5):290–301.
1999 Tecnologías prehispánicas de la obsidiana: los centros de producción de la región de Zináparo-Prieto, Michoacán. Cuadernos de Estudios Michoacanos 9. México: CEMCA.

Darras, Véronique, with Alain Demant and Jean Louis Joron
2005 Economía y poder: la obsidiana entre los tarascos de Zacapu, Michoacán (fase Milpillas 1200 a 1450 d.C.). *In* Reflexiones sobre la industria lítica. Leticia Gonzalez and Lorena Mirambell, eds. Pp. 243–298. Colección Científica 475. Mexico: INAH.

Drennan, Robert D.
1984 Long-distance transport costs in Prehispanic

Mesoamerican.   American   Anthropologist
86(1):105–111.

Feinman, Gary M.
  1999 Rethinking Our Assumptions: Economic Spe-
         cialization at the Householf scale In Ancient
         Ejutla, Oaxaca, Mexico. *In* Pottery and People: A
         Dynamic Interaction. James Skibo and Gary Fein-
         man, eds. Pp. 81–98. Salt Lake City: University
         of Utah Press.

Feinman, Gary, and Linda Nicholas
  1995 Household craft specialization and shell or-
         nament manufacture in Ejutla, Mexico. Expedition
         37(2):14–25.
  2007 Craft Production in Classic Period Oaxaca:
         Implications for Monte Alban's Political Economy.
         In Craft Production Complex Societies. Multicraft
         and Producer Perspectives. Izumi Shimada, ed. Pp.
         97–19. Salt Lake City: Utah Press University.

Feinman, Gary, with Linda M. Nicholas, and William
         Middleton
  1993 Craft activities at the prehispanic Ejutla site,
         Oaxaca, Mexico. Mexicon 15(2):33–41.

Hassig, Ross
  1985 Trade, Tribute, and Transportation: the Sixteenth-
         Century Political Economy of the valley of
         Mexico. Norman: University of Oklahoma Press.

Healan, Dan M.
  1986 Technological and nontechnological aspects
         of an obsidian workshop excavated at Tula,
         Hidalgo. *In* Economic Aspects of Prehispanic
         Highlan Mexico. Barry Isaac, ed. Pp. 133–152.
         Research in Economic Anthropology, supplement
         2. Greenwich, Connecticut: JAI Press.

Healan, Dan, with Janet Kerley, and George Bey III
  1983 Excavation and Preliminary Analysis of an
         Obsidian Workshop in Tula, Hidalgo. Journal of
         Field Archaeology 10:127–145.

Hirth, Kenneth G.
  1995 The investigation of obsidian craft production
         at Xochicalco, Morelos. Ancient Mesoamerica
         6:251–258.
  2006 Obsidian Craft Production in Ancient Central
         Mexico. Archaeological Research at Xochicalco.
         Salt Lake City: University of Utah Press.

Hirth, Kenneth G., ed.
  2003 Mesoamerican Lithic Technology. Experi-
         mentation and Interpretation. Salt Lake City:
         University of Utah Press.

Hirth, Kenneth, and Bradford Andrews, eds.
  2002 Pathways to Prismatic Blades: A study In
         Mesoamerican obsidian core-blade technology.
         Cotsen Institute of Archaeology. Los Angeles:
         University of California.

Inomata, Takeshi
  2007 Classic Maya Elite Competition, Collabora-
         tion, and Performance in Multicraft Production. *In*
         Craft Production in Complex Societies. Multicraft
         and Producer Perspectives. Izumi Shimada, ed.
         Pp. 120–136. Salt Lake City: University of UTAH
         Press.

Lumholtz, Carl
  1986 [1904] El México desconocido: cinco años
         de exploración entre las tribus de la Sierra Madre
         Occidental, en la tierra caliente de Tepic y Jalisco,
         y entre los tarascos de Michoacán, México.
         México: Instituto Nacional Indigenista.

Michelet, Dominique
  1992 El Centro-Norte de Michoacán: características
         generales de su estudio arqueológico regional. *In*
         El proyecto Michoacán 1983–1987. Dominique
         Michelet, ed. Pp. 12–54. Cuadernos de Estudios
         Michoacanos 4. México: CEMCA.
  1998 Topografía y prospección sistemática de los
         grandes asentamientos del Malpaís de Zacapu:
         claves para un acercamiento a las realidades
         sociopolíticas. *In* Génesis, Culturas y Espacios
         en Michoacán. Véronique Darras, ed. Pp. 47–60.
         México: CEMCA.
  In press Vivir diferentemente. Los sitios de la fase
         Milpillas (1250–1450 d.C.) en el Malpaís
         de Zacapu (Michoacán)/To live differently: the
         Milpillas phase (1250–1450 D.C.) sites in the
         Malpais of Zacapu (Michoacan). *In* El urbanismo
         en Mesoamérica/Urbanism in Mesoamerica, vol.
         2. Instituto Nacional de Antropología e Historia/
         Pennsylvania State University, University Park,
         PA.

Michelet, Dominique, with Marie Charlotte Arnauld, and
         Marie France Fauvet-Berthelot
  1989 El proyecto del CEMCA en Michoacan.

Etapa I: un balance. Trace 16:70–87. México: CEMCA.

Michelet, Dominique, with Gregory Pereira and Gérald Migeon
2005 La llegada de los Uacúsechas a la región de Zacapu, Michoacán: datos arqueológicos y discusión. Reacomodos demográficos del Clásico al Posclásico en el centro de México. Linda Manzanilla, ed. Pp. 137–154. México: UNAM.

Migeon, Gérald.
1990 Archéologie en pays tarasque. Structure de l'habitat et ethnohistoire des habitations tarasques de la région de Zacapu au Postclassique Récent. Ph.D. dissertation. University of Paris I.
1998 El poblamiento del Malpaís de Zacapu y de sus alrededores, del Clásico al Posclásico. *In* Génesis, Espacios y Culturas en Michoacán. Véronique Darras, ed. Pp. 35–46, México: CEMCA.

Migeon, Gérald, and Grégory Pereira
2007 La secuencia ocupacional y cerámica del cerro Barajas, Guanajuato, y sus relaciones con el centro, el occidente y el norte de México. *In* Dinámicas culturales entre el Occidente, el Centro-norte y la cuenca de México, del Preclásico al Epiclásico. Brigitte Faugère, ed. Pp. 201–230. Zamora: El Colegio de Michoacán.

Parry, William J.
2001 Production an Exchange of obsidian tools in late Aztec city-states. Ancient Mesoamerica 12:101–111.
2002 Aztec Blade Production Strategies in the Eastern Basin of Mexico. *In* Pathways to Prismatic Blades: A study in Mesoamerican Obsidian Core-Blade Technology. Kenneth Hirth and Bradford Andrews, eds. Pp. 37–46. Cotsen Institute of Archaeology. Los Angeles: University of California.

Pollard Perlstein, Helen
1987 The Political Economy of Prehispanic Tarascan Metallurgy. American Antiquity 52(4):741–752.
2003 Development of Tarascan Core: The Lake Patzcuaro Basin. *In* The Postclassic Mesoamerican World. Michael Smith and Frances Berdan, eds. Pp. 227–237. Salt Lake City: University of Utah Press.

Pollard Perlstein, Helen, and Thomas Vogel
1994 Implicaciones políticas y económicas del intercambio de obsidiana des Estado tarasco. *In* Arqueologia del Occidente de México. Eduardo Williams and Roberto Novella, eds. Pp. 158–182. Zamora: El Colegio de Michoacán.

Relación, de Michoacán.
1977 [1541] Relación de las ceremonias y ritos y población y gobierno de la provincia de Michoacán. Reproducción facsimilar del Ms IV de El Escorial, Balsal Editores, Morelia.

Santley, Robert
1984 Obsidian Exchange, Economic Stratification, and the Evolution of Complex Society in the Basin of Mexico. *In* Trade and Exchange Society in Early Mesoamérica. Kenneth Hirth, ed. Pp. 43–86. Albuquerque: University of New Mexico.

Santley, Robert, with Janet Kerley, and Ronald Kneebone
1986 Obsidian Working, Long-distance Exchange, and the Politico-Economic Organization of Early States in Central Mexico. *In* Economic Aspects of Prehispanic Highland Mexico. Barry Isaac, ed. Pp. 101–132. Research in Economic Anthropology, Supplement 2. Greenwich, Connecticut: JAI Press.

Shimada, Izumi
2007 Craft Production in Complex Societies. Multicraft and Producer Perspectives. Foundations of Archaeological Inquiry. Salt Lake City: University of Utah Press.

Spence, Michael W.
1981 Obsidian Production and the State of Teotihuacan. American Antiquity 46:769–788.
1984 Craft production and polity in early Teotihuacan. *In* Trade and Exchange in Early Mesoamerica. Kenneth Hirth, ed. Pp. 87–110. Albuquerque: University of New Mexico Press.
1986 Locational Analysis of Craft Specialization Areas in Teotihuacan. *In* Research in Economic Anthropology: Economic Aspects of Prehispanic Highland Mexico, Supplement 2. Barry Isaac, ed. Pp. 75–100. Greenwich, Connecticut: JAI Press.
1987 The Scale and Structure of Obsidian Production in Teotihuacan. *In* Teotihuacan: Nuevos Datos, Nuevas Síntesis, Nuevos Problemas. Emily

McClung de Tapia and Evelyn Childs Rattray, eds. Pp. 429–450. México: IIA- Universidad Nacional Autónoma de México.

Titmus, Gene, and John Clark
2003 Mexica Blade Making with Wooden Tools: Recent Experimental Insights. *In* Mesoamerican Lithic Technology. Experimentation and Interpretation. Kenneth Hirth, ed. Pp. 72–97, Salt Lake City: University of Utah Press.

Warren, Benedict J.
1968 [1533] Minas de cobre de Michoacán. Anales del Museo Michoacano 6:35–52.

8

Residential Pottery Production in Mesoamerica

Christopher A. Pool
University of Kentucky

O f all of the crafts pursued in ancient Mesoamerica, making pottery would seem to have been the most ubiquitous. Pottery sherds are the most common artifacts at most Mesoamerican sites by one or two orders of magnitude, literally reaching into the millions for large sites. That ubiquity is partly a consequence of the durability of ceramics in the archaeological record and their susceptibility to breakage, which required regular replenishment of ceramic inventories. It is also reflective of the wide range of utilitarian and symbolically charged functions served by ceramic vessels, which included storing liquids and dry goods, preparing and serving food and drink, and use as censers and braziers in ritual ceremonies.

Despite the volume of pottery that was used and discarded by consumers, understanding the organization of pottery production is not a simple matter. As compared to the manufacture of flaked stone tools, for example, the residues of pottery manufacture are relatively scarce and often ambiguous (Rice 1987:177–180; Stark 1985: 164–177). Pottery-making implements were often general purpose items, made of perishable materials, and commonly recycled from other uses. Whereas the reductive technology of flaking stone produces residues from each stage of production, building pots up from clay depletes the raw material, leaving few residues (Rice 125–128; Rye 1981: 66–83). As discussed below, identification of ceramic production relies heavily on manufacturing errors incurred when pots are fired – an occurrence potters try to avoid – and the identification of firing facilities, which may mimic cooking hearths and roasting pits. Furthermore, sherds from vessels that crack during firing may be indistinguishable from those of vessels broken in use, making it necessary to use assemblage characteristics of high sherd densities and skewed type frequencies to detect possible production localities (e.g., Santley et al. 1989; Stark 1985).

Over the last three decades ethnoarchaeological and archaeological research on pottery production has steadily improved our ability to identify production loci and, consequently, to infer the contexts and organization of pottery production. In the pages that follow I provide an overview of pottery production in ancient Mesoamerica, as it is currently understood. Space does not allow an exhaustive review of the ceramic production literature for Mesoamerica (but see Stark 1985 and chapters in Bey and Pool 1992, Pool and Bey 2007). Instead, I discuss sites and studies to illustrate the range of variability in prehispanic pottery production in Mesoamerica, and to underscore particular interpretive issues. An inescapable conclusion of this overview is that most pottery production was carried out as housework in residential settings, but that the intensity and volume of production varied greatly among those residential settings. In other words, residential production does not necessarily mean low in volume or intensity.

Following this overview I examine residential pottery production as a risk-reduction strategy drawing on excavated contexts of the Late Formative, Terminal Formative, and Classic periods in southern Veracruz at the sites of Bezuapan, Tres Zapotes, and Matacapan (Figure 1). This discussion highlights contexts within which low-intensity (and probably intermittent) production, multi-crafting, and elite residential production were employed as well as the ecological and social risk factors that appear to have contributed to potters adopting these production strategies.

ARCHEOLOGICAL PAPERS OF THE AMERICAN ANTHROPOLOGICAL ASSOCIATION, Vol. 19, Issue 1, pp. 115–132, ISSN 1551-823X, online ISSN 1551-8248. © 2009 by the American Anthropological Association. All rights reserved. DOI: 10.1111/j.1551-8248.2009.01016.x.

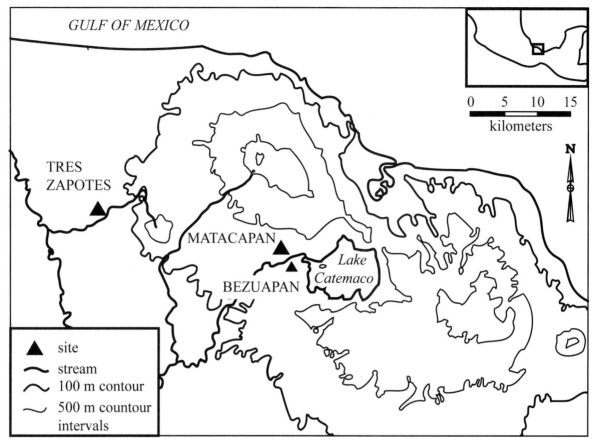

Figure 1. Map of Tuxtlas region, showing sites discussed in the text.

An Overview of Mesoamerican Pottery Production

The systematic study of ancient pottery production in Mesoamerica is barely thirty years old. Before the 1970s only a handful of pottery production contexts had been reported, including the Postclassic period site of Las Peñitas, Nayarit (Bordaz 1964); the Classic site of San Juan Icaquixtla, Puebla (Cook de Leonard 1953); and La Lima, Honduras (Stone and Turnbull 1941), but even those were open to question. By 1985 Barbara Stark (1985:Table 7.1) was able to list 25 sites and areas with some reported evidence for pottery production, including sites in Hidalgo, the Valley of Mexico, Oaxaca, Tabasco, Guatemala, Belize and El Salvador. In the intervening time more pottery production localities have been reported from southern Veracruz (Arnold et al. 1993; Ohnersorgen 2001; Pool 1990, 2003; Santley et al. 1989; Stark 1985; 1989; 1992; 2007; Stark and Garrity 2004), Ejutla, Oaxaca (Balkansky et al. 1997; Feinman and Nicholas 2000, 2007), Otumba, Mexico (Charlton et al. 2000; 2007), and the Tepexi region of Puebla (Rattray 1990).

Since the mid-1980s, ceramic production studies in Mesoamerica have benefited from careful efforts such as those of Stark (1985, 2007; see also Santley et al. 1989; Pool 1992) to define explicit criteria for the detection and identification of production localities based on ethnographic and ethnoarchaeological as well as archaeological studies. Implements commonly associated with pre-industrial ceramic production include vessel molds, stone smoothers and polishers, scrapers, incising tools, and grinding stones. Unfortunately, with the exception of distinctively-shaped molds and tools with clay residues, these implements often have multiple uses, including activities not associated with pottery production. Firing facilities can offer more secure evidence for pottery production, particularly when they have distinctive characteristics of construction and use-alteration. An example is that of true kilns, which separate the pottery load from the fire, unlike ovens or firing pits (Arnold 1985). Once thought to have been a Spanish introduction, true kilns have now been securely identified in prehispanic Mesoamerican contexts in Oaxaca (Winter and Payne 1976), southern Veracruz (Santley et al. 1989; Pool 1990, 1997), and at Tula, Hidalgo (Healan 1977). Kilns identified at the Classic period site of Matacapan, Veracruz, were distinctive enough in their materials, construction, and development of vitrified interiors and interior-to-exterior color zonation to permit identification of fragments of destroyed kilns in surface collections (Santley et al. 1989). Firing pits (or "pit kilns") and open firings undoubtedly were more common, but their remains are more difficult to detect in survey and may closely resemble roasting pits and cooking hearths; they therefore must be confirmed through their contexts and association with other implements and production residues. Those residues or by-products may include severely deformed, overfired, waster sherds, which provide some of the strongest evidence for ceramic production. More numerous than deformed wasters in most production contexts are "de facto wasters" without obvious deformation, resulting from vessels discarded because they cracked during firing or were otherwise defective (Stark 1985: 181, 1992: 188).

When combined with more overt indicators, high sherd densities and unusual frequency distributions of ceramic types and vessel forms offer evidence for the accumulation of such de facto wasters (Stark 1985:173, 181–182). Today, the "double criterion" of high sherd density in combination with deformed wasters or other overt indicators has become the "gold standard" for detecting ceramic production localities in surface survey (Stark 2007: 168). Nevertheless, our ability to detect ceramic production is biased toward locations with greater production volumes, higher degrees of specialization, and/or more salient kinds of production facilities. As a result, identified ceramic production loci are particularly scarce for earlier time periods and certain regions, most notably including the Maya lowlands. For such cases we must continue to rely heavily on clues from technological and distributional evidence.

It seems likely that the bias against the detection of smaller, lower volume production localities with less investment in facilities under-represents certain social identies, especially the poor and women, although the precise degree of underrepresentation is uncertain. Ethnographically in Mexico and Central America, most traditional potters are women, and female potters are the rule for low-volume production as well as production in residential contexts, including production for exchange in "household industries" (e.g., Arnold 1991; Deal 1998; Rice 1987: 187–188; Reina and Hill 1978). Male potters are found more often in cases of high-volume production (Rice 1987: 184) and when disabilities prevent them from performing agricultural and wage labor (e.g., Arnold 1991: 28). In the context of the present volume, the gender of crafters is a significant issue, especially sense multicrafting and intermittent crafting represent opportunities for broadening and restructuring the participation of household members in economic pursuits. Unfor-

tunately, direct archaeological identification of the sex of ceramic crafters is very rare. One of the very few exceptions is Barbour's (1976) analysis of fingerprints to identify statistical tendencies in the sex of the producers hand-modeled and mold-made figurines at Teotihuacan, Mexico.

Contexts of Early Pottery Production in Mesoamerica

The earliest pottery traditions in Mesoamerica are associated with the Initial Formative period (2000–1500 cal. B.C.) when cultivation of domesticated plants started to become widespread and settlements became less mobile than previously. Pottery first appeared between 1900 and 1750 cal. B.C. on the Pacific coast of Chiapas, in the valleys of highland Mexico, and possibly on the Gulf Coast of northern Veracruz (Clark and Cheetham 2005; Clark and Gosser 1995 discuss claims for earlier Mesoamerican pottery). The highland complexes so far are known from small village or hamlet sites and a rock shelter. Their simple bowl, jar, and *tecomate* (neckless jar) forms and the lack of decoration on pottery of the Espiridión and Purrón phases (in the highland valleys of Oaxaca and Tehuacán, respectively) suggest a utilitarian emphasis. In contrast, the equally early Barra phase of the Soconusco region on the Chiapas coast includes bowls, tecomates, and tall fluted vessels, typically slipped and burnished, with an astounding variety of incised, punctated, fluted, and gadrooned decoration and paints in black, red, orange and white or buff (Clark and Gosser 1995). In the Mazatán region of the Soconusco, where it is best described, Barra phase settlement also appears to have been more substantial and to have encompassed a broader range of settlement size, including numerous hamlets and three larger villages, up to 10 ha in size (Clark 1994:551). In short, the Barra phase pottery emphasized forms of social display, perhaps associated with feasting (Clark and Blake 1994), in the context of a population that was larger and arguably more socially diverse than contemporaneous pottery-using societies in the Mexican highlands. Although we have no direct evidence on the organization of pottery production, such a setting would have offered some potential for producing and exchanging pottery as a complement to the household economy, expanding in the succeeding Locona phase (1700–1550 cal. B.C.) with the emergence of Mesoamerica's first rank society and further elaboration of pottery forms and decoration, particularly in serving vessels (Clark and Blake 1994).

Pottery making was well-established throughout Mesoamerica by the beginning of the Early Formative period (ca. 1500–1000 cal. B.C.), and some of that production was exchanged well beyond the household or the local area. After about 1400 cal. B.C. the "Early Horizon" style incorporating distinctive carved and incised motifs on black, white, and differentially fired black-and-white pottery appears across much of Mesoamerica. Instrumental neutron activation analysis (INAA) has demonstrated interregional exchange of Early Horizon pottery from the Coatzacoalcos basin around the Olmec site of San Lorenzo, Veracruz, to central Mexico, Oaxaca, central Chiapas, and the Soconusco, as well as local production in these areas of pottery with Early Horizon motifs (Blomster et al. 2005; Neff et al. 2006a, 2006b). Occasional exchange of vessels among these regions and from one or more to San Lorenzo remains a possibility, and suggestions of such exchange based on petrographic analysis (e.g., Stoltman et al. 2005, Sharer et al. 2006) merit further testing, although recent petrographic analyses of source materials and sherds from San Lorenzo are at odds with some of the assumptions of previous studies regarding the mineralogy of clays and ceramic pastes in the Coatzacoalcos basin (Guevara 2004; Cheetham et al. 2009). The Early Formative period also offers the earliest reported Mesoamerican firing facilities. Not far from San Lorenzo, at San Carlos, Kruger (1999) excavated a set of shallow pits with burned walls, the most complete of which measured 2.8 m long by 0.7 m wide. The pits contained ash and charcoal as well as adobe blocks and irregular lumps of fired clay. Kruger interprets these pits as firing features and cites the occurrence of underfired sherds and polishing stones as additional evidence of pottery production at the site. Notably, the San Carlos features occur within a domestic context. In contrast, circular kilns or ovens attributed to the Tlatempa phase in Puebla and Tlaxcala appear to have served several nearby households (Abascal 1976).

Later Pottery Production in Mesoamerica

Identified ceramic production loci remain scarce for the Middle Formative period (but see Castanzo, this volume), but the situation improves markedly for later periods. Late Formative (ca. 400 B.C.–A.D. 100) or Terminal Formative (A.D. 100–300) production loci have been identified at Papayal, Bezuapan, and Tres Zapotes in the Tuxtlas region of southern Veracruz (Szatkowski-Reeves 2002; Pool 1997, 2003, and below), at Santo Domingo Tomaltepec in the Valley of Oaxaca (Whalen 1981), and at site Ts73 in the Tehuacan Valley of Puebla (Redmond 1979). All but the last are associated with residential occupation. In contrast, the Ts73 production locality was placed within the defensive wall of a hilltop center. It contained four rectangular stone-lined pits interpreted as horizontal kilns, as well as other implements and by-products, including high densities of El Riego Gray

sherds and wasters (Stark 1985:Table 7.1). Redmond (1979) interprets the Ts73 production locality as a non-domestic workshop producing the El Riego Gray ceramic type under direct control of elite administrators. El Riego Gray pottery also appears to have been produced without elite control at contemporaneous settlements within the Tehuacan Valley (Redmond 1979; Stark 1985; 171).

Many ceramic production localities of the Classic (ca. A.D. 300–900) and Postclassic (ca. A.D. 900–1500) periods have been detected in surface surveys and excavations from El Salvador to Central Mexico. Here I describe a few of the more completely investigated examples to illustrate the variation in the organization of ceramic production after the expansion of urban settlement and state-level political organization in Mesoamerica. My emphasis here is on areas outside of the Tuxtlas region, which is the focus of the rest of this paper.

Household 1 of the Cerén site in El Salvador, spectacularly preserved under volcanic ash, provides an example of low-volume production within a household setting. A lump of tempered clay matching the mineralogical composition of utilitarian pottery and an andesite flake scraper with use-wear consistent with smoothing pottery provide evidence for pottery manufacture (Sheets 1992:44). Here pottery production appears to have been conducted as part of the general activities of household maintenance. Fancier decorated pottery is thought to have been acquired from outside the household.

As evidenced by surface collections and excavations in five production areas, ceramic production in Classic period Matacapan encompassed a broad range of production contexts with different levels of intensity within residential contexts, as well as at least one elite-sponsored "attached" producer (Santley et al. 1989). The non-residential character of a large production complex on the outskirts of Matacapan, discussed below, is a matter of debate (e.g., Arnold et al. 1993; Balkansky et al. 1997). Stark's (1992) study of ceramic production from surface collections in the Mixtequilla area of south-Central Veracruz suggests that production was generally of low intensity as compared with the largest of the Matacapan production areas, although differences in surface collection strategies and the use of more stringent analytical criteria may affect this perception (Stark 2007). Examples of more restricted, and presumably more specialized, production include Middle Postclassic *comales* (tortilla griddles) (Curet 1993) and bichrome bowls (Stark and Garraty 2004) and Late Classic orange bowls, although these examples also seem to have been carried out in residential contexts (Stark 2007).

Good examples of multi-crafting that include pottery manufacture in a residential context come from Ejutla and

El Palmillo in the Valley of Oaxaca (Feinman and Nicholas 2000, 2007). In an excavated residential terrace at the hilltop site of El Palmillo, crafting focused primarily on the manufacture of chert tools and maguey fiber textiles. Low-volume production of utilitarian pottery was carried out for local, if not household, consumption (Feinman and Nicholas 2007:200–208). Pottery production was more intensive in a residential context excavated at Ejutla, as evidenced by over 60 ceramic molds (including 15 figurine molds) and 900 wasters that included fragments of figurines, *comales*, and *sahumadores* (incense burners). The ceramic products were evidently fired in four shallow pits filled with ash, charcoal, burnt rock, wasters, kiln furniture and fired clay concretions (Feinman and Nicholas 2007:198). Multicrafting in this domestic context included high-volume shell working and lower-volume lapidary work in onyx, greenstone, and other non-local stones.

In the hyper-urban setting of Classic period Teotihuacan, pottery production was carried out within residential "apartment" compounds that served to organize the domestic and economic activities of large extended households of 60–100 people. High sherd densities and skewed type distributions suggest the presence of as many as 200 localities within the city that were involved in ceramic production (Millon 1981), about 30 of which specialized in the production of the San Martín Orange type. Excavations at the Tlajinga 33 compound confirmed the production of San Martín Orange ollas and basins as well as obsidian lapidary items (Widmer and Storey 1993). Contrasting with this residential context of utilitarian pottery production, Munera Bermúdez (1985) found evidence for the production of censers and ceremonial items in "priests' workshops" in the Ciudadela in central Teotihuacan. Interestingly, Thin Orange, the pottery type most strongly associated with Teotihuacan interaction throughout Mesoamerica, was not manufactured at Teotihuacan, but in the Tepexi region of southwestern Puebla. Rattray's (1990) excavations identified Thin Orange workshops associated with residences in the Tebernal and Jagüey sites along the Río Carnero.

To summarize, the growing literature on pottery production in Mesoamerica makes certain points clear (see also Pool and Bey 2007). First, the vast majority of pottery in Mesoamerica was produced in residential contexts. Reported exceptions include the production of censers and ceremonial items in "priests' workshops" at the Ciudadela in Teotihuacan (Munera Bermúdez 1985) and areas of concentrated firing facilities interpreted as non-residential workshops in Puebla-Tlaxcala (Abascal 1976) the Tehuacan Valley (Redmond 1979) and at the Comoapan locality on the outskirts of Matacapan, Veracruz (Arnold et al. 1993; Santley et al. 1989). There is some doubt about the non-

residential character of the Puebla-Tlaxcala and Comoapan cases, however; houses were reported near the Puebla-Tlaxcala kilns (Abascal 1976), and the absence of residential contexts in or near the Comoapan production area has been questioned (Balkansky et al. 1997; Feinman and Nicholas 2000; Pool 1990:247; Stark 2007). Although I am willing to accept the possibility that some pottery production took place away from residential contexts, it was at best rare, and would not change the picture of residential production as the norm in ancient Mesoamerica.

Second, there was wide variation in the intensity and overall volume of production in residential contexts and in the social status of the households in which production took place. Such variation even appears to have occurred among contemporaneous production localities within the same site, for example, at Matacapan (Pool 1990; Santley et al. 1989) and Tres Zapotes (Pool 2003, 2005). Much of this variation can be seen as a consequence of households implementing different mixes of risk reduction strategies under specific economic and historical circumstances. Finally, opportunities to enhance the household economy by producing pottery for exchange appear to have great antiquity in Mesoamerica, extending back to the Early Formative period and perhaps even the Initial Formative in the Soconusco.

Residential Pottery Production in the Tuxtlas Region

In this section I discuss residential pottery production at three sites in the Tuxtlas region of southern Veracruz, Mexico. Matacapan is a predominantly Classic period site located in the upper Río Catemaco valley in the central Tuxtla Mountains. It contains many production localities, including a large ceramic production complex called Comoapan for the modern village that has grown up around it. Bezuapan was included in Santley's Matacapan survey but is a separate village site about 500 m to the southeast, which contains substantial Late Formative and Protoclassic period components as well as Classic. Tres Zapotes is a well known site with a long, continuous sequence of Early Formative to Late Classic occupation located just west of the Tuxtla Mountains proper where the piedmont meets the alluvial plain of the Papaloapan basin (Figure 1).

Low-volume Production at Matacapan

Matacapan has provided some of the most detailed and comprehensive data on ceramic production in Mesoamerica (Figure 3). Santley and associates (1989) identified 41 ceramic "production areas" based on surface collections

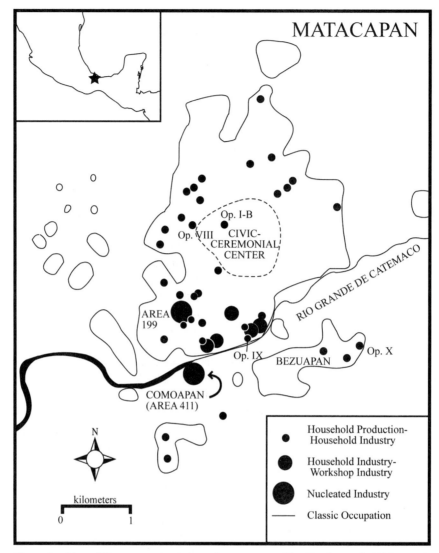

Figure 2. Map of Matacapan showing production areas. After Santley et al. 1989: Fig. 1.

containing high sherd densities (defined as the upper tercile of sherd frequencies in standard 3 × 3 m collection units[1]) in combination with overfired sherds and/or fragments of kilns (Santley et al. 1989:113). Excavations tested four of the surface-identified production areas and one other that did not appear on the surface (Pool 1990; Santley et al. 1984). The Comoapan production area, located on the outskirts of Classic-period Matacapan, has received the most attention, owing to its characterization as a nucleated industry or, more controversially, a non-residential manufactory (Arnold et al. 1993; Pool 1990:247; Santley et al. 1989:119). The inference of intensive, high-volume production at Comoapan was based on its size (ca 4 ha), its concentration of firing facilities and extensive waster dumps (36 circular updraft kilns and 13 dumps were identified; many more cer

tainly were destroyed or buried by modern construction), and its highly skewed ceramic assemblage (over 75% rim sherds of one ceramic type in two jar forms). Santley favored the manufactory characterization, in large part due to the failure of survey and excavations to identify associated domestic contexts (Santley et al. 1989:119).

Frequently lost in the debate over the scale, intensity, and context of production at Comoapan, however, is the fact that the other 40 production areas identified in survey were in areas of residential occupation (Arnold and Santley 1993; Santley et al. 1989:116;) (Figure 1). Variation in the extent, sherd densities, and proportional area with firing indicators for these residential production areas, suggested that they encompassed wide variation in the scale and intensity of production. Following Peacock's (1982) nomenclature, Santley

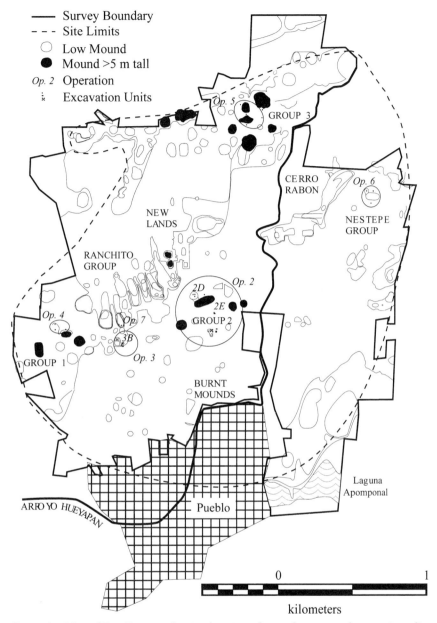

Figure 3. Map of Tres Zapotes showing location of mound groups and excavations discussed in the text.

et al. (1989:118) classified them as ranging from less intensive "household production/household industry" (HP-HI, 35 cases) to more intensive "household industry/workshop industries" (HI-WI, 5 cases) and one "nucleated industry" (NI, Area 199) in a residential zone. An additional "tethered" production locality was encountered in excavation behind a range structure in a civic-ceremonial complex of central Matacapan. Costin (1991:5) correctly noted that this production area was equivalent to an "attached production" facility in Brumfiel and Earle's (1987) terminology.

Excavations in two of the HP-HI production areas, Area 120 in western Matacapan and Area 249 in Bezuapan, recovered evidence of firing as well as common domestic refuse. These excavations also confirmed the low intensity of production, based on maximum sherd densities in disposal contexts, which in the case of Area 120 were lower than for any other excavated production area (838 sherds/cu m, Pool 1990:Table 5). Indeed, the evidence for production at Bezuapan was initially ambiguous, and was only confirmed in a second season of excavation (Pool 1997).

These small, low intensity production areas would appear to be good candidates for the intermittent production that Hirth (chapter 2) describes as a household diversification and risk reduction strategy. It is difficult to believe that the low volume of pottery production that appears to be indicated would have been sufficient to support even a small household through exchange for staples. Climatic constraints, often in combination with a seasonal pattern of labor requirements complementary to agricultural production, may also favor intermittent production of ceramics to a greater extent than the manufacture of lithic artifacts. Seasonal rainfall patterns have a particularly strong effect on pottery production, with periods of high precipitation and humidity resulting in longer drying schedules, damp fuel, reduced firing temperatures, and increased probablitiy of failure during firing (Arnold 1985:70–71). In the Tuxtlas, an intense and prolonged rainy season from June through November favors a highly seasonal pattern of production among modern potters (Arnold 1991:16, 18–20), and I expect the same was true in the past. Deadwood collected early in the dry season and cut wood allowed to dry during the season offer better, more abundant fuel sources than in the rainy season when stores of firewood for cooking and heating are dwindling. Incidentally, the annual aggregate fuel consumption for pottery production at Classic period Matacapan is estimated at between 25 and 50 metric tons of fuelwood or its equivalent. While impressive, this only represents 0.7% to 1.5% of aggregate domestic fuel consumption, based on a peak population of 3500–14,000 at Matacapan and minimum fuel consumption rates of about 2.1 kg/person/day in rural hamlets tropical lowland settings in Central America (Pool 1993; Jones and Otavalo 1981). Recently demonstrated regional demand for Coarse Orange jars (Stoner 2002; Stoner et al. 2008) would at best double these percentages, which suggest that intensified pottery production was a minor addition to stresses placed on fuel wood by population growth. The recovery of ash and carbonized fruits of the coyol palm from kilns excavated at Matacapan suggests some potters compensated for fuel scarcity by using the less desirable, but renewable, supply of leaf fronds from this economically useful tree (Pool 1993: 406–408).

Dry season pottery production is also complementary to peak agricultural labor requirements in the central Tuxtlas, which occur in May through August, although in the predominantly agricultural households studied by Philip Arnold (1991), potters must also schedule production activities around moderate labor loads associated with dry season planting (Killion 1987:186, Fig. 13). For pottery-producing households such as those in the Tuxtlas, who derive a substantial portion of their livelihood from farming, seasonally

intermittent ceramic production is a particularly viable risk-reduction strategy. Nevertheless, it often is difficult to prove, as opposed to assume, that a household cultivated crops. Our best evidence that this was the case comes from bell-shaped pits associated with these contexts. Such bell-shaped pits are usually interpreted to have begun their use-life as storage facilities for harvested crops, although they usually end their use-life as convenient trash pits or burial pits. This was the ultimate fate of a bell-shaped pit near the ruined kiln in Area 120. In Bezuapan, however, four bell-shaped pits were filled with ash from a volcanic eruption that terminated the Protoclassic occupation of the site, indicating that they were all open and in use at the same time, apparently when stores had almost been exhausted (in fact, a rat was trapped in the bottom of one pit by the eruption). If households were acquiring resources by regular exchange for produced wares, such storage would seem unnecessary.

Amber VanDerwarker's (2006) paleoethnobotanical research offers further evidence that Late Formative, Protoclassic and Early Classic Bezuapan households cultivated maize on or near the houselot. Low ratios of maize kernels to cupules (0.30 to 0.61 vs. 5 to 15.3 for Late Formative and Early Classic contexts at the nearby village site of La Joya) strongly suggest that maize was processed in the houselots, rather than being brought there already shelled (note, however, that the reverse is not true; high kernel/cupule ratios could result from shelling maize away from the houselot in outfields, as is suspected for La Joya) (VanDerwarker 2006:102–105). Consistent with the evidence from kernel/cupule ratios, an undulating ground surface preserved under the same volcanic ash that filled the bell-shaped pits suggests the presence of a ridged garden or infield at the edge of the houselot. Therefore, it is probable that Protoclassic pottery production at Bezuapan was carried out as an intermittent activity that complemented agricultural production.

Multi-crafting at Bezuapan and Tres Zapotes

The Bezuapan excavations revealed a sequence of three village houselots dating from the Late Formative and Protoclassic periods (Pool 1997; Pool and Britt 2000). The earliest, from the Late Formative period, included a house which had burned, leaving burned poles and ash from palm thatch on its floor. The second, from the Protoclassic period, was overlain by a thin, discontinuous deposit of volcanic ash that also filled one bell-shaped pit, and the third was sealed by the volcanic ash that filled the bell-shaped pits described above, and which lay up to 120 cm thick on the old ground surface. Each of these occupations produced some indicators of pottery production (Pool 1997:58). In addition, unutilized basalt flakes, mainly associated with the first (n = 18) and the third (n = 13) occupations, suggest some production of basalt implements. The third houselot (also Protoclassic) yielded a perforated sherd disk, which may have been used as a spindle whorl. While the evidence is not conclusive that craft production at Bezuapan was for exchange, it does appear that there was an increase in the range of household craft activities from Houselot 2 to Houselot 3.

Contemporaneous with these developments, the faunal record at Bezuapan indicates an increasing reliance on small animals. including a diversification of terrestrial mammals associated with agricultural disturbance, with the biggest change coming between Houselot 2 and Houselot 3 (Vanderwarker 2006:176–178; Tables 5.28 and 5.29). The Protoclassic Bezuapan residents also increased their reliance on tree fruits such as avocados, zapotes, and coyol palm nuts (VanDerwarker 2006:107–108, Figures 4.14 and 4.15). VanDerwarker (2006:177–179, 196–197) attributes this diversification of the household subsistence base to increased risk from the heightened volcanic activity documented at Bezuapan and elsewhere in the Tuxtlas (Santley et al. 2000). Occurring at the same time, multicrafting at Bezuapan may be seen as one of a suite of strategies mobilized to avoid or mitigate risk (see Hirth, chapter 2).

The Protoclassic period also yielded evidence for multicrafting at Tres Zapotes, a large regional center about 20 km west of Bezuapan. Excavations conducted in 2003 in the nonelite residential context of Operation 3B (Figure 3) uncovered two shallow firing pits. These heavily oxidized features were located to the north of a house indicated by a prepared sandstone pavement. One, in Unit 26, was a shallow (ca. 10 cm) keyhole-shaped depression, about 80 cm in diameter, with the entrance to the east. The other, in Units 23 and 28 was a circular pit, 100–120 cm in diameter, 35 cm deep, and filled with large blocks of highly fired mud, which appear to be the walls or covering of the firing feature (Figures 4A and 4B). Associated with both features and the surrounding deposits were small pieces of bubbled, vitrified slag, which also was observed on surfaces of the fired mud fragments. Also associated were 31 vitrified, bubbled, and warped overfired sherds, all of coarse utilitarian types typically formed as ollas. The most common vessels, however, were differentially fired plates and bowls with divergent walls. An unusual bottle form with a wide, elaborately carved rim flange, so far recovered only from this context, suggests occasional production for ceremonial purposes as well.

Pottery production was not the only craft pursued in Operation 3B, however. The excavations also produced evidence for obsidian blade production in the form of cores,

Figure 4. Excavated firing pits at Tres Zapotes, Operation 3B. Left, Unit 28; Right, Unit 26. Photograph by the author.

macrodebitage, and debitage from macro-core reduction and polyhedral core reduction, including error recovery blades (Charles Knight, personal communication). In all, blade production residues represent 7.0% of the obsidian from Operation 3B, as compared to an average of 3.6% from all excavated contexts. Basalt working is also evidenced in the form of microdebitage, macrodebitage, and preforms for stone bowls made from recycled metates (Jaime-Riverón and Pool 2009). Bowl preforms have not been identified in other contexts at Tres Zapotes, nor, for that matter, at Bezuapan, suggesting that recycling of metates into bowl forms was not a regular feature of Late Formative and Protoclassic household maintenance. Furthermore, with the exception of Operation 3B, stone bowls are rare outside elite and civic-ceremonial contexts at Tres Zapotes (Jaime-Riverón and Pool 2009). It is possible, therefore, that this component of craft production in Operation 3B may have been on consignment for elites.

Charcoal from the Unit 23/28 firing pit yielded a radiocarbon date of 1940±60 BP (cal A.D. 90, cal 2σ

40 B.C.-A.D. 240), squarely within the Protoclassic period, and broadly contemporaneous with the last two occupations at Bezuapan. What is particularly interesting is that Tres Zapotes also suffered a volcanic eruption during the Protoclassic (Wendt 2003; Ortiz 1975). Thus, like Bezuapan, this diversification of craft activities correlates with a period of increased subsistence risk from volcanic hazard.

Attached Elite Residential Production at Tres Zapotes

In chapter two, Hirth also challenges us to consider: (1) how important attached versus independent production was in a society's political economy and (2) how it conformed to organizational strategies used in *all* households to intensify production. As it happens, the excavations in Operation 3B were conducted as part of broader investigation to address similar questions regarding the political economy of Tres Zapotes in the Late and Protoclassic period. Based on surface collections from our intensive survey I suggested that attached specialists in elite contexts at Tres Zapotes manufactured essentially the same suite of utilitarian and service wares that were made by independent producers in non-elite contexts (Pool 1999). This ran counter to theoretical expectations that attached specialists should produce wealth goods for elites and independent specialists should produce staple goods for an unrestricted demand crowd, as suggested by Elizabeth Brumfiel and Tim Earle in 1987.

In a subsequent publication (Pool 2003) I noted that elite-sponsored production of widely circulating service vessels and more utilitarian cooking/storage vessels had parallels in other times and places, such as Maya production of utilitarian items in response to state demand (Earle 1981), part-time attached specialists supplementing employment (Clark and Parry 1990; Lewis 1996), mit'a and mitmaqkuna pottery production for the Inca state (Costin 1996), "duplicated professions" in Mesopotamia (Stein and Blackman 1993), Roman estate production of bricks and amphorae (Peacock 1982), and pottery production in the household of the King of Baganda (Roscoe 1965). The particular form that elite-sponsored production of pottery took at Tres Zapotes appeared to be geared toward supplying the quotidian needs of the elite household. I argued that this should be considered "attached production" because the producers are not free to distribute their products to an unspecified demand crowd, but "produce items on command for elites and the social and political institutions they control (Costin 1991: 7)" meeting the *sine qua non* of attached specialization. My broader point, however, was that we should analytically separate the sociopolitical context of production from the

products manufactured by specialists (see also Costin 2001: 298–299). By doing so we can explore a wider range of political-economic arrangements than the attached-wealth good/independent-utilitarian good dichotomy encompasses.

Later, I linked the development of this "elite household production[2]" at Tres Zapotes to the implementation of corporate (or collective) politico-economic strategies (Blanton et al. 1996) by an alliance of elite groups, represented in the Late and Terminal Formative periods by four widely-spaced mound-plaza complexes. Because this "Confederation" model implies less vertical social differentiation than an alternative, Centralized model, it would be expected that differences in access to strategic and highly valued goods between elites and non-elites would be less pronounced (though likely existent), and elite craft patronage would be geared toward supply of common household items as well as highly crafted goods (see Reents-Budet et al. 2000 for a Classic Maya example), resulting in less differentiation in the products of attached and independent specialists.

Using the same criteria as were developed at Matacapan (high sherd density combined with either waster sherds or fragments of firing features ["kiln debris"]), we identified 41 ceramic production areas at Tres Zapotes, which we differentiated on the basis of context, size, and production intensity. Excavations in two of these areas confirmed pottery production. I have already described the independent residential production area tested by Operation 3B. The other, Operation 2D, is attached, physically, to an elite residence-cum-administrative structure (Figure 3). Compared to other surface collected areas, both were classified as small and of low intensity.

In situ firing features were not encountered in our excavations in the attached production locus of Operation 2D, but we did encounter a dump containing kiln debris, overfired sherds, and raw clay lumps in levels 20 – 25 of Unit 10. Sherd densities are generally high, exceeding 1000 sherds/cu m above level 22 in all but 3 levels. Kiln debris, however, occurs regularly only below level 11 and it is concentrated in the dump around level 23. Wasters occur only below level 14. Taking these three lines of evidence into account, it appears that, although ceramic production residues were concentrated in the dump, ceramic production occurred in the vicinity of Unit 10 through the deposition of level 15, and possibly through level 12. Radiocarbon dates from correlated strata in levels 25 and 10 of Unit 9 bracket these deposits between 2220 ± 40 BP (cal 2σ 390 – 180 B.C. with cal 230, 290, and 360 B.C. intercepts) and 2060 ± 40 BP (cal 2σ 180 B.C. – A.D. 30 with a cal 50 B.C. intercept), that is, within the Late Formative period.

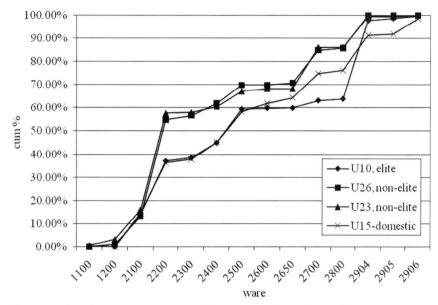

Figure 5. Cumulative percentage curve of wares in production levels of Unit 10 (Operation 2D), Units 23 and 26 (Operation 3B) and domestic levels of Unit 15 (Operation 2E). See text for discussion.

Levels 11–23 in Unit 15 of Operation 2E offer an example of a non-production domestic context for purposes of comparison. these levels contained midden deposits, packed earth floors, and bell-shaped pits from domestic occupations prior to the construction of the plaza of Group 2. Two over-fired sherds were recovered from these deposits, but no kiln debris. At an average of 430 sherds/cu m, ceramic densities were the lowest of any context considered in this paper. Level 18 is radiocarbon dated in the Late Formative period at 2090±50 BP (cal 2σ 340 – 320 B.C. and 210 B.C. – A.D. 20 with a cal 100 B.C. intercept).

To test the hypothesis that elite and non-elite residential production areas at Tres Zapotes manufactured a similar suite of products, I compare the assemblages from selected excavation units in the two production areas, Operations 2D (Unit 10) and 3B (Units 23 and 26), and the domestic assemblage, Operation 2E (Unit 15). Following the procedure employed in the previous analysis of the surface collections (Pool 2003), I begin with a comparison of percentages of ceramic wares defined by paste characteristics. Next I briefly compare the diversity of ceramic types in the two assemblages. Finally I compare forms in the two assemblages. All calculations are based on frequencies of rim sherds. In comparing the composition of these assemblages it is necessary to keep in mind that none of them are "pure" ceramic production assemblages, but contain some admixture of ceramics derived from residential activities. In the case of Unit 10 ceremonial activities may be represented in addition to elite residential activities.

Variation in Wares

As Figure 5 illustrates, the principal difference in the representation of ceramic wares was between the elite production context of Operation 2D (Unit 10) and the non-elite production context of Operation 3B (Units 23 and 26). One difference is that ware 2904 (Polished Orange) is more common in the former (34% to about 14%, and ware 2200 (Differentially Fired) is more common in the latter (about 42% to 23%). This difference is primarily chronological, with Polished Orange achieving its maximum popularity in the Late Formative period and specific types of Differentially Fired ware increasing in popularity in the Terminal Formative period (Ortiz 1975). Both of these are service wares primarily manufactured as plates and bowls. Significantly, if these two wares are added together, the combined percentages are nearly identical for the two production areas (57% for Unit 10 compared to 56% for Units 23 and 26). The Operation 3B Units also have higher percentages of ware 2700, which consists primarily of necked ollas. This is consistent with their domestic context and the fact that many of the sherds identified as overfired were of this ware. Nevertheless, taking chronological variation into account, the percentages of wares associated with the two production areas are remarkably similar. The Late Formative domestic assemblage from Unit 15 tracks that of Unit 10 very closely except that it has more coarse wares (2600 – 2800) and fewer Polished Orange sherds. This suggests that Late Formative attached specialists did produce, and that their patrons used, more of this service ware (confirmed by the recovery of an

Table 1. Richness indices for contexts at Tres Zapotes.

	N	S	R = S/logN
Unit 10 Levels 15–26	855	93	31.71933
Unit 23	348	35	13.77097
Unit 26	113	33	16.07342
Unit 15 Levels 11–24	323	72	28.69438

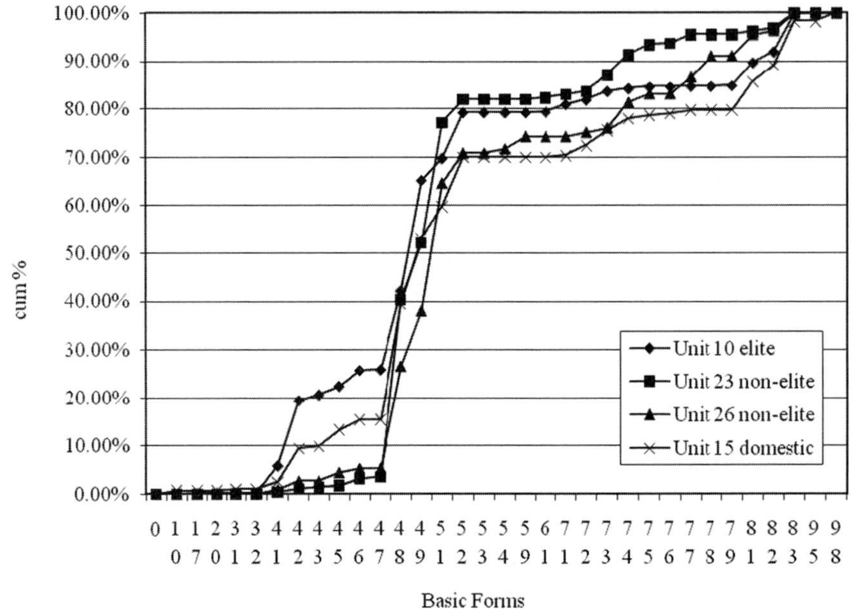

Figure 6. Cumulative percentage curve of basic vessel forms in production levels of Unit 10 (Operation 2D), Units 23 and 26 (Operation 3B) and domestic levels of Unit 15 (Operation 2E). Forms 41–59 are plates and bowls, 61–79 are necked jars, and 81–83 are neckless jars. See text for discussion.

overfired Polished Orange sherd) than was typical in domestic contexts.

Typological Diversity

The foregoing strongly suggests that the excavated elite and non-elite production contexts were comparable in terms of the evenness of their assemblages, with the most common wares in each setting comprising 34–42%. A separate component of diversity is richness, referring to the number of categories relative to the size of an assemblage. There are several measures of richness, each with advantages and disadvantages. Here I employ that developed by Odum et al. (1960), given by the formula R = S/logN, where R is richness, S is the number of categories, and N is the number of specimens (Table 1). Odum's formula is not ideal, but has the advantage of taking into account sample size and not requiring an estimate of the standard deviation of the number of categories, which we cannot yet estimate for a representative sample of contexts. Inspection of Table 3 suggests

that the attached production area represented by Unit 10 is indeed richer in its assemblage than the independent production area represented by Units 23 and 26. However, the richness of the assemblage for Unit 10 is similar to that for the domestic contexts from Unit 15, also from the Late Formative period, which leads me to suspect that the difference has more to do with chronological difference in typological variation (and quite possibly differences in the degree to which our classification subdivides types and varieties for types prevalent in these two periods).

Variation in Forms

Figure 6 illustrates variation in basic form categories among the analyzed contexts. Differences among the production contexts occur primarily in specific forms of bowls and plates (codes 41–59). Compared to Units 23 and 26, Unit 10 has more slightly convergent bowls (Form 42) and plates with curved divergent walls (Form 49), but fewer plates with straight divergent walls (Form 48) or convex divergent walls

(Form 51). Medium to tall-necked ollas (Forms 71–79) are more common overall in Units 23 and 26, while neckless or short necked forms (including *tecomates* [Form 81] and *macetas* [Form 83]) are somewhat more common in Unit 10. This is consistent with the well-documented general increase in necked ollas over the course of the Formative period (Coe and Diehl 1980; Ortiz 1975; Ortiz and Santley 1988) and does not represent a substantial difference in the functional emphases of the two assemblages.

Finally, it should be noted that attached craft production in Operation 2D was not confined to pottery. Basalt flakes and microdebitage indicate groundstone production, and numerous flakes of mica concentrated to the east of the platform suggest multicrafting. Of these, only the nonlocal mica is clearly associated with prestige good production.

The three-way comparison presented here among a Terminal Formative independent production context, a Late Formative attached production context, and a Late Formative non-production domestic context suggests the following conclusions.

1. The Late Formative domestic assemblage was remarkably similar to the attached production context of the same period except for a higher proportion of utilitarian jars and a lower proportion of serving vessels, especially in Polished Orange ware. This accords with the general expectation that elite households require more serving vessels and have greater access to well-finished pottery. It is important to recognize, however, that all wares are represented in non-elite contexts. Elite access to "fancy" pottery was in no way exclusive, as reflected in the similar richness of types in these two contexts.
2. Overall, the analyzed production contexts contained higher proportions of serving vessels than the non-production context (though Unit 26 was more similar in this regard). While this might suggest that specialized production in the Late and Terminal Formative periods emphasized service wares, surface collections suggest a more variable picture, with other production areas, in elite and nonelite contexts and of varying scale and intensity, showing greater emphasis in utilitarian wares (Pool 2003:Table 5.3).
3. Ceramic assemblages in the elite and nonelite production contexts were similar in their proportions of functionally equivalent wares and forms. What differences exist are attributable to chronological factors. Clearly it would be preferable to compare production contexts with greater contemporaneity; analyses in progress for other excavations should soon provide such data. Nevertheless, this observation generally supports the inference from surface collections that elite and nonelite production areas

manufactured similar products during the florescence of Tres Zapotes. On the other hand, evidence from surface collections had suggested that the similarity would result from the elite context producing utilitarian vessels for quotidian uses of cooking and storage. Instead, in this comparison at least, the similarity in assemblages evidently results from the independent production context producing more serving vessels than in the domestic control sample of Unit 15.

Conclusions

Hirth (chapter 2, this volume) challenges us to consider residential craft production, whether in non-elite or elite contexts, as a household diversification and risk reduction strategy. The data on ceramic production from the Tuxtlas region generally bear out his expectations in several respects. Multicrafting in nonelite residential contexts of the Protoclassic period at Bezuapan and Tres Zapotes correspond with increased volcanic activity and, presumably, greater subsistence risk – a conclusion born out by botanical and faunal data (VanDerwarker 2006). Demonstrating intermittent production is more difficult, but production at Bezuapan and in Area 120 at Matacapan was small scale and associated with bell-shaped pits that suggest these households also stored agricultural products rather than periodically exchanging crafts for them. Given the seasonal rainfall regime in the Tuxtlas, it is likely that ceramic production, including that carried out as part of a multicrafting strategy, was intermittent and would not have interfered with peak labor demands for agriculture.

Pottery manufacture in elite residential contexts at Tres Zapotes appears to have produced the same general suite of products as in nonelite contexts. In part this simply reflects widespread access to well-made serving vessels across the social spectrum. However, it also can be seen as another kind of risk reduction, one in which elite households in a less centralized political economy, as compared to Matacapan, found it effective and prudent to provision themselves rather than to rely on a politically riskier strategy of meeting their needs through consignments or taxation of independent producers.

Notes

1. Santley et al. (1989:112) initially defined "high density" as the mean of all collection squares plus one standard deviation. The upper tercile criterion was later adopted as preferable to one based on the mean because the density distribution is positively skewed (Arnold and Santley 1993; Pool 1990:202; Pool and Santley 1992). Working in the

Mixtequilla region of southern Veracruz, Stark (1992) defined high density as the upper decile of the surface density distribution. See Stark (2007:165–171) for a thorough review of the effects of differing data recovery methods and analytical techniques on the inference of ceramic production from surface data in the southern Gulf lowlands of Mesoamerica.

2. Such elite household production resembles both the "Intensified household production" type of attached production identified by Costin (1996: 211) and the production by "embedded specialists" in elite households in North American Northwest Coast Indian societies, as proposed by Kenneth Ames (1995). The emphasis here, however, is on the production of quotidian items for the elite household rather than production of surplus goods "for circulation within the political economy (Costin 1996: 211). Ames's (1995: 158) concept of embedded specialists as "full- or part-time specialists whose vocation is a part of the household or local economy, and the specialist's activity is integral to the functioning of that economy", is closer, but his emphasis is also on elite goods, "The crucial point here is that when they were part of the elite, they produced elite goods, not as dependents of an elite class, but as part of their *roles* as elite individuals" (Ames 1995: 174).

References

Abascal, Rafael
1976 Los Primeros Pueblos Alfareros Prehispánicos. *In* El Proyecto Arqueológico Puebla-Tlaxcala. Suplemento. Comunicaciones, Puebla-Tlaxcala, III. G. Cook, ed. Pp. 40–52. Puebla, México: Fundación Alemana para la Investigación Científica.

Ames, Kenneth M.
1995 Chiefly Power and Household Production on the Northwest Coast. *In* Foundations of Social Inequality. T. Douglas Price and Gary M. Feinman, eds. Pp. 155–187. New York: Plenum Press.

Arnold, Dean E.
1985 Ceramic Theory and Cultural Process. Cambridge: Cambridge University Press.

Arnold, Philip J.
1991 Domestic Ceramic Production and Spatial Organization: A Mexican Case Study in Ethnoarchaeology. Cambridge, U.K.: Cambridge University Press.

Arnold, Philip J., et al.
1993 Intensive Ceramic Production and Classic-Period Political Economy in the Sierra De Los Tuxtlas, Veracruz, Mexico. Ancient Mesoamerica 4:175–191.

Arnold, Philip J., and Robert S. Santley
1993 Household Ceramics Production at Middle Classic Period Matacapan. *In* Prehispanic Domestic Units in Western Mesoamerica. R.S. Santley and K.G. Hirth, eds. Pp. 227–248. Boca Raton: CRC Press.

Balkansky, Andrew K., Gary M. Feinman, and Linda M. Nicholas
1997 Pottery Kilns of Ancient Ejutla, Mexico. Journal of Field Archaeology 24:139–160.

Barbour, Warren
1976 The Figurines and Figurine Chronology of Ancient Teotihuacan. Ph.D. dissertation, University of Rochester.

Blanton, Richard, et al.
1996 A Dual-Processual Theory for the Evolution of Mesoamerican Civilization. Current Anthropology 37:1–14.

Blomster, Jeffrey P., Hector Neff, and Michael D. Glascock
2005 Olmec Pottery Production and Export in Ancient Mexico Determined through Elemental Analysis. Science 307:1068–1072.

Bordaz, Jacques
1964 Pre-Columbian Ceramic Kilns at Peñitas, a Post-Classic Site in Coastal Nayarit, Mexico. Ph.D. dissertation, Columbia University.

Brumfiel, Elizabeth, and Timothy K. Earle
1987 Specialization, Exchange and Complex Societies: An Introduction. *In* Specialization, Exchange and Complex Societies. E. Brumfiel and T.K. Earle, eds. Pp. 1–9. Cambridge: Cambridge University Press.

Charlton, Thomas H., Deborah L. Nichols, and Cynthia L. Otis Charlton
2000 Otumba and Its Neighbors, Ex Oriente Lux. Ancient Mesoamerica 11:247–265.

Charlton, Thomas H., et al.
2007 Aztec Otumba, Ad 1200–1600: Patterns of the Production, Distribution, and Consumption of Ceramic Products. *In* Pottery Economics in Mesoamerica. C.A. Pool and G.J. Bey, III, eds. Pp. 237–266. Tucson: University of Arizona.

Clark, John E.
1994 The Development of Early Formative Rank Societies in the Soconusco, Chiapas, Mexico. Ph.D. dissertation, University of Michigan.

Clark, John E., and David Cheetham
2005 Cerámica del Formativo de Chiapas. *In* La Producción Alfarera en el México Antiquo, Volume I. B. L. Merino Carrión and A. García Cook, eds. Pp. 285–433. Colección Científica No. 484. Mexico City: INAH.

Clark, John E., and Dennis Gosser
1995 Reinventing Mesoamerica's First Pottery. *In* The Emergence of Pottery: Technology and Innovation in Ancient Societies. W.K. Barnett and J.W. Hoopes, eds. Pp. 209–221. Washington, DC: Smithsonian Institution.

Clark, John E., and William J. Parry
1990 Craft Specialization and Cultural Complexity. Research in Economic Anthropology 12:289–346.

Coe, Michael D., and Richard A. Diehl
1980 In the Land of the Olmec, Vol. 1, the Archaeology of San Lorenzo Tenochtitlán. Austin: University of Texas Press.

Cook de Leonard, Carmen
1953 Los Popolocas de Puebla: Ensayo de una Identificación Etno-Demográfica e Histórico-Arqueológica. Revista Mexicana de Estudios Antropológicos 13(423–445).

Costin, Cathy L.
1991 Craft Specialization: Issues in Defining, Documenting, and Explaining the Oganization of Production. Advances in Archaeological Method and Theory 3:1–56.
1996 Craft Production and Mobilization Strategies in the Inka Empire. *In* Craft Specialization and Social Evolution: In Memory of V. Gordon Childe. Bernard Wailes, ed. Pp. 211–

155. Philadelphia: University of Pennsylvania Museum.
2001 Craft Production Systems. *In* Archaeology at the Millenium: A Sourcebook. G. Feinman and T. D. Price, eds. Pp. 273–326. New York: Kluwer Academic/Plenum Publishers.

Earle, Timothy K.
1981 Comment on P. Rice, Evolution of Specialized Pottery Production: A Trial Model. Current Anthropology 22(3):230–231.

Feinman, Gary M.
2000 High-Intensity Household-Scale Production in Ancient Mesoamerica: A Perspective from Ejutla, Oaxaca. *In* Cultural Evolution: Contemporary Viewpoints. G.M. Feinman and L. Manzanilla, eds. Pp. 119–142. New York: Kluwer Academic.

Feinman, Gary M., and Linda M. Nicholas
2007 Household Production and the Regional Economy in Ancient Oaxaca: Classic Period Perspectives from Hilltop El Palmillo and Valley-Floor Ejutla. *In* Pottery Economics in Mesoamerica. C.A. Pool and G.J. Bey, III, eds. Pp. 184–211. Tempe: University of Arizona.

Guevara, María Eugenia
2004 La Cerámica de San Lorenzo Tenochtitlán. Origen y Naturaleza. Unpublished Master's thesis, UNAM.

Healan, Dan M.
1977 Architectural Implications of Early Life in Ancient Tollan, Hidalgo, Mexico. World Archaeology 9:140–156.

Jaime Riverón, Olaf, and Christopher A. Pool
2009 The Impact of Volcanic Hazards on the Ancient Olmec and Epi-Olmec Economies in the Los Tuxtlas Region, Veracruz, Mexico. *In* The Political Economy of Hazards and Disasters. Eric C. Jones and Arthur D. Murphy, eds. Pp. 133–154. Lanham; Alta Mira Press.

Jones, Jeffrey R., and Augusto Otavalo
1981 Diagnóstico Socio-Económico Sobre el Consumo y Producción de Leña en Fincas Pequeños en Nicaragua. Report submitted to the IRENA-CATIE-ROCAP, Turrialba, Costa Rica.

Killion, Thomas W.
1987 Agriculture and Residential Site Structure among Campesinos in Southern Veracruz, Mexico: A Foundation for Archaeological Inference. Unpublished Ph.D. dissertation, University of New Mexico.

Kruger, Robert P.
1999 Investigations of a Rural Olmec Settlement in Southern Veracruz. 64th Annual Meeting of the Society for American Archaeology, Chicago, Illinois, 1999.

Lewis, Brandon S.
1996 The Role of Attached and Independent Specialization in the Development of Sociopolitical Complexity. Research in Economic Anthropology 17:357–388.

Millon, René F.
1981 Teotihuacan: City, State, and Civilization. *In* Supplement to the Handbook of Middle American Indians, Vol. 1: Archaeology. V.R. Bricker and J.A. Sabloff, eds. Pp. 198–243. Austin: University of Texas Press.

Munera Bermúdez, Luis Carlos
1985 Un Taller de Cerámica Ritual en la Ciudadela. Teotihuacan. Tesis de Licenciatura, Escuela Nacional de Antropología e Historia, México.

Neff, Hector, Jeffrey P. Blomster, Michael D. Glascock, Ronald L. Bishop, M. James Blackman, Michael D. Coe, George L. Cowgill, Ann Cyphers, Richard A. Diehl, Stephen Houston, Arthur A. Joyce, Carl P. Lipo, and Marcus C. Winter
2006a Smokescreens in the Provenance Investigation of Early Formative Mesoamerican Ceramics. Latin American Antiquity 17:104–118.

Neff, Hector, Jeffrey P. Blomster, Michael D. Glascock, Ronald L. Bishop, M. James Blackman, Michael D. Coe, George L. Cowgill, Richard A. Diehl, Stephen Houston, Arthur A. Joyce, Carl P. Lipo, Barbara L. Stark, and Marcus C. Winter
2006b Methodological Issues in the Provenance Investigation of Early Formative Mesoamerican Ceramics. Latin American Antiquity 17:54–76.

Ohnersorgen, Michael Anthony
2001 Social and Economic Organization of Cotaxtla in the Postclassic Gulf Lowlands. Dissertation, Arizona State University.

Ortíz Ceballos, Ponciano
1975 La Cerámica de Los Tuxtlas. Unpublished Maestría thesis in archaeology, Universidad Veracruzana.

Ortíz Ceballos, Ponciano, and Robert S. Santley
1988 La Cerámica de Matacapan, Ms. On File, Department of Anthropology, University of New Mexico. Albuquerque, New Mexico.

Peacock, D. P. S.
1982 Pottery in the Roman World. London: Longman.

Pool, Christopher A.
1990 Ceramic Production, Resource Procurement, and Exchange at Matacapan, Veracruz, Mexico. Ph.D. disseratation, Tulane University.
1992 Integrating Ceramic Production and Distribution. *In* Ceramic Production and Distribution: An Integrated Approach. G.J. Bey, III and C.A. Pool, eds. Pp. 275–313. Boulder, Colorado: Westview Press.
1993 Quest for Fire: Fuel Costs and Pottery Manufacture at Matacapan, Veracruz. *In* Culture and Environment: A Fragile Coexistence: Proceedings of the Twenty-Fourth Annual Conference of the Archaeological Association of the University of Calgary. Ross W. Jamieson, Sylvia Abonyi, and Neil Mirau, eds. Pp. 395–409. Calgary: The Archaeological Association of the University of Calgary.
1997 Prehispanic Kilns at Matacapan, Veracruz, Mexico. *In* The Prehistory and History of Ceramic Kilns. P.M. Rice and W.D. Kingery, eds. Pp. 149–171. Westerville, OH: The American Ceramic Society.
1999 Variability in Ceramic Production in the Classic Period of Southern Veracruz, Mexico. Paper presented at the Annual meeting of the American Anthropological Association, Chicago, 1999.
2000 Why a Kiln? Firing Technology in the Sierra De Los Tuxtlas, Veracruz (Mexico). Archaeometry 42(1):61–76.
2003 Ceramic Production at Terminal Formative and Classic Period Tres Zapotes. *In* Settlement Archaeology and Political Economy at Tres Zapotes, Veracruz, Mexico. C.A. Pool, ed.

Pp. 56–68. Monograph 50. Los Angeles: Cotsen Institute of Archaeology, University of California.

2005 Further Investigation of Ceramic Production and Political Economy at Tres Zapotes, Veracruz, Mexico. Paper presented at the 104th Annual Meeting of the American Anthropological Association, Washington, DC., 2005.

Pool, Christopher A., and George J. Bey, III
2007 Conceptual Issues in Mesoamerican Pottery Economics. *In* Pottery Economics in Mesoamerica. C.A. Pool and G.J. Bey, III, eds. Pp. 1–38. Tempe: University of Arizona.

Pool, Christopher A., and Georgia Mudd Britt
2000 A Ceramic Perspective on the Formative to Classic Transition in Southern Veracruz, Mexico. Latin American Antiquity 10(2):139–161.

Rattray, Evelyn
1990 Nuevos Hallazgos Sobre los Orígenes de la Cerámica Anaranjado Delgado. *In* La Epoca Clásica: Nuevos Hallazgos, Nuevas Ideas. A. Cardos de Méndez, ed. Pp. 89–106. Mexico City: Instituto Nacional de Antropología e Historia.

Redmond, Elsa
1979 A Terminal Formative Ceramic Workshop in the Tehuacan Valley. *In* Prehistoric Social, Political, and Economic Development in the Area of the Tehuacan Valley: Some Results of the Palo Blanco Project. R.D. Drennan, ed. Pp. 111–125. Ann Arbor: Museum of Anthropology, University of Michigan.

Reents-Budet, Dorie, Ronald L. Bishop, Jennifer Taschek, and Joseph W. Ball
2000 Out of the Palace Dumps: Ceramic Production and Use at Buenavista Del Cayo. Ancient Mesoamerica 11:99–121.

Rice, Prudence
1987 Pottery Analysis: A Sourcebook. Chicago: The University of Chicago Press.

Roscoe, John
1965 The Baganda: An Account of Their Native Customs and Beliefs. London: Frank Cass & Co. Ltd.

Rye, Owen
1981 Pottery Technology: Principles and Reconstruction. Washington, DC: Taraxacum.

Santley, Robert S., and Philip J. Arnold
1996 Prehispanic Settlement Patterns in the Tuxtla Mountains, Southern Veracruz, Mexico. Journal of Field Archaeology 23:225–249.

Santley, Robert S., Philip J. Arnold, and Christopher A. Pool
1989 The Ceramics Production System at Matacapan, Veracruz, Mexico. Journal of Field Archaeology 16:107–132.

Santley, Robert S., Stephen Nelson, Benjamin Reinhardt, Christopher A. Pool, and Philip J. Arnold
2000 When Day Turned to Night: Volcanism and the Archaeological Record from the Tuxtla Mountains, Southern Veracruz, Mexico. *In* Environmental Disaster and the Archaeology of Human Response. G. Bawden and R.M. Reycraft, eds. Pp. 143–161. Albuquerque, New Mexico: Maxwell Museum of Anthropology.

Santley, Robert S., Ponciano Ortiz Ceballos, Thomas W. Killion, Philip J. Arnold, and Janet M. Kerley
1984 Final Field Report of the Matacapan Archaeological Project: The 1982 Season. Research Papers Series, No. 15. Albuquerque: Latin American Institutue, University of New Mexico.

Sharer, Robert J., Andrew K. Balkansky, James Burton, Gary M. Feinman, Kent V. Flannery, David C. Grove, Joyce Marcus, Robert G. Moyle, T. Douglas Price, Elsa M. Redmond, Robert G. Reynolds, Prudence M. Rice, Charles S. Spencer, James B. Stoltman, and Jason Yaeger
2006 On the Logic of Archaeological Inference: Early Formative Pottery and the Evolution of Mesoamericna Societies. Latin American Antiquity 17:90–103.

Sheets, Payson D.
1992 The Cerén Site: A Prehistoric Village Buried by Volcanic Ash in Central America. Fort Worth, Texas: Harcourt Brace Jovanavich.

Stark, Barbara L.
1985 Archaeological Identification of Pottery-Production Locations: Ethnoarchaeological

and Archaeological Data in Mesoamerica. *In* Decoding Prehistoric Ceramics. B. Nelson, ed. Pp. 158–194. Carbondale, IL: Southern Illinois University Press.

1989 Patarata Pottery: Classic Period Ceramics of the South-Central Gulf Coast, Veracruz, Mexico. Tucson: University of Arizona Press.

1992 Ceramic Production in Prehistoric La Mixtequilla, South-Central Veracruz, Mexico. *In* Ceramic Production and Distribution: An Integrated Approach. G.J. Bey, III and C.A. Pool, eds. Pp. 175–204. Boulder, Colorado: Westview Press.

2007 Pottery Production and Distribution in the Gulf Lowlands of Mesoamerica. *In* Pottery Economics in Mesoamerica. C.A. Pool and G.J. Bey, III, eds. Pp. 147–183. Tucson: University of Arizona.

Stark, Barbara L., and Christopher P. Garraty
2004 Evaluation of Systematic Surface Evidence for Pottery Production in Veracruz, Mexico. Latin American Antiquity 15:123–143.

Stein, Gil J., and M. James Blackman
1993 The Organizational Context of Specialized Craft Production in Early Mesopotamian States. Research in Economic Anthropology 14:29–59.

Stone, Doris, and C. Turnbull
1941 A Sulua-Ulua Pottery Kiln. American Antiquity 7:39–47.

Stoner, Wesley D.
2002 Coarse Orange Pottery Exchange in Southern Veracruz: A Compositional Perspective on Centralized Craft Production and Exchange in the Classic Period. Unpublished M.A. thesis, University of Kentucky.

Stoner, Wesley D., Christopher A. Pool, Hector Neff, and Michael D. Glascock
2008 Exchange of Coarse Orange Pottery in the Middle Classic Tuxtla Mountains, Southern Veracruz, Mexico. Journal of Archaeological Science 35:1412–1426.

Szatkowski-Reeves, Tammy L.
2002 Specialized Production and Economic Change in the Late Formative Community of Papayal, Veracruz, Mexico. Paper presented at the 67th Annual Meeting of the Society for American Archaeology, Denver, Colorado, 2002.

VanDerwarker, Amber M.
2006 Farming, Hunting, and Fishing in the Olmec World. Austin: University of Texas Press.

Wendt, Carl J.
2003 Buried Occupational Deposits at Tres Zapotes: The Results from an Auger Testing Program. *In* Settlement Archaeology and Political Economy at Tres Zapotes, Veracruz, Mexico. C.A. Pool, ed. Pp. In Press. Los Angeles: Cotsen Institute of Archaeology, University of California.

Whalen, Michael
1981 Excavations at Santo Domingo Tomaltepec: Evolution of a Formative Community in the Valley of Oaxaca, Mexico. Memoirs of the Museum of Anthropology 12. Ann Arbor: University of Michigan.

Widmer, Randolph J., and Rebecca Storey
1993 Social Organization and Household Structure of a Teotihuacan Apartment Compoiund: S3 W1: 33 of the Tlajinga Barrio. *In* Prehispanic Domestic Units in Western Mesoamerica. R.S. Santley and K.G. Hirth, eds. Pp. 87–104. Boca Raton: CRC Press.

Winter, Marcus C., and William O. Payne
1976 Hornos para Cerámica Hallados en Monte Alban. Boletín del Instituto Nacional de Antropología e Historia Epoca II, 16:37–40.

9

Ceramics on the Side: Pottery Making as an Augmentation of Household Economy in the Valley of Puebla during the Formative Period

Ronald A. Castanzo
University of Baltimore

Economic specialization is considered to be a fundamental component of cultural evolution throughout much of the world. However, conceptually, developmentally, and in terms of measurement, craft specialization remains controversial (Arnold and Nieves 1992; see Arnold 1999; Longacre 1999; Michaels 1989; Schortman and Urban 2004; Spielmann 2002). Traditionally, the degree of specialization exhibited by a household has been considered as lying along a continuum from no specialization, through part-time specialization, to full-time specialization, based on the extent to which the household is dependent on craft activity for subsistence. Thus, specialization has implicitly connoted reliance by a household on other households. Theoretical problems with this relationship have recently been outlined by Costin (2007), and recent data from the Valley of Puebla casts doubt on the utility of the traditional view of craft specialization. I argue that Formative Period households there were engaged in pottery production for exchange when such households had no apparent need for subsistence assistance from other households.

Ceramics are associated with the beginning of the Formative Period (beginning as early as 2000 BC) in the central highlands of Mexico, the most salient feature of which initially was the spread of a farming and village life (García Cook and Merino Carrión 1989a; Hirth 1987; Sanders et al 1979:94–95; Weaver 1993:49). By the close of the Formative Period early in the first millennium AD, village life had given way to significant urbanization in several locations in the central and southern highlands, most notably at Teoti-

huacan and Cuilcuilco in the Basin of Mexico (Charlton and Nichols 1997; Sanders and Santley 1983), Monte Alban in the Valley of Oaxaca (Blanton et al. 1993:69–87), and Tlalancaleca in Puebla-Tlaxcala (García Cook & Merino Carrión 1989a). Ranking, and later social stratification, as well as the rise of state-level societies, also characterize the Formative Period (Blanton 1978:57; Blanton et al. 1993:79; Flannery and Marcus 1983a, 1983b, 1983c; García Cook 1981, 1976:40–41; Sanders et al. 1979:106; see Cordova et al. 1994; Millon 1988). The ways in which families and communities interacted economically were also increasing in complexity. Evidence of trade in both utilitarian and elite goods is clear in the highlands during the Formative Period (Drennan and Nowack 1984; Grove et al. 1976; Pires-Ferreira 1975:57–62).

Because of the work of Acatzingo-Tepeaca Project (Castanzo and Hirth 2008) and the Tepeaca Kiln Project (see below), over the past fifteen years, our knowledge of the Formative Period in the area of the town of Tepeaca has increased tremendously. This area lies just off the southern edge of the region of Puebla-Tlaxcala extensively investigated by García Cook a generation ago (García Cook 1981, 1976; García Cook & Merino Carrión 1989a, 1989b, 1977). The Tepeaca region is long known to have played a vital economic role in the highlands of Mexico, from prehispanic times up to the present day (Berdan 1985; Berdan & Anawalt 1992:99; Gormsen 1978; Licate 1981:10–11; Tyrakowski 1978). Since 2003, we have turned our attention to the investigation of lime processing and ceramic firing pits that were located during the survey of the region in the mid-1990's. This chapter focuses on excavations conducted during the summer of 2007 about 10 km to the northeast of Tepeaca. Five ceramic firing facilities were uncovered along with numerous examples of production debris. This paper explores the social context of their use in an attempt to get at the dynamics of the local development of crafting activity.

Ceramic Technology in the Mexican Highlands

Presumably, the earliest ceramics in the Mexican highlands were produced through open firing (i.e., above ground in a bonfire), which is still common in much of the world today (Rice 1987:153–158). This is the simplest method of clay firing, requiring no infrastructural investment, but control over the firing environment is limited (Sillar 2000; see Sillar and Tite 2000). Open firing, while probably widespread in ancient Mexico, is difficult to identify in archaeological contexts because of the ephemeral nature of the activity. Later, at least by Middle Formative times, people began to fire ceramics in pits. In the literature, these features are frequently referred to as "pit kilns" since clay items to be fired are placed in depressions or cavities dug in the ground (Rice 1987:158). In practice, there is a fine line between the open firing method and the pit kiln, since the excavation of small craters is often done at the start of the open firing process (Hill 1994; Wandibba 2003). Using a semi-subterranean chamber to fire ceramics may allow for greater control over the firing environment and raise the upper limit of the temperature that can be achieved. A major drawback of pit firing facilities is that the fuel is still in contact with the vessels, which increases variability in the firing environment and the potential for product damage.

In Puebla-Tlaxcala, firing pits (some of which provided a nearly completely enclosed firing environment) have been found dating to Middle Formative times and later (Abascal 1996[1975]). At Classic Period Ejutla in Oaxaca, ceramic firing pits ranging in size from 2 to 4 m wide and 40 to 70 cm deep were discovered, as were large concentrations of wasters, potsherds, and other production byproducts (Balkansky et al. 1997; Feinman 1999; Feinman and Balkansky 1997). In addition to pit kilns, updraft kilns have been found at prehispanic sites. Updraft kilns contain separate chambers for firing ceramics and for burning fuel, and a more completely enclosed environment for firing in the form of walls and perhaps a roof (Rice 1997, 1987:159–160; Tite 1999). Updraft kilns of stone and adobe were used at Classic Period Monte Alban (Feinman and Balkansky 1997; Payne 1982) and dozens have been found at Classic Period Matacapan in

Veracruz (Arnold and Santley 1993; Pool 2000, 1997; Pool and Santley 1992; Santley et al. 1989).

The finding of firing facilities is, however, rare in Mesoamerica. The identification of pottery manufacturing at archaeological sites has mostly relied upon artifactual support, such as wasters, concentrations of potsherds, assemblage characteristics, tools, etc. (Arnold and Santley 1993; Curet 1993; Santley et al. 1989; Stark 1985). Using some of these kinds of materials as confirmation of ceramic fabrication is problematical, however (Hayashida 1999; Santley et al. 1989; Underhill 1991; Urban et al. 1997).

In terms of vessel forms and surface treatments, a few general statements can be made regarding the pottery of Puebla-Tlaxcala and, specifically, the Tepeaca area. A number of wares and forms existed during the Early Formative Period in Western Puebla-Tlaxcala, corresponding to the Tzompantepec Phase in the local chronology (García Cook & Merino Carrión 1988). Several later Formative forms, surface treatments, and styles, are represented in Early Formative assemblages, but the high frequency of *tecomates*, especially large ones filling the roles that jars later filled, is distinctive to this time. In the Tepeaca area, the Early Formative is not well-represented, although some of the material drawn from kiln feature K3 may date to this period (see below). The first recognizable period of occupation, based on surface reconnaissance and the limited amount of excavation performed in the area, is the Middle Formative Period, which is currently estimated at 950–550 BC, but some revision in dates will be necessary after materials from the 2007 season are fully analyzed. White-slipped bowls, many of type *Tenextepec*, are a distinctive characteristic of this period and composite silhouette and, to lesser extent, *tecomate* forms predominate (Castanzo 2002:Appendix A). The application of white slip occurs solely on vessels, or in combination with red slip or natural burnished surfaces. By the Late Formative Period (550–150 BC), however, white-slipped vessels became far less common, although their use persisted for the remainder of the Formative Period. Red-slipped *Tlaquexpa* and natural/burnished *Tecococatl* vessels increase in abundance. Both types come in a variety of forms, including subhemispherical, composite silhouette, and restricted-mouth bowls, and jars of various sizes. Incision is a very common form of decoration during this time, especially on bowls.

Ceramic Manufacturing on Cerro Tlaquexpa

In 2003, the Tepeaca Kiln Project began attempting to locate and describe hundreds of features identified as kilns from 1994 to 1998 as part of the Acatzingo-Tepeaca Project

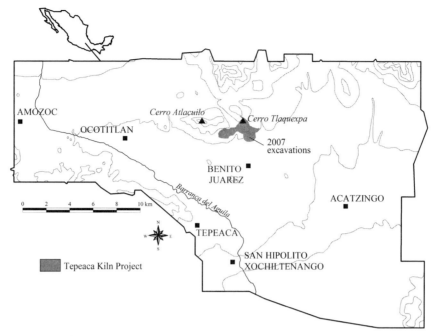

Figure 1. The Acatzingo-Tepeaca Project survey area showing the focus of the Tepeaca Kiln Project in the 2003 and 2007 field seasons.

(PAT). PAT was an intensive regional surface reconnaissance designed to study prehispanic regional demographic development in a 560 km² area of the Valley of Puebla. In 2003, we focused on Cerro Tlaquexpa and the eastern portion of Cerro Atlacuilo, areas of sizable Formative Period occupation (Castanzo 2003) (Figure 1). The Tepeaca Kiln Project has catalogued 89 features, of which 36 were identified as the remains of kilns used in the processing of lime. The remainder were largely indeterminate in terms of function based on surface remains. In the 2003 season, two lime processing pits/pit kilns were excavated that dated to early in the Middle Formative Period (Castanzo and Anderson 2004). Lime is today, and apparently was also in prehispanic times, an important local product. Tepeaca was the only Aztec province known to have paid some of its tribute in lime (Berdan and Anawalt 1992:100). Several features believed to be pottery firing facilities in 2003 became the focus area of the 2007 season.

In 2007, the Tepeaca Kiln Project focused on an apparent Formative Period pottery production area in the southeastern corner of the 2003 study area (Figure 2). The area is heavily eroded with *tepetate* exposed in many places. Nine firing features had been identified as possible ceramic manufacturing facilities based on the high densities of potsherds. We excavated at four locations on the eroded hillside, designated "Operations" A through D. In each location, the remains of one firing feature could be seen partially exposed

at the edge of an earth island. In all, a total of five firing pits and eight truncoconical pits (note the pyramidal form in Figure 3A) were uncovered. Truncoconical pits were filled with refuse, which included tools, materials, and waste products associated with ceramic production. In firing features, fill appeared to be entirely secondary, although it did include material associated with ceramic manufacturing. Large concentrations of sherds, wasters, lumps of clay, and tools that were likely used in preparing clay for vessel forming, were recovered in excavated contexts and on the ground surfaces adjacent to excavation operations.

The excavated facilities all had the same basic structure, essentially truncoconical, although each had at least some irregularity in morphology. Such is the degree of erosion on Cerro Tlaquexpa, today, that no preserved residential structures were uncovered, nor were any living/work surfaces positively identified. *Tepetate* is at or near the surface today all over the hill. However, based on the manner in which the firing facilities were produced, the situation may have been generally similar a few thousand years ago, although probably with far less *tepetate* actually exposed.

To construct one of these facilities, the prehispanic inhabitants dug through the overlying earth and into the *tepetate,* hollowing-out a hole with a diameter of at least 70 cm (Figure 3). The walls of the features are heavily oxidized reddish orange, with some flecks of carbon embedded. Facility floors are carbonized, gray to black in color. As

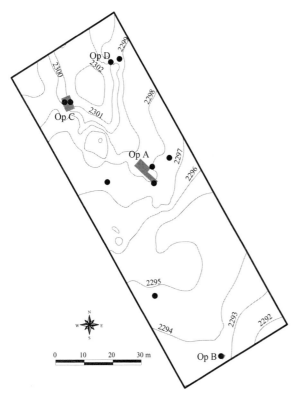

Figure 2. Location of the 2007 excavations (shaded) and associated firing facilities (solid circles) on Cerro Tlaquexpa

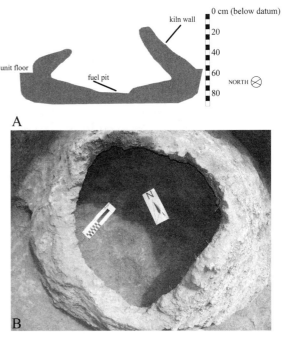

Figure 3. (A) Firing facility K91 profile (in an approximately northwest-southeast plane); (B) Facility K91 in Operation C.

mentioned above, the structures themselves were irregular in form with variable depths and widths (Figure 4). After the excavation of several ceramic firing facilities, it is clear that they can be easily distinguished from lime processing pits in morphology (Table 1). Their appearances at the surface are also quite different. Both are circular/ovular features in *tepetate*, but lime pits are larger, carbonized (black) rings, whereas ceramic kilns are smaller, heavily oxidized (orange to red) rings. Furthermore, lime processing pits often appear as piles of limestone rubble at the surface.

Waster sherds were found in excavated contexts. Sherds were classified as wasters if they appeared either to be fragments of vessels misfired in their manufacturing or fragments of pottery used as "kiln furniture" (i.e., used in the placement or propping up of clay items during the firing process) (see Pool 2003) (Figure 5). In addition to potsherds that represent wasters/furniture, a misfired or re-fired figurine was found (evidence of firing can be seen on the broken edge under the neck). Many fired lumps of clay were also found, in addition to two fragments of probable ceramic clay pounders (Figure 5A), used in clay preparation and vessel formation. Surface collections made in the immediate vicinities of excavation units contained many wasters, although many date to later time periods than the excavated

contexts. These suggest pottery-making was practiced on the hillside for centuries, if not millennia, in prehistory.

The 24 excavated square meters of Operation C may contain the remains of a Late Formative Period ceramic production area (Figure 6). Firing Facilities K91 and K92 lie approximately 1.5 m apart. They are both smaller than the other three firing features excavated (K92 very much so). K91 has been radiocarbon dated to 810 ± 30 BC (1σ), which places it in line with an Olmec figure found in nearby refuse pit TP7. In the southeastern corner of Operation C, running up against the southern edge of K91, as much as 60 cm of fill with high clay content was also discovered.

Abutting this clay lens on its western edge was a sand-filled feature 25 cm thick in the central area of the operation. The upper extent of this feature reached 114 cm in width and was difficult to trace, aside from the existence of sandy fill that tapered off at the edges in unit matrix. Small masses of clay-rich fill were found within this sandy matrix. In the lower portion of this feature, a trough was clearly carved in the underlying *tepetate*, several centimeters deep and as much as 57 cm wide. While the upper end of the feature was located, its length at the time of its use will never be known because the edge of Operation C corresponds closely to the southern edge of a large earth island and has eroded away. Since the south end of the trough lay 7 cm below its north end, a gradient existed. Figure 6 depicts a reconstruction of how this feature probably appeared when it was formed.

Figure 4. Excavated firing facilities on Cerro Tlaquexpa: (A) K3 in Operation A; (B) K10 in Operation B; (C) K6 in Operation D; (D) K92 in Operation C.

Table 1. General morphometrics of the ceramic firing and lime processing facilities.

Designation	Product	Maximum aperture width (cm)	Depth (cm)	Diameter at base (cm)	General pit morphology
K3	Ceramic	100	68	198	Truncoconical
K6	Ceramic	106	70	171	Truncoconical
K10	Ceramic	91	90	138	Truncoconical
K91	Ceramic	70	58	128	Truncoconical
K92	Ceramic	99	34	76	Truncoconical?
K50	Lime	250	60	n/a	Subhemispherical
K51	Lime	200	40	n/a	Subhemispherical

Of course, the question of the contemporaneity of the firing features, the clay deposit, the sand deposit, and trough remains unanswered (a question which planned radiocarbon dating may not be able to resolve). However, all of these features occur in broadly overlapping layers of the operation. The function of the sand deposit/trough associated with the two kilns is unknown. Perhaps, it served as a water channel and had little to do directly with pottery making. Another possibility, though, is that the sandy fill is what remains of a levigation pit used in the processing of local clays. The location of the clay-rich area on the side of sand deposit supports this idea. Potters may have been dumping earth and water in the levigation pit and skimming off the clay slurry and dumping it on the side of the pit. The beginning of the clay area was 20 to 30 cm above the beginning of the sand which represents what would have fallen out of

suspension during the levigation process. Soil samples taken in 2007 at a nearby *barranca* were rich in clay and sand. In the coming year, we will attempt to extract the clay content of this soil through levigation in the laboratory. Neutron activation will be used to compare any clay extracted to clays used to produce pottery on Cerro Tlaquexpa (see below).

Why Did the People of Cerro Tlaquexpa Make Pottery?

Wasters, raw materials, tools, not to mention the ceramic firing and lime processing pits themselves, all point to a significant degree of craft production and raw materials processing in the area. An important question is: for whom were the operators of these facilities producing? Certainly,

Figure 5. Production debris: (A) tool probably used in clay preparation recovered from TP7 in Operation C; (B) wasters (perhaps originally handles) recovered from feature K6; (C) waster from upper levels of Operation C; (D) wasters from inside K91.

the digging of a lime pit of the kinds excavated in 2003, and the quarrying and transportation of the limestone needed for one firing, was well within the capabilities of a single household. While the production of the ceramic firing facilities, as well, would have been within the means of a relatively small group of people, would families have produced one to satisfy their own needs? Of course, perhaps groups of families may have dug and used the same facility. Open firing (still practiced by some potters in the region today) would have sufficed for the number of vessels a single household might require in any given year.

The differences between open firing and firing in the Tlaquexpa pit facilities are clear; it is a reasonable assumption that the change in technology corresponded with changes in the way potters perceived their product and the role it played in their lives (see Sillar and Tite 2000), such as a shift away from production exclusively for household use to production for exchange. Importantly, though, especially in the case of K92, it is not clear that all of the kinds of pottery a typical family might use (particularly large jars) could have been produced in these facilities.

For the purposes of this paper, domestic craft specialization is considered to be household production that is not solely for consumption by the household (Costin 1991; see Blackman et al. 1993; Rice 1991; Stark 1992). From a cultural evolutionary perspective, the start point presumably is a situation in which all (at least, non-elite) families are subsistence farmers. Such families provide for their own food and also manufacture any material items (tools, clothing, pottery, etc.) they need. Importantly, though, as argued by Hirth (chapter two, this volume), these households may have engaged in intermittent craft production to augment their domestic economy. At the other end of the continuum of economic specialization from the subsistence farmer lies the full-time specialist. However, domestic craft specialization may have always played a role in household economic pursuits.

Household specialization has traditionally implied some level of reliance on other households for subsistence. Some households no longer produce enough food to satisfy their own needs; they produce something else that can be converted ultimately into food through exchanges with others. From a developmental standpoint, this shift in economic focus may stem from need (Harry 2005). That is, some households turn to craft specialization to supplement flagging returns from their agricultural pursuits. If this is correct, evidence of craft specialization should be accompanied by evidence of subsistence stress and uncertainty; evidence, perhaps, that a population is close to, or perhaps already is, exceeding food production potential.

An analysis of regional carrying capacity can be used to gauge potential subsistence stress on the local population

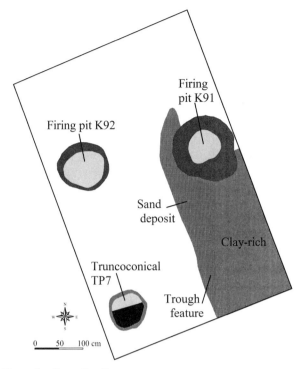

Figure 6. Operation C.

during the Middle and Late Formative Periods. A modified 2,500 ha grid was placed over an approximately 560 km² area of the eastern Valley of Puebla (Castanzo 2002:152–153). This zone corresponds to the limits of the Acatzingo-Tepeaca Project survey conducted in the mid-1990s. Three variables were considered in gauging the agricultural potential of land: soil quality, potential for floodwater irrigation, and the caloric content of maize (Castanzo 2002:156–163). A detailed soil survey conducted by the Fundación Alemana para la Investigación Científica, Puebla (Werner 1978), provided data regarding the relative utility of local soils for maize agriculture. Soils were placed in one of four categories: "good", "satisfactory", "poor", and "unusable". Slope data were used to estimate the potential of the land for floodwater irrigation. There is ample evidence for irrigation in the Puebla-Tlaxcala region during the Formative Period. García Cook (1981, 1976:17) has found evidence of irrigation and drainage canals associated with agricultural terracing after around 1200 BC. An extensive irrigation network was also constructed at Formative Amalucan (Fowler 1969). In addition to two aspects of land quality, the fact that the maize plant itself went through changes during the time period in question was also taken into account. Data concerning diachronic changes in maize caloric content were based on Sanders' (1976) work in the Basin of Mexico.

The grid square (which has 7.1 km maximum internal linear distance) within which the settlement on Cerro

Tlaquexpa rests overlooks some of the most productive land in the study area (Figure 7). During the Middle and Late Formative times, there were approximately 1,780 ha of land available potentially for floodwater irrigation and another 400 ha potentially available for rainfall agriculture. Approximately 1,300 people lived in this grid square during Middle and Late Formative times (Castanzo 2002:169,171; see Castanzo and Hirth 2008). Assuming all land was in rainfall agriculture, the local population was at approximately one-half of its carrying capacity. If local farmers were utilizing floodwater irrigation to its maximum extent, the local population would have only been at about one-fifth of carrying capacity (Castanzo 2002:169,171). Furthermore, the regional population would have been anywhere from about one-sixth to one-third (again, depending on how much land was brought into floodwater irrigation) of the carrying capacity of the area.

Assuming the people residing on Cerro Tlaquexpa were producing ceramics (and perhaps also lime) for exchange, subsistence stress does not seem to be the driving force, given the productive potential of the land just to the north of the town of Tepeaca. Thus, the notion is flawed that the development of economic specialization arises out of a cultural context in which all households are subsistence farmers who produce craft and other material items only for their own use. Since it is likely that the Middle and Late Formative Period families of Cerro Tlaquexpa could satisfy their own subsistence needs, they appear to have been engaging in intermittent crafting (Hirth chapter two, this volume) in order to augment their household economies. Such pursuits may have given them a means to acquire materials, utilitarian and otherwise, that they did not or could not produce themselves. Their extra-subsistence activities may have also been used as a buffer in times when agricultural production did fall below acceptable levels (Halstead and O'Shea 1989; see Hirth chapter two, this volume).

The excavated remains of the pit firing features provide one variable in establishing the context (domestic vs. non-domestic) and intensity of production. Production in a purely domestic setting generally represents lower intensity activity than production taking place in a non-domestic context (Peacock 1982:6–10; see Santley et al. 1989; Tite 1999). Inferring the context of production from the intensity of production is problematical, however, since households may exhibit high levels of output (Costin 1991; Feinman 1999; see Costin 2001). Of course, whether or not a workshop is "attached" to an elite household is an important consideration (Costin 2001; Costin and Hagstrum 1995; Hagstrum 1985), although there is nothing to suggest such a relationship associated with the features excavated in 2007. Furthermore, the nature of the firing facility itself can suggest a level of

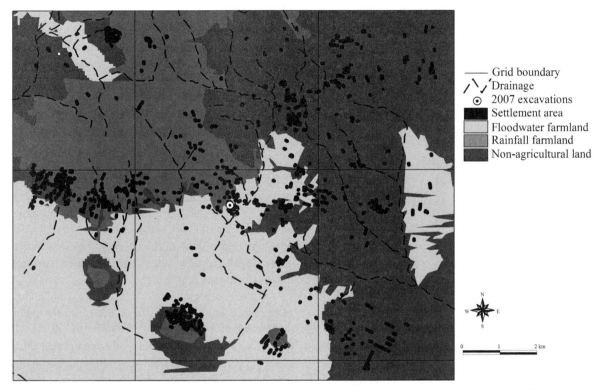

Figure 7. Land use and settlement in the vicinity of the Cerro Tlaquexpa ceramic production area during the Middle Formative Period and the Late Formative Period (950–150 BC).

intensity of production. Although not a perfect relationship, updraft kilns, as compared to open firing, are reflective of a higher level of output (Arnold 1990; Pool 1997; see Pool 2000). Thus, the firing pits of Tlaquexpa may lie between these two firing methods in terms of intensity.

Unfortunately, mainly due to the heavily eroded nature of the hillside, we could not identify any architecture or living surface associated with the pit features. Therefore, the context of production cannot be directly inferred. However, based on the structure of the facilities and their size (together with what is known about the local cultural setting at the time), I assume that these pits were utilized by household units. In modeling ceramic production variability on the Gulf Coast, Pool (2003) argues that, in dispersed populations, one would expect to find lower-intensity production largely by households, and relatively small consuming populations. Such a situation may have obtained in the Tepeaca area during most of the Formative Period.

Conclusion and Future Research

Although much remains to be learned regarding the role of craft production in the lives of the people of the Tepeaca area during the Formative Period, the available evidence sug-

gests that ceramic production was an activity in which local households were engaged for centuries. In pottery-making (and perhaps lime production, as well, since we know the role this region has played in this regard going back to prehispanic times), the intensity of behavior appears to be at a level greater than would be expected to satisfy the needs of a single household. Importantly, there is nothing to suggest that families *had* to engage in this behavior. Agricultural potential, with available technology (including the caloric potential of maize itself), was far in excess of what would have been needed to satisfy the needs of the local population. Local families were likely subsistence farmers, engaging in ceramic production "on the side" as a way to offset ever present subsistence risks (Halstead and O'Shea 1989) and give them a means of acquiring other kinds of goods and materials they did not make or to which they did not have direct access.

The analyses of materials recovered during the 2007 field season are ongoing. These endeavors provide other avenues to study the dynamics of the development of pottery production in the Tepeaca area of Puebla. These analyses include a standardization study, focusing on subhemispherical *Tlaquexpa* bowls. This form appears to occur out of proportion to what one would expect at a Late Formative Period site in this region. There are two possibilities for this: (1) these red-slipped vessels were more abundant during this period of time than could be ascertained from surface data collected during the 1990's or (2) the people of Cerro Tlaquexpa were specializing in the production of this ware. Although the pit kilns/firing facilities appear small (especially K92), many of these red bowls could be stacked to produce a sizeable batch. Disproportionate amounts of certain ceramic types or vessel forms can be used as supporting evidence of craft specialization in conjunction with other lines of evidence (Curet 1993; see Arnold and Santley 1993; Santley et al. 1989; Stark 1985).

Morphometrics are currently being collected on rim sherds, both from the 2007 season and from collections from the Acatzingo-Tepeaca Project of the 1990's, so that coefficients of variation (standard deviation/mean x 100) can be calculated (Costin and Hagstrum 1995; Magness-Gardiner 2003). It has been argued that higher degrees of standardization in vessel formation are indicative of greater amounts of time and focus on the activity in question, although the relationship is not a perfect one (Arnold 1991; Blackman et al. 1993; Hagstrum 1985; Longacre 1999; McClure 2007; Mills 1995; Rice 1991, 1987:202–203; Roux 2003). There are problems associated not only with measuring ceramic variability, but also with understanding product standardization in its proper cultural context (Arnold 1992; Arnold and Nieves 1992).

In addition to a study of standardization, instrumental neutron activation analysis (INAA) of hundreds of samples of sherds and clays is being applied to the issue of local household craft production (see Arnold et al. 1991; Bishop et al. 1990, 1982; Blackman 1986; Glascock 1992). Chemical compositional analysis has been used in the study of craft specialization with mixed results. A number of factors can affect the success of this approach, especially the degree of chemical homogeneity of local clays and the degree to which individual potters behaviorally alter the elemental profile of their clays. Poblome et al. (2002) applied a number of compositional analytical techniques in their study of the organization of pottery production in 7th century AD Turkey. Although there may theoretically be measurable standardization in the chemical composition of the products of an individual workshop, inter-workshop variation may obscure any standardization that may be present (Blackman et al 1993). Based on their work in the Yucatan, Mexico, Arnold et al. (2000) argue it is not possible to identify individual workshops in regions of high geologic homogeneity using clay sourcing when sources are separated by 3 km or less. Also shown, however, was that community-level production can be discerned in the regional pattering of compositional groups.

In addition to using INAA to measure standardization, it is being used to characterize the regional exchange of ceramics. This technique has added to our understanding of pottery production and exchange in a wide diversity of cultural settings, including the Anasazi of what is now Utah State between AD 1200 and 1300 (Neff et al. 1997), the Lowland Maya (Bishop 1994), and 17th-16th century BC Crete (Garrigós et al. 2001), to name a few. The Tepeaca Kiln Project will compare competing models of exchange in an effort to test the hypothesis that a market system was in operation by the close of the Formative Period in the Tepeaca area. It is hoped that chemical compositional analysis, together with the study of the character of the excavated and surface-collected pottery assemblages, and the nature and context of the firing facilities, will allow for a more complete picture of the dynamics of craft production than has been possible in many areas of Mesoamerica.

References

Abascal, Rafael
1996 [1975] Los Hornos Prehispánicos de la Región de Tlaxcala. *In* Antología de Tlaxcala, Volumen I. Ángel García Cook and B. Leonor Merino Carrión, comps. Pp. 321–332. Instituto Nacional de Antropología e Historia, Gobierno del Estado de Tlaxcala.

Arnold, Dean E., H. Neff, and M. D. Glascock
2000 Testing Assumptions of Neutron Activation Analysis: Communities, Workshops and Paste Preparation in Yucatán, Mexico. Archaeometry 42(2):301–316.

Arnold, Dean E.
1999 Advantages and Disadvantages of Vertical-Half Molding Technology: Implications for Production Organization. *In* Pottery and People, a Dynamic Interaction. James M. Skibo and Gary M. Feinman, eds. Pp. 59–80. Salt Lake City: The University of Utah Press.

Arnold, Dean E.
1992 Commentary on Section II. *In* Chemical Characterization of Ceramic Pastes in Archaeology, Hector Neff, ed. Pp. 159–166. Madison: Prehistory Press.

Arnold, Dean E., and Alvaro L. Nieves
1992 Factors Affecting Ceramic Standardization. *In* Ceramic Production and Distribution, an Integrated Approach. George J. Bey III and

Christopher A. Pool, eds. Pp. 93–114. Boulder: Westview Press.

Arnold, Dean E., Hector Neff, and Ronald L. Bishop
1991 Compositional Analysis and "Sources" of Pottery: An Ethnoarchaeological Approach. American Anthropologist 93(1):70–90.

Arnold, Philip J.
1991 Dimensional Standardization and Production Scale in Mesoamerican Ceramics. American Antiquity 2(4):363–370.

Arnold, Philip J.
1990 The Organization of Refuse Disposal and Ceramic Production within Contemporary Mexican Houselots. American Anthropologist 92:915–932.

Arnold III, Philip J., and Robert S. Santley
1993 Household Ceramics Production at Middle Classic Period Matacapan. *In* Prehispanic Domestic Units in Western Mesoamerica: Studies of the Household, Compound, and Residence. Robert S. Santley and Kenneth G. Hirth, eds. Pp. 67–86. Boca Raton: CRC Press.

Balkansky, Andrew K., Gary M. Feinman, and Linda M. Nichols
1997 Pottery Kilns of Ancient Ejutla, Oaxaca, Mexico. Journal of Field Archaeology 24:139–160.

Berdan, Frances F.
1985 Markets in the Economy of Aztec Mexico. *In* Markets and Marketing. S. Plattner, ed. Pp. 339–367. Lanham: University Press of America.

Berdan, Frances F., and Patricia R. Anawalt
1992 The Codex Mendoza. Berkeley: University of California Press.

Bishop, Ronald L.
1994 Pre-Columbian Pottery: Research in the Maya Region. *In* Archaeometry of Pre-Columbian Sites and Artifacts. David A. Scott and Pieter Meyers, eds. Pp. 15–65. Marina Del Rey: The Getty Conservation Institute.

Bishop, Ronald L., Robert L. Rands, and George R. Holley
1982 Ceramic Compositional Analysis in Archaeological Perspective. *In* Advances in Archaeological

Method and Theory, Vol. 5. Michael B. Schiffer, ed. Pp. 275–330. New York: Academic Press.

Bishop, Ronald L., Valetta Canouts, Patricia L. Crown, and Suzanne P. De Atley
1990 Sensitivity, Precision, and Accuracy: Their Roles in Ceramic Compositional Data Bases. American Antiquity 55(3):537–546.

Blackman, M. James
1986 Precision in Routine INAA over a Two-Year Period at the NBSR. *In* NBS Reactor: Summary of Activities July 1985 through June 1986. F. J. Shorten, ed. Pp. 122–1126. NBS Technical Note 1231. Washington, DC: U.S. Department of Commerce National Bureau of Standards. U.S. Government Printing Office.

Blackman, M. James, Gil J. Stein, and Pamela B. Vandiver
1993 The Standardization Hypothesis and Ceramic Mass Production: Technological, Compositional, and Metric Indexes of Craft Specialization at Tell Leilan, Syria. American Antiquity 58(1):60–80.

Blanton, Richard E.
1978 Monte Albàn: Settlement Patterns at the Ancient Zapotec Capital. New York: Academic Press.

Blanton, Richard E., Stephen A. Kowalewski, Gary M. Feinman, and Laura M. Finsten
1993 Ancient Mesoamerica: A Comparison of Change in Three Regions. Cambridge: University Press.

Castanzo, Ronald A.
2003 Tepeaca Kiln Project, Final Report. Report submitted to the Foundation for the Advancement of Mesoamerican Studies Inc., Florida: Crystal River.

Castanzo, Ronald A.
2002 The Development of Socioeconomic Complexity in the Formative Period Central Puebla-Tlaxcala Basin, Mexico. Unpublished Ph.D. Dissertation, Pennsylvania State University, University Park, Pennsylvania.

Castanzo, Ronald A., and Kenneth G. Hirth
2008 El Asentamiento del Periodo Formativo en la Cuenca Central de Puebla-Tlaxcala, México. *In* Ideología Política y Sociedad en el Periodo

Formativo. Ann Cyphers and Kenneth G. Hirth, eds. México: Universidad Nacional Autónoma de México.

Castanzo, Ronald A., and J. Heath Anderson
2004 Formative Period Lime Kilns in Puebla, Mexico. Mexicon 26(4):86–90.

Cordova F. de A., Carlos, Ana L. Martin del Pozzo, and Javier L. Camacho
1994 Palaeolandforms and Volcanic Impact on the Environment of Prehistoric Cuicuilco, Southern Mexico City. Journal of Archaeological Science 21:585–596.

Charlton, Thomas H., and Deborah L. Nichols
1997 Diachronic Studies of City-States: Permutations on a Theme. *In* The Archaeology of City-States: Cross-Cultural Approaches. Deborah L. Nichols and Thomas H. Charlton, eds. Pp. 169–207. Washington: Smithsonian Institution Press.

Costin, Cathy L.
2007 Thinking about Production: Phenomenological Classification and Lexical Semantics. *In* Rethinking Craft Specialization in Complex Societies: Archaeological Analyses of the Social Meaning of Production. Zachary Hruby and Rowan Flad, eds. Pp. 143–162. Archaeological papers of the American Anthropological Association no. 17. Berkeley: University of California Press.

Costin, Cathy L.
2001 Production and Exchange of Ceramics. *In* Empire and Domestic Economy. Terence N. D'Altroy and Christine Hastorf, eds. Pp. 203–241. New York: Kluwer Academic/Plenum Publishers.

Costin, Cathy L.
1991 Craft Specialization: Issues in Defining, Documenting, and Explaining the Organization of Production. *In* Archaeological Method and Theory. Michael B. Schiffer, ed. Pp. 1–56. Tucson: The University of Arizona Press.

Costin, Cathy L., and Melissa B. Hagstrum
1995 Standardization, Labor Investment, Skill, and the Organization of Ceramic Production in Late prehispanic highland Peru. American Antiquity 60(4):619–639.

Curet, Antonio
1993 Regional Studies and Ceramic Production Areas: An Example from La Mixtequilla, Veracruz, Mexico. Journal of Field Archaeology 20:427–440.

Drennan, Robert D., and Judith A. Nowack
1984 *In* Trade and Exchange in Early Mesoamerica. Kenneth G. Hirth, ed. Pp. 157–178. Albuquerque: University of New Mexico Press.

Feinman, Gary M.
1999 Rethinking our Assumptions: Economic Specialization at the Household Scale in Ancient Ejutla, Oaxaca, Mexico. *In* Pottery and People, a Dynamic Interaction. James M. Skibo and Gary M. Feinman, eds. Pp. 81–98. Salt Lake City: The University of Utah Press.

Feinman, Gary M., and Andrew Balkansky
1997 Ceramic Firing in Ancient and Modern Oaxaca. *In* The Prehistory and History of Ceramic Kilns. Prudence M. Rice and W. David Kingery, eds. Pp. 129–148. Westerville: The American Ceramic Society.

Flannery, Kent V., and Joyce Marcus
1983a The Cloud People: Divergent Evolution of the Zapotec and Mixtec Civilizations. New York: Academic Press.

Flannery, Kent V., and Joyce Marcus
1983b The Growth of Site Hierarchies in the Valley of Oaxaca: part I. *In* The Cloud People: Divergent Evolution of the Zapotec and Mixtec Civilizations. Kent V. Flannery and Joyce Marcus, eds. Pp. 53–64. New York: Academic Press.

Flannery, Kent V., and Joyce Marcus
1983c The Origins of the State in Oaxaca (Introduction to Chapter 4). *In* The Cloud People: Divergent Evolution of the Zapotec and Mixtec Civilizations. Kent V. Flannery and Joyce Marcus, eds. Pp. 79–83. New York: Academic Press.

Fowler, Melvin L.
1969 A Preclassic Water Distribution System in Amalucan, Mexico. Archaeology 22:208–215.

García Cook, Ángel
1981 The Historical Importance of Tlaxcala in the Cultural Development of the Central Highlands.

In Handbook of Middle American Indians: Supplement 1 Archaeology. Jeremy A. Sabloff, ed. Pp. 244–276. Austin: University of Texas.

García Cook, Ángel
1976 El Desarrollo Cultural Prehispánico en el Norte de Valle Poblano-Tlaxcalteca: Inferencias de una Secuencia Cultural, Espacial y Temporalmente Establecida. Serie Arqueología, Departamento de Monumentos Prehispánicos, 1. Mexico: Instituto Nacional de Antropología e Historia.

García Cook, Ángel, and B. Leonor Merino Carrión
1989a El Formativo en la Región Tlaxcala-Puebla. *In* El Preclasico o Formativo, Avances y Perspectivas, Seminario de Arqueologia "Dr. Roman Piña Chan". Pp. 161–193. Mexico City: Instituto Nacional de Antropología e Historia.

García Cook, Ángel, and B. Leonor Merino Carrión
1989b Historia Prehispanica del Valle Poblano. Puebla: Gobierno del Estado de Puebla, Secretaria de Cultura.

García Cook, Ángel, and B. Leonor Merino Carrión
1988 Notas sobre la Ceramica Prehispanica en Tlaxcala. *In* Ensayos de Alfareria Prehispanica e Historica de Mesoamerica. Mari Carmen Serra and Carlos Navarrete, eds. Pp. 275–342. Mexico: Universidad Nacional Autonoma de Mexico.

García Cook, Ángel, and B. Leonor Merino Carrión
1977 Notas Sobre Caminos y Rutas de Intercambio al Este de la Cuenca de Mexico. Comunicaciones 14:71–82. Fundación Alemana para la Investigación Científica, Puebla.

Garrigós, Jaume B. I., Vassilis Kilikoglou, and Peter M. Day
2001 Chemical and Mineralogical Alteration of Ceramics from a Late Bronze Age Kiln at Kommos, Crete: The Effect on the Formation of a Reference Group. Archaeometry 43(3):349–371.

Gormsen, Erdmann
1978 Weekly Markets in the Puebla Region of Mexico. *In* Market-place Trade: Periodic Markets, Hawkers, and Traders in Africa, Asia, and Latin America. Robert H. T. Smith, ed. Pp. 240–264. Vancouver: Centre for Transportation Studies, University of British Columbia.

Glascock, Michael D.
1992 Neutron Activation Analysis. *In* Chemical Characterization of Ceramic Pastes in Archaeology. Hector Neff, ed. Pp. 11–26. Madison: Prehistory Press.

Grove, David C., Kenneth G. Hirth, David E. Bugè, and Ann M. Cyphers
1976 Settlement and Cultural Development at Chalcatzingo. Science 192:1203–1210.

Hagstrum, Melissa B.
1985 Measuring Prehistoric Ceramic Craft Specialization: A Test Case in the American Southwest. Journal of Field Archaeology 12:65–75.

Halstead, Paul, and John O'Shea
1989 Introduction: Cultural Responses to Risk and Uncertainty. *In* Bad Year Economics: Cultural Responses to Risk and Uncertainty. Paul Halstead and John O'Shea, eds. Pp. 1–7. Cambridge: Cambridge University Press.

Harry, Karen G.
2005 Ceramic Specialization and Agricultural Marginality: Do Ethnographic Models Explain the Development of Specialized Pottery Production in the Prehistoric American Soutwest? American Antiquity 70(2):295–319.

Hayashida, Frances M.
1999 Style, Technology, and State Production: Inka Pottery Manufacture in the Leche Valley, Peru. Latin American Antiquity 10(4):337–352.

Hill, David V.
1994 Technological Analysis: Making and Using Ceramics on Black Mesa. *In* Function and Technology of Anasazi Ceramics from Black Mesa, Arizona. Marion R. Smith, Jr., ed. Pp. 23–45. Southern Illinois University at Carbondale.

Hirth, Kenneth G.
1987 Formative Period Settlement Patterns in the Rio Amatzinac Valley. *In* Ancient Chalcatzingo. David C. Grove, ed. Pp. 343–367. Austin: University of Texas Press.

Licate, Jack A.
1981 Creation of a Mexican Landscape, Territorial Organization and Settlement in the Eastern Puebla

Basin, 1520–1605. Chicago: Department of Geography, The University of Chicago.

Longacre, Willliam A.
1999 Standardization and Specialization: What's the Link? *In* Pottery and People, a Dynamic Interaction. James M. Skibo and Gary M. Feinman, eds. Pp. 44–58. Salt Lake City: The University of Utah Press.

Magness-Gardiner, Bonnie
2003 Pottery Production and Demand in a Middle Bronze Age Levantine village: Ceramic Specialization and Rural Development. *In* The Near East in the Southwest, Essays in Honor of William G. Dever. Beth A. Nakhai, ed. Pp. 117–129. Boston: American Schools of Oriental Research.

McClure, Sarah B.
2007 Gender, Technology, and Evolution: Cultural Inheritance Theory and Prehistoric Potrees in Valencia, Spain. American Antiquity 72(3):485–508.

Michaels, George H.
1989 Craft Specialization in the Early Postclassic of Colha. *In* Research in Economic Anthropology, Supplement 4: Prehistoric Maya Economies of Belize. Patricia A. McAnany and Barry L. Isaac, eds. Pp. 139–183. Greenwich: JAI Press Inc.

Millon, René
1988 The last years of Teotihuacan Dominance. *In* The Collapse of Ancient States and Civilizations. Norman Yoffee and George L. Cowgill, eds. Pp. 102–164. Tucson: The University of Arizona Press.

Mills, Barbara J.
1995 Assessing Organizational Scale in Zuni Ceramic Production: A Comparison of Protohistoric and Historic Collections. Museum Anthropology 19(3):37–46.

Neff, Hector, Daniel O. Larson, and Michael D. Glascock
1997 The Evolution of Anasazi Ceramic Production and Distribution: Compositional Evidence from a Pueblo III site in South-Central Utah. Journal of Field Archaeology 24:473–492.

Payne, William O.
1982 Kilns and Ceramic Technology of Ancient Mesoamerica. *In* Archaeological Ceramics. Jacqueline S. Olin and Alan D. Franklin, eds. Pp. 189–192. Washington, DC: Smithsonian Institution Press.

Peacock, David P. S.
1982 Pottery in the Roman world: An Ethnoarchaeological approach. London: Longman.

Pires-Ferreira, Jane W.
1975 Formative Mesoamerican Exchange Networks with Special Reference to the Valley of Oaxaca. Memoirs of the Museum of Anthropology, University of Michigan, no. 7. Ann Arbor: University of Michigan.

Poblome, Jeroen, Patrick Degryse, Willy Viaene, Raoul Ottenburgs, Marc Waelkens, Roland Degeest, and Jean Naud
2002 The Concept of a Pottery Production Centre. An Archaeometrical Contribution from Ancient Sagalassos. Journal of Archaeological Science 29:873–882.

Pool, Christopher A.
2003 Ceramic Production at Terminal Formative and Classic Period Tres Zapotes. *In* Settlement Archaeology and Political Economy at Tres Zapotes, Veracruz, Mexico. Christopher A. Pool, ed. Pp. 56–68. Los Angeles: The Cotsen Institute of Archaeology.

Pool, Christopher A.
2000 Why a Kiln? Firing Technology in the Sierra de los Tuxtlas, Veracruz (Mexico). Archaeometry 42(1):61–76.

Pool, Christopher A.
1997 Prehispanic Kilns at Matacapan, Veracruz, Mexico. *In* The Prehistory and History of Ceramic kilns. Prudence M. Rice and W. David Kingery, eds. Pp. 149–172. Westerville: The American Ceramic Society.

Pool, Christopher A., and Robert S. Santley
1992 Middle Classic Pottery Economics in the Tuxtla Mountains, Southern Veracruz, Mexico. *In* Ceramic Production and Distribution, an Integrated Approach. George J. Bey III and Christopher A. Pool, eds. Pp. 205–234. Boulder: Westview Press.

Rice, Prudence M.
   1997 Introduction and Overview. *In* The Prehistory and History of Ceramic Kilns. Prudence M. Rice and W. David Kingery, eds. Pp. 1–10. Westerville: The American Ceramic Society.

Rice, Prudence M.
   1991 Specialization, Standardization, and Diversity: A Retrospective. *In* The Ceramic Legacy of Anna O. Shepard. Ronald L. Bishop and Frederick W. Lange, eds. Pp. 257–279. Niwot: University Press of Colorado.

Rice, Prudence M.
   1987 Pottery Analysis, a Sourcebook. Chicago: The University of Chicago Press.

Roux, Valentine
   2003 Ceramic Standardization and Intensity of Production: Quantifying Degrees of Specialization. American Antiquity 68(4):768–782.

Sanders, William T.
   1976 The Agricultural History of the Basin of Mexico. *In* The Valley of Mexico, Studies in Pre-hispanic Ecology and Society. Eric R. Wolf, ed. Pp. 101–159. Albuquerque: University of New Mexico Press.

Sanders, William T., and Robert Santley
   1983 A Tale of Three Cities: Energetics and Urbanization in Prehispanic Central Mexico. *In* Prehistoric Settlement Patterns: Essays in Honor of Gordon R. Willey. Evon Vogt and Richard Leventhal, eds. Pp. 243–291. Albuquerque: University of New Mexico Press.

Sanders, William T., Jeffrey R. Parsons, and Robert S. Santley
   1979 The Basin of Mexico: Ecological Processes in the Evolution of a Civilization. New York: Academic Press.

Santley, Robert S., Philip J. Arnold III, and Christopher A. Pool
   1989 The Ceramics Production System at Matacapan, Veracruz, Mexico. Journal of Field Archaeology 16:107–132.

Schortman, Edward M., and Patricia A. Urban
   2004 Modeling the Roles of Craft Production in Ancient Political Economies. Journal of Archaeological Research 12(2):185–226.

Sillar, Bill
   2000 Dung by Preference: The Choice of Fuel as an Example of how Andean Pottery Production is Embedded within Wider Technical, Social, and Economic Practices. Archaeometry 42(1):43–60.

Sillar, Bill, and Michael S. Tite
   2000 The Challenge of 'Technological Choices' for Materials Science Approaches in Archaeology. Archaeometry 42(1):2–20.

Spielmann, Katherine A.
   2002 Feasting, Craft Specialization, and the Ritual Mode of Production in Small-Scale Societies. American Anthropologist 104(1):195–207.

Stark, Barbara L.
   1992 Ceramic Production in Prehistoric La Mixtequilla, South-Central Veracruz, Mexico. *In* Ceramic Production and Distribution, an Integrated Approach. George J. Bey III and Chrisopher A. Pool, eds. Pp. 205–234. Boulder: Westview Press.

Stark, Barbara L.
   1985 Archaeological Identification of Pottery Production Locations: Ethnoarchaeological and Archaeological data in Mesoamerica. *In* Decoding Prehistoric Ceramics. Ben A. Nelson, ed. Pp. 175–204. Carbondale: Southern Illinois University Press.

Tite, Michael S.
   1999 Pottery Production, Distribution, and Consumption-the Contribution of the Physical Sciences. Journal of Archaeological Method and Theory 6(3):181–233.

Tyrakowski, Konrad
   1978 El Tianguis Central de Tepeaca, Función e Importancia de un Mercado Complejo. Comunicaciones 15:47–60.

Underhill, Anne P.
   1991 Pottery Production in Chiefdoms: the Longshan Period in Northern China. World Archaeology 23(1):12–27.

Urban, Patricia A., E. Christian Wells, and Marne T. Ausec
    1997 The Fires without and the Fires within: Evidence for Ceramic Production Facilities at the Late Classic Site of La Sierra, Naco Valley, Northwestern Honduras, and in its Environs. *In* The Prehistory and History of Ceramic Kilns. Prudence Rice, ed. Pp. 173–194. Westerville: The American Ceramic Society.

Wandibba, Simiyu
    2003 Ceramic Ethnoarchaeology: Some Examples from Kenya. *In* East African Archaeology: Foragers, Potters, Smiths, and Traders. Chapurukha M. Kusimba and Sibel B. Kusimba, eds. Pp. 59–70. Philadelphia: University of Pennsylvania Museum of Archaeology and Anthropology.

Weaver, Muriel P.
    1993 The Aztecs, Maya, and their Predecessors: Archaeology of Mesoamerica. San Diego: Academic.

Werner, Gerd
    1978 Los Suelos de la Cuenca Alta de Puebla-Tlaxcala y sus Alrededores. Puebla: Fundación Alemana para la Investigación Científica.

10

Production and Use of Orchid Adhesives in Aztec Mexico: the Domestic Context

Frances F. Berdan
California State University San Bernardino
Edward A. Stark
Redlands East Valley High School
and
Jeffrey D. Sahagún
California State University San Bernardino

This chapter examines an aspect of craft production typically hidden from view: the production and use of natural materials as adhesives. In Aztec-period Mexico, adhesives were not only a rather ordinary and "invisible" aspect of craft production (compared, say, to flashy feathers or precious stones), they may also be considered a dependent or auxiliary industry. As such, they only have meaning when attached (literally) to something else. In other words, glues are made in association with other activities. It is this very auxiliary feature that makes a study of adhesives particularly informative – not only do glues and gums serve to adhere specific materials, they also provide windows through which to view more general economic interconnections. In the spirit of this more general perspective, our examination of Aztec adhesives offers special insights into the multifaceted world of economic production, distribution, and consumption in ancient households.

In terms of production: many different natural products served as adhesives; adhesive products were available in a wide range of ecological zones; the scheduling of production processes was generally harmonious with other typical rural household activities; the production of adhesives could make use of an age- and gender-differentiated labor pool, such as commonly found in household settings; adhesives

were easy to make, utilizing a small and cheap toolkit that was already available in most domestic contexts; and the materials were not re-cycled. Overall, fresh adhesives were constantly needed and investment in this production effort would have represented little risk.

In terms of economic distribution: adhesives were potentially storable for significant periods of time, they could be processed for convenient transport, and partially processed adhesives were sold in markets.

And in terms of consumption: adhesives were needed and used on a wide array of manufactured objects, were required for both luxury and utilitarian wares, and were used in both manufacturing and repairing processes; adhesives were a high-demand item not particularly subject to large fluctuations in demand; mosaic makers, who were necessary adhesive consumers, often acquired adhesives already partially-processed, and there are indications that the elite craft of mosaic manufacturing was carried out, at least in some cases, in household contexts.

This chapter examines these dimensions more closely by focusing on orchids as adhesives, drawing on data primarily from ethnohistoric documents, ethnographic investigations, experimental research, and chemical analyses. In Aztec Mexico orchid gums were applied primarily to feather

ARCHEOLOGICAL PAPERS OF THE AMERICAN ANTHROPOLOGICAL ASSOCIATION, Vol. 19, Issue 1, pp. 148–156, ISSN 1551-823X,
online ISSN 1551-8248. DOI: 10.1111/j.1551-8248.2009.01018.x.

mosaics which were used as military regalia, ritual paraphernalia and in elite daily life, displays and gifts. Therefore, this chapter also ascertains the role of orchids in producing these exquisite devices.

Essentials of the Production of Orchid Adhesives in Aztec Mexico

The Aztecs (more properly Mexica) and their neighbors produced adhesives from a variety of natural vegetal substances. In addition to the orchids discussed here, numerous substances were used as adhesives by the Aztecs and their neighbors. Copal was prominent, found as an adhesive on several extant stone mosaics (see Berdan et al., n.d.; McEwan et al. 2006). Pine resin has also been encountered on stone mosaics, occasionally mixed with copal (McEwan et al. 2006), and excellent recent studies of copal and pine resin have been conducted by Victoria Lona (2004) and Tripplett (1999). A recent experiment reconstructing an Aztec macquahuitl used a mixture of copal and pine resin (Cervera Obregón 2007). Beeswax also appears as an adhesive, in one case on a feather mosaic (Filloy Nadal et al. 2006) and in others as a repair or probable repair (Berdan et al. n.d., McEwan et al. 2006). Gum from the stems of the *tzinacancuitlaquahuitl* ("bat-excrement tree") secured obsidian blades to clubs, and when mixed with an unspecified resin, was effective in sealing letters and other papers in colonial times (Hernández 1959, I: 187; II: 407). A different type of adhesive was obtained from the glutinous roots of *tecpatli* plants and was used specifically to capture small birds (Hernández 1959, I: 177–178). These sticky roots (probably mashed and mixed with water) were spread on the grass or sticks at the birds' known dining and drinking spots, thus ensnaring the unwary birds (Sahagún 1963: 133; Plata Contreras and Montes Meneses 1982: 268). Additionally, gum from mesquite (Nahuatl: *mizquitl*) trees provided "an excellent gum Arabic" (Hernández 1959, II: 32–33), and that from acacia was used for mending pottery (Martínez Cortés 1974: 111–112). The fruit of the *chapona* tree, common in southern Mesoamerica, produces a glutinous latex; it is used today in El Salvador to seal cigarette papers (Miranda 1998: 249). Several of these substances also had medicinal value (Berdan et al. n.d.). The Huasteca region produces valuable gum plants: Alcorn (1984) mentions the use of gums from the orchid *Encyclia cochleata* in the gluing of musical instruments, and a Nahua man from the same region identified a small tree as *tzacuhtli* (glue), although it is clearly not an orchid (Alan Sandstrom, personal communication, April 1998). The use of this last gum suggests that there were more known natural adhesives than were recorded in the available documentation.

Resource Availability

The wide variety of plants that produced useful, sticky gums meant that adhesive substances were broadly available to the Mesoamerican population. Among these was an orchid (or orchids) termed *tzacuhtli*, although there is some disagreement as to the identification of this orchid. It was initially identified as Encyclia pastoris (an epiphytic orchid) by La Llave and Lexarza (1881), and others, such as Urbina (1903) and Martínez Cortés (1974) have followed this lead. However, we feel this identification is unlikely for a number of reasons. Primary among them is that this plant, as depicted in Hernández (1959, I: 119), more closely resembles a terrestrial rather than an epiphytic orchid. Encyclia pastoris develops only one or two pseudobulbs annually that grow along the rhizome or "creeping ground stem" (Wiard 1987: 26). This process tends to separate rather than clump the pseudobulbs; the image in Hernández shows the bulbs "clumped." We feel that the description and depiction more closely resemble a terrestrial *Bletia* or *Govenia* orchid.

Among these various orchids, some were considered "better" adhesives than others. So, for instance, we read that *tzacuhtli* offered "an excellent and very tenacious adhesive" while its close relative *chichiltictepetzacuxochitl* (probably Laelia autumnalis or Laelia speciosa, epiphytic orchids [see Linares and Bye 2006: 51; Berdan et al., n.d.]) produced a "less esteemed" gum, although we are not told why (Hernández 1959, I: 117). One clue to these differences is provided by our gum-processing experiments, which revealed that the roots of terrestrial orchids are easier to process and yield stronger gums than the pseudobulbs of epiphytic orchids, which tend to be much more fibrous than the roots of terrestrial ones, and therefore more difficult to reduce to a fine, usable powder. Furthermore, not all adhesive substances "worked" equally well for all types of projects. Our experiments with various plant gums suggest that they varied significantly in adhesive qualities, especially depending on their specific applications. For example, delicate, transparent orchid gums were perfectly suited for the manufacture of feather mosaics while the thicker and gummier copal and pine resins worked especially well with fine greenstone mosaics.

Specific plants yielding the orchid adhesives were found in somewhat different regions and ecological zones; gum-yielding orchids were (and are) found in highlands, lowlands, and points in between. Some places were known for these products. For instance, the northern Puebla town of Tzauctlan (from *tzacuhtli*) was noted for a locally available orchid and its desirable gum, at least in the early 17th century. So while gummy orchids as a whole were widely available, it was not the case that any specific variety sought was locally available. Nonetheless, gum-producing plants (orchids in this case) were found in rural and especially in forested areas, and were particularly accessible to rural householders.

Scheduling

The scheduling of gum acquisition and production responded to several factors. The first of these involves the natural availability and life cycle of the resources. Orchid roots/pseudobulbs are available year-round. However, there are some meaningful scheduling patterns, revealed ethnographically and suggested experimentally. First, we have discovered that the adhesive quality of orchid gums is tied to the plant's life cycle: while orchids yield adequate adhesives at any time of year, young bulbs attached to leaves and spikes are stickier than older bulbs of the same plant, and they are also easier to process. Therefore, these plants will yield the highest-quality gum during their active growing periods. This is typically during the rainy season, which is also usually the busiest time in the agricultural cycle (see Costin 1991: 17).

The second factor concerns how these resource patterns relate to the overall rhythms of household production. Collection of orchid roots or pseudobulbs can be an intermittent task, although we must rely on ethnographic parallels to suggest that this was the case in Aztec times. Where such gums are still used today, they are normally gathered on an "as-needed" basis (see below). Collection of orchid gums may produce no particular labor hardship for a rural household, as these plants are often found in and around areas of milpa agriculture. Nonetheless, in their scheduling of orchid-gum gathering, a household may need to choose between expediency (collecting older roots/bulbs in the dry season) and quality (exploiting younger roots/bulbs in the busier rainy season).

And third, special events periodically may have called for the production of gums "on the spot." For instance, today the Tarahumara collect terrestrial orchid roots (*Bletia sp.*) in late winter-early spring to provide adhesives in their manufacture of musical instruments for use in Easter celebrations. They follow this timing despite the fact that the plants are not readily visible at that time of year (Wyndham 2004).

Figure 1. Children making glue for featherwork mosaic-makers.

Division of Labor

Collecting and processing plant gums is not a particularly arduous or complicated undertaking and could have drawn on virtually any able-bodied member of a household's diverse labor pool: male or female, young or old. For instance, children may have served as knowledgeable collectors and processors of orchids and their gums. Among the Tarahumara, children easily identify orchid gum plants, even in the dry season (Felice Wyndham, personal communication, August 2006). In the Huasteca, school children collect the sap of a small tree for glue (Alan Sandstrom, personal communication 1998). Similarly, Tzotzil school children boil the bulbs of two orchid species and use them for glue (Breedlove and Laughlin 2000: 267). In the sixteenth century, children (or young apprentices) made the orchid gums for the luxury featherworking artisans (Figure 1; Sahagún 1959: 95; 1956: 84). Children were certainly capable of contributing to this enterprise. In another vein, some of the orchid gum processing involves grinding dried bulbs and roots, drawing on techniques and motions finely-honed by women of most rural households (see below).

Transferability of Technology and Techniques

Orchid gums are readily acquired and easily produced for use. The toolkit is small and consists almost entirely of materials already present in a rural household. The good news: any given household requires essentially no capital investment to undertake this auxiliary production activity. The bad news: the process is virtually invisible in the archaeological record, as the implements used in processing gums are redundant with other, usually more prominent, household activities.

The ethnohistoric record gives us three recipes for producing adhesives from orchids. Hernández (1959, I: 118–19) tells us that the roots (or perhaps pseudobulbs) were cut into small pieces, dried in the sun, ground into a powder, and "prepared." Sahagún (1961: 87; 1956: 150) provides two recipe variations: the plant (roots or pseudobulbs) was trimmed, pulverized with a stone, and sold uncooked. Alternatively, the roots were cleaned, soaked, pounded, dried in the sun, and then finely ground up after they were dry. It is entirely possible that these different procedures were applied to different types of orchids. Also, our re-creation of the recipes offered by Sahagún suggests that the techniques described by him were not well suited to storage and transport; it is possible that these recipes were more commonly used more immediately by the consuming household itself (Wyndham 2004). Whatever procedure was employed, the necessary tools would have been readily available in most rural households: digging stick, cutting blade (obsidian worked well for us), *molcajete* or similar grinding implement, storage/carrying container, and bowl and stick for mixing the concoction. Our experiments also suggest that some kind of sieve would have been especially useful in rendering the dried material into a sufficiently fine powder. It was also convenient that the techniques used in orchid gum collection and preparation would have mimicked existing, well-honed household skills: digging roots, slicing plants, and grinding up vegetal material.

Risk

With this relatively minimal investment, households took very little risk in undertaking this additional economic activity. The tool kit was available and unspecialized, the techniques replicated those already well known within rural households, and the labor requirements could be fulfilled by a range of household members and be scheduled sporadically and opportunistically. In addition, since orchid adhesives were not recycled, and their applications were not particularly seasonal, there was a relatively continuous demand for these products. The collecting and processing of orchid gums fits well into Kenneth Hirth's notion of "intermittent crafting" presented in chapter two of this volume. It "compliments and diversifies the to-

tal household subsistence strategy" [page 21] as an auxiliary enterprise unlikely to develop as a fully specialized activity.

Essentials of the Distribution of Orchid Adhesives in Aztec Mexico

In its initial stages, the production of adhesives from orchids was largely a partial industry; that is, full preparation of the product often did not take place in those households engaged in its collection. As such, much of this production would have been geared toward external consumers, reaching them through central Mexico's extensive market system (see Brumfiel 1987). Fortunately, properly dried and powdered orchid gums could be stored for long periods of time and could be efficiently transported. However, our experiments revealed that, if not fully dried, the orchid material will quickly mold. Drying the sliced orchids during the rainy season may have been a bit tricky, although thorough drying only required 48 hours or less in our experiments. We also conducted preliminary experiments with making "cakes" of the powders as a means of transporting them; the jury is still out on this possibility.

The glue (*tzacuhtli*) sellers are listed among those who sold their products in the urban Tlatelolco marketplace; it was therefore a sufficiently significant item to warrant its own description (Sahagún 1961: 87). Nonetheless, we probably should not get too excited by this: the glue seller is bracketed by the broom and pine resin sellers, with rubber, liquidambar, smoking tube, and bitumen sellers nearby in this rather miscellaneous area of the market (ibid.). Like most of the other vendors in Sahagún's account, the glue-sellers were not above adulterating their product by selling it "coarsely ground, with pulverized maize stalks, with ground grains of maize, with ground beans" (ibid.). This also suggests a higher value for the glue than for maize and beans.

Tzacuhtli glues were sold in the market as a powder. This is not surprising, as our experiments have shown that the orchid roots and pseudobulbs lose an average of 90% of their weight when processed into a powder, and that they also preserve well in that form (Berdan et al., n.d.). This also makes practical economic sense, especially if the sources of the orchids were at some distance from the market, and given that all transport was on foot or by canoe (see also Costin 1991: 14). This points to sequential production events, with the initial processing occurring at the sources of the raw material, and the final gum-making provided by the consumers who, in this case, were for the most part also producers themselves, manufacturing complex luxury objects.

Essentials of the Use of Orchid Adhesives in Aztec Mexico

Being sold in the market, these pre-processed materials were available to all consumers: commoners and elites, independent and attached specialists. It is likely that among the purchasers were the fine mosaic makers, since orchid gums were essential to the manufacturers of fine feather mosaics. If we look briefly at these luxury specialists, we see the movement of partially-processed gums from farming households to more upscale settings. What was the institutional context of these subsequent settings? Is there evidence to suggest that these luxury endeavors also took place in households?

The feather mosaic manufacturers, using orchid gums as an essential element in their enterprises, operated as both independent and attached specialists (Costin 1991; Brumfiel and Earle 1987). Sahagún (1959: 91–92) distinguishes among three types of featherworkers: those of the palace and serving as artisans of the ruler (*tecpan amanteca*), those of the royal treasury house (*calpiscan amanteca*), and those who operated privately (*calla amanteca*). Each specialized in particular types of featherwork, the last group, according to the good friar, working "exclusively in devices which they made (and) sold: perhaps shields, or shirts of yellow parrot feathers – whatsoever they made" (Sahagún 1959: 91–92). This is interesting, since Costin (1991: 11–12) suggests, reasonably, that "emblems of power and prestige" would more likely be produced by attached specialists under the watchful eye of the elite and powerful. Yet here we have an instance of objects displaying such information being produced by independent artisans.

The first two types of featherworkers, attached to the palace and the state storehouses, produced the ruler's fancy array, specially designed warrior and elite regalia (Figure 2), palatial decorations and probably temple and ceremonial adornments. These attached artisans would have had access to imperial resources in producing their exquisite creations for the ruler and his elite world. Tribute, ending up in the royal coffers, included regular supplies of precious feathers, fine stones, gold and shells. In addition, these artisans had access to the ruler's personal aviary and zoo.

The private artisans would have had to acquire their materials in the marketplace or perhaps through other more informal channels. In the Tlatelolco market, the merchant of fine feathers and the vendor of unspecified feathers occupied different areas of the market – the one in the high-rent district, the other surrounded by vendors of dyes and herbs (Sahagún 1961: 61, 92). The latter individual split and spun small back and breast feathers, the very ones used extensively by the mosaic makers, especially in the under layers of their creations (Sahagún 1959).

The feathers aside, orchid gums are only recorded as being available in the markets (and not through tribute), and therefore all featherworkers would most likely have obtained that item there. This also would have included certain other individuals (such as accomplished warriors) who possessed feather mosaic objects and required gums for repairs. Unfortunately, there is precious little information on how repairs (of anything) were made. One clue, from Durán (1994: 167), states that individual warriors were responsible for repairs to their own shields following a military engagement. Perhaps these warriors repaired their shields in their own households, perhaps they employed professional featherworkers to do the work.

The construction of feather mosaics was a complicated process, requiring finely-honed skills and a wide array of materials. Even a cursory perusal of the booty and inventories listed in Saville (1920), and an examination of extant mosaic pieces reveals that most fancy objects made of luxury materials (e.g., feathers, shells, precious stones and metals) were manufactured using combinations of these materials. So while Sahagún describes these crafts as separate enterprises, the artisans were quite interdependent and relied on each others' expertise and materials. This may have been most easily facilitated among various attached specialists who quite likely worked at palaces in close proximity to one another.

Feather mosaic fashioning involved a number of steps, some of which could be easily divided among a number of workers. These creations were built up of layers of feathers attached to paper and unspun cotton; it would have been efficient to have several artisans working simultaneously on these separate pieces (see Filloy Nadal et al. 2006). Indeed, Sahagún (1959: 93–96) phrases his descriptions in terms of at least more than one artisan. Juan de Torquemada is more specific in describing the fashioning of colonial feather creations by native artisans:

> ...if there are twenty artisans, they all make an image together, and dividing among themselves the figure of the image, into so many parts, however many there are, each one [artisan] takes his piece to make it at his house, and afterwards each one returns with it [the finished piece], and they all join together, and in this way the perfect and completed image results, as if one artisan had done the work (1969, vol. III: 210; translation, underlining and brackets: FB).

Close examination of a 16th century colonial feather triptych at the Metropolitan Museum of Art in New York City (by Berdan in 2000) is mute testimony to this process described by Torquemada. The workmanship of this piece clearly reveals the input of at least three different artisans, one for each part of the tripartite artifact. The most

Figure 2. Achieved warriors in their feathered regalia.

meticulous work is found in the middle section (probably executed by a master artisan), while the featherworker constructing the left panel was more adept than his partner on the right. In addition to variable skill level, these artisans also had different manners of executing similar motifs. For instance, little brick motifs created by the middle (master) artisan were all fashioned individually and then set together to make the overall design; the little bricks on the side panels were laid in strips. The final product is not so ideally uniform in quality and style as Torquemada's description suggests.

While these examples derive from colonial times, featherwork continued to be carried on much as it had been in preconquest times. The major change was in the imagery of the works which largely followed Christian iconography. Nonetheless, Sahagún (1959: 92) emphasizes that "As the ancient feather workers left (and) established their traditions, so (those of today) go on learning their craft; for the same expert work is demanded for ornamenting today" (latter half of the 16th century).

Torquemada's mention of featherworking tasks accomplished in individual households is intriguing. So too are some other suggestions of household production of these luxury objects. The Codex Mendoza (Berdan and Anawalt 1992, vol. III: folio 57r) depicts four craft symbols relevant at the birth of a baby boy (Figure 3). The accompanying text indicates that "they carried [the baby boy] with

The midwife

The symbols

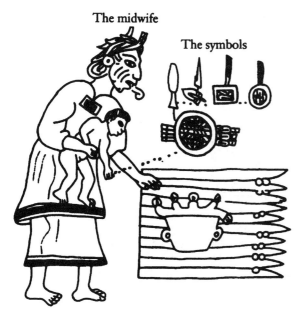

Figure 3. Symbols associated with the birth of a child.

Master featherworker

Son of the master

Figure 4. A father teaches featherworking skills to his son.

his symbol in his hand; and the symbol was the tool used by the infant's father, whether of the military or professions like metalworker, woodcarver, or whatever other profession" (Berdan and Anawalt 1992, vol. IV: folio 56v). Among the symbols is that of the featherworker. Further, this same codex (Berdan and Anawalt 1992, vol. IV: folio 70r) illustrates a master featherworker teaching his son the trade (Figure 4). The Spanish explanation (Berdan and Anawalt 1992, vol. IV: folio 69v) specifies that "the masters of the trades taught the professions to their sons, from childhood, so that when grown to manhood they might pursue these trades and spend their time usefully." Some of their early "useful time" was undoubtedly spent in mixing orchid gums for the mosaics, as this was the task of "the children who were being trained" (Sahagún 1959: 95). Nor were the girls and women neglected in these activities. A noble girl was exhorted by her father to understand "how to be an artisan, how to be a feather worker" (Sahagún 1969: 96). These statements indicate family-oriented and family-transmitted enterprises.

With the household mobilized, the creation of actual feathered objects required a well-honed organization of production activities. Some of these were necessarily sequenced (such as the placement of precious feathers on top of ordinary ones), others were on-going (such as the dyeing of feathers), while others were on-call (such as the mixing of the orchid gums). This last activity, the domain of children, highlights the intermittent nature of gum-making. Yet intermittent as it was, it was not random but rather was tied tightly to the activities of the other artisans in the household.

The question remains as to whether these sources refer to independent or attached featherworkers (or both). The descriptions would readily fit independent artisans, particularly in their need to mobilize the full range of household labor. Attached featherworkers were, according to Sahagún (1959: 91), housed separately by the ruler: "He gave them a house of their own. The feather artisans of Tenochtitlan and Tlatelolco mingled with one another." This suggests that these luxury artisans were resettled and perhaps grouped close to the ruler's palace. It also suggests that this "housing" was not just a place to work, but a place to live, probably with the artisan's full household and full array of age and gender contributors. If so, then the descriptions of featherworking as a household enterprise would hold for both independent and attached artisans. We recognize that this pertained specifically to Tenochtitlan, where our information is most abundant. However, ornate featherworking was a pervasive and valued activity carried on throughout Mesoamerica in the Postclassic period, and long preceded the hegemony of the Aztecs.

A Brief Conclusion

This chapter has approached the matter of household economies from the perspective of one small industry: the production, distribution, and consumption of orchid gums as adhesives. In its initial production stages in rural settings, it was embedded in and consistent with other household tasks and demands. Partially processed, it was conveniently transported to markets where it would have been frequently purchased by manufacturers of complicated and exquisite feather mosaics. In this new, high-end setting, the orchid powders were finally processed into strong yet delicate gums by the feather artisans. In the final analysis, more than one type of household was involved in rendering these gums into their final form, and these households differed considerably in status and complexity of economic production activities.

How may we characterize this little yet essential industry? In the first place, Kenneth Hirth's concept of intermittent crafting is particularly apt, whether the activities took place in rural agricultural or luxury crafting households. Second, this was an auxiliary industry or contingent craft, in that it was necessarily attached to other production activities. Third, we may also consider this a transfer industry, in that it utilized extant technologies, techniques, and labor and hence reduced overhead and risk. And finally, it was also a partial industry in terms of any single household, requiring available and predictable channels of exchange for its sequential production stages. In general, this brief foray into Aztec-period orchid adhesives suggests that investigations into such small-scale and relatively invisible aspects of technology have the potential to yield insights into the interconnections of different levels of complex economic systems.

References

Alcorn, Janis B.
1984 Huastec Mayan Ethnobotany. Austin: University of Texas Press.

Berdan, Frances F., and Patricia Rieff Anawalt
1992 The Codex Mendoza. 4 vols. Berkeley: University of California Press.

Berdan, Frances F., David F. Maynard, and Edward A. Stark
n.d. Reconstructing Aztec Super Glue. Manuscript in preparation.

Breedlove, Dennis E., and Robert M. Laughlin
2000 The Flowering of Man: A Tzotzil Botany of Zinacantan. Washington: Smithsonian Institution Press.

Brumfiel, Elizabeth M.
1987 Elite and Utilitarian Crafts in the Aztec State. *In* Specialization, Exchange, and Complex Societies. Elizabeth M. Brumfiel and Timothy K. Earle, eds. Pp. 102–118. Cambridge: Cambridge University Press.

Brumfiel, Elizabeth M., and Timothy K. Earle
1987 Specialization, Exchange, and Complex Societies: an introduction. *In* Specialization, Exchange, and Complex Societies. Elizabeth M. Brumfiel and Timothy K. Earle, eds. Pp. 1–9. Cambridge: Cambridge University Press.

Cervera Obregón, Marco
2007 El *macuahuitl*: una arma del posclásico tardío en Mesoamérica. Arqueología Mexicana XIV(84):60–65.

Costin, Cathy Lynne
1991 Craft Specialization: Issues in Defining, Documenting, and Explaining the Organization of Production. Archaeological Method and Theory 3:1–56.

Durán, Diego
1994 The History of the Indies of New Spain. Doris Heyden, transl. Norman: University of Oklahoma Press.

Filloy Nadal, Laura, Felipe Solís Olguín, and Lourdes Navarijo
2006 Un eccezionale mosaico di piume azteco: il "coprecalice" del Museo Nacional de Antropología. *In* Gli Aztechi tra passato e presente. Alessandro Lupo, Leonardo López Luján, and Luisa Migliorati, eds. Pp. 105–115. Roma: Carocci editore.

Hernández, Francisco
1959 Historia natural de Nueva España. 2 vols (vols. 2 and 3 of Obras Completas). Mexico City: Universidad Nacional de Mexico.

La Llave, P. de la, and J. Lexarza
1881 Novorum Vegetabilium, 1824. Mexico. Reprint by the Sociedad Mexicana de la Historia Natural, Mexico.

Linares, Edelmira, and Robert Bye
2006 Las Plantas Ornamentales en la Obra de Francisco Hernández. Arqueología Mexicana XIII(78):48–57.

Martínez Cortés, Fernando
1974 Pegamentos, gomas y resinas en el México prehispánico. Mexico: Secretaría de Educación Pública. SepSetentas 124.

Maynard, David, and Frances F. Berdan
n.d. The Adhesive and Repair Material on Pakal's Mask. *In* Mysteries of a Maya Face: The Funerary Mask of Pakal II. Boulder: University Press of Colorado. In press.

McEwan, Colin, Andrew Middleton, Carolina Cartwright, and Rebecca Stacey

2006 Turquoise Mosaics from Mexico. London: The British Museum.

Miranda, Faustino
1998 Vegetación de Chiapas. Third edition. Mexico: Gobierno de Chiapas and Conaculta.

Molina, Fray Alonso de
1970 Vocabulario en lengua castellana y mexicana, y mexicana y castellana. Mexico: Editorial Porrua.

Plata Conreras, Buenaventura, and Jorge Montes Meneses
1982 Liga (Iostephane heterophylla Cav.) Planta Usada Popularmente Como Pegamento y Cicatrizante. *In* Memorias del Simposio de Etnobotánica. Alicia Bárcenas, Alfredo Barrera, Javier Caballero, and Leonel Durán, eds. Pp. 266–270. Mexico: Instituto Nacional de Antropología e Historia.

Sahagún, Bernardino de
1956 Historia General de las Cosas de Nueva España. Angel Maria Garibay K., ed. Mexico: Editorial Porrua.
1959 Florentine Codex: General History of the Things of New Spain, Book 9: The Merchants. Charles E. Dibble and Arthur J. O. Anderson, eds. and trans. Salt Lake City: University of Utah Press.
1961 Florentine Codex: General History of the Things of New Spain, Book 10: The People. Charles E. Dibble and Arthur J. O. Anderson, eds. and trans. Salt Lake City: University of Utah Press.
1963 Florentine Codex: General History of the Things of New Spain, Book 11: Earthly Things. Charles E. Dibble and Arthur J. O. Anderson, eds. and trans. Salt Lake City: University of Utah Press.
1969 Florentine Codex: General History of the Things of New Spain, Book 6: Rhetoric and Moral Philosophy. Charles E. Dibble and Arthur J. O. Anderson, eds. and trans. Salt Lake City: University of Utah Press.

Saville, Marshall H.
1920 The Goldsmith's Art in Ancient Mexico. New York: Museum of the American Indian Heye Foundation, Indian Notes and Monographs.

Torquemada, Juan de
1969 Monarquia Indiana. 3 vols. Mexico: Editorial Porrua.

Tripplett, Kirsten Jill
1999 The Ethnobotany of Plant Resins in the Maya Cultural Regions on Southern Mexico and Central America. Ph.D. dissertation, University of Texas at Austin.

Urbina, Manuel
1903 Nota acerca de los 'tzauhtli' u orquídeas mexicanas. Anales del Museo Nacional de Mexico, 2a. época I:54.

Victoria Lona, Naoli
2004 El Copal en las Ofrendas del Templo Mayor de Tenochtitlan. Tesis para Licenciada en Arqueología, Escuela Nacional de Antropología e Historia, INAH. Mexico.

Wiard, Leon A.
1987 An Introduction to the Orchids of Mexico. Ithaca: Comstock Publishing Associates.

Wyndham, Felice
2004 Learning Ecology: Ethnobotany in the Sierra Tarahumara, Mexico. Ph.D. dissertation: University of Georgia.

Yetman, David
2002 The Guarijios of the Sierra Madre. Albuquerque: University of New Mexico Press.

11

Intermittent Domestic Lapidary Production during the Late Formative Period at Nativitas, Tlaxcala, Mexico

Kenneth G. Hirth
Penn State University
Mari Carmen Serra Puche
Universidad Nacional Autónoma de Mexico
Jesus Carlos Lazcano Arce
Universidad Nacional Autónoma de Mexico
and
Jason De León
University of Washington

"The lapidary [is] well reared, well advised; a counselor, informed in his art; an abrader, a polisher; one who works with sand; who glues [mosaic] with thick glue, works with abrasive sand, rubs [stones] with fine cane, makes them shine...The bad lapidary... scrapes [the stones] who roughens them; who raises a clattering din. [He is] stupid, bird[-like]. He scrapes [the stones]; roughens, shatters, pulverizes, ruins, damages them; raises a clattering din." (Sahagún 1961:28)

Lapidary work was an important craft in prehispanic Mesoamerica. Lapidary craftsman made a variety of the precious ornamental regalia worn by rulers and elite members of society. These regalia ranged from beads, labrets and earspools, to pendants and mosaic masks. Sahagún identifies the lapidary craftsman by the work done and the technology employed to produce finished goods. In the preceding epigraph Sahagún identifies the lapidary as one who abrades, cuts, drills, polishes, and fashions a variety of materials. While Sahagún (1959:80–81, 1961:28) focuses on the precious materials that the lapidary processed (jade, turquoise, amethyst, opal, and rock crystal), archaeological investiga-

tions indicate that they also worked an array of semi-precious items including shell, slate, pyrite, and obsidian (Charlton et al. 1991; Di Peso 1974; Hempenius Turner 1987; Otis Charlton 1993).

The study of prehispanic lapidary work is important for two reasons. First, most of the items produced were items of personal adornment and costume regalia. These goods helped mark the status of the individuals who wore them and were used in ceremonies and ritual enactments at all levels of society. Lapidary items were high value goods that were used in burial and ritual contexts throughout Mesoamerica from the Early Formative period onward. Second, lapidary work is one of the prestige good production systems that can be readily studied using archaeological data. Although production debitage is small, lapidary work produces durable waste in the form of cutout debitage, shatter, partially drilled and broken pieces, tools, adhesives, and abrasives (Charlton et al. 1991; Costin 1991; Kenoyer et al. 1991; Kovacevich 2007; Rochette, this volume; Widmer, this volume). Study of where lapidary work took place,

ARCHEOLOGICAL PAPERS OF THE AMERICAN ANTHROPOLOGICAL ASSOCIATION, Vol. 19, Issue 1, pp. 157–173, ISSN 1551-823X, online ISSN 1551-8248.

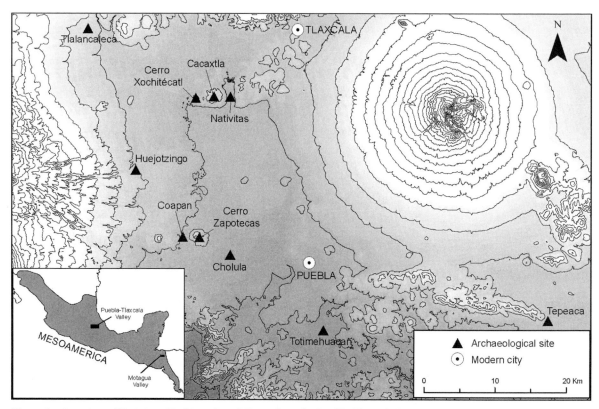

Figure 1. Location of Nativitas, Xochitecatl, and Cacaxtla in the Puebla-Tlaxcala Basin.

and how these goods were controlled and distributed is fundamental to the study of the structure and operation of prestige goods economies throughout Mesoamerica and elsewhere.

During the Formative period, many areas of Mesoamerica were organized as ranked societies in which the circulation of prestige goods played an important role in regulating social relations within and between groups (Aizpurúa and McAnany 1999; Clark and Blake 1994; Dalton 1977; Lesure 1999; Smith and Schortman 1989). Emerging elite are believed to have sponsored the production of prestige goods and controlled their distribution as a strategy of building social clientages within society (Brumfiel and Earle 1987; Earle 2002; Hayden 2001; Lesure 1999; Peregrine 1991; Schortman and Urban 1992). While the prestige goods economy is an important theoretical framework for understanding the emergence of complex society, very little is known about how prestige goods were produced, used, or circulated in social contexts in Mesoamerica.

This presentation examines the evidence for lapidary craft production recovered in 1998 and 2000 at the rural site of Nativitas, Tlaxcala, Mexico (Figure 1). Excavations here recovered evidence for the manufacture of jade beads and other small lapidary items from a Late Formative (550–150

B.C.) household located on Terrace 5 (Figure 2). The location of a lapidary craftsman manufacturing high value prestige goods in a rural domestic workshop was an unexpected surprise. The obvious questions were how was this household obtaining the raw material it worked and for whom was it producing the finished goods? The Terrace 5 household was not located near a civic-precinct or attached to an elite residence, which suggests that the artisan was an independent craftsman who produced lapidary goods as a part the household's normal subsistence regime. We characterize the lapidary as being male because that is how Sahagún (1961:28) describes and depicts this artisan in the Florentine Codex. Nevertheless, the work is not physically demanding and would not preclude female participation in production activities. The evidence for lapidary production is presented here along with a discussion of what crafting on Terrace 5 indicates about the organization of domestic craft production during the Late Formative period. This evidence consists of worked and unworked raw material, partially worked and broken artifacts, and several types of tools used in lapidary manufacturing. Nativitas lapidary production is best modeled as intermittent production by an artisan residing in a household whose primary activities were focused on subsistence agriculture.

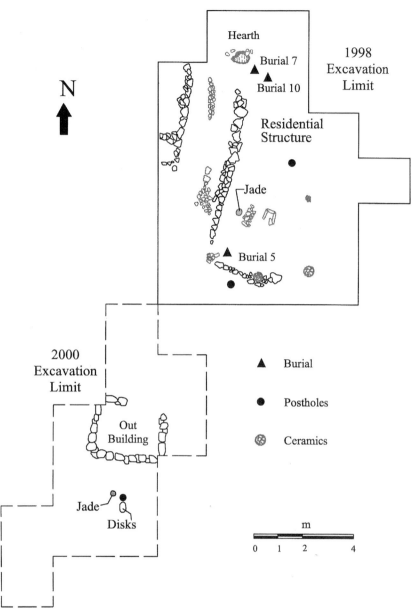

Figure 2.   Terrace 5 Features.

The Site of Nativitas

The site of Nativitas is located in the eastern hill region of the Bloque Nativitas-Xochitécatl in the northern Puebla-Tlaxcala valley 23 km northwest of the city of Puebla, Mexico (Figure 1). The Bloque Nativitas-Xochitécatl consists of a series of low hills and mesas covering approximately 10 sq km. It was an important area of prehispanic settlement in the northern valley of Puebla-Tlaxcala, with major occupations during the Late Formative (550–150 B.C.) and Epiclassic periods (A.D. 650–850) (Serra Puche 1998).

Two well known sites are located here. The earliest of these was the large site of Xochitécatl which was the center of a powerful chiefdom during the Late Formative period (Armillas 1995a, 1995b; Dávila 1975; Serra Puche 1998; Spranz 1970, 1978). The other important center was the site of Cacaxtla which rose to power during the Epiclassic period after the decline of Teotihuacan (Armillas 1995a; Foncerrada de Molina 1993). Both of these sites are located along the western margins of the Bloque Nativitas-Xochitécatl where they overlook the agriculturally productive Puebla-Tlaxcala valley.

Settlement survey has documented prehispanic occupation throughout the Bloque Nativitas-Xochitécatl (García Cook 1981; Serra Puche 1998). One important area was the hill overlooking the modern town of Nativitas, located three km east of the important civic-ceremonial center of Xochitécatl. The site of Nativitas was a dispersed rural community with two major occupations. The earliest was during the Late Formative period, contemporaneous with the site of Xochitécatl, while the later coincided with the growth of Cacaxtla.

Both the Late Formative and Epiclassic were periods of regional competition within the Puebla-Tlaxcala valley (García Cook 1981; Mountjoy and Peterson 1973). During the Late Formative period the Puebla-Tlaxcala valley appears to have been divided up into a series of competing chiefdoms with large centers located at Xochitécatl, Tlalancaleca, Totimehuacan, Coapan, and possibly Cholula (Carballo and Pluckhahn 2007; Dávila 1975; García Cook 1981; Mora 1975) (Figure 1). The Epiclassic was also a period of political turmoil and regional competition in Central Mexico after the decline of Teotihuacan (Diehl and Berlo 1989). During both periods a good portion of rural settlement appears to have moved to the margins of the valley and onto defendable hillsides. This seems to have occurred at the end of the Classic period around Cholula where significant rural population growth occurred on Cerro Zapotecas located 3 km west of the Cholula pyramid (Mountjoy and Peterson 1973) (Figure 1). The occupation at Nativitas grew in response to these larger regional conditions and provided agricultural support for the centers of Xochitécatl and Cacaxtla.

Excavations were conducted at Nativitas between 1998–2004 and 2007–2008 as part of the ongoing *Proyecto Arqueológico El Hombre y sus Recursos en el Sur del Valle de Tlaxcala* under the direction of Mari Carmen Serra Puche and Carlos Lazcano Arce (Serra Puche et al. 1998, 2000).[1] These excavations uncovered a series of domestic structures dating to the Late Formative and Epiclassic-Early Postclassic period. Specifically, excavations on Terrace 5 in 1998 and 2000 uncovered the remains of a Late Formative residential group that contained evidence for lapidary work which is the focus of this discussion.

The layout of the Terrace 5 residence is illustrated in Figure 2. Excavations identified the partial remains of a rock wall residential building and a small associated outbuilding along with associated floors, artifactual debris, burials, and other features (Serra Puche et al. 1998, 2000). The main residential structure probably had a roof made of perishable material that was supported by posts identified during excavation. One burial (number 5) was recovered inside the structure at the southwest corner of the residence. Two additional burials (7 and 10) were located near a hearth feature

outside the residence near its northwestern corner. Additional rock alignments were identified along the western edge of the excavation but it could not be determined what these might represent. A compact earthen floor was identified across the interior of the structure. Ceramic and lithic remains were recovered from this floor which, together with its layout, confirm that it was a residential building.

The area immediately south of the residential structures was a patio area that contained a small 2 × 3 m outbuilding with a stone foundation. A compact earthen pedestrian surface was identified in several areas of the patio as well as inside the small outbuilding. The old patio surface could be identified on the south side of the outbuilding which was important because evidence for lapidary work was associated with the earthen floor of the patio.

The evidence for lapidary work was found on the occupation surface in two areas at Terrace 5. The first work area was excavated in 1998 and is located inside and along the western wall of the residential structure (Figure 2). A total of 977 chert microdrills and 420 jade fragments were recovered from two excavation squares in this area.[2] The second work area was identified during the 2000 field season. This area was located on the patio surface 1.5 meters south of the small outbuilding. Production debris was concentrated in unit S113E259, square 4, around a circular organic stain that appeared to be the remains of a wooden post. While this post may have supported a roofed over work area, the concentration of debitage around its base suggests that it more likely was a half-post set vertically in the ground as a low work station. The production debris concentrated around this post consisted of 3,919 pieces of jade debitage, 169 chert microdrills, 41 small basalt grinding disks, and one perforated stone disk that may have been a tool used with the grinding disks (Figure 3). Both the jade debitage and the small basalt disks occurred in compact concentrations 20–30 cm in diameter adjacent to one another; the chert drills were scattered around them (Figure 4). An additional 80 chert microdrills and 27 jade fragments were found in the three adjacent excavation squares to the north and south of unit 4.

The evidence indicates that there were two lapidary work areas in the Terrace 5 domestic structure. The patio was the main area used for crafting. It is here that most of the jade debitage was recovered along with chert drills and the basalt disks used in lapidary work. The second work area was inside the east structure and had higher concentrations of chert drills than jade debitage. Whether this was where the drills were made or just where they were stored is unclear. Both of these work zones are small, with concentrated production debitage suggesting highly discrete production areas within the household like those Clark (1991a, 1991b)

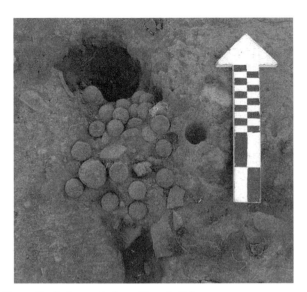

Figure 3. Patio post hole and basalt disks.

Figure 4. Patio concentration of jade. Oval shows jade concentration.

reports for flaked stone reduction among the Lacandon. Unfortunately, problems with the land owner early in the 2000 field season forced excavations to be terminated before the patio and the remainder of the structures on Terrace 5 could be completely investigated. The lapidary production debris and technological categories from these excavations are described below.

Jade Production Debitage

Lapidary debitage consists of 4,657 small pieces of apple green jade recovered from the two production areas. The majority of this material (96.7%, n = 4505) consists of small irregular jade fragments (Table 1). These fragments are percussion shatter, produced when nodules and laminar pieces of jade were intentionally fragmented into small pieces ranging from 3–20 mm in length (Figure 5). In their unmodified form these pieces resemble a coarse gravel and could be misinterpreted as waste. Close inspection, however, reveals that these jade fragments are actually the first stage in a sequence of small bead manufacture produced by intentionally breaking jade nodules into sections using percussion. It is this first stage of production that Sahagún refers to as "shattering" in the epigraph to this chapter.

Also included with this irregular jade debitage were a small number of unfinished and broken artifacts that include bead blanks, partially drilled bead preforms, broken beads, two small tubular beads, and one small earspool (Figures 6–7, Table 1). While small in number (3.3%, n = 152), these unfinished artifacts provide the complete picture of how the manufacturing process proceeded from fragmenting the jade nodule through the final finishing of a completed bead.

Visual inspection of the jade pieces revealed virtually no variation in color or type of raw material. The majority of the jade is a homogenous, high quality light green jade identical to jade recovered from the Motagua Valley (Garber et al. 1993; Hammond et al. 1977; Hirth and Hirth 1992, 1993; Kovacevich 2007; Rochette, this volume). The homogeneity in color and texture suggests that the majority of the fragments, preforms, and beads were processed from a few jade nodules recovered from the same deposits. No weathered surface or exterior cortex was noted on any of the pieces, indicating that these nodules arrived either as cobbles collected from alluvial deposits or in some partially processed form. Analysis using INAA and LA-ICP-MS of three of these jade pieces at California State University, Long Beach by Hector Neff confirmed that the raw material was a Motagua source.[3] Only one piece of extraneous material was recovered from the excavations. This piece was also analyzed and the results indicate that it was similar to artifacts recovered from the Alta Verapaz region of Guatemala (Hector Neff, personal communication).

The focus of lapidary work was the production of small jade beads. Manufacture was a four-step process and employed a relatively simple technology. First, nodules were broken into small pieces to create a wide range of shapes and sizes. Second, a small jade fragment was selected from

Table 1. Counts of greenstone, chert microdrills and basalt grinding artifacts and debitage recovered on Terrace 5.

Greenstone Production Debitage	Frequency	Percent
Percussion Fragments and Shatter	4,505	96.7
Bead Preform	29	.6
Partially Drilled Preform	44	1.0
Bead Fragment	76	1.6
Tubular Bead	2	>.1
Small Earspool	1	>.1
Total Greenstone	4,657	100.0
Chert Microdrills	**Frequency**	**Percent**
Raw Material	4	.3
Flakes with Cortex	18	1.5
Interior Flakes	79	6.4
Triangular Blades	53	4.3
Prismatic Blades	137	11.2
Microdrill Preforms	3	.2
Large Microdrills	72	5.9
Medium Microdrills	246	20.1
Small Microdrills	125	10.2
Microdrill Fragments	51	4.2
Unidentified Fragments and Shatter	438	35.7
Total Chert Microdrills	1,226	100.0
Basalt Grinding Disks	**Frequency**	**Percent**
Disk Preforms	2	4.9
Single Convex Disks	7	17.1
Bi-Convex Disks	18	43.9
Double Convex Disks	14	34.1
Total Basalt Grinding Disks	41	100.0

Figure 5. Jade percussion shatter.

Figure 6. Jade bead preforms.

the percussion fragments and was shaped into a rough bead preform by grinding and abrading (Figure 6). These bead preforms were often intentionally irregular or slight rectangular in form so that they could be stabilized in a small jig or die. Third, once stabilized, bead preforms were then drilled to create a suspension hole for the bead. Drilling was a difficult task and bead preforms occasionally broke or were abandoned before completion, examples of which were re-

covered in the collections (Figure 7). Fourth, after drilling beads were brought to their finished form and polished to a medium to high luster (Figure 8).

The initial stage of breaking jade nodules into fragments might seem like a wasteful way to process a high value commodity like jade. However, from the perspective of the craftsmen it was a time saving and effective way to produce small workable raw material in short amount of time. Pieces that were too small for bead production could have been used in the manufacture of small decorative mosaics, although

Figure 7. Broken perforated beads.

Figure 8. Finished jade beads.

Figure 9. Chert drills.

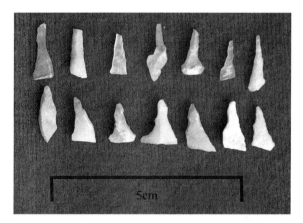

Figure 10. Chert drill tips.

there is no indication that any mosaic work took place on Terrace 5. While effective, this technique did produce waste and it is interesting that despite the Motagua jade source being 1200 km away, the Nativitas lapidaries were more interested in saving time than making efficient use of every piece of raw material by sawing pieces into usable preforms. Of course what is waste? Small fragments could have been exchanged to other artisans making mosaics or processed into a grinding compound used to cut both jade and other softer materials. Furthermore, jade may not have been as scarce as we sometimes think it was and may have circulated and been accessible to domestic craftsmen through inter-regional exchange networks.

The use of percussion to segment and section jade nodules apparently was a common technique used by lapidaries in Mesoamerica. The epigraph from Sahagún at the beginning of this chapter illustrates this point. Although he refers to the bad lapidary as a person who shatters, pulverizes, and damages the stone, Sahagún (1961:26) seems to be describing both a commonly used technique and its misapplication at the same time. Fragmentation by percussion seems to have been a regular aspect of lapidary work since he

describes good lapidaries as regularly "breaking" raw material when they worked amethyst and bloodstone. After breakage, craftsmen could then select the piece of stone to be worked (Sahagún 1959:81). This is the same pattern found archaeologically by Kovacevich (2007) and Rochette (this volume) in the Maya region.

Lapidary Microdrills

Drills are an indispensable component of the lapidary toolkit needed to produce jade beads. A total of 1,226 small microdrills and microdrill preforms were recovered from Terrace 5 (Figures 9–10). These drills are small, averaging 12.8 mm in length (SD = 2.6) and 6.6 mm in width (SD = 1.6). They vary in shape from short to long depending on their intended usage and stage of use. Short drills were used for initial hole drilling and have blunt edges. Longer drills were needed for interior hole drilling and the perforation of thick beads. The diameter of drill tips ranges from .8–2.0 mm in width depending on their length and degree of

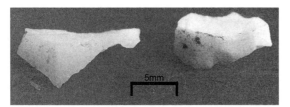

A

B

Figure 11. Microdrill manufacturing byproducts. A) Core platforms removed from chert microcores during core rejuvenation, B) Triangular chert blade used as a preform for preparing a microdrill.

wear (Figure 10). The shape of the microdrills suggests that they were end hafted into a shaft (e.g. see Aldenderfer 1991, Figure 8; Aldenderfer et al. 1989) that was rotated by hand or with the help of a bow drill (Figure 9).

Microdrills were manufactured from small microblades and flakes of white chert that were removed using pressure from small hand-held cores like those documented for small core obsidian blade production at Xochicalco (Flenniken and Hirth 2003; Hirth this volume). The different stages of drill preparation found in the assemblage makes it clear that microdrills were manufactured by the artisans who used them at Terrace 5 (Figure 11). The complete microdrill manufacturing sequence was recovered beginning with initial core shaping, removal of triangular and prismatic blades, core

rejuvenation, shaping drill preforms and finished microdrills, to their final use, breakage, and eventual discard (Table 1).

Although no complete cores were found, the shape of the chert microblades and the core platforms removed during core rejuvenation (Figure 11A) indicate that microcores were conical in form. The most frequent preforms used to make microdrills in the collections were small blades with a triangular cross-section (Figure 11B). Microdrills usually were shaped with long tapering tips that often broke off during use. Tips were probably reshaped on blades several times until all the usable length was exhausted; then drills were discarded. Few chert flakes other than microdrill preforms were found in the collections. This is logical because the same material used to drill jade beads would also make a useful abrasive to shape jade preforms and finished pieces. It is likely that most small waste flakes and broken microdrills were recycled into abrasives to use in grinding activities (Flenniken and Hirth 2003).

Three lines of evidence corroborate that the microdrills recovered at Terrace 5 were used to drill jade beads. The first and most obvious is that all drills occur together with drilled pieces of jade. This is a first order expectation for lapidary production and occurs in the jade production areas at Cancuen (Kovacevich 2007). Second, the chert drills were hard enough to drill and abrade the jade recovered in the workshop. These drills have a MOHS hardness of 7.0 compared to a MOHS hardness of 6.5–7.0 for the jade in the collection. Third, the size of the microdrills corresponds to the size of the holes drilled in the whole and broken jade beads recovered in the Terrace 5 workshop. Together these lines of evidence confirm the practice of lapidary work on Terrace 5.

In addition to jade, one small onyx vessel in the shape of an incurving wall bowl or tecomate was recovered inverted over a red jar as part of an offering associated with the construction of the house. Inside the onyx bowl was a green stone figure lying on its back (Figure 12). While cache and burial offerings are always difficult to interpret, the location of the figure inside the covered jar may represent the spirit of the household head or the craftsman residing here. While onyx is easier to work than jade, no production debitage of this material was recovered at Terrace 5. It is likely that the greenstone figure was made in the workshop while the onyx bowl came into the household as a gift or trade item.

Basalt Grinding Disks

One interesting set of artifacts was a cluster of 41 small convex basalt disks recovered on the patio surface adjacent

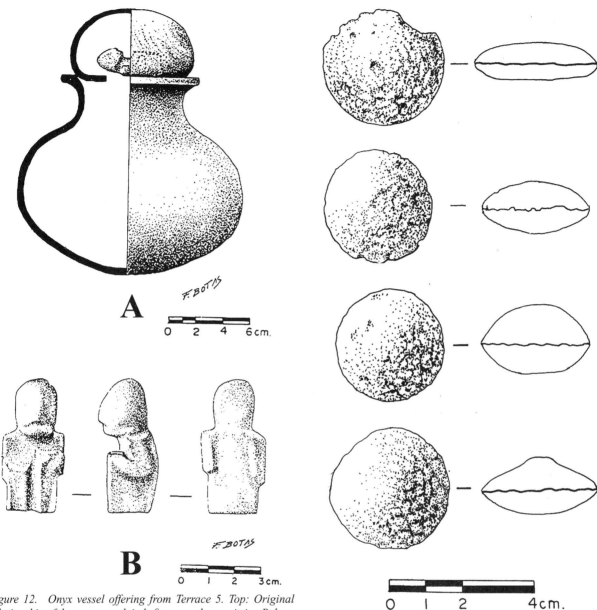

Figure 12. Onyx vessel offering from Terrace 5. Top: Original relationship of the onyx vessel, jade figure, and ceramic jar, Below: drawing of the jade figure 5. Drawing by Fernando Botas.

Figure 13. Basalt grinding disks Upper Row: single convex, Middle Rows: bi-convex, Bottom Row: double-convex on one side, convex on the other Drawing by Fernando Botas.

to the large concentration of jade debitage (Figure 3). These disks range from 25.8 to 32.6 mm in diameter (X = 29.6, SD = 1.63) and were manufactured from a fine grained vesicular basalt. There small size and compact grouping suggest that they may have been stored in a perishable bag or basket. The disks occur in three forms: single convex, bi-convex disks and double-convex disks (Figures 13 and 14). Single convex disks are flat on one side and convex on the other; they range from 11–21 mm in thickness (Figure 13, upper). Bi-convex disks are lozenge shaped, have a convex profile on both sides, and average 12.3 mm in thickness (Figure 13, middle). Double-convex disks have an

additional convex protrusion on one or both sides which makes them thicker (19.7 mm) than simple bi-convex disks (Figure 13, lower). As with the chert microdrills, the recovery of a piece of unworked raw material along with two disk preforms within this cache indicates that basalt disks were made within the Terrace 5 household.

Although the exact function of these disks remains unclear, microscopic examination of their surfaces reveals that they were used as grinding disks. Wear is found on the exterior surfaces of all three forms and rotational striations

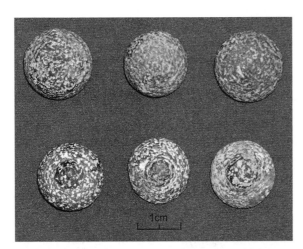

Figure 14. Basalt grinding disks: Upper: Biconvex disks, Lower: Double-convex disks.

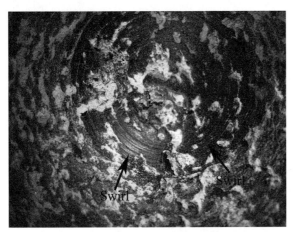

Figure 15. Striations on biconvex basalt disk. White areas on photograph are vesicles in the disks that are filled with residue of grinding slurry.

are evident on the convex surface of several double-convex disks (Figures 14 (lower) and 15). In several cases these striations appear in what seems to be a thin layer of resin covering the surface of the disk. The slightly vesicular nature of the basalt made them especially well adapted for grinding because the vesicles could hold abrasives in a wet slurry. Traces of this slurry can still be viewed in many of these vesicles (Figure 15).

The shape of the disks and the wear on their surfaces suggests that they were used to polish or abrade concave surfaces like those found on jade plaques and pyrite mirrors, although neither were found in the production debris. A more likely possibility is that some disks were used to polish the frontal surfaces and throats of small earspools, a broken example of which was recovered in the jade debitage. This could account for the formation of the double-convex disks as they are similar to ear spool polishers recovered

3cm

Figure 16. Drop of mastic found with grinding disks on Terrace 5.

from Kaminaljuyu (Kidder et al. 1946: Fig 153a). It is also possible that they were used to shape other materials such as wood, reed, or bone. Whatever their function, we believe they were used in abrading and/or polishing activities within the workshop.

Adhesives

An interesting technological element was the recovery of a small amount of what appears to be resin from the patio work area that may have been used as an adhesive in conjunction with lapidary activities (Figure 16). This material was found together with the basalt grinding disks and presence of this material adhering to the surface of several disks indicates that they were used together. The amount of adhesive preserved is small and it is unclear if it is a carbonized organic resin (Berdan et al., this volume) or *chapopote* imported from the Gulf Coast (Wendt, this volume). Possible functions in a lapidary context would include use as adhesive in hafting microdrills to shafts, in mounting grinding disks in composite lapidary tools, or in finishing decorative mosaics. As mentioned above, this last use is problematic since no mosaic inlays were recovered from Terrace 5. Nevertheless, it is clear that this material was employed as a cement or binder with the basalt grinding disks since it covers their surfaces and displays circular striations (see Figure 15).

Intermittent Production and Multicrafting at Terrace 5

The Terrace 5 workshop represents a unique and intriguing situation. In most respects, the residents of the Terrace 5 household resemble other Late Formative agricultural households excavated at Nativitas. Its residential architecture and ceramic and lithic inventories are the same as those found in other domestic contexts (Serra Puche 1998, 2009). What sets the residents of the Terrace 5 household apart from other houses excavated at Nativitas (Serra Puche et al.

1998, 2000) is their involvement in small-scale lapidary production. Both of the lapidary work areas identified in this residence only show evidence for working one material, jade. Although this may be a result of sampling error, there is no indication that materials such as onyx, shell, or other metamorphic stones from neighboring areas of Central Mexico were worked into beads or other types of artifacts. Clearly the frequency and intensity of jade work was limited by the distance and difficulty of getting raw material from the Motagua source.

The logical conclusion is that lapidary production was an intermittent craft activity within the Terrace 5 household. How it contributed to the overall economic well being of the household is less clear, although the burial information suggests that the residents of this household were prosperous. Cache and burial offerings recovered from this household include some unique and important materials including a slate pendant, pieces of green stone, a green stone figure, an onyx vessel, and a complete tortoise shell along with the usual ceramic vessels. Likewise, several pieces of green stone were included as part of the offering with burial 5 indicating that jade use was not restricted to only elite. Finally, the scale of production suggests that there was no more than one artisan involved in this work at any one time, and then only on an intermittent basis.

While this would seem to be a good case for single commodity craft production, the situation is a bit more complex than first appearances suggest. The cache of 41 basalt disks in the patio work area raises the possibility that they were used in processing materials other than jade. Although they may have been employed in the manufacture of ear spools as suggested above, there was only one partial jade ear spool recovered in this assemblage and the percussion technology used to shape beads is not conducive for preforming earspools. These basalt disks could reflect the practice of a separate craft either in perishable materials or some type of raw material that was not recovered in the excavated portion of the residence.

All craftsmen need tools to carry out their craft. Where and how prehispanic craftsmen obtained them is rarely discussed although it is important for: (1) identifying craft production in the archaeological record, and (2) understanding what skills an artisan needed to practice his or her trade (Clark 1990). The manufacture of tools by craftspersons to practice his or her craft was called *contingent production* in chapter 2 and there are two indications for this kind of production at Terrace 5.

The first form of contingent production was the manufacture of the chert microdrills needed to perforate jade beads. Technological evidence indicates that these drills were produced within the household using a hand-held microblade reduction strategy like that used to produce obsidian blades at Xochicalco (Flenniken and Hirth 2003). Small pressure microblades are the perfect preform for manufacturing the small chert drills that were an indispensible component of lapidary toolkits. Chert microdrills have been recovered in crafting contexts in Oaxaca (Feinman and Nichols 2000; Parry 1987), the Maya region (Aldenderfer 1991; Kovacevich 2007), and Central Mexico (Hirth 2006; Hirth et al. 2006), as well as elsewhere in the Americas (Arnold 2001; Preziosi 2001). Chert microdrills certainly were produced at Terrace 5 and we suspect that microblade production was a regular part of the technological toolkit of all lapidaries who needed drills to create suspension holes in hard substances. The presence and use of microblade technology underscores that craftsmen needed diverse skills to produce and use the tools of their craft. It is highly unlikely that Terrace 5 craftsmen could have obtained microdrills from outside their household even if they wanted to since they don't occur in, and weren't produced for, general household consumption anywhere that we know of in Central Mexico. It is more likely that microblades and the microdrills were made by an individual in this household using a specialized flaked stone pressure technology to do so.

Another example of contingent production that shows this same level of ingenuity is the manufacture of the basalt grinding disks (Figures 3, 13 and 14). To our knowledge no tools of this type, much less a whole cache, have ever been reported in Mesoamerica. These materials represent a highly specialized toolkit of the type sometimes recovered in mortuary contexts with individuals inferred to be craftsmen (e.g. Kidder et al. 1946, Minor Grave 7). The unique and specialized nature of these tool kits is the best argument for their manufacture by the craftsmen who used them.

Contingent production is a consistent dimension of the multicrafting activities carried out at Terrace 5. While lapidary skills were required to manufacture jade beads, the ability to produce flaked (microblades, microdrills) and ground stone tools (basalt grinding disks) also were required as contingent crafting skills. Only one craft activity resulted in the production of jade items for use outside the household; the other two produced a few critical tools consumed within the household as part of the manufacturing process (c.f. Anderson and Hirth 2009; Hirth and Castanzo 2006). The important point is that craftsmen needed to possess multiple skills to perform their tasks. This is a dimension of multicrafting that needs to be recognized in any analysis of domestic craft production.

In chapter two it was argued that intermittent crafting provided households with a way of maximizing their overall subsistence productivity while minimizing risk through activity diversification. Households strive to be self-sufficient for their food needs, and as a result can produce specialized, low demand commodities that augment household productivity without endangering their survivability. In some ways small scale craft production with low or periodic demand may have been optimal for households because it more closely matches their labor availability and output capacity. What is important is that high output is not a requirement for successful production since intermittent crafting provides a flexible, low risk solution to meeting prehispanic demand.

One of the advantages of intermittent crafting is that there is no real restriction on the types of goods that households can produce. Households are free to produce both utilitarian and wealth items *as long as* they can procure the raw materials, master the knowledge necessary to manufacture them, and distribute the finished products to intended consumers, whether elite or non-elite. Moreover, it is overtly biased to expect a sharp division between the production of utilitarian and wealth goods in non-elite households *before* investigation begins. This is a topic for empirical research, not *a priori* determination. While elite households certainly were motivated to obtain wealth goods in large quantities, the model of intermittent production does not preclude the production of wealth goods in non-elite households for purposes of exchange. The key variables, of course, are whether exotic raw materials are generally accessible (see Rochette, this volume) or intentionally restricted and whether the technical knowledge and training are readily available. If resources and training are not widely available then the production of wealth goods may more closely conform to the expectations of attached production under elite control.

Conclusions

The evidence suggests that prestige goods in the form of jade beads, a few small earspools, and at least one small greenstone figure were manufactured during the Late Formative period in small quantities by artisans residing in a rural, non-elite household at the site of Nativitas, Tlaxcala. The evidence for lapidary production consists of small fragments of jade percussion shatter, bead blanks, partially drilled bead preforms, broken beads, and incompletely finished items including small tubular beads and one small ear spool. It is likely that the greenstone figure was manufactured here even though no direct evidence in the form of sawed jade cutoffs was recovered in the workshop debris. A total of 4,657 pieces of high quality jade were recovered along with 1,226 microdrills and 41 abrading disks. The scale of production in the Terrace 5 domestic workshop was both small and intermittent. There were no full-time special-

ists in this residence, and crafting probably was incorporated as an additional production activity into a domestic household whose primary activity was subsistence agriculture. It is a good illustration of intermittent crafting as discussed in this volume.

What is particularly important about lapidary production at Nativitas is that high value items do *not* appear to have been produced under the control of supervising elite. Instead, the domestic workshop was located in a non-elite, rural context. It was far removed from high ranking elite on Xochitecátl and the craftsmen at Nativitas were not part of an elite household. Nevertheless, the jade used in the workshop originates in the Rio Motagua valley over 1200 km away, well beyond the *presumed* procurement sphere of a normal household.

The Nativitas example of craft production from Terrace 5 raises important questions about what specialization means as an analytical category in studying craft production (e.g. Clark 1995; Costin 1991; Flad and Hruby 2007; Rice 1981). The lapidary work at Terrace 5 reflects the use of a highly specialized microdrill technology in what by all appearances is an ordinary, small rural household. The basalt grinding disks are specialized and unique tools that have not been reported elsewhere in Mesoamerica. The scale of jade bead production is very low and production is restricted to a narrow range of forms made from an exotic commodity. Without question, artisans were engaged in a "specialized" activity, but it implies nothing about the complexity, scale, integration, or organization of work.

An important question for a broader understanding of Mesoamerican economic systems is how production was integrated into the broader political economy of Late Formative Central Mexico. There are two possible ways this production could have been organized: either as a form of independent commercial production at the household level or as a form of consignment production. In both cases production would have taken place in domestic contexts by independent craft producers.

The commercial model would argue that production was undertaken by independent craft specialists who obtained jade on their own independently of elite involvement through long distance exchange. The fact that craftsmen were located in rural contexts is not a problem in and of itself because it conforms to the pattern of dispersed independent craft specialists reported at the time of the Conquest from the neighboring regions of Huejotzingo and Tlaxcala (Anguiano 1987; Brumfiel 1987). I find this explanation plausible given the many innovative ways that households make use of economic opportunities. The only problem with this explanation is accounting for how jade in the form of unworked nodules could have reached the Puebla-Tlaxcala valley from the Rio Motagua jade source. While problematic, we still understand very little about the extent or structure of Formative period trade networks anywhere in Mesoamerica (see for example Neff et al. 2006a, Neff et al. 2006b, Sharer et al. 2006). That jade moved over long distances through household procurement networks is a possibility that ought not be discarded before we have the empirical data to do so.

An alternative and equally possible explanation is that Nativitas lapidary production represents a form of consigned production from elites at Xochitecátl. This explanation would place the procurement of raw material in the hands of the elites who subsequently made it available for work in a small domestic workshop like Terrace 5. In the consignment model the relationship between patron and artisan can take several forms. It could be a service performed for direct payment or part of the *tequitl* (service) obligation that independent craftsmen fulfilled for their lord as part of fealty or tribute obligations (Carrasco 1978). Consigned production cannot, in my view, by construed as attached production because there is no prolonged dependence of the craftsman on the sponsoring patron. In both possibilities cited above, consignment production is possible *only* when independent craftsmen are already present and supporting themselves through both craft and subsistence activities. In most instances independent craft specialization is a *precondition* for any kind of periodic consigned production and the patron is dependent on the presence of these craftspersons for the manufacture of specialty items.

Prestige goods certainly were important in the chiefdom societies of Formative period Mesoamerica. What is *not* clear at this time, is what the relationship was between the craftsmen who produced them and the elite who consumed them. The data for lapidary production at Terrace 5 suggests that the connection between elite and the craftsmen who produced prestige goods may be more distant than current prestige goods models suggest. If there is one thing that is true about the history of science it is that theory abounds in the absence of data. It is only as solid empirical data are collected on craft production that we will begin to understand if and how elite were involved in the manufacture of prestige goods in Central Mexico during the Formative period. That evidence has not as yet been found.

It is true that elite have a vested interest in increasing the flow and accumulation of prestige goods. But we cannot assume that elite maintained exclusive control over the production of prestige goods during the Formative period *before* we find evidence for craftsmen closely associated with, or directly attached to, elite households. At this point it would be a mistake to interpret the evidence for craft production at Nativitas in light of a theory of elite control that has yet to be confirmed in Mesoamerica during the Formative period. What we can say with confidence is that Nativitas craftsmen were independent artisans who engaged in the intermittent production of small amounts of lapidary goods that contributed to both the household's social life and domestic economy. Whether independent artisans of the type found at Nativitas were an anomaly or a foundational feature of craft production will not be resolved until comprehensive research is conducted on all aspects of the Mesoamerican economy in both the rural and urban contexts where work occurred.

Notes

1. The Terrace 5 excavations were conducted under the supervision of Mari Carmen Serra Puche and Jesus Carlos Lazcano Arce. Kenneth Hirth was invited to analyze the lithic materials from Xochitécatl and Nativitas during the summer of 2004 and he is indebted to the directors of the project for the opportunity to examine these materials. Jason De León assisted in the analysis of the flaked stone lithic materials, in particular the analysis of the chert microdrills.

2. An additional 291 jade fragments were also recovered from the 1998 excavations whose provenance was misplaced in the lab. It is likely that these materials also came from these two excavated squares.

3. Four pieces of jade were analyzed by Hector Neff using INAA and LA-ICP-MS at the IIRMES lab at the California State University at Long Beach. Three pieces of jade were selected that appeared representative of the majority of pieces in the collection. Samples 1 and 3 fall within his Motagua Dark group based on enriched chromium levels. This group includes three samples from the Pakal mask at Palenque and two samples from Burial 5 at the Pyramid of the Moon, Teotihuacan. Sample 2 falls within his Motagua Light group based on low chromium levels; this group also includes two samples from Burial 5 at the Pyramid of the Moon, Teotihuacan. The fourth sample was an unusual material with a grey color. It is distinguished from the other samples by high potassium, rubidium, barium, and rare earth elements; it groups materials from the Alta Verapaz region of Guatemala which is its presumed source area. Analysis of these materials was made possible through NSF grant BCS 0604712.

References

Aizpurúa, Isaza, and Patricia McAnany
   1999 Adornment and Identify: Shell Ornaments from Formative K'axob. Ancient Mesoamerica 10:117–127.

Aldenderfer, Mark
1991 Functional Evidence for Lapidary and Carpentry Craft Specialties in the Late Classic of the Central Peten Lakes Region. *Ancient Mesoamerica* 2:205–214.

Aldenderfer, Mark, Larry Kimball, and April Sievert
1989 Microwear Analysis in the Maya Lowlands: The Use of Functional Data in a Complex Society Setting. *Journal of Field Archaeology* 16:47–60.

Anderson, J. Heath, and Kenneth Hirth
2009 Obsidian Blade Production for Craft Consumption at Kaminaljuyu. Ancient Mesoamerica 20:163–172.

Anguiano, Marina
1987 Annexo II. División del trabajo en Tlaxcala a Mediados del Siglo XVI. *In* Padrones de Tlaxcala del Siglo XVI y Padrón de Nobles de Ocotelolco. Teresa Rojas, ed. Pp. 25–48. Mexico City: CIESAS, Colección Documentos 1.

Armillas, Pedro
1995a Cacaxtla, Xochitecatl y Otros Lugares de la Zona Arqueológica de Cacaxtla. *In* Antología de Cacaxtla, Volumen 1. Angel Garcia Cook and Beatriz Merino Carrión, eds. Pp. 68–72. Mexico City: INAH.
1995b Informe del Levantamiento Topográfico de la Zona Arqueológica de Cacaxtla. *In* Antología de Cacaxtla, Volumen 1. Angel Garcia Cook and Beatriz Merino Carrión, eds. Pp. 49–67. Mexico City: INAH.

Arnold, Jeanne
2001 The Origins of a Pacific Coast Chiefdom: The Chumash of the Channel Islands. Salt Lake City: University of Utah Press.

Brumfiel, Elizabeth
1987 Elite and Utilitarian Crafts in the Aztec State. *In* Specialization, Exchange, and Complex Societies. Elizabeth Brumfiel and Timoth Earle, eds. Pp. 102–118. Cambridge: Cambridge University Press.

Brumfield, Elizabeth, and Timothy Earle
1987 Specialization, Exchange, and Complex Societies: An Introduction. *In* Specialization, Exchange, and Complex Societies. Elizabeth

Brumfiel and Timothy Earle, eds. Pp. 1–9. Cambridge: Cambridge University Press.

Carballo, David, and Thomas Pluckhahn
2007 Transportation Corridors and Political Evolution in Highland Mesoamerica: Settlement Analysis Incorporating GIS for Northern Tlaxcala, Mexico. Journal of Anthropological Archaeology 26:607–629.

Carrasco, Pedro
1978 La Economía del México Prehispánico. *In* Economía Política e Ideología en el México Prehispánico. Pedro Carrasco and Johanna Broda, eds. Pp. 13–74. México: Editorial Nueva Imagen.

Charlton, Thomas, Deborah Nichols, and Cynthia Otis Charlton
1991 Aztec Craft Production and Specialization: Archaeological Evidence from the City-State of Otumba, Mexico. World Archaeology 23:98–114.

Clark, John
1990 Fifteen Falacies in Lithic Workshop Interpretation: An Experimental and Ethnoarchaeological Perspective. *In* Etnoarqueología: Primer Coloquio Bosch-Gimpera. Yoko Sugiyama and Mari Carmen Serra, eds. Pp. 497–512. Mexico City: UNAM.
1991a Flintknapping and Debitage Disposal among the Lacandon Maya of Chiapas, Mexico. *In* Ethnoarchaeology of Refuse Disposal. E. Staski and L. Sutro, eds. Pp. 63–78. Anthropological Research Papers No. 42. Tempe: Arizona State University.
1991b Modern Lacandon Lithic Technology and Blade Workshops. *In* Maya Stone Tools: Selected Papers from the Second Maya Lithic Conference. Thomas Hester and Harry Shafer, eds. Pp. 251–265. Madison: Prehistory Press.
1995 Craft Specialization as an Archaeological Category. Research in Economic Anthropology 16:267–294.

Clark, John, and Michael Blake
1994 The Power of Prestige: Competitive Generosity and the Emergence of Rank Societies in Lower Mesoamerica. *In* Factional Competition and Political Development in the New World. Elizabeth Brumfiel and John Fox, eds. Pp. 17–30. Cambridge: Cambridge University Press.

Costin, Cathy
1991 Craft Specialization: Issues in Defining, Documenting, and Explaining the Organization of Production. *In* Archaeological Method and Theory. Michael Schiffer, ed. Pp. 1–56. Tucson: University of Arizona Press.

Dalton, George
1977 Aboriginal Economies in Stateless Societies. *In* Exchange Systems in Prehistory. Timothy Earle and Jonathon Ericson, eds. Pp. 191–212. New York: Academic Press.

Dávila, Patricio
1975 La Fase Tezoquipan (Protoclásico) de Tlaxcala. *In* Arqueología I, XIII Mesa Redonda de la Sociedad Mexicana de Antropología, Pp. 107–115.

Di Peso, Charles
1974 Casas Grandes. The Medio Period. Volume 2. Dragoon and Flagstaff, Arizona: The Amerind Foundation and Northland Press.

Diehl, Richard, and Janet Berlo
1989 Mesoamerica after the Decline of Teotihuacan A.D. 700–900. Washington, DC: Dumbarton Oaks.

Earle, Timothy
2002 Bronze Age Economics. Boulder: Westview Press.

Feinman, Gary, and Linda Nicholas
2000 High-Intensity Household-Scale Production in Ancient Mesoamerica: A Perspective from Ejutla, Oaxaca. *In* Cultural Evolution: Contemporary Viewpoints. Gary Feinman and Linda Manzanilla eds. Pp. 119–142. New York: Kluwer Academic/Plenum Publishers.

Flad, Rowan, and Zachary Hruby
2007 "Specialized" Production in Archaeological Contexts: Rethinking Specialization, the Social Value of Products, and the Practice of Production. *In* Rethinking Craft Specializatin in Complex Societies: Archaeological Analysis of the Social Meaning of Production. Zachary Hruby and Rowan Flad, eds. Pp. 1–19. Arlington: Archaeological Papers of the American Anthropological Association, Number 17.

Flenniken, J. Jeffrey, and Kenneth Hirth
2003 Handheld Prismatic Blade Manufacture in Mesoamerica. *In* Mesoamerican Lithic Technology: Experimentation and Interpretation. Kenneth Hirth, ed. Pp. 98–107. Salt Lake City: University of Utah Press.

Foncerrada de Molina, Marta
1993 Cacaxtla. La Iconografía de los Olmeca-Xicalanca. Instituto de Investaciones Estéticas. Mexico City: UNAM.

Garber, James, Kenneth Hirth, David Grove, and John Hoopes
1993 Ritual use of Jade in Mesoamerica. *In* Jade and Ritual in Mesoamerica. Fred Lange, ed. Pp. 211–231. Provo:University of Utah Press.

García Cook, Angel
1981 The Historical Importance of Tlaxcala in the Cultural Development of the Central Highlands. *In* Handbook of Middle American Indians, Supplement 1, Archaeology. Victoria Bricker and Jeremy Sabloff, eds. Pp. 244–276. Austin: University of Texas Press.

Hammond, N, A. Spinall, S. Feather, J. Hazelden, T. Gazard, and S. Agrell
1977 Maya Jade: Source Location and Analysis. *In* Exchange Systems in Prehistory. Timothy Earle and Jonathon Ericson, eds. Pp. 35–67. New York: Academic Press.

Hayden, Brian
2001 Richman, Poorman, Beggarman, Chief: The Dynamics of Social Inequality. *In* Archaeology at the Millennium: A Sourcebook. Gary Feinman and Douglas Price, eds. Pp. 231–272. New York: Kluwer Academic Press.

Hempenius Turner, Margaret
1987 The Lapidaries of Teotihuacan, Mexico: A Preliminary Study of Fine Stone Working in the Ancient Mesoamerican City. *In* Teotihuacan. Nuevos Datos, Nuevas Síntesis, Nuevos Problemas. Emily McClung de Tapia and Evelyn Rattray, eds. Pp. 465–471. Mexico City: UNAM.

Hirth, Kenneth
2006 Obsidian Craft Production in Ancient Central Mexico. Salt Lake City: University of Utah Press.

Hirth, Kenneth, Bradford Andrews, and J. Jeffrey Flenniken
2006 A Technological Analysis of Xochicalco Obsidian Blade Production. *In* Obsidian Craft Production in Ancient Central Mexico. Kenneth Hirth, ed. Pp. 62–95. Salt Lake City: University of Utah Press.

Hirth, Kenneth, and Ronald Castanzo
2006 An Experimental Study of Use-wear Striation on Obsidian Prismatic Blades. *In* Obsidian Craft Production in Ancient Central Mexico. Kenneth Hirth, ed. Pp. 318–327. Salt Lake City: University of Utah Press.

Hirth, Kenneth, and Jason De León
2009 A Lapidary Tool Assemblage and Craft Production in a Late Formative Household: Terrace 5, Nativitas, Tlaxcala. *In* Vida y Tradición en el Sitio de Nativitas. Mari Carmen Serra Puche and Jésus Carlos Lascano Arce, eds. Mexico City: UNAM. (In press)

Hirth, Kenneth, and Susan Hirth
1992 Objektbeschreibungen: The El Cajon Jades. *In* Die Welt der Maya. A. Eggrebrecht and N. Grube, eds. Pp. 300, 368–530-551. Mainz am Rhein: Roemer un Pelizaeus-Museum, Hildescheim, Verlag Philipp von Zabern.
1993 Jade and Marble: An Analysis of their Style and Ritual Usage in Prehistoric Central Honduras. *In* Jade and Ritual in Mesoamerica. Fred Lange, ed. Pp. 173–190. Provo: University of Utah Press.

Inomata, Takeshi
2001 The Power and Ideology of Artistic Creation: Elite Craft Specialists in Classic Maya Society. Current Anthropology 42:321–349.

Kenoyer, Johnathan M., Massimo Vidale and Kuldeep Kumar Bhan
1991 Contemporary Stone Beadmaking in Khambhat, India: Patterns of Craft Specialization and Organization of Production as Reflected in the Archaeological Record. World Archaeology 23:44–63.

Kidder, Alfred V., Jesse D. Jennings and Edwin M. Shook
1946 *Excavations at Kaminaljuyu, Guatemala.* Publication 561. Washington, D.C.: Carnegie Institution of Washington.

Kovacevich, Brigitte
2007 Ritual, Crafting and Agency at the Classic Maya Kingdom of Cancuen. *In* Mesoamerican Ritual Economy. E. Christian Wells, and Karla Davis-Salazar, eds. Pp. 67–114. Boulder: University of Colorado Press.

Lesure, Richard
1999 On the Genesis of Value in Early Hierarchical Societies. *In* Material Symbols: Culture and Economy in Prehistory. John Robb, ed. Pp. 23–55. Center for Archaeological Investigations. Carbondale: Southern Illinois University.

Mora, Raziel
1975 El Preclásico de Tlaxcala: fases Tezompantepec, Tlatempa y Texoloc. Arqueología I, XIII Mesa Redonda de la Sociedad Mexicana de Antropología, Pp. 97–106.

Mountjoy, Joseph, and David Peterson
1973 Man and Land in Prehispanic Cholula. Vanderbilt Publications in Anthropology No. 4, Nashville.

Neff, Hector, Jeffrey Blomster, Michael Glascock, Ronald Bishop, M. James Blackman, Michael Coe, George Cowgill, Richard Diehl, Stephen Houston, Arthur Joyce, Carl Lipo, Barbara Stark, and Marcus Winter
2006a Methodological Issues in the Provenance Investigation of Early Formative Mesoamerican Ceramics. Latin American Antiquity 17:54–76.

Neff, Hector, Jeffrey Blomster, Michael Glascock, Ronald Bishop, M. James Blackman, Michael Coe, George Cowgill, Ann Cyphers, Richard Diehl, Stephen Houston, Arthur Joyce, Carl Lipo, and Marcus Winter
2006b Smokescreens in the Provenance Investigation of Early Formative Mesoamerican Ceramics. Latin American Antiquity 17:104–118.

Otis Charlton, Cynthia
1993 Obsidian as Jewelry: Lapidary Production in Aztec Otumba, Mexico. Ancient Mesoamerica 4:231–243.

Peregrine, Peter
1991 Some Political Aspects of Craft Specialization. World Archaeology 23:1–11.

Preziosi, Aimee
2001 Standardization and Specialization: The Channel Island Microdrill Industry. *In* The Origins of the Pacific Coast Chiefdom. The Chumash of the Channel Islands. Jeanne Arnold, ed. Pp. 151–163. Salt Lake City: University of Utah Press.

Rice, Prudence
1981 Evolution of Specialized Pottery Production: A Trial Model. Current Anthropology 22:219–240.

Sahagún, Fray Bernardino de
1959 Florentine Codex. General History of the Things of New Spain, Book 9, The Merchants. Charles Dibble and Arthur Anderson, trans., Monographs of the School of American Research, No. 14, Part 10, Santa Fe.
1961 Florentine Codex. General History of the Things of New Spain, Book 10, The Merchants. Charles Dibble and Arthur Anderson, trans., Monographs of the School of American Research, No. 14, Part 11, Santa Fe.

Schortman, Edward
1989 Interregional Interaction in Prehistory. American Antiquity 54:52–65.

Schortman, Edward and Patricia Urban
1992 Resources, Power, and Interregional Interaction. New York: Plenum.

Serra Puche, Mari Carmen
1998 Xochitecatl. Tlaxcala: Gobierno del Estado de Tlaxcala.

Serra Puche, Mari Carmen, and Jésus Carlos Lascano Arce
2009 Vida y Tradición en el Sitio de Nativitas. Mexico City: UNAM. (In press)

Serra Puche, Mari Carmen, et al.
1998 *Proyecto Arqueológico "El Hombre y sus Recursos en el sur del Valle de Tlaxcala durante el Formativo y el Epiclásico."* Informe Técnico de Excavación Febrero-Abril/1998.
2000 *Proyecto Arqueológico "El Hombre y sus Recursos en el sur del Valle de Tlaxcala durante el Formativo y el Epiclásico. Sitio Nativitas"* Informe Técnico Parcial de Excavación, 2a Temporada, Enero-Abril/2000.

Sharer, Robert, Andrew Balkansky, James Burton, Gary Feinman, Kent Flannery, David Grove, Joyce Marcus, Robert Moyle, T. Douglas Price, Elsa Redmon, Robert Reynolds, Prudence Rice, Charles Spencer, James Stoltman, and Jason Yaeger
2006 On the Logic of Archaeological Inference: Early Formative pottery and the Evolution of Mesoamerican Societies. Latin American Antiquity 17:90–103.

Smith, Kipp, Rita, and Edward Schortman
1989 The Political Impact of Trade in Chiefdoms. American Anthropologist 91370–385.

Spranz, Bodo
1970 Investigaciones Arqueológicas en el Cerro Xochitacatl, Tlaxcala. Temporada 1969–1970. Comunicaciones 1:37–38.
1978 Die Pyramiden vom Cerro Xochitecatl, Tlaxcala (Mexico)/Las Pirámides del Cerro Xochicalco, Tlaxcala (Mexico). Wiesbaden: Franz Steiner Verlag.

12

Elite Household Multicrafting Specialization at 9N8, Patio H, Copan

Randolph J. Widmer
University of Houston

Evidence of well-developed craft specialization among the Classic Lowland Maya is found in elaborate ritual paraphernalia recorded in iconography and recovered from grave furnishings, offerings, and other ritual cache materials (Adams 1970, 1977; Becker 1973; Culbert 1973; Hammond 1982; Willey 1982; Schele and Miller 1986). Much of the research devoted to Classic Maya craft specialization has focused on the procurement, production, and distribution of lithic materials (Shafer and Hester 1983, 1985; Hester and Shafer 1984; Mallory 1984), with some discussion of specialized production of jewelry (Becker 1973), eccentrics (Hruby 2007), ceramics (Fry 1980; Price 1980), marine shell celt production (Eaton 1974), stone sculpture (Haviland 1974; Abrams 1994, 1987), and greenstone lapidary work (Walters 1979; Kovasevich 2007).

In spite of this research, few actual loci of lapidary activity producing finished jewelry and other wealth goods have been identified for the Late Classic Maya. At Dziblchaltun several caches containing fragments of worked marine shell and greenstone were recovered (Andrews and Andrews 1980) that were originally interpreted as jeweler's caches. Further study, however, indicates that these materials are actually disintegrated mosaic objects and not associated with craft production (Andrews and Andrews 1980:128–129). The difficulty with identifying lapidary production is that the materials worked are valuable and finished artifacts leave the place of manufacture. Even the debitage from production is used in caches and offerings in burials (Moholy-Nagy 1990)!

This does not mean that no lapidary workshops have been identified. Aldenderfer (1991a, 1991b) has identified a Late Classic jade lapidary craft area associated with an elite community adjacent to the site of Yaxha. Likewise, investigations at the Late Classic site of La Sierra in the Naco Valley of Honduras have identified evidence of marine shell processing (Schortman et al. 1992: 81–82). Jade and pyrite workshops have also been identified at the site of Cancuen in Guatemala (Kovacevich 2007; Kovacevich et al. 2001) where jade beads and ornament blanks, and pyrite mirrors were manufactured by non-elites. Elite shell, bone and pyrite manufacture have also been identified at the site of Aguateca (Emery and Aoyama 2007; Inomata 2007). While evidence exists for lapidary workshops during the Late Classic Period, little is understood about the intensity of production and the manufacture of jewelry because finished lapidary artifacts are generally the focus of investigation. The evidence for lapidary craft remains relatively rare in spite of the prominence representation of finished goods in Maya art and burial offerings. Extensive test pitting (474 test pits) and complete excavation of eight Late Classic rural sites in the Copan Valley have not yielded any evidence of non-domestic economic activity in the Copan Valley (Webster et al. 1999; Webster and Freter 1988). To date, two Classic period Maya lapidary workshops associated with elite sites have been discovered, one at Aguateca (Emery and Aoyama 2007; Inomata 2001, 2007) and the other at the elite Type IV mound group 9N-8 Patio H, Copan (Widmer 1986, 1997).

This study examines the structure and organization of elite craft production in Patio H in group 9N-8 at Copan (Figures 1 and 2). The evidence for craft specialization at Patio H included materials associated with lapidary

ARCHEOLOGICAL PAPERS OF THE AMERICAN ANTHROPOLOGICAL ASSOCIATION, Vol. 19, Issue 1, pp. 174–204, ISSN 1551-823X, online ISSN 1551-8248. © 2009 by the American Anthropological Association. All rights reserved. DOI: 10.1111/j.1551-8248.2009.01020.x.

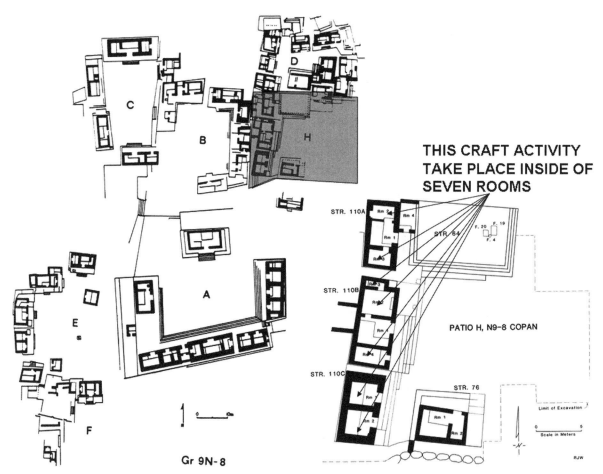

THIS CRAFT ACTIVITY
TAKE PLACE INSIDE OF
SEVEN ROOMS

Figure 1.   Patio Group 9N-8 with the location of Patio H.

production of wealth goods manufactured from shell, green-stone, and other metamorphic stones, as well as evidence for weaving, and feather working. The identification of craft activity was aided by the collapse of roofs and rapid abandonment of the buildings leaving valuable materials *in situ* as *de facto* refuse on the work surfaces of buildings. Of particular interest is the detailed nature of the multi-crafting activity that took place within Patio H, 9N-8 and the distinctive cultural contexts of this production. This craft production is both sacred and secular in nature and the architectural, artifactual, mortuary, and iconographic evidence for this work is described here along with pre-liminary interpretations for what they tell us about the or-ganization of elite domestic crafting. It is likely that one of the reasons elite crafting has not been identified in other Maya sites is due to the inability of traditional excava-tion strategies to identify areas where work was carried out.

Cultural Formation Processes and Craft Production

The finished products of craft production are usually not found at production sites since finished goods would be delivered elsewhere, unless circumstances resulted in their in situ preservation in archaeological context. Under typi-cal situations, only micro-debitage will be found because the media worked are often exotic and valuable material, i.e., marine shell, greenstone, or pyrite. Even small pieces of debitage from these objects can be utilized as mosaic elements (Inomata 2001) or inlays for teeth. Furthermore, the methods of manufacturing craft items from greenstone and shell (e.g. grinding, abrasion, and polishing) produce sand and grit sized by-products not large enough to be re-coverable by traditional excavation techniques. For work in wood, bark, feathers, or hide no debitage would be preserved. In addition, the removal of serviceable tools used in craft

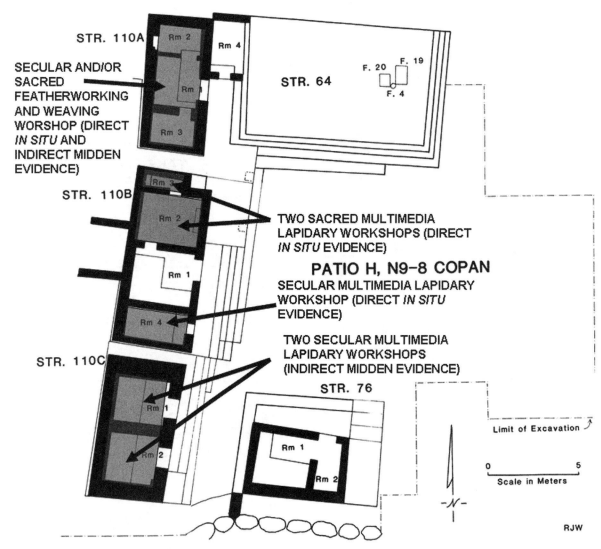

Figure 2. Location of Multi-craft Workshops with Patio H, 9N-8.

production when sites were abandoned further complicates and obscures the ability to identify craft workshops. However, differential discard patterns of exhausted tools and debitage from craft activity should allow for the identification of craft workshops and the kinds and rate of production activities carried out in them.

Research Methodology

All architectural elements were mapped *in situ*, and detailed plan maps and building cross-section drawings were prepared. All in situ soil matrices directly above bench and floor surfaces were distinguished from overlying rubble and fill, carefully hand troweled, and sifted through 6 mm mesh screen. Eight liters of soil, where possible, was collected

from each provenience, floated to remove the light fraction organic materials and the remaining heavy fraction screened through 1 mm mesh sieves. An additional 0.5 liters was retained for pH, chemical, petrographic, pollen, and sedimentary analysis.

Patio proveniences were treated somewhat differently, with the standard 2 × 2 meter grid units divided into four 1 × 1 quadrants. Three were excavated by hand without screening, while the soil from the southwest quadrant was sifted through 6 mm mesh screen. This was done to evaluate the degree of bias between screened and non-screened samples considered necessary for comparative purposes since Patio H was the only Patio in 9N-8 where substantial screening was employed.

The artifacts from these excavations were classified according to functional and technological criteria, counted and weighed, and contour maps of their spatial distribution prepared using the SYMAP contour mapping program for both the adjusted 6mm screened patio proveniences and the 1mm fine wet screened proveniences. This was done to ascertain if the artifacts from secondary sheet midden deposits in the patio could be associated with their room of origin, and, if so, to directly compare them with the artifact frequencies from their respective floor and bench surfaces. The value ranges for artifact types from the 6mm samples were divided into five equal quintiles that formed the contour intervals. Trend surface maps were produced for the 6mm samples while simple interpolated maps were produced for the 1mm samples. This difference in map type was necessary because of small sample sizes and the numerous zero values for many of 1mm proveniences.

The data recovered and analyzed from the excavation of Patio H, 9N-8 reveal four lines of evidence that indicate the presence of lapidary craft specialization in this patio: architectural, artifactual, mortuary, and iconographic.

Architectural Evidence for Craft Production

Mound Group 9N-8 is a residential compound composed of at least ten residential patios. Eight of these patios cluster around an elevated platform on which Patio A, the largest and most substantial residential house group, and Patio B are located (Figure 1). Patio H is located adjacent to Patio A on its northeast margin and Patio B on its western margin. Although Patio H is peripheral to this platform and situated at a lower elevation, the patio group is spacious and composed of several substantial structures (Figure 2). Three of the buildings (Structures 110A, 110B, 110C) form a range structure situated on a long platform, whose height is over one meter, on the west end of the group. These buildings are accessed by a single staircase in front of Structure 110B, with an additional staircase later added to it for access to Structure 110C. All of these structures have evidence of crafting activities.

Four buildings, Structures 76, 110A, 110B, and 110C, are interpreted as containing residential rooms. These buildings are partitioned into two to four rooms, most of which contain a sleeping bench, and each room opens directly onto the patio through a door. Examples of this layout include Rooms 1 and 4 of Structure 110A, Rooms 1 and 4 of Structure 110B, and Rooms 1 and 2 in Structure 110C;. Alternatively a room may be accessed from a central vestibule at the front of the building as is the case for Rooms 1 and 2 of Structure 76, and Rooms 2 and 3 of Structure 110A (see Figure 2). Two of the buildings, Structures 110A and 110C,

have vaulted roofs while Structure 110B had a substantial beam and mortar roof with a staircase that accessed its roof. These are clearly the residences of very high status elites.

The notable exceptions to this architectural pattern are Rooms 2 and 3 of Structure 110B. These rooms appear purposely constructed to have restricted access and are not directly accessible from outside the building. Room 2 of Structure 110B can only be accessed by a narrow 50 cm gap between the northern end of the bench face of Room 1 and its northern wall. This gap leads to a door opposite the northern end of the bench. Room 3 is a narrow slot-like room with an even more restricted entrance that is only accessible through Room 2. Room 3 is located in the extreme northwest corner of Structure 110B, an area with the greatest linear distance from the entrance to the room suite of Structure 110B. The small, secluded, and unusual room layout suggests a limited range of possible activities, none of which were purely residential. Room 2 has the largest floor area of any room in Patio H and has a narrow, low, small bench against the center of the eastern wall; this is the smallest bench of any room in Patio H and is too small to be a sleeping bench. As will be demonstrated, it functioned as a storage shelf for tools and materials used in craft production.

The unusual layouts of Rooms 2 and 3 suggest distinct non-domestic activities. The secluded nature of the rooms with restricted access suggests that secretive activities took place inside them that might relate to esoteric, religious behavior, even restricted from other elites. Despite their restricted access these rooms have a central position within the patio suggesting that the activities that took place in Rooms 2 and 3 had played a primary role within Patio H and 9N-8 as a whole. All of the 16 rooms of Structures 110A-C and Structure 64 are accessed by the single staircase and its lateral addition, which leads up directly to Room 1 of Structure 110B.

Room 3 of Structure 110A also has an unusual layout that indicates that it had a non-domiciliary (sleeping) function. This room has an elevated floor accessed by a staircase from the central room of the structure (Room 1) and lacks a bench. Additionally, there are three vertical gaps in the eastern wall of Rooms 2 and 3 that serve as windows for letting in sunlight. The architectural layout and the restricted access of these rooms suggest that the activities that took place within them were of special importance.

Artifactual Evidence for Lapidary Craft Production

Structures 110A and 110B were destroyed by some catastrophic event, presumably an earthquake, which caused

Figure 3. In Situ Features in Room 2, Structure 110B, 9N-8.

their roofs to collapse and seal cultural remains, including many tools and artifacts in situ on their floor and bench surfaces. The result of this catastrophic event is that it is possible to view, in a very detailed way, the actual artifacts used in rooms, a rare situation for most Late Classic Maya rooms which were continually swept clean (Haviland 1963; Webster 1987). The copious amount of de facto refuse recovered facilitates the reconstruction of the activities that took place within rooms.

The strongest evidence for craft specialization in Patio H is provided by the *in situ* materials found on the interior surfaces of Rooms 2 and 3 of Structure 110B (Figures 3–4). Apparently the earthquake took place at night, or occurred so suddenly that valuable, useful material could not be retrieved, thereby freezing in time the artifacts that reveal the actual behaviors and activities that took place in these rooms. Room 2 of Structure 110B contains the widest range of artifacts that reflect craft activity taking place in a sacred, ritual context.

A ceramic censer (Feature 7), with copious amounts of charcoal, was located in the west central area of the room directly on the floor surface of Room 2, Structure 110B (Figures 3–4). This censer is thought to have provided light for the apparently windowless room by functioning as a receptacle for a torch. Although there is no evidence for windows on the east wall, because of low preserved wall height, the secretive nature of entry would seem to preclude them. Windows were not found on the north or east walls that were preserved to a sufficient height to reveal them if they were present.

Also found in the room was a crushed jar near a worked olivine-basalt river cobble, Feature 8 (Figures 3–4). The cobble had a flat, ground facet and was associated with numerous fragments of mussel shell. This worked cobble, although faceted, is not a polishing stone. Its flat faceted surface was ground and polished smooth, but has numerous striations on its face. These scratches cannot be attributed to use as a polishing or grinding tool since the striations occur at every conceivable angle, criss-cross each other, and are characteristically straight. Furthermore, all of the striations are clear and there were not affected by grinding or polishing, which would have obliterated these scratches. This cobble appears to have served as an anvil or cutting platform where some unknown material was cut with chert or obsidian tools. A casual experiment demonstrated that olivine-basalt can be scratched with obsidian, and can producing striations similar to those observed on the faceted cobble. The mussel shell remains are problematic due to their highly fragmentary condition. Whether they functioned as tools (scrapers or knives) or as craft material utilized for their nacerous finish is unknown. Feature 8 is interpreted as a work station for craft production.

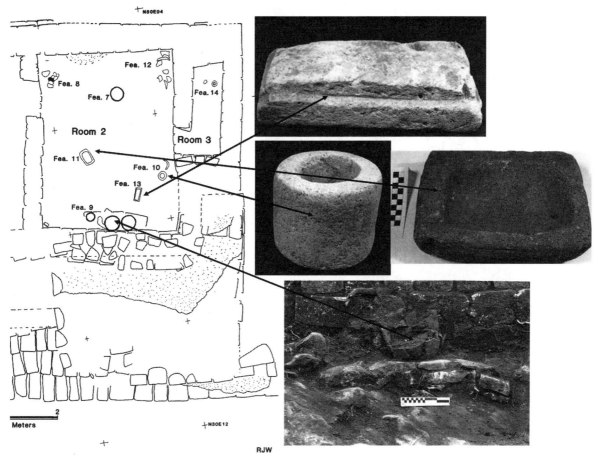

Figure 4. Plan Drawing of Room 2, Structure 110B with Artifacts and Feature 9.

Another workstation has been identified in Room 2 of Structure 110B. It contains a number of tools labeled as features in an area near the east central region of the room. Feature 10 (Figures 3–4) consists of a volcanic tuff stone that was fashioned into a hollow cylinder with straight interior and exterior walls. It appears to be a finished artifact and its association with other tools on the floor and bench of this room suggest it is involved in some way with craft production. Two highly speculative functions, based solely on form, are its use as a roller or perhaps a mold for shaping the cylindrical walls of ceramic beakers. Associated with this tuff cylinder is half of a small ceramic bowl whose remaining portion could not be found nearby in spite of careful searching. It may be that vessel 4 of Feature 9, located in the southeast corner of the room, is its remaining portion. If it is, the extreme distance between these portions, 2.2 meters, would indicate the severity of the quake. Unfortunately, it was not until after the ceramic analysis was performed that it was realized that the two vessels might be related and so the possible match has not been checked.

Feature 11 (Figures 3–4, 6) is also associated with the second workstation. It consists of rectangular bi-concave stone grinding palette that was plotted in situ. It is similar to a metate, but has two shallow basin-shaped rectangular depressions forming the working surfaces, one on each face. However, only one of the faces, the one found facing up, exhibited any evidence of use (Figure 4). Its surface was concave, sloping gently from the outer edge or rim. The shallow basin-shaped depression on the reverse face was unused (Figure 4). The obverse side might have had a similar form that was ground down through use. Possibly the reverse side would have been used when the obverse side was no longer serviceable. It is also possible that the artifact was being manufactured and the reverse face would have eventually been finished to resemble the obverse face. However, no tools or grinding implements were found in the vicinity of the palette, suggesting that it might have been a finished product. The fact that the palette has an elevated rim suggests that it was used to prepare a liquid or loose powdery material of considerable value, perhaps pigment

Figure 5. Feature 9 Work Table with Ceramic Vessels.

for paint. The soil from the surface of the palette was removed by brush and retained for chemical analysis, which has not as yet been performed.

Feature 13 (Figures 3–4), is a rectangular "brick-like" cut tuff block, with an expanded lateral basal molding. The surface of the block is irregular and has gouges and abrasions in several areas. This artifact is probably an unfinished box lid, although no stone box was associated with it. However, a box could have been fabricated from wood and not preserved, or the lid was manufactured before the box was manufactured. This feature is also associated with the second workstation within this room.

Storage Bench for Craft Tools and Materials

Feature 9 (Figures 4–6) is the most spectacular group of artifacts recovered from this workshop. This feature consists of a narrow, low, shelf-like bench situated up against the central eastern interior wall of Room 2, Structure 110B. Although this bench is located directly adjacent to the second workstation, it seems likely that it is functionally associated with all the workstations in Rooms 2 and 3 of Structure 110B. Three ceramic vessels were situated on the surface of this bench. Vessel 1, the northernmost vessel on the bench, is a Sisero cylinder. This vessel served as a storage container for both tools and raw materials that were found in its interior. Included in the interior matrix of Vessel 1 were 10 obsidian prismatic blade sections. Five of these were plotted in situ while the remaining five were recovered from the lower

soil matrix of the vessel. Four of these blade sections were dated using obsidian hydration and yielded a two sigma range of AD 713 – AD 1126 putting the workshops within the Late Classic through Postclassic time span. This soil was fine screened through one mm mesh sieves for micro-artifacts. All 10 obsidian blades were examined for use-wear under a binocular microscope at 20X magnification and classified according to the categories developed by Hay (1978). The 20 edges, two each per blade, exhibited the following wear categories: 14 light to heavy sawing edges, 1 planing bit on top of a sawing edge, one light slicing, and 4 unutilized edges. Specific edge-wear and blade metric attributes, where available, are presented in Table 1. It is suggested that these blade fragments represent hafted tools that were stored in a quiver-like manner and used for working the artifacts recovered from the bench. These obsidian tools were undoubtedly hafted on wooden handles.

In addition to the obsidian tools, five pieces of cut and worked *Spondylus* marine shell fragments were plotted *in situ* in the jar along with an *Olivella* shell bead. A large solitary unmodified potsherd was found at the bottom of the vessel. All of these artifacts were located in the lower 7 cm of soil matrix within this vessel. A small fragment of worked/fractured olivine-basalt was situated on the front edge of the bench up against the western margin of Vessel 1 and a worked deer antler tine tool was located and plotted in situ on the bench between the eastern wall of the room and Vessel 1. The distal end of the antler tine tool has been ground to a point and polished by use, suggesting it functioned as an awl for working on material softer than

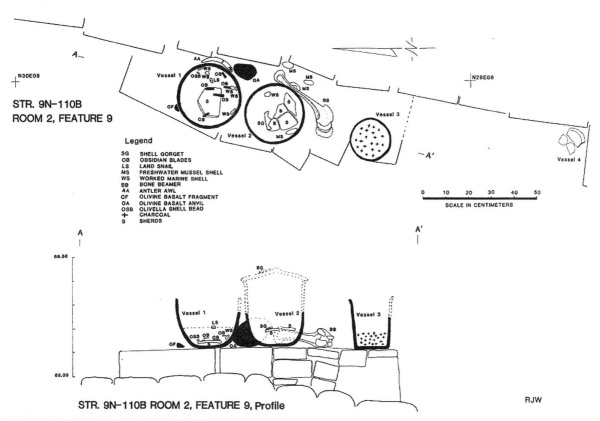

Figure 6. Feature 9 Plan Map and Profile.

Table 1. Metric and edge-wear Attributes of the Obsidian Blades from Vessel 1, Feature 9.

	Specimen	Length (mm)	Width (mm)	Thickness (mm)	Weight (gm)	Blade	Edge-wear	
							Edge 1	Edge 2
Recovered from Soil Matrix	A	59.0	12.4	2.9	3.22	midsection	shallow, heavy dense sawing	shallow, heavy dense sawing
	B	26.5	13.2	2.8	1.12	midsection	deep, light sawing	deep, light sawing
	C	20.0	11.4	2.4	.64	distal	none	none
	D	22.8	14.5	3.2	1.15	platform	none	light slicing
	E	13.9	14.3	3.1	.77	midsection	shallow, moderate, dense sawing	none
Plotted *in situ*	1	32.5	13.6	2.7		midsection	shallow, moderate sawing	very shallow, moderate sawing
	2	38.9	14.6	3.8		midsection	heavy, dense, shallow sawing	planning over very dense sawing
	3	48.0	9.0	2.3		distal	dense, shallow (plunge core) sawing	light shallow sawing[1]
	4	57.1	11.9	3.2		distal	dense, shallow sawing	dense, shallow sawing
	5	29.8	1.06	3.6		platform[2]	dense, shallow sawing	dense, shallow sawing

[1]Concentrated away from the distal end; also a single notch, perhaps for hafting
[2]Two notches on opposite edges just below the platform for apparent hafting

bone. The proximal end of the tine tool has a chisel-like flattened beveled surface also polished through use, suggesting it functioned as a gouge or smoother used to work soft materials like leather or hide. A small olivine-basalt faceted pebble is located on the bench just south of the bone gouge.

Vessel 2, a Sisero caldero, was centrally located on the bench. It contained a fragment of worked *Spondylus*, a small fragment of mussel shell and a portion of a ceramic censer lid broken into five pieces. More importantly it contained a fragment of star shaped marine-shell gorget that will be discussed shortly.

A large worked femur beamer, probably from a jaguar, and several fragments of mussel shell were located on the bench between Vessel 2 and the eastern wall of the room. A long groove extending the length of the distal diaphysis of the jaguar femur was formed by removing part of the shaft. The hollow groove was probably used as a smoother or polisher with the epiphyses used as handles. A medium such as leather, bark, wood or cloth was probably worked with this tool. A Sepulturas censer with cacao pod adornos (Vessel 3) was situated on the southern end of the bench adjacent to Vessel 2. It contained copious amounts of charcoal but no other artifacts were found inside. This censer functioned as either a light source for the room, as a container for a torch, or else burned incense as part of the ritual prescription for artifact manufacture, perhaps both. The censor lid found in Vessel 2 may have originated from this vessel.

Half of an unfinished star shaped gorget made of marine conch shell was found resting on top of the censer lid and covered by the sherds from the crushed wall of Vessel 2 in the bottom of Vessel 2. Its matching fragment was found on the floor surface in front of the bench. When fitted together, the gorget is an eight-pointed star with a large central hole with two small holes for suspension drilled on its margin (Figure 7). The gorget has been modified to such an extent as to render identification of the species impossible. However, based on its size, color, curvature, and texture, it is unquestionably of Atlantic/Caribbean origin, probably *Busycon*. This artifact is unique in the Classic Maya region although it is depicted iconographically, a topic that will be considered shortly. It seems that this gorget originally was either outside Vessel 2 or perhaps resting on a lid covering the vessel and then was broken by collapsing roof debris, causing it to be deposited in two separate locales.

The gorget is unfinished and its method of fabrication is typical for Mesoamerican shell working, with the points of the star apparently cut by obsidian blades (Castro and Arellano 2009; Bautista 2009; Espinosa 2009; Solis and Cantu 2009; Melgar et al. 2009). This is observed in the shape of the cutting grooves on the gorget, which are shallow, have straight V-shaped sides, and overlap with one another as a

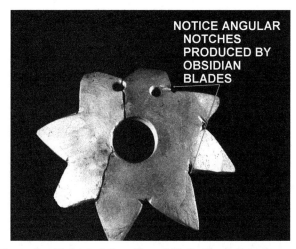

Figure 7. Unfinished Star Shaped Shell Gorget from Room 2, Structure 110B.

result of cutting through the relatively thick shell. These grooves are consistent with the heavy sawing of hard material observed on some of the obsidian blades from Vessel 1 (See Table 1). The number of obsidian blades required to produce this artifact would be high, since marine shell is very hard.

The use of obsidian blades as cutting tools to produce this shell gorget seems to be an incredibly slow, cumbersome, and wasteful method of manufacture but these patterns of manufacture have been replicated in experiments conducted on shell by researchers at the Templo Mayor museum in Mexico City (Castro and Arellano 2009; Bautista 2009; Espinosa 2009; Solis and Cantu 2009; Melgar et al. 2009). Also, even though this production is not industrial, it seems that other manufacturing techniques, such as string and sand or use of harder cutting material such as chert, could have been employed, but they were not. It is argued that the seemingly wasteful production of this artifact is a ritual requirement in its manufacture because of its sacred context and function. It is suggested that the ritual prescription for its production required the use of obsidian, which although hardly rare or exotic at Copan, has a more limited distribution within the Copan region than chert (Webster et al. 1999). The more time, resources, and expense put into the item, the greater its value, and probably more important, the greater its sanctity. Thus, from a purely economic point of view its production using obsidian blades makes no sense, but from a sociopolitical, religious or ritual perspective it does. After all, these craft specialists were elites, who were removed from basic food production. The strategy was not cost-effective, but the creation of a religiously charged, sacred object would need to be produced under strict ritual prescriptions in a special sacred place. Room 2 of Structure

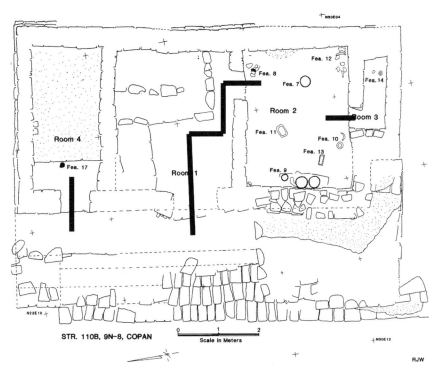

Figure 8. Direct and Indirect Room Access in Structure 110B.

110B was an isolated location where esoteric artifacts were produced from exotic and costly material (Figure 8). That this was the case will be elaborated below.

Other de facto refuse found in Room 2, Structure 110B includes a crushed Casaca Striated olla in the northwest corner of the room. This was labeled Feature 12 (Figures 3–4) and probably served as a chamber pot, water storage jar, or had some other utilitarian function.

Room 3 of Structure 110B, unlike Room 2, had very little cultural material on its floor, only three obsidian blade sections. However, two important artifacts indicative of ritual crafting were located in this room: a straight-sided cylindrical sandstone cup with double basins was found lying directly adjacent to a small olivine-basalt celt (Figures 9–10). The blunt end of this celt or hacha as it is called in Mesoamerica, is roughened by pecking and is thought to have been used in working the unfinished side of the cup. The double-ended cylindrical cup is, to my knowledge, a unique artifact, probably religious/ritual in function. The fact that craft production took place in such a small, confined room suggests a sacred context of craft production. This double-ended cylindrical cup is, to my knowledge, a unique artifact, probably religious/ritual in function.

Room 4 also contained *in situ* tools and craft items on its floor and bench surface in quantities indicating craft production. However, craft production here does not seem to have been sacred/esoteric in nature. An olivine-basalt faceted pebble identical to that found in Feature 8 was plotted *in situ* on the floor immediately in front of the bench (Figure 11) where it appears to have fallen from the edge of the bench onto the floor during the earthquake. A sandstone abrading tool was recovered in three pieces from the floor. A large whole marine cowry shell with a facet ground on its surface was recovered from the bench (Figure 12). A dove shell and *Olivella* shell were also recovered from this room. This flat, rectangular shaped palette has a series of well-worn sharpening grooves on both sides. The grinding apparently was from sharpening pointed bone or wood tools and produced two concave faces with multiple groove impressions that are almost worn through (Figure 12).

Unlike Rooms 2, 3, and 4 of Structure 110B, Room 1 had no *in situ de facto* refuse on its floor or bench surface. Since this room has a direct exit, useful or valuable artifacts might have been removed during the earthquake.

Structure 110A also contained *in situ de facto* refuse indicative of specialized multi-crafting activity (Figures 13–14). A large Casaca striated ceramic jar was located *in situ* in the northwest corner of the Room 1 bench. The vessel was crushed when the wall between room 1 and Room 2 collapsed, scattering fragments onto the floor. Other artifacts found in this room include three spindle whorls and three bone needles.

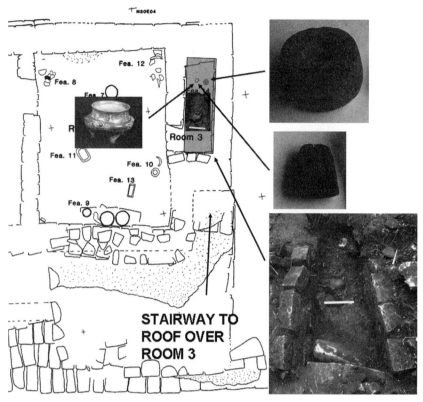

Figure 9. Unfinished Stone Cup and Hacha in Room 3, Structure 110B under Child Burial in Rubble of Abandoned Structure and Above Burial Niche.

Figure 10. Unfinished Stone Cup and Tool Used in Its Manufacture Room 3, Structure 110B.

Figure 11. Olivine Basalt Work Platform In Situ in Room 4, Structure 110C.

Room 3 of Structure 110A has an elevated floor without a bench and contained a portion of a pedestaled metate, a faceted olivine-basalt anvil, and an intricately carved bone

spatula on its elevated floor surface. Bone spatulas are known to have been used by Aztec feather workers for gluing feathers to fabric (Sahagun 1959:162–169), and the faceted anvil would provide a surface for the cutting of feathers by

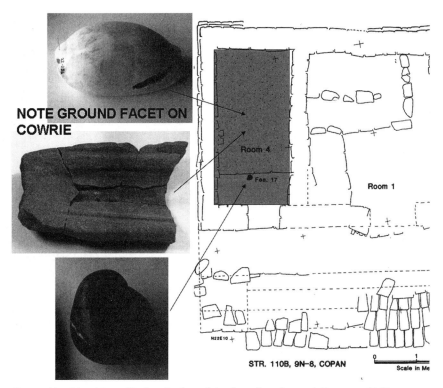

Figure 12. Plan Map of In Situ Tools and Artifacts from Room 4, Structure 110B.

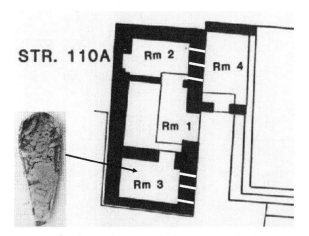

Figure 13. Featherworking Spatula from Room 3, Structure 110A.

obsidian blades. It is suggested that Room 3 functioned as a workshop involved in cloth production, embroidering of marine shell, feather working (cutting and gluing), and perhaps cutting hide for the production of elite costumes. This crafting is further supported by the existence of three window slots built into the eastern walls of Rooms 2 and 3 (Figures 13–14). I argue that these windows provide light for the room interiors. This type of activity would be con-

sonant with the other specialized elite lapidary craft activity found in Patio H.

Although Structure 110C (Figure 15) did not contain *de facto* refuse in either of its two room, there is substantial evidence that crafting took place here. In fact, this structure probably had the highest rate of craft production of any building in Patio H since the highest density of sheet refuse, perhaps the best indication of amount of crafting, is found in front of this structure. The absence of *de facto* tools is probably a result of curation, since the roof did not collapse during the earthquake. Secular crafting is believed to have been practiced here because the configurations of the rooms of this structure have a typical domiciliary floor plan with a sleeping bench facing an open doorway. This would suggest craft production is much more frequent for the patio as a whole than reflected in the ritual workshop, and that secular craft production for elite prestation, ceremony, or ritual was the primary economic and sociopolitical function of the patio.

Primary Room Deposits and Sheet Refuse

As valuable as *in situ* de facto deposits are for reconstructing activities, they represent only a small interval of time and do not represent the full range of craft activities

Figure 14. Reconstructed Structure 110A with Room Layouts and Window Slots.

Figure 15. Photograph of Structure 110C Reconstructed.

practiced throughout the occupation of Patio H. Instead, discarded primary refuse found on room floor and bench surfaces would be more representative of room activities than useful tools and/or finished artifacts subject to curation. However, since rooms would periodically have been swept clean of debris, the sheet refuse and midden accumulations on the patio surface adjacent to building entrances would be expected to contain the most complete record of the activities that originally took place in these buildings. This supposition was confirmed in the excavations.

Table 2. Frequency by Count of Obsidian Blades from Patio H.

Structure	Room	Inside Room		Patio in Front of Structure		Combined Structure and Patio	
		N	%	N	%	N	%
110A	1	31	13.5				
	3	28	12.2				
	4	6	2.6				
	TOTAL	65	28.4	186	12.2	251	14.3
110B	1	74	32.3				
	2	13	5.6	490	32	580	37.9
	3	3	1.3				
	4	36	15.7	341	22.3	377	24.6
	TOTAL	126	55	831	54.3	957	54.4
110C	1	13	5.7	196	12.8	209	13.6
	2	25	10.9	316	20.7	341	22.3
	TOTAL	38	16.6	512	33.5	550	31.3
GRAND TOTAL		229	100.0	1529	100.0	1758	100.0

The highest density of artifacts in the Patio H excavations was recovered from a narrow strip, less than four meters wide, against the eastern (front) base of Structure 110. The SYMAP contour maps indicate that the highest densities of artifact types and micro-debitage material types, both by count and weight occurred immediately in front of the entrances, suggesting that they represent secondary refuse swept from the rooms adjacent to them. This allows a direct comparison of artifacts from the midden/sheet refuse areas in front of rooms with artifacts in their interior rooms. Obsidian blade sections were used for this comparison. The high density of artifacts in these middens indicates that most activities took place within room interiors or on the platform terraces in front of the rooms, activity, since blades were directly involved in this craft from the *in situ* evidence. Table 2 provides the frequencies of obsidian blades from room interior surfaces for Structures 110A, 110B, and 110C and their adjacent patio aprons. Obsidian blade use appears most intense in Rooms 1, 2, and 3 of Structure 110B where 39.2% of the blades from room interiors were found. In fact the rooms of Structure 110B had the highest obsidian blade frequency, accounting for 55.0% of all blades. However, these data are misleading because of the way differential sweeping might bias room frequencies. High frequencies artifacts, including four bone needles, 44 fragments of marine shell including an *Olivella* bead, and 10 fragments of exotic stone were recovered in the patio in front of Structure 110A. These artifacts directly functionally complement the feather spatula, and the three spindle whorls that were found in Room 3 of this structure, and the seven bone needles recovered in Room 1 of Structure 110A.

Now that the existence of crafting has been established at 9N-8 Patio H it is necessary to understand the rate of production that took place in these workshops. A method of evaluating the relative rate of craft production was developed utilizing obsidian blade frequency in different archaeological deposits. This assumes of course that obsidian blade tools were used in crafting and relate to differential use in this activity. This method is referred to as the Index of Activity and is simply the number of exhausted blade sections found in middens in front of rooms divided by the number of blades that were found within the room. The idea is that the greater the number of blade sections found in the midden compared to the number found inside of the rooms is a relative measure of greater use of obsidian blade tools and hence greater craft activity. These data are presented in Table 3. Based on the Index of Activity, Structure 110C has twice the obsidian blade use as 110B (13.47 compared to 6.59), and 4.7 times that of Structure 110A. This last figure is undoubtedly even lower since the patio apron for Structure 110A also served as the discard area for the six rooms behind Structures 110A and 110B (Figure 1), that are not included in this study. This emphasizes the lower obsidian blade use associated with the costume craft activities in Structure 110A since costume manufacture would utilize fewer obsidian blades than the lapidary activity in Patio H.

The data suggest that although Rooms 2 and 3 in Structure 110B have a specialized architectural layout, the intensity of obsidian use is less than in Rooms 1 and 2 of Structure 110C. This reinforces the ritual nature of craft activities in Rooms 2 and 3 of Structure 110B, which has already been observed in architectural and *de facto in situ* artifact evidence.

Table 3. Calculation of Obsidian Index of Activity.

Structure	Room	Room Floor(N)	Room Bench (N)	Room Total (N)	Patio (N)	Index of Activity[1]
110A	1	13	18	31	139[2]	2.35
	2[3]	n/a	n/a	n/a		
	3	28	n/a	28	included in Room 1	
	4	6	n/a	6	47[2]	7.83
	TOTAL	47	18	65	186	2.86
110B	1	10	64	74	490	5.44
	2	13	n/a	13	included in Room 1	
	3	3	n/a	3	included in Room 1	
	4	19	17	36	341	9.47
	TOTAL	45	81	126	831	6.59
110C	1	13	0	13	196	15.07
	2	15	10	25	316	12.64
	TOTAL	28	10	38	512	13.47
GRAND TOTAL		120	109	229	1529	6.67

[1] Patio N/Total Room N

[2] Rooms 1 and 4 share a common midden; Room 1 also includes refuse from Rooms 2 and 3. Therefore, values are weighted by the number of rooms accessed by the middens through a common door.

[3] Data from Room 2 have not been included; it is assumed that 25% of the midden is derived from Room 2

This pattern of less crafting activity in Rooms 1 and 2 of Structure 110B is also observed in the density of material debitage from the patio surface. The buildings and midden deposits with the highest densities and greatest range of exotic materials (i.e. marine shell, basalt, exotic stone such as schist, greenstone, and pyrite) are from Structures 110A and 110C, not 110B (Table 4, Figures 16–18). These data substantiate the hypothesis that two different types or contexts of crafting took place in Patio H: 1) a low output mode associated with restricted access and specialized layouts of Rooms 2 and 3 in Structure 110B and Room 3 of Structure 110A, and the open access, non-restricted, and non-specialized room layout with a higher rate of craft production within Structure 110B, Room 4, and Structures 110A Rooms 1 and 4, and 110C. These data suggest that a low production ritual lapidary craft specialization can be distinguished from higher production secular lapidary craft activity that utilizes the same media but in a different cultural context, profane versus sacred. These two distinctive patterns are further supported by mortuary data.

Mortuary Evidence for Craft Specialization

The argument for the sacred nature of Rooms 2 and 3 of Structure 110B, and its associated craft activities is also supported by mortuary evidence. A Postclassic interment of a child, Burial 22–4 was placed in a clean earth grave excavated into the rubble of Room 3. This is the only Postclassic burial found in Patio H. The interment of this child in Room

3 together with a staircase leading directly above this room is religiously important and clearly indicates the site of an ancestral shrine.

A massive tomb the same size as Room 2 of Structure 110B was found under its floor and was contemporary with its occupation (Figure 19). This tomb contained the remains of five individuals, four adult males and a child. The last adult interred in the tomb, had extreme cranial deformation and unusually developed muscle attachment ridges on his arms and wrists compared with other Copan skeletons (Rebecca Storey, personal communication). This morphological condition indicates a differential use of the hands and arms in physical labor. This individual is clearly an elite based on the size of the tomb, the largest in Patio H, and the cranial deformation, which had to be performed when the individual is a child. Additionally, the tomb has a niche in its northern wall. In it was a frog pot. Room 3 of Str.110 B is directly above this niche, as is the Post Classic child burial with its shoe pot offering in the rubble of Room 3.

It is tempting to suggest that a censor was positioned on the roof of Room 3 of Structure 110B that was accessed by the staircase leading from the front of the building. This would allow non-elites to participate publicly in ancestor veneration in what would otherwise be restricted internal space of Room 3. This tomb is the most architecturally elaborate and costly and contains the most lavish grave goods of any burial context in 9N-8 (Storey, personal communication). It is doubted that the exaggerated muscle attachments resulted from agriculture or other generalized labor and seems more likely associated with lapidary activity.

Table 4. Distribution of Selected Artifacts in Rooms and Adjacent Patio. (a) marine shell; (b) exotic stone; (c) bone needles.

Structure	Room	1 mm screened		6 mm screened		combined screened		Index of Activity[1]
		N	weight (gm)[2]	N	weight (gm)[3]	N	Weight (gm)	
110A	1	3	0.45	12	11.0	15	11.45	2.93
	3	4	0.21	0	0	4	0.21	11.00
	4	3	0.05	0	0	3	0.05	14.67
	TOTAL	10	0.71	12	11.0	22	11.71	2.00
	Adjacent Patio	18	.58	26	53.0	44	53.58	
110B	1	0	0	0	0	0	0	
	2	5	0.30	61	78.0	66	78.30	0.71
	3	0	0	0	0	0	0	
	4	5	0.27	1	283.0	6	283.27	7.83
	TOTAL	10	.57	62	361	72	361.57	0.65
	Adjacent Patio	39	1.29	8	127.0	47	128.29	
110C	1	1	0.02	0	0	1	0.02	57.00
	2	3	0.08	0	0	3	0.08	19.00
	TOTAL	4	0.10	0	0	4	0.10	14.25
	Adjacent Patio	49	0.68	8	67.0	57	67.68	
110A	1	7	0.12	0	0	7	0.12	1.43
	3	0	0	1	<0.1	1	<0.1	10.00
	4	0	0	0	0	0	0	
	TOTAL	7	0.12	1	<0.1	8	<0.22	1.25
	Adjacent Patio	10	0.20	0	0	10	0.20	
110B	1	2	0.16	0	0	2	0.16	9.00
	2	3	0.08	1	<0.1	4	<0.18	4.50
	3	0	0	0	0	0	0	
	4	10	0.10	0	0	10	0.10	1.80
	TOTAL	15	0.34	1	<0.1	16	<0.44	1.12
	Adjacent Patio	18	0.56	0	0	18	0.56	
110C	1	1	0.01	1	<0.1	2	<0.11	12.00
	2	0	0	1	<0.1	1	<0.1	24.00
	TOTAL	1	0.01	2	<0.2	3	<0.21	8.00
	Adjacent Patio	17	0.81	7	<0.1	24	<0.91	
110A	1	4	1.06	3	3.2	7	4.26	0.57
	3	0	0	0	0	0	0	
	4	0	0	0	0	0	0	
	TOTAL	4	1.06	3	3.2	7	4.26	0.57
	Adjacent Patio	3	0.14	1	0.6	4	0.20	
110B	1	0	0	0	0	0	0	
	2	0	0	0	0	0	0	
	3	0	0	0	0	0	0	
	4	1	0.06	0	0	1	0.06	4.00
	TOTAL	1	0.06	0	0	1	0.06	4.00
	Adjacent Patio	2	?	2	0.4	4	?	
110C	1	0	0	0	0	0	0	
	2	0	0	0	0	0	0	
	TOTAL	0	0	0	0	0	0	
	Adjacent Patio	3	0.14	3	0.7	6	0.74	

[1] patio N/room N
[2] 1 mm samples weighed to 0.01 gm accuracy
[3] 6 mm samples weighed to 0.1 gm accuracy

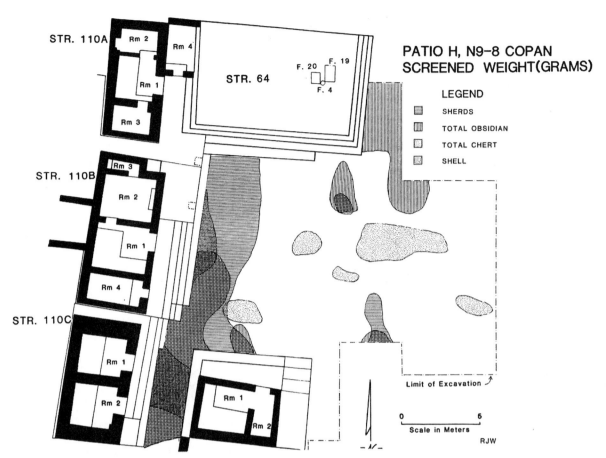

Figure 16. Map Overlays of the Highest Frequency Quintile Contour for Six Millimeter Screened Artifact Categories by Weight.

Another adult was interred with grave goods that included a complete *Spondylus* shell with two fragments of unworked greenstone inside. This offering (Figure 20) contains the same material worked in the room above, suggesting that the individual interred with them was a lapidary specialist. All of these factors seem to indicate the sacred nature of this tomb and the elite status context of its interments.

The tomb is unusual because it is only one of two in 9N-8 that contain multiple interments. This may be a family sepulcher in which important lineage members were interred. It seems that two of the individuals buried in this tomb were involved in craft activity and at least one if not all of these interred individuals were deified ancestors based on the iconographic data present at 9N-8.

Iconographic Evidence for the Ritual Nature of Craft Production

Star-shaped gorgets, with a large central circular perforation, and two suspension holes are depicted in only four iconographic contexts at Copan, to include a bench in Group 8N-11 (Webster et al. 1998, hieroglyphic bench in Structure 82C of 9N8, Patio A.

Star-shaped shell gorgets, with a large central circular perforation, and two suspension holes are depicted in only five iconographic contexts at Copan, to include two on a carved bench in Group 8N-11 (Webster et al. 1998) and three on the carved bench and Structure 82C of 9N-8, Patio A. These gorgets are associated with Pauah Tuns (God N) patrons of scribes and painters (Figures 21–22) (Schele and Miller 1986:54, Fash 1986:338),

Fash (1986:337–338) considers the Pauah Tuns to be the patron deity of the lineage or family of Plaza A, 9N-8. The discovery of Pauah Tuns on the bench at 8N-11 somewhat changes this interpretation. It now seems that the shell gorget functions as a symbol of linkage to the main ruler in the Acropolis. I agree with this interpretation and consider the shell gorget recovered in Patio H and depicted iconographically at Copan in the bench of Structure 82C

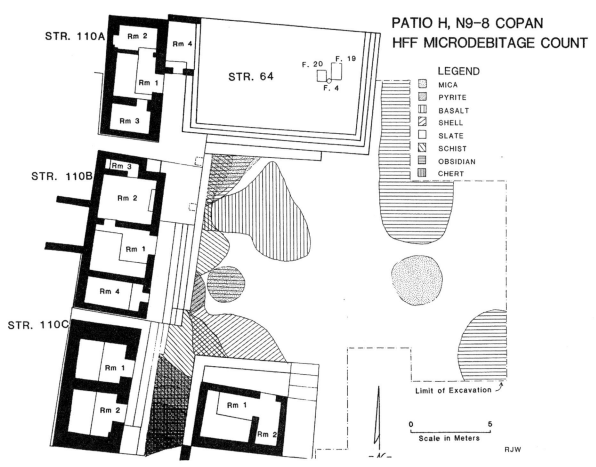

STR. 110A
Rm 2
Rm 4
Rm 1
Rm 3

STR. 64
F. 20 F. 19
F. 4

PATIO H, N9-8 COPAN
HFF MICRODEBITAGE COUNT

LEGEND
MICA
PYRITE
BASALT
SHELL
SLATE
SCHIST
OBSIDIAN
CHERT

STR. 110B
Rm 3
Rm 2
Rm 1
Rm 4

STR. 110C
Rm 1
Rm 2
Rm 1
Rm 2

Limit of Excavation

0   5
Scale in Meters

RJW

Figure 17. Map Overlays of the Highest Frequency Quintile Contour of One Millimeter Screened Microdebitage Material Categories by Count.

of 9N-8 Patio A to represent a supernatural badge or symbol linking the deities of the supernatural world with the living apical ancestor of living lineage heads. This is depicted iconographically on the hieroglyphic bench in Patio A (Figure 22), where three supernatural Pauah Tuns wearing shell gorgets, two of which are illustrated in Figure 21, are holding up the hieroglyphic bench. A fourth figure, also holding up the hieroglyphic bench and facing the Pauah Tuns, is a protagonist that wears a simple necklace of beads instead of a shell gorget. Fash (1986:337–338, Figure 22) considers this figure to represent the deified ancestor of the protagonist in the bench of Patio A, 9N-8. Since no living protagonists are depicted wearing star-shaped shell gorgets, this artifact is considered a supernatural symbol of divine right of lineage headship and is different from the scribe symbol depicted on living protagonists.

The Demographic Composition of the Patio H Workshops

The architectural, artifactual, mortuary, and iconographic evidence provide insight into the demographic composition of sacred and secular craft activity in Patio H. Two patterns of lapidary craft activity have been identified in Patio H, those that took place in rooms whose benches had domiciliary functions as well as crafting and multi-crafting that occurred in the architecturally distinct and specialized rooms that lacked domiciliary benches suggesting exclusive use of craft workshops. The former areas that have evidence of crafting are correlated with secular, but nonetheless elite, craft production, while the latter are correlated exclusively with ritual or sacred craft activity. It is proposed that at least three individuals were engaged in both secular and sacred activities. I suggest that they lived in Rooms 1 and 2 of

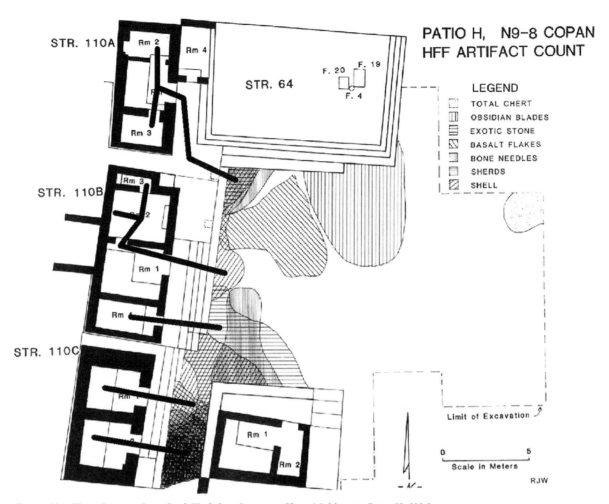

Figure 18. Waste Streams from Craft Workshop Rooms to Sheet Middens in Patio H, 9N-8.

Structure 110C, and Room 4 of Structure 110B where they produced a wide range of secular, elite craft items. They slept in these rooms and probably consumed meals there as well as evidenced by serving bowl sherds found in the middens in front of these rooms. These rooms served as both domiciles and craft workshops.

I contend that these same individuals used Rooms 2 and 3 of Structure 110B on an intermittent basis exclusively to craft sacred esoteric paraphernalia. These rooms have identical layouts each with sleeping benches across the rear wall opposite their central doorways. All of these rooms are accessed by a single staircase in front of Structure 110B. It is suggested that a single artisan resided in each of these rooms and slept there.

The interpretation that three individuals were involved in sacred crafting is supported by the existence of three spatially discrete workstations in these rooms. These are: 1) Feature 8 in Room 2 of Structure 110B; 2) the area in the

vicinity of Features 9, 10, 11, and 13 in Room 2 of Structure 110B; and; 3) and Feature 14 in Room 3 of Structure 110B. Most of the time artisans worked on secular craft items in their own residences. During certain periods, perhaps sacred or ritual calendrical occasions, they would engage in esoteric craft production in Rooms 2 and 3 of Structure 110B.

There is no clear evidence of craft activity in Room 1 of Structure 110B, the room containing the Large L-shaped bench discussed earlier since no features were located there and the fact that the midden is shared with Rooms 2 and 3 make isolating activities from the midden context problematic. A total of 7 obsidian blades were recovered from Room 1 with 64 found on the bench. This would suggest some crafting but they could be tools used in another area for use, perhaps even Rooms 2 or 3. No other tools, anvils, or debitage were found in the room suggesting that crafting did not occur there. Instead, the proximity and exclusive access of this room to Rooms 2 and 3 suggests its resident might

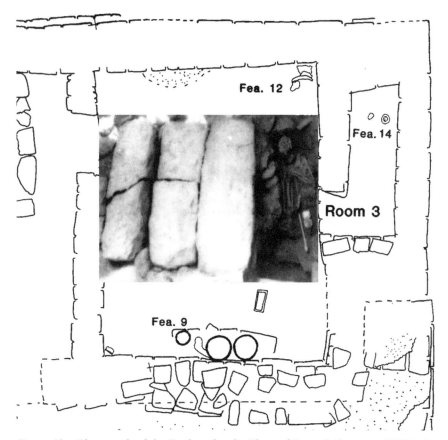

Figure 19. Photograph of the Tomb under the Floor of Room 2, Structure 110B in its location within Structure 110B.

Figure 20. Photograph of Grave Goods from the Tomb under the Floor of Room 2, Structure 110B.

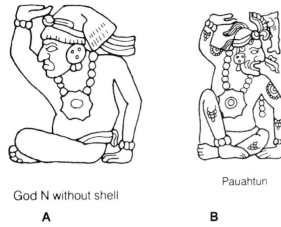

God N without shell   Pauahtun

A   B

Figure 21. Drawings of Pauahtuns with Star Shaped Shell Gorgets from the Bench of Structure 82C, Patio A.' 9N-8, Copan. Figure A is on the right bench support while Figure B is on the left bench support.

have been a priest involved exclusively with esoteric craft activity either by direct participation in crafting or by supervising it within a ritual context. Thus, a minimum total of four individuals were involved in lapidary craft production with three people directly participating in secular multi-crafting and possibly sacred production, and perhaps an additional elite involved exclusively with the sacred, ritual process, although not necessarily producing craft items. However, it might also be the case that only a single a priestly artisan was engaged in all of the multi-crafting in the sacred workshops.

A somewhat different demographic patterning is observed for the costume craft workshop. A dedicated non-domiciliary workshop, Room 3 of Structure 110A, was utilized by two artisans that resided in Rooms 1 and 4 of Structure 110C as inferred from sleeping benches in these rooms. The workstations for Structure 110A are inferred from the locations of the window slats that facilitated light, the lack of floor area in from of the bench in Room 2, and the absence of floor and bench configuration in Room 3 (see Figures 13–14). The room, room access, and bench configuration of Room 4 of Structure 110A is similar to that of the rooms in structure 110C, which were shown to be secular workshops. This might suggesting that secular craft activity was going on there as well but there is no evidence for this and the presence of a shared midden. The combined evidence indicates a total of six artisans involved in multi-crafting a Patio H.

While it is clear that both secular and sacred elite multi-crafting took place in Patio H, it is not certain whether there was a division of tasks among the elite artisans in Patio H, with some producing secular artifacts for use, while others produced the sacred esoteric artifacts for the Ahau

ruler of 9N-8. No tombs or burials were associated with Structure 110C either behind it, in front of it or under the floors and benches of its two rooms. This might suggest that individuals buried within the tomb beneath Room 2, Structure 110B might have resided or worked in Structure 110C. Distinctive room floor plans appear linked to the type of craft products produced within them. This interpretation is consonant with the number of work stations noted within the ritual workshop.

The gender associations of the multi-crafting in Patio H will now be discussed. The review of gender and crafts specialization among the Postclassic Maya of the Yucatan (Clark and Houston 1998) clearly indicates that weaving, carding, spinning of yarn and seam stressing were activities conducted by both men and women suggesting that both were involved in craft activity in Patio H. The differences in crafting activities between Structure 110A and those in Structures 110B and 110C does not appear to be related to social status distinctions, since Structure 110A is a substantial building with a vaulted roof indicating elite occupation. It is possible that the female residents of Structure 110A lived and worked in this building but did not participate in crafting activities in Structure 110B and 110C and vice versa. While it is clear that engendered craft activities took place in separate structures, the residential location and kinship relationship of the male and female artisans is not. Rooms 1 and 4 of Structure 110A could represent married male and female domestic space while rooms 2 and 3 may represent female craft areas. But it could also be the case that all of Structure 110A represents a sacred workshop with the women that crafted there residing in Structure 110C, and Room 4 of 110B. It is likely that all of the individuals associated with Structures 110A-C were members of the same high status social group with different engendered craft occupational specialties.

Inomata (2001: 327–328) suggests that the wife of the scribe living in Structure M8–10 at Aguateca sewed ornaments onto cloth. This might suggest that the artisans are married, a possibility for the craft specialist at the House of the Scribe at M8–10, Aguateca. If the women in Patio H were married to the men living in Structure 110C, or Room 4 of Structure 110B, then there might be no "domestic" costume making taking place in this structure, only sacred or chiefly production. This would also explain the single room with a bench in it. However, the fact that male and female craft production took place in different structures simply means that husbands were the artisans in Structures 110B and 110C and wives were the specialists in Structures 110A.

Cathy Costin (1991, 2001) has developed the dichotomy between independent and attached artisans may not be analytically useful at sites sociopolitically and economically

Figure 22. Patio A, Structure 82C Hieroglyphic Bench with Pauahtuns.

organized like Copan (Lass 1998). The data from Patio H, 9N-8 suggest that craft production is clearly attached rather than independent. But attached in what manner? I argue that this attached status is through consanguinal relationships and represents one of the highest social positions in the society, and crafters were in fact sibs of the ruler. As such it represents a priestly artisan. In chiefdoms sacred elite craft production has a strong hereditary component (Ames 1995; Lass 1998; Spielmann 1998). In most middle range societies, elites are usually only interested in the production of the most valuable items, such as feather working in Hawai'i (Lass 1998:26). In some elite production, skilled crafters are sought out and attached to elite households either through warfare or other means of recruitment because of their crafting skill (Ames 1995; Spielmann 1998; Lass 1998). However, there is no reason to suggest that a household cannot produce its own skilled artisans. Brumfiel (1998:147) has shown that among the Aztec the ruler's sons were taught crafts such as gold working and lapidary manufacture in special rooms. The same may have been occurring in Room 2 of Structure 110B. Of course it could also be the case that some of the children of the Ahau left the patio group to be specifically trained by lapidary specialists to return later to produce elite goods.

With respect to females a similar pattern could exist but if there were a strong patrilocal residence pattern these women would move to another residence or even polity.

However, their skills would be valued if not even a requirement of marriage so there similar training probably did take place. This would be extremely desirable for costume making skill would be highly desirable and would facilitate recruitment of skilled artisans into Patio H through marriage. The upshot of this discussion is that it appears that all recruitment of artisans is within kinship to include both consanguineal and affinal ties rather than recruitment from external non-kinship mechanisms.

The Role of Sacred and Secular Craft Production at Patio H, 9N-8

While there has been much discussion of the nature of ritual craft specialization, crucial information is often omitted in these discussions. Where, for example, was the physical location of craft production and what is the nature of its location relative to the status and ritual organization of the site? Excavation at Patio H, provides these missing data. There are two very important contextual observations regarding star-shaped shell gorgets that have an important bearing on the nature of sacred craft production in 9N-8. Shell gorgets are never depicted being worn by human protagonists, either living or dead, and they are exclusively associated with Pauah Tun deities. Furthermore, they have never been found in burials, dedicatory caches or other offerings. Rather they were a highly curated artifact, passed down from generation to generation or destroyed after use. Furthermore, the unique occurrence of this artifact also indicates that it is a rare artifact.

The production of this type of artifact may have required special, even sacred conditions for its manufacture the knowledge for which may have been limited to select elites. Secretive rituals may have been involved in transforming the raw material from a profane substance to a sacred item and this might explain why the artifact was produced in the isolated Room 2 of Structure 110B. The use of obsidian blades as saws in the fabrication of this artifact may be a ritual requirement in creating the sacred. The Maya believe that obsidian was created when lightning hit the ground and so this material is considered sacred (Schele and Miller 1986:73). Thus obsidian blades are sacred objects and would imbue the material they worked sacred power (Schele and Miller 1986:73). Obsidian blades are used as offerings and also in rituals involved in bloodletting and the obsidian mirror is symbol of God K (Schele and Martin 1986:49). At the Aztec Templo Mayor, secular craft artifacts of exotic materials are fabricated using chert (Melgar et al. 2009) while shell and stone lapidary offerings from sacred contexts were made from obsidian blades. The tomb beneath the floor of Room 2 might have been considered the gateway to the underworld/cosmos with the ancestors in the tomb providing the link to the supernatural world to bring it into the everyday world of the Maya.

Production in Room 3 of Structure 110B was at a very low intensity. Artisans appear to have "wasted" time and resources on the production of these artifacts, although this is probably a component of supernatural ritual required for manufacture in an isolated and secretive place. After all, the artifacts produced were probably considered supernatural in context, if not origin, and probably required some religious ritual to validate their sacred or supernatural character. Furthermore, since the artifacts produced were probably religious and sociopolitical paraphernalia, the production output would be low. Artisans clearly were elite, based on the substantial architecture of Structure 110B, and the mortuary context of the artisans themselves. These include the large and elaborate formal tomb, the extreme cranial deformation of one of the individual in burial 22–41, and the jade inlaid teeth and articulated Spondylus shell with two pieces of unworked greenstone inside it that was associated with burial 22–40. It is suggested that these elites are probably priests that are high ranking lineage members and relatives of the lineage leader residing in Patio A.

It is possible that the star-shaped shell gorget may have been made for the lineage leader of Patio A as a symbol of his ancestral right to rule. Since this lineage is associated with scribes, and Pauah Tuns were the patron deities of scribes (Fash 1986, D. Stuart Personal communication), the link between Patio A and H seems obvious. It is likely that the priests/artisans producing these ritual items are the younger brothers and/or male offspring of the scribe or lineage ruler of Patio A. Such an interpretation is consistent with ethnographic situations where the younger brothers of paramount chiefs serve as priests/shamans and artisans. This is observed in Polynesia (Goldman 1970; Sahlins 1958), the southeastern U.S. (Goggin and Sturtevant 1964; Murdock and White 1972), and more specifically among the Maya (Roys 1943). It may even be the case that the tomb in Structure 110B was the burial ground of the artisan priest for 9N-8 and that these buried ancestors, perhaps now deified provided the necessary bridge between the supernatural world and the political religious world of the Maya. It could also be the case that the tomb under Room 2 of Structure 110B was the burial crypt for the Ajau of Patio A, since no elaborate Late Classic tomb was found in Patio A, making an even more direct link to the artifacts produced in the room above. In any event, the space in which the artisan produced the ritual paraphernalia was clearly sacred and not accessible by even most members of the patio.

This gorget may have served an even more important function since the ultimate occupation of Patio H occurs well after the fall of the last king of the Copan dynasty (Freter 1987). It may be the case that the star-shaped shell gorget is an attempt by the lineage head of 9N-8 to claim divine right to rule and to establish a paramouncy or political dynasty reintegrating the independent and probably declining lineages remaining in the Copan valley. As interesting as this hypothesis may appear it is impossible to test because the 9N-8 was abandoned before this star-shaped gorget could be finished. Structure 110A may also have been involved in sacred production based on its unique slotted windows designed to admit light into secluded rooms that like Rooms 2 and 3 of Structure 110B. Feather working and beading were elite activities associated with the highest levels of status at Copan. Also, there is a burial under the bench of Room 2 of Structure 110A. This female had cranial deformation was buried with a jade pendant and clearly represents a woman of high status but did not have a formal tomb, and no teeth were preserved to indicate the existence of inlaid or filed teeth, which are correlated with the highest female mortuary at 9N-8. Nevertheless, this woman was high status from birth and represented the highest status female buried in 9N-8. This woman had a status equivalent to the men buried under the floor of Room 2 of Structure 110B.

Secular Craft Production

In spite of the sacred craft production found at Patio H, the bulk of the lapidary craft output was secular in nature. There is no difference in the types of media worked in the two types of craft workshops, although there are other differences between them. With the exception of obsidian blade sections and faceted olivine-basalt cobbles, all tools and artifacts differ between the two types of workshops. However, not to much should be made of this distinction since the same artisans worked in both workshops and could therefore move tools to different places as required. However, there was a dedicated work bench in the sacred workshop of Room 2 suggesting otherwise that there were sacred tools confined to sacred spaces. A few tools were found *in situ* in secular workshops suggesting that a sacred/secular dichotomy of tools did exist, if not by functional type then by location.

It is impossible to determine the full range of types of artifacts produced in the four secular workshops since only a few finished artifacts were found. These include a small rim sherd of a travertine bowl found on the bench surface in Room 2 of Structure 110C, two phallic effigies of slate, 11.0, × 1.5 cm. in size, found in the midden in front of Structure 110C, and a broken drilled greenstone pendant. All other material is waste debris from the production process. Likewise, it is also impossible to adequately assign sheet refuse debris to individual rooms within Structure 110B, which contain both secular and sacred workshops. However, the refuse originating from the rooms of Structure 110C, where only secular production was practiced, has higher frequencies of all classes of material than that from structure 110B. The high rate of production and relatively low frequency of finished artifacts consumed by the patio group, other than greenstone in features, caches, and burials throughout 9N-8, suggest that not only were these workshops producing elite paraphernalia for consumption within Group 9N-8, but also for other elites at Copan since no other such workshop has been identified at Copan in spite of extensive excavations of other elite patio groups in the Copan pocket (Fash 1986; Webster et al. 1998).

Since the costume workshop in Room 3 of Structure 110A was involved in non-lapidary production, it is impossible to compare its intensity of craft output with those in Structures 110B and 110C. It would seem that the refuse produced from costume production would be very low. Only obsidian blades would be discarded used and their use rate would be much lower than those involved in lapidary or wood working activity. This lower obsidian use has been empirically verified. Nonetheless, since both 110A and 110B produced elite secular paraphernalia, it is felt that their rates of craft output were probably the same.

It should be re-emphasized that the craft production in Structures 110B and 110C was not restricted to lapidary activities. Wear patterns on obsidian blades, sharpening abraders, bone tools, and the faceted cobbles all suggest that softer, probably perishable material such as wood and hide was also worked reinforcing the notion of multi-crafting. No bark beaters were recovered in Patio H, suggesting that bark cloth was not processed, nor was there any evidence of ceramic production. However, this should not rule out the possibility that finished vessels were painted and/or burnished at this location for firing elsewhere. There is no question that the craft activities are multimedia in material composition and the predominance of lapidary materials may be a function of preservation. Because elite paraphernalia and regalia were produced in these workshops, it is possible that a wide array of other materials including hides, feathers, wood, bone and other perishable media also were fabricated into craft items. This is apparent since many of the tools recovered can not be linked directly with lapidary production nor do they appear to be typical domestic items found in either high status or low status Late Classic Maya households in the Copan Valley (Webster et al. 1999; Webster 1988; Webster and Freter 1988). It is clear that the craftsmen in Patio H were producing a diverse set of craft items for elite consumption, with most of this production used for public display, probably as body ornamentation, dress, or accessories. Unfortunately, the complete range of items produced cannot be directly inferred from the archaeological evidence because of differential preservation.

Conclusion

Six elite multi-crafting household workshops have been identified at an elite Type IV Late (Terminal?) Classic Maya compound, 9N-8 (Table 5). Three of these workshops, Rooms 1 and 2 in Structure 110C, and Room 4 in Structure 110B have identical floor plans similar to other domestic elite residence at Copan. Unlike other elite residences, those in Patio H were involved in the production of elite secular portable lapidary artifacts fabricated from exotic materials such as marine shell and greenstone and costumes composed of spun yarns woven into cloth with beading and feather work. One set of workshops (Rooms 2 and 3 in Structure 110B) has a distinctive architectural layout with a secluded work area over a burial crypt; this area contained multiple work stations and engaged in multi-crafting of differing media at the same time. This workshop is where highly sacred

Table 5. Crafting Activities Identified In Patio H, 9N-8.

Structure	Room	Secular Context	Sacred Context
110A	1	Seamstressing Spinning of Yarn	
	2	Spinning of Yarn Weaving	
	3	Feather working Seamstressing Weaving of Cloth Spinning of Yarn Hide/feather cutting Beading of Cloth	
110B	2		Shell Ornament Production Stone Ornament Production Hide cutting Sawing of unspecified media Grinding of Pigment
	3		Stone Cup Production
	4	Shell Ornament Production Bone/wood sharpening Hide Cutting	
110C	1 & 2	Shell Ornament Production Stone Ornament Production	

artifacts were fabricated under strict ritual supervision of an attendant 110A) and had two workshop rooms where elite costuming costumes were produced by at least two artisans. These workshops could also be sacred since they do not have direct access.

The multi-crafting that took place in 9N8-Patio H served two groups. One of these was the Ahau or ruler of the compound 9N-8 whose residence centered on the hieroglyphic bench In Structure 82C of Patio A. Crafts persons in Patio H provided him and probably his close kinsmen with the ritually charged sacred artifacts that functioned as his symbols of divinity and authority including costume, jewelry, and ritual paraphernalia. The second group served by this crafting was the elite residents of Patio H of 9N-8. While not requiring the special ritual charged sacred items, they nonetheless were consumers of high status craft goods. These consumers probably also included high status residents of other patios in the compound of 9N-8. It might even be the case that consumers in other patios of 9N-8 received the elite lapidary and costume items produced in Patio H from the Ahau of Patio A. This seems reasonable since the Ahau probably supplied the raw material for their production as is typical of chiefly trade in Mesoamerica and hence controlled the multi-crafting.

Craft output for jewelry and lapidary ritual paraphernalia was low since this items have long use-lives and new artifacts would only be needed when individuals reached an age when they changed social position. On the other hand,

the perishable and fragile nature of clothing and costumes, particularly feather work, would require considerable upkeep and repair and so crafting in this context probably had a higher rate than more durable artifacts.

Secular production of lapidary items is thought to have been intermittent because most craft activity occurred in domestic rooms and not in rooms or ateliers set aside for this purpose. The same can be said for textile production. If the secular craft workshops of 9N-8 are typical of other elite compounds at Maya centers, then it suggests that elite secular crafting was relatively infrequent, had a low production output, and involved relatively few individuals. At the Classic Maya site of Aguateca, for instance, most stone tools used to process meat and hide were only occasionally used to work bone and shell (Emery and Aoyama 2007:77).

On the other hand, I argue that the production of sacred paraphernalia is a continuous rather than intermittent process even though the rate of craft output was low. The reason for this interpretation is that sacred craft production areas had a distinct architectural layout that clearly was not domestic. These areas are characterized by indirect access, room locations that lack sleeping benches, and architectural features such as tool and raw material storage facilities (Feature 9). The inefficient means of manufacture identified in these areas require more time for manufacture than secular production. This conclusion is based on experimental work carried out by researchers at research laboratories at the Templo Mayor museum in Mexico City that demonstrate the shell artifacts manufactured with obsidian tools take four times as long to manufacture than those made with chert tools (Castro and Arellano 2009; Melgar et al. 2009). The differential use of obsidian and chert tools for working shell has been observed archaeologically at Monte Alban where chert is used for manufacturing shell jewelry in low status residences and obsidian is used in manufacturing marine shell jewelry in high status contexts (Melgar et al. 2009).

Likewise, weaving and feather working is a very labor intensive activity and was probably a continuous crafting activity as well. The fact that the textile craft workshop had special windows to admit light and a distinct room layout different from most buildings in 9N-8 indicates continuous use of these rooms at least in the mornings when they would be lit by the eastern sun.

It is important to note that this is the only residential patio group within 9N-8 where this type of crafting took place, and even in Patio H, it is restricted to the three buildings on the western side of the courtyard. At Copan, it seems that elite lapidary and costume craft production was exclusively the activity of high ranking elites and not the output of satellite rural communities as has been suggested for other Maya areas (Fry 1980; Rands and Bishop 1980; Shafer and Hester 1985, 1986) since no such evidence has been found there in spite of extensive survey and intensive testing and complete excavations of settlements (Webster and Gonlin 1987; Webster and Freter 1988). Crafting was concentrated within a single architectural unit having three conjoined buildings with specialized room configurations. At 9N-8 this elite crafting provided the greenstone pendant and *Spondylus* shell offering in Feature 20 of Structure 64, the ceremonial yoke and hachas found in Structure 81, Patio A, as well as the greenstone beads, pendants, shell pendants, and tooth inlays of various media. All of these artifacts have been found in archaeological contexts in 9N-8, and it is suggested that the lapidary artisans of Patio H, and artisans were also involved in producing clothing. The activities involved in producing these costumes include spinning and weaving, embroidering, and the cutting and gluing of feathers. The craft production that took place in the buildings of Structure 110 probably produced most of the items, elements, and paraphernalia depicted in the elite costume and ceremonies recorded in Late Classic Maya art and epigraphy for which no archaeological examples are preserved.

The Patio H artisans might also have produced "surplus" elite items in quantities greater than those needed within 9N-8 although there is no direct evidence for this. Such materials perhaps could be traded or exchanged for other items, particularly raw material. They might also have

been required as tribute or obligation to higher rulers or as bride-price when male lineage members married.

The multi-crafting revealed at Patio H is an elite activity that is confined to a single patio group that specialized in this function within a larger patio complex. This implies kin based control of craft production at the lineage or patio group level. The buildings of Structure 110 were the only craft workshops of this type located at 9N-8 or any other sites excavated during the various Copan projects. However, it is not suggested that these were the only such workshops at Copan. It is probably the case that other elite, Type IV, or perhaps all compounds, in the Copan Valley each have had their associated craft shops serving their elite residents. But if this is the case and elite craft activity did not take place in satellite communities, then why have such workshops not been previously discovered?

The failure to identify similar craft workshops both at Copan and other Classic Maya sites appears to be a sampling issue. Intensive excavation or test sampling of the entire area of elite residences may be required to adequately determine the existence of low output workshops. This is particularly problematic since high status multi-crafting using exotic materials appears to have taken place within households that look like typical elite domestic residences. For example, no craft workshops were identified at 9N-8 until Patio H was excavated. Even here, three of the workshops do not differ architecturally from the typical Maya domestic structure. This patio represents less than ten percent of the total area of 9N-8. Furthermore, it is not the largest or most impressive patio within the mound group and therefore might not be a candidate for excavation if a single group was chosen for investigation.

Furthermore, the craft output in these workshops was extremely low and would not be obvious without a rigorous methodology explicitly developed to collect microdebitage unless unusual circumstances like those seen in Room 2 of Structure 110B preserved *in situ* deposits on production surfaces. For example, would it be possible to infer craft activity in Rooms 2 and 3 of Structure 110B on solely architectural criteria? I doubt it, although this is what most Maya archaeologists have to resort to ascertain room function. Further complicating this situation are the two different contexts of craft production. The ritual component of craft production with a specialized architectural configuration might be ascertained archaeologically, but could secular craft activity that took place in residential domiciles be identified without the association of tools and production debitage as were recovered at Patio H? What is needed to identify craft workshop areas are intersite and intrasite comparisons of debitage frequencies from midden and other primary contexts associated with rooms and buildings. Only in this manner can the type and level of craft activity be recognized in lieu of unusual and rare accidents of preservation like those found at 9N-8, Copan and at Aguateca, Guatemala (Inomata 2001, 2007; Emery and Aoyama 2007).

What the results suggest is a part-time or intermittent involvement in crafting. This should be no surprise since these artisans were elites and continuous labor would not be expected from them as it would be from commoners. For adult males, warfare would be an alternative important activity that required their time and labor. For women, Stone Lee (1995) has shown that elite women within 9N-8 were not as involved in domestic activities as non-elite women on the basis of bone robusticity studies.

Classic Maya elite craft production at 9N-8 took the form of multi-crafting of exotic materials in Patio H. Elite multi-crafting workshops among the Maya should not be characterized by large rooms or buildings littered with craft debris and finished products. Instead, households engaged in the production of elite high status artifacts should be small, architecturally indistinguishable from domestic residences, and characterized by low production outputs, few finished products, and only modest amounts of production debitage. This is in keeping with the economic and political context of this production, by elites for elites. It is expected that other Classic Maya multi-crafting workshops that manufactured elite high status artifacts will be discovered when archaeologists employ methodologies similar to the ones used here. It is essential to recognize the role of site formation processes in craft production since without a fortuitous earthquake the more obvious evidence would be almost non-existence. However, the use of fine-scaled recovery methods will mitigate these site formation problems and allow the presence of workshops of this type to be revealed. Even without the fortuitous earthquake that preserved all of the crafting tools and artifacts _in situ_, it would have been possible to identify multi-crafting at Patio H of 9N-8 just as was possible to do so at the site of S3W1:33 at Teotihuacan were only limited _in situ_ features were recovered. Nonetheless, the use of the fine-scaled recovery technique allowed the identification of a lapidary workshop (Widmer 1993).

Acknowledgements

I would like to thank the Instituto Hondureno de Anthropología e Historia, Gerentes Ricardo Agurcia F., and Victor Cruz, and Lic. Vito Veliz for the permission and support that made this work possible. I would also like to thank William T. Sanders for inviting me to participate in the supervision of the Patio H excavation of the Projecto Arqueologico Copan, Phase II and for his valuable comments on the manuscript. I would also like to thank Linda Schele, William L. Fash, and David Stuart for their considerable help in providing iconographic information and background for me. I however except full responsibility for the use and interpretations presented here. I would also like to thank William T. Sanders, Kenneth L. Brown, and Rebecca Storey who have provided considerable discussion and comment on the manuscript throughout its preparation and of course Ken Hirth for the opportunity of participating it the session leading to this work.

References

Abrams, Elliot M.
1987 Economic Specialization and Construction Personnel in Classic Period Copan. American Antiquity 52:485–499.
1994 How the Maya Built Their World: Energetics and Ancient Architecture. Austin: University of Texas Press.

Adams, Robert E. W.
1970 Suggested Classic Period Occupational Specialization in the Southern Maya Lowlands. _In_ Monographs and Papers in Maya Archaeology. William Bullard, ed. Pp. 487–498. Papers of the Peabody Museum, Vol. 61. Cambridge, Massachusetts: Harvard University.
1977 Prehistoric Mesoamerica. Boston: Little, Brown.

Aldenderfer, Mark
1991 Functional Evidence for Lapidary and Carpentry Craft Specialties in the Late Classic of the Central Peten Lakes Region. Ancient Mesoamerica 2:205–214.

Ames, Kenneth M.
1995 Chiefly power and Household Production on the Northwest Coast. _In_ Foundations of Social Inequality. T. Price and Gary M. Feinman, eds. Pp. 155–187. New York: Springer.

Andrews, E. Wyllis, IV, and E. Wyllis. Andrews V
1980 Excavations at Dziblichaltun, Yucatan, Mexico. Tulane: Middle American Research Institute Tulane University Pub. 48.

Bautista, Clara P.
2009 Estudio Technilogico de los Ornamentos de Conchka Usados en la Consagracion de la Piramide de la Luna de Teotihuacan, Mexico.

Paper presented in the session Producction de Bienes de Prestigio Ornamentales y Votivos de la America Antigua. 53rd International Congress of Americanists. Mexico City, Mexico, 20 July 2009.

Becker, Marshall J.
1973 Archaeological Evidence for Occupational Specialization Among the Classic Period Maya at Tikal, Guatemala. American Antiquity 38:396–406.

Brumfiel, Elizabeth M.
1998 The Multiple Identities of Aztec Craft Specialization. *In* Craft and Social Identity. Cathy L. Costin, and Rita P. Wright, eds. Pp. 145–152. Archaeological Papers of the American Anthropological Association, 8. Arlington, Va: American Anthropological Association.

Castro, Adrian V., and Belem Z. Arellano
2009 Los Peces de Madreperla de la Ofrenda 41 del Templo Mayor de Tenochtitlan. Paper presented in the session Producction de Bienes de Prestigio Ornamentales y Votivos de la America Antigua. 53d International Congress of Americanists. Mexico City, Mexico, 20 July 2009.

Clark, John E.
1995 Craft specialization as an archaeological category. Research in Economic Anthropology 16:267–294.

Clark, John E., and Stephen D. Houston
1998 Craft Specialization, Gender, and Personhood among the Postconquest Maya of Yucatan, Mexico. *In* Craft and Social Identity. Cathy L. Costin and Rita P. Wright, eds. Pp. 31–46. Archaeological Papers of the American Anthropological Association, 8. Arlington, Va: American Anthropological Association.

Costin, Cathy L.
1991 Craft Specialization: Issues in Defining, Documenting, and Explaining the Organization of Production. *In* Archaeological Method and Theory, Vol. 3. Michael B. Schiffer, ed. Pp. 1–56. Tucson: University of Arizona Press.
1998 Introduction: Craft and Social Identity. *In* Craft and Social Identity. Cathy L. Costin and Rita

P. Wright, eds. Pp. 1–16. Archaeological Papers of the American Anthropological Association, 8. Arlington, Va: American Anthropological Association.
1998 Housewives, Chosen Women, Skilled Men: Cloth Production and Social Identity in the Late Prehispanic Andes. *In* Craft and Social Identity. Cathy L. Costin and Rita P. Wright, eds. Pp. 123–144. Archaeological Papers of the American Anthropological Association, 8. Arlington, Va: American Anthropological Association.
1993 Textiles, Women, and Political Economy in Late Prehispanic Peru. Research in Economic Anthropology 14:3–28.

Costin, Cathy L., and Rita P. Wright, eds.
1998 Craft and Social Identity. Archaeological Papers of the American Anthropological Association, 8. Arlington, Va: American Anthropological Association.

Culbert, T. Patrick, ed.
1973 The Classic Maya Collapse. Albuquerque: University of New Mexico Press.

Eaton, Jack D.
1974 Shell Celts from Coastal Yucatan, Mexico. Bulletin of the Texas Archaeological Society 45:197–208.

Emery, Kitty F., and Kazu Aoyama
2007 Bone, Shell, and Lithic Evidence for Crafting in Elite Maya Households at Aguateca, Guatemala. Ancient Mesoamerica 18: 69–89.

Espinosa, Alicia R.
2009 La Produccion de Objetos Manufacturados en Strombus gigas, Procedentes de Kohunlich, Quintana Roo, Mexico. Paper presented in the session Producction de Bienes de Prestigio Ornamentales y Votivos de la America Antigua. 53d International Congress of Americanists. Mexico City, Mexico, 20 July 2009.

Fash, William L.
1986 La Fachada Esculpida de la Estructura 9N-8: Composicion, Forma e Iconographica. *In* Excavaciones en el Area Urbana de Copan, Tomo I.William. T. Sanders, ed. Pp. 319–382. Tegucigalpa: Instituto Hondureño de Anthropologia e Historia.

1991   Scribes, Warriors, and Kings. London: Thames and Hudson.

Freter, AnnCorinne.
1987   The Classic Maya Collapse at Copan, Honduras: A Regional Settlement Perspective. PhD dissertation, Pennsylvania State University. Ann Arbor: University Microfilm.

Fry, Robert E.
1980   Models of Exchange for Major Shape Classes of Lowland Maya Pottery. *In* Models and Methods in Regional Exchange. Robert E. Fry, ed. Pp. 3–18. Society for American Archaeology Papers 1. Washington, D.C.: Society for American Archaeology.

Goggin, John W., and William T. Sturtevant
1964   The Calusa: A Stratified Nonagaricultural Society, (with Notes on Sibling Marriage). *In* Explorations in Cultural Anthropology: Essays in Honor of George Peter Murdock. Ward H. Goodenough, ed. Pp. 179–219. New York: McGraw Hill.

Goldman, Irving
1970   Ancient Polynesian Society. Chicago: University of Chicago Press.

Hammond, Norman
1982   Ancient Maya Civilization. New Brunswick, New Jersey: Rutgers University Press.

Haviland, William A.
1963   Excavation of Small Structures In The Northeast Quadrant of Tikal, Guatemala. PhD Dissertation, University of Pennsylvania. Ann Arbor: University Microfilm.
1974   Occupational Specialization at Tikal, Guatemala. American Antiquity 39:494–496.
1981   Dower houses and minor center at Tikal, Guatemala. *In* Lowland Mayan Settlement Patterns. Wendy Ashmore and Robert Sharer, eds. Pp. 89–117. Albuquerque University of New Mexico Press.

Hay, Conran A.
1978   Kaminaljuyu Obsidian: Lithic Analysis and the Economic Organization of a Prehistoric Maya Chiefdom. Ph.D. Dissertation, Pennsylvania State University. Ann Arbor: University Microfilms.

Hester, Thomas R., and Harry J. Shafer
1984   Exploitation of Chert Resources by the Ancient Maya of Northern Belize, Central America. World Archaeology 16(2):157–173.

Inomata, Takaeshi
2007   Knowledge and Belief in Artistic Production by Classic Maya elites. *In* Rethinking Craft Specialization in Complex Societies: Archaeological Analyses of the Social Meaning of Production. Zachary X. Hruby and Rowan K. Flad, eds. Pp. 129–141. Washington, D.C.: Archaeological Papers of the American Anthropological Association, Number 17.

Kovacevich, Brigitte
2007   Ritual, Crafting, and Agency at the Classic Maya Kingdom of Cancuen. *In* Mesoamerican Ritual Economy: Archaeological and Ethnological Perspectives. E. Cristian Wells and Karla L. Davis-Salazar, eds. Pp. 67–114. Boulder: University of Colorado Press.

Kovacevich, Brigitte, Tomas Barrientos, Michael Callahan, and Karen Pereira
2001   La economia en el reino clasico de Cancuen: Evidncia de produccion, especializacion e intercambio. *In* XV Simposio de Investigaciones Arqueologicas en Guatemala, 2001. J. P. Laporte, H. Escobedo, and B. Arroyo, eds. Pp. 365–375. Guatemala: Minesterio de Cultura y Deportes, Instituto de Antropologia e Historia, and Asssociation Tikal.

Lass, Barbara
1998   Crafts, chiefs, and Commoners: Production and Control in Precontact Hawai'i. *In* Craft and Social Identity. Cathy L. Costin and Rita P. Wright, eds. Pp. 19–30. Archaeological Papers of the American Anthropological Association, 8. Arlington, Va: American Anthropological Association.

Longyear, John M.
1952   Copan Ceramics: A Study of Southeastern Maya Pottery. Carnegie Institution of Washington, Pub. 597.

Mallory, John K.
1984   Late Classic Maya Economic Specialization: Evidence from the Copan Obsidian Assemblage. PhD dissertation, Pennsylvania State University, Ann Arbor, Michigan: University Microfilms.

Moholy-Nagy, Hattula.
1990 The Misidentification of Mesoamerican Lithic Workshops. Latin American Antiquity 1:268–279.

Rands, Robert L., and Ronald L. Bishop
1980 Resource Procurement Zones and Patterns of Ceramic Exchange in the Palenque Region, Mexico. *In* Models and Methods in Regional Exchange. Robert. E. Fry, ed. Pp. 19–46. Washington, D.C.: Society for American Archaeology Papers 1.

Reents-Budet, Dorie
1998 Elite May Pottery and Artisans as Social Indicators. *In* Craft and Social Identity. Cathy L. Costin and Rita P. Wright, eds. Pp. 71–89. Archaeological Papers of the American Anthropological Association, 8. Arlington, Va.: American Anthropological Association.

Roys, Ralph
1943 The Indian Background of Colonial Yucatan. Washington, D.C.: Carnegie Institution of Washington Pub. 548.

Sahagun, Bernardino de
1959 Florentine Codex: General History of the Things of New Spain, Book Nine, the Merchants. Arthur J. O. Anderson and Charles E. Dibble, eds. Santa Fe: School of American Research and the University of Utah Press.

Sahlins, Marshall D.
1958 Social Stratification in Polynesia. Seattle: University of Washington Press.

Sanders, William T., and David L. Webster
1984 Preliminary Report of Copan Second Phase 1983 Field Operations. University Park: Pennsylvania State University.

Sanders, William T.
1986 Introduccion. In Excavaciones en el Area Urbana de Copan, Tomo I. William T. Sanders, ed. Pp. 9–26. Tegucigalpa: Instituto Hondureño de Anthropologia e Historia.

Schele, Linda, and Mary E. Miller
1986 The Blood of Kings: Dynasty and Ritual in Maya Art. Fort Worth: Kimbell Art Museum.

Schiffer, Michael B.
1976 Behavioral Archaeology. New York: Academic Press.
1983 Towards the Identification of Formation Processes. American Antiquity 48:675–706.
1987 Formation Processes of the Archaeological Record. Albuquerque: University of New Mexico Press.

Shafer, Harry J., and Thomas R. Hester
1983 Ancient Maya Chert Workshops in Northern Belize, Central America. American Antiquity 48:519–543.
1986 Maya Stone-Tool Craft Specialization and Production at Colha, Belize: Reply to Mallory. American Antiquity 51:158–166.

Solis, Reyna B., and Osvaldo S. Cantu
2009 La Produccion de Bienes Pestigio en Concha de Tula, Hidalgo. Paper presented in the session Producction de Bienes de Prestigio Ornamentales y Votivos de la America Antigua. 53rd International Congress of Americanists. Mexico City, Mexico, 20 July 2009.

Melgar, Emiliano R., Reyna B. Solis, and Ernesto G. Licon.
2009 Produccion y Prestigio en Concah y Lapidaria de Monte Alban. Paper presented in the session Producction de Bienes de Prestigio Ornamentales y Votivos de la America Antigua. 53rd International Congress of Americanists. Mexico City, Mexico, 20 July 2009.

Spielmann, Katherine A.
1998 Ritual Craft Specialists in Middle Range Societies. *In* Craft and Social Identity. L. Cathy and Rita P. Wright, eds. Pp. 153–160. Archaeological Papers of the American Anthropological Association, 8. Arlington, Va: American Anthropological Association.
2002 Feasting, Craft Specialization, and the Ritual Mode of Production in Small-Scale Societies. American Anthropologist 104:195–207.

Stone Lee, Carla
1995 A Bioarchaeological Study of Differential Food Access and Activity Type at an Elite Late Classic Maya Site: Copan, Honduras. M. A. Thesis, University of Houston.

Storey, Rebecca
  1980 Chiefdom Demography in Archaeological Perspective. Paper presented at the 38th annual meeting of the Southeastern Archaeological Conference, Atlanta, Georgia.

Taylor, Peter J.
  1977 Quantitative Methods in Geography. Boston: Houghton Mifflin Company.

Thompson, J. Eric S.
  1968 The Bacabs: Their Portraits and their Glyphs. Cambridge, Massachucetts: Memoirs of the Peabody Museum of American Archaeology and Ethnology Vol. 61:469–486.

Walters, Gary
  1979 Preliminary Results of the 1979 San Augstin Acasagustlan Archaeological Project, Guatemala. Mexicon 2(4):55.

Webster, David L., ed.
  1987 The House of the Bacabs. Copan: A Study of Iconography, Epigraphy, and Social Context of a Maya Elite Structure. Washington, D.C.: Dumbarton Oaks Precolumbian Publication Program.

Webster, David L., and E. M. Abrams
  1983 An Elite Compound at Copan, Honduras. Journal of Field Archaeology 10:285–296.

Webster, David L., William L. Fash, and Elliot M. Abrams
  1986 Excavaciones en el Conjunto 9N-8, Patio A (Operacion VIII). *In* Excavaciones en el Area Urbana de Copan, Tomo I. William T. Sanders, ed. Pp. 155–318. Tegucigalpa: Instituto Hondureño de Anthropologia e Historia.

Webster, David L., and AnnCorinne Freter
  1988 The Demography of Late Classic Copan. *In* Prehistoric Maya Demography. P. Culbert and D. Rice, eds. Pp. 37–62. Albuquerque: University of New Mexico Press.

Webster, David L., AnnCorinne Freter and Nancy Gonlin
  2000 Copan: The Rise and Fall of an Ancient May Kingdom. Belmont, California: Wadsworth.

Webster, David L., AnnCorinne Freter, and Rebecca Storey
  1997 Analysis of Copan Obsidian Hydration and 14C Condorance Experiments. Report to the Foundation for Advancement of Mesoamerican Studies, Inc.

Webster, David L., Barbara W. Fash, Randolph J. Widmer, and Scott Zeleznik
  1998 The Skyband Group: Investigation of a Classic Maya Elite Residential Complex at Copan, Honduras. Ancient Mesoamerica 25:319–343.

Widmer, Randolph J.
  1987 Excavaciones en el Conjunto 9N-8, Patio H (Operacion XXII). *In* Excavaciones en el Area Urbana de Copan, Tomo V. William T. Sanders, ed. Pp. 155–318. Tegucigalpa: Instituto Hondureño de Anthropologia e Historia.
  1997 Especializacion Economica en Copan. Yaxkin 15: 141–160.

Willey, Gordon R.
  1982 Maya Archaeology. Science 215:260–267.
  1986 The Structure of the Ancient Maya Society: Evidence From the Southern Maya Lowlands. American Anthropologist 58:

Willey, Gordon R., and Richard M. Leventhal.
  1979 A Preliminary Report on Prehistoric Maya Settlements in the Copan Valley. *In* Maya Archaeology and Ethnology. Norman Hammond and Gordon R. Willey, eds. Pp. 75–102. Austin: University of Texas Press.

Willey, Gordon R., Richard M. Leventhal, and Willaim L. Fash.
  1978 Maya Settlement in the Copan Valley. Archaeology 31:32–43.

13

Jade in Full: Prehispanic Domestic Production of Wealth Goods in the Middle Motagua Valley, Guatemala

Erick T. Rochette
Penn State University

Household craft production was an important part of both the domestic and political economy in many preindustrial societies, including those of prehispanic Mesoamerica (Brumfiel 1987; Feinman 1999; Sinopoli 1988; Wattenmaker 1998). The organization of this production varied according to political, cultural, historical, and ecological factors. Maya scholars often highlight this variation by contrasting the organization of production of two classes of goods: utilitarian and "prestige" or wealth goods. This dichotomy of production systems is more often based on assumptions about the structure of political and power relations in ancient Maya polities than on empirical evidence. As the argument goes, elites sought to control the production and/or distribution of wealth goods, while paying less attention to the control of the production and exchange of utilitarian goods (Aoyama 1999; Ball 1993; Foias 2007; Inomata 2001; Rathje 1975; West 2002). These models often posit that attached craft producers, and in some cases elites themselves, crafted wealth goods (c.f. McAnany 1993). As Takeshi Inomata (2001:321) notes for the Classic Maya, "this system of production contrasts with those of many other complex societies, in which non-elite artisans produced prestige goods."

Recent archaeological research in the Middle Motagua Valley, Guatemala (Rochette 2009; Rochette and Pellecer-Alecio 2008) and elsewhere in the Maya area (Aoyama 2007; Emery and Aoyama 2007; Kovacevich 2007; Wells and Davis-Salazar 2007a) demonstrate that current models of craft production are inadequate and have resulted in in-

complete reconstructions of the organization of prehispanic Maya economies. This new evidence indicates that the organization of wealth goods production was more varied than previously believed and suggests that a simple dichotomy between wealth and utilitarian goods production obscures more than it clarifies the nature and organization of prehispanic economies. Recognizing the instrumental role that both elite and non-elite households played as production units of utilitarian and wealth goods is essential for any reconstruction of the organization of ancient Maya craft production systems. This paper presents evidence for non-elite, household production of jadeite and other wealth goods in the Middle Motagua Valley (MMV), Department of Zacapa, Guatemala (Figure 1).

Craft Production and Archaeology

Archaeologists have long recognized that elites often seek to maintain and increase their power by controlling the production and/or distribution of valuable or necessary resources, materials or finished goods (e.g. Brumfiel and Earle 1987; Frankenstein and Rowlands 1978). Despite the variety of means by which elites might achieve these ends, more studies focus on defining the role of elites in controlling the distribution and exchange of wealth goods rather than on how production was organized within particular polities or societies (Hirth 1992, 1996). In this paper, I use the more general term "wealth goods" to refer to what have traditionally been called "prestige goods" in the literature to avoid

ARCHEOLOGICAL PAPERS OF THE AMERICAN ANTHROPOLOGICAL ASSOCIATION, Vol. 19, Issue 1, pp. 205–224, ISSN 1551-823X, online ISSN 1551-8248. © 2009 by the American Anthropological Association. All rights reserved. DOI: 10.1111/j.1551-8248.2009.01021.x.

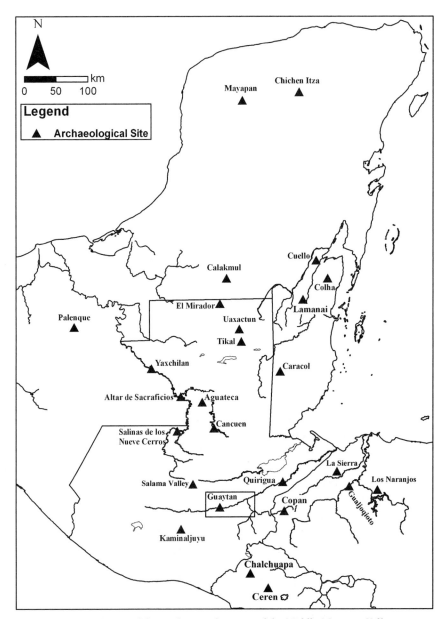

Figure 1. Maya Area, with box indicating location of the Middle Motagua Valley.

interpretive problems related to the term "prestige good," which implies a particular type of "prestige goods system" to many scholars.

A particular concern for many archaeologists has been documenting variation in the organization of craft production systems (Clark and Parry 1990; Costin 1991, 2001). One of the most prominent models dichotomizes craft production based on the nature of the goods produced and the degree to which production is controlled by political elites (Brumfiel and Earle 1987; Earle 1981). In this model, it is argued that everyday utilitarian goods tend to be produced by independent specialists who produce for general demand, while wealth or prestige goods tend to be produced by attached specialists who produce for patrons on demand (Brumfiel and Earle 1987: 5). Although this distinction is useful, it has been criticized as overly typological and too closely tied to cultural evolutionary trajectories (Arnold and Munns 1994; Clark and Parry 1990; Costin 1991). Recent research documenting variability in the organization of systems of craft production within particular societies (e.g.

Costin 1996; Masson and Freidel 2002; Underhill 1991; Wright 1998) demonstrates the need to refine these earlier models to clarify the relationship between political and economic structures (Costin 2001: 274).

A central debate among Mayanists has been about the nature of Classic Maya political organization and how it articulated with economic systems within and between polities (e.g. Blanton et al. 1996; Demarest 1992; Fox et al. 1996; Masson and Freidel 2002). Although scholars have proposed a variety of models of Classic Maya political and economic organization, they have consistently argued that elites controlled the production and distribution of wealth goods and used this control to enhance or otherwise validate their position within society (Foias 2002, 2007; Rice 1987). In particular, scholars note that because of their high value and their symbolic content, controlling the production and distribution of wealth goods would have been essential for the maintenance of power by Classic Maya elites (Aoyama 1995; Emery and Aoyama 2007: 164; Inomata 2001, 2007). Additionally, by controlling wealth goods and their production, Maya elites effectively controlled the "materialization" (c.f. DeMarris, Castillo and Earle 1996) of ideologies and rituals that legitimated their elevated position within society.

Controlling the production of wealth goods can also be a particularly effective strategy for enhancing or legitimating political authority, because doing so means having *de facto* control of their distribution (Lewis 1996). Elites may attempt to control craft production systems in a number of ways. They may sponsor production in attached facilities or undertake production within their own households (e.g. Ball 1993; Inomata 2001), or they may obtain finished or semi-finished craft products from non-elite households within or outside of their polities though a variety of extractive or exchange mechanisms. Alternatively, production of wealth goods may be an activity in which nonelite households engaged when the necessary resources to do so were available (i.e. as an *intermittent craft)* as part of a *domestic economy*, creating a situation in which the ability of elites to control distribution and acquisition of these finished goods was of paramount importance. As Hirth (this volume, Chapter 2) and others (e.g. Feinman 1999) note, domestic, household-level craft production appears to have been the norm both archaeologically and ethnographically in Mesoamerica.

These propositions lead to two basic questions. First, was the production of wealth goods controlled or directed in any demonstrable way by ancient Maya elites? Demonstrating control of the production of craft goods by elites is a notoriously difficult task for archaeologists, and this is especially the case for the ancient Maya (Graham 2002). Clear evidence of large-scale elite management of the production of wealth goods, has proved elusive in the Maya area (but see Foias 2007; Kovacevich 2007). This situation is partially attributable to the very characteristics from which wealth goods derive their value: their scarcity, the (often exotic) raw materials from which they are manufactured, and the specialized skills and knowledge sometimes needed to craft them properly (Wells and Davis-Salazar 2007b). These factors have often made it difficult for archaeologists to document many clear examples of wealth goods production in the Maya area. Where there is evidence for elite involvement, it is sometimes argued to be within the context of a "palace economy" in which elites produced goods within their own households for their own uses (Ball 1993; Ball and Taschek 1991; Inomata 2001; Widmer, this volume). Some scholars have argued for non-elite participation in the production of wealth goods (Ball 1993; Potter and King 1995; Rands and Bishop 1980), but the evidence for this participation is not straightforward and is open to interpretation.

Following from this, we must also ask a second question: were all wealth goods used in the same manner by ancient Maya elites and commoners? Decades of research at ancient Maya centers has demonstrated the disproportionate consumption of highly crafted exotic objects by the elite. Nevertheless, a major interpretive problem for understanding how wealth goods production was organized derives from an insufficient recognition of the varied uses of many of these goods in the Maya area. Emphasis is often placed on the raw material from which they were produced, rather than on the stylistic characteristics of particular forms of wealth goods. This is especially true for artifacts produced from exotic raw materials such as jadeite. Jadeite objects were certainly of high value in the Maya world and beyond, but not all of these objects were treated with the same reverence nor used in the same contexts (Freidel 1993; Taube 2005).

The variety of ways in which wealth goods were used by individuals and social groups of differing status can been seen at a few sites in the Maya area. At the site of Cuello, Belize, jadeite use varied temporally. During the Early Middle Preclassic period (1250–650 BC), jade was recovered (although rarely and in small quantities) in a diverse range of burial assemblages, with few indications of differentiation between individuals (Hammond 1999). During the subsequent Late Middle Preclassic period (650–400 BC), jade continues to be rare in burial assemblages, but is found only with adult males, in contexts that suggest jade beads were worn as jewelry (probably bracelets), and in combination with shell ornaments. Hammond (1999: 55) interprets the overall pattern at Late Middle Preclassic Cuello to be reflective of social differentiation that was not evident previously. In a study of Late Classic (A.D. 600–900) artifact distribution in the Copan Valley, Zeleznik (2002) concluded that although jadeite was found more frequently and with greater artistic and stylistic elaboration in elite contexts, it was still present at all levels of the social hierarchy.[1] While jadeite was certainly a raw material with strong cosmological and symbolic associations, its use was not restricted to elites. Hirth's (1992:23) admonition is applicable in this regard:

> "Archaeologists must discard the notion that the circulation of primitive valuables through interregional exchange networks was stimulated by a desire to obtain status markers. . .and begin to examine the more specific ways in which primitive valuables are used in the formation of status hierarchies"

A number of scholars (e.g. Fields 1991; Freidel 1993; Freidel et al. 2002; Garber 1993; Proskouriakoff 1974; Taube 2005) have documented the many symbolic associations that jadeite held for the ancient Maya, both as a raw material and in particular artifact forms. For the Classic Maya, it was a symbolic expression of rulership and authority, wealth, water, maize, centrality, wind and the breath-soul (Fields 1991; Miller and Samayoa 1998; Taube 2000, 2005). Freidel (1993) argues that jadeite and other worked greenstones were used for both ritual and mundane purposes from as early as the Middle Preclassic until the time of Spanish conquest. These symbolic associations were not restricted to the elite strata of Maya society, but were also present among non-elite Maya. Thus, the use of jadeite (or greenstone) beads as symbolically and ritually significant objects appears to have been a shared practice between both ancient Maya commoners and elite.

Elites would have sought to manipulate the shared recognition between themselves and commoners of the cosmological significance of jadeite in ways that legitimated their authority. What we should examine are the ways in which elite and commoner uses of jadeite and jadeite objects both overlapped and diverged. Lesure (1999) suggests that to better understand the use and significance of valuable goods, we should focus on understanding how different artifact forms produced from the same raw material(s) were used, both in terms of the kinds of social relationships they mediated and the way particular artifact forms were valued. Although such a nuanced understanding and examination of wealth goods is beyond the scope of this paper, recognizing the diversity of uses of jadeite artifacts demonstrates that simply labeling them wealth or "prestige" goods fails to capture adequately their role in Maya society.

This contextual diversity has implications for our understanding of how elites might have sought to control both raw jadeite and its production into finished artifacts. Characterizing the production of wealth goods as full/part-time or attached/independent specialization does little to advance our understanding of how production was organized. Fur-

thermore, this oversight prevents us from fully recognizing how different types of wealth and utilitarian goods were exchanged or transferred both amongst and between elites and commoners.

Put simply, if jadeite consumption varied widely, then it cannot be assumed that control over the raw material, its production and exchange mechanisms did not similarly vary. During the Colonial period, Spanish colonial administrators used a variety of pre-existing tribute and exchange networks to mobilize resources in the Maya area and throughout Mesoamerica (e.g. Feldman 1971; Restall 1997). It is likely that prehispanic elites also used multiple exchange and distribution networks to meet their needs. Understanding the variety of ways resources were mobilized is crucial if we are to accurately reconstruct Classic Maya systems of craft production and political economy. Recent archaeological research in the Middle Motagua Valley provides new data about how the Classic Maya organized wealth goods production and the nature of domestic craft production.

The Middle Motagua Valley

The Middle Motagua Valley (MMV) is located in east-central Guatemala and includes the Motagua River Valley between the modern communities of Paloamontonado and Río Hondo (Smith and Kidder 1943); it is generally considered an extension of the southeastern zone of the Maya lowlands (Smith and Gifford 1965). The MMV lies entirely within the *tierra caliente* climate zone, with an average annual temperature of 32 degrees centigrade and an average annual rainfall of 500 millimeters, which occurs almost exclusively during the rainy season between May and October (Simmons, Tarrano and Pinto 1959). The environment on the valley floor is arid and semi-desert; low, thorny scrub brush and other xerophytic vegetation dominate. Today, agriculture is only practical on the floodplains of the Motagua River and a few of its tributaries, where it can produce large surpluses. Elsewhere, rainfall agriculture of maize and other subsistence crops is practiced with varying success. This inhospitable environment for agriculture is an environmental characteristic that has implications for household sustainability in the region, a point to which I will return later.

The MMV was first recognized as an important jadeite[2]-bearing region when Robert Leslie documented extensive jadeite sources at Manzanotal in 1952 (Foshag and Leslie 1955); it is the only positively-identified source area exploited in prehispanic Mesoamerica (Harlow 1993; Taube et al 2004). Outcrops occur in the mountains surrounding the valley, and jadeite cobbles and boulders can be found in the Motagua River and most of its tributaries.

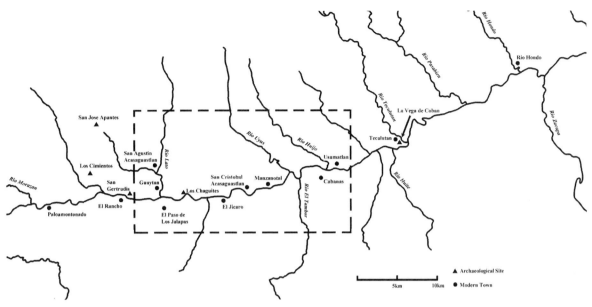

Figure 2. Middle Motagua Valley, with hatched lines indicating extent of map in Figure 3.

Today, local independent prospectors collect jadeite as raw material for sale to shops in Antigua by exploiting outcrops and by collecting cobbles in the many *quebradas* that scar the region.

Previous research in the Middle Motagua Valley

Excavations and surface survey by the Carnegie Institute in the 1930's (Kidder 1935; Smith and Kidder 1943) led to the designation of the area between the towns of Paloamontonado and Río Hondo as the "Middle Motagua Culture" based on the presence of a unique tomb style and the lack of carved stelae. Nevertheless, widespread evidence of jade artifact production was not identified until the 1970's during research conducted by Hammond and colleagues (Hammond et al. 1977) and by Walters (1980, 1982). Based on surface survey and limited excavations at Guaytan, Walters (1982) proposed a tentative model in which small workshops at non-elite sites passed raw or partially worked jadeite to higher-order sites with more complex workshops, which performed the final stages of artifact production. In his model, the most complex workshops were associated with the most highly ranked centers and production was done by attached specialists. Despite Walters' important and pioneering work, we are still left with a vague description of the jadeite-processing industry in the MMV.[3] Therefore, I felt that more focused and rigorous archaeological research in the region had the potential to produce a powerful new data

set regarding the structure of the local craft production industry. The results of the first field season are presented here. The data suggest that many of the assumptions regarding the organization of Classic period Maya wealth goods production are incomplete and that recognizing the importance of domestic craft production of jadeite artifacts is necessary to fully recognize the structure of this system.

Middle Motagua Valley Survey and Excavation Data

From October to December 2005, Licenciado Mónica Pellecer Alecio and I carried out a program of archaeological survey and excavation as part of the Proyecto de Investigación Sobre la Producción de Jade en el Río Lato (Rochette 2009; Rochette and Pellecer 2007) in the Middle Motagua Valley, centering on the region around the Lower Lato River Valley (Figure 2). Archaeological surface survey identified a total of 28 sites, ranging from artifact scatters without associated architecture to clusters of residential and civic-ceremonial architecture (Figure 3). Based on the survey results, we created a five-level settlement hierarchy for the MMV based on: the number of mounds/structures, mound/substructure heights, the presence of multi-roomed masonry superstructures, and the presence of 'elite/ceremonial' features such as ballcourts and stelae (Table 1). The presence of characteristics listed on the right are not confined to each specific site type, but may be present in higher-order site types as well. For example,

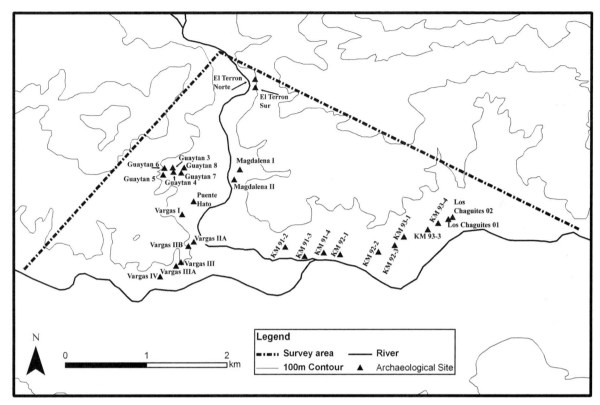

Figure 3. Lower Lato Valley survey area (note that the Motagua River served as the southern boundary to the survey area).

Table 1. Definition of site hierarchy in the Middle Motagua Valley.

Hierarchical Site Type	Characteristics
Type I	Unmounded or no architecture (i.e. only cultural material/artifacts)
Type II	Low mounds only (all less than 1 m tall)
Type III	All mounds less than 2 m tall
	Multi-roomed masonry substructures
Type IV	Some mounds greater than 2 m tall
	Multi-roomed masonry superstructures with high (> .5 m) stone walls
Type V	Multi-roomed masonry structures over 2 m tall
	Vaulted funerary monuments greater than 4 m tall
	Ballcourt (not found at all Type V sites)

Vargas IIA is a Type V site, and includes a ballcourt, one multi-roomed structure over 2 meters tall, and two 2 meter tall vaulted funerary monuments,[4] but also includes three low substructure platforms of less than 50 cm in height.

Test excavations focused on the southern periphery of the site of Guaytan (Guaytan 3, Guaytan 4), as well as adjacent areas (Guaytan 5, Guaytan 7, Guaytan 8) that showed evidence of jadeite artifact production. In addition, we excavated multiple test pits in concentrations of debitage at Magdalena I. Although we were unable to locate *in situ* production evidence, we did recover a large amount of jadeite and other lapidary and shell production evidence, mostly found within subfloor and structure fill that were compara-

ble to artifacts found on the surface, including chert drills, obsidian blade fragments and flakes, ceramic sherds, jadeite flakes, partial beads, and sawn pieces. All levels of our test excavations yielded ceramics that date to the Late Classic period.

Regardless of size, number of structures or location, surface collections and excavations at *all* sites yielded evidence of jadeite artifact production (Figure 4). Although jade production evidence was recovered at all Middle Motagua Valley sites, in most instances it was not concentrated in particular portions of sites, but was instead found distributed sporadically throughout many areas at many sites. At only a few sites can we infer that debitage was associated

Jade Flakes **Jade Bead Preforms** **Broken Jade Bead**

Hollow Drill Cores **Fragments with Ground Facets** **Cut Fragment**

Figure 4. Examples of jadeite artifact production evidence from Middle Motagua Valley surface collections and excavations.

with particular structures or structure groups on the basis of the surface collections. Where this was possible, the current data suggest that the physical scale and structure of production units varied significantly; some of these contexts are described below (see Rochette 2009 for further details).

At Vargas IIA (Type V site), jadeite production evidence in the northern part of the site was concentrated approximately 15 m to the north of Structure 1, a large mound of unknown function that has been heavily looted. The next-closest structure is 25 m to the east. Structure 1 occupies part of a possible a large civic-ceremonial group, as it is located 30 m across a flat plaza area from another large mound, which we were unable to examine closely because it was on the property of another landowner. Production evidence included over 250 jade artifacts, and included all stages of jadeite bead production (e.g. jadeite nodules, flakes, cores from the use of hollow drills, and beads broken in the process of manufacture) and some associated production tools (including chert drill bits and a stone with circular depressions that may have been used for grinding or polishing jadeite beads) as well as sawn pieces. Additionally, we col-

lected evidence of production of jasper and other unidentified stone beads in the same contexts. While it is unclear why production evidence was concentrated in this area, it is notable that it was found closest to elite architecture. Nevertheless, it appears that the structure served some domestic purpose, because *comal* fragments were recovered near the structure, as was a fragment of a basalt *metate*, both of which suggest probable domestic activity. Ceramics from looter's trenches and surface collections indicate occupation from the Late Preclassic through the Late Classic periods, and include locally-made Usulutan imitations and likely imported Usulutan ceramics (Craig Goralski 2005, personal communication).

At Vargas III (Type III site), we encountered an extensive scatter of jadeite production debitage in the southwestern and western portions of the site, much of it possibly eroded from the structures located upslope. The site consists of 12 structures arranged along the southern slopes to the north of the Motagua River. Another series of three groups of low platform structures (two to three structures per group, nine structures in all) is located in the southwestern portion

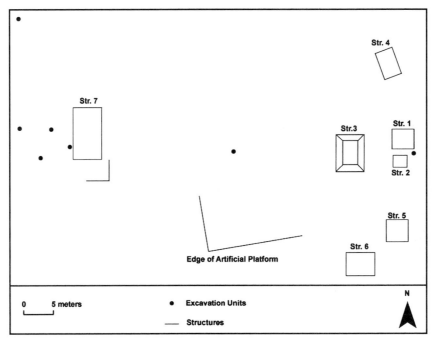

Figure 5. Map of southern portion of Magdalena I.

of the site. The majority of the structures in the northeastern sector are 1 m-tall domestic platform terraces built into gently-sloping terrain; there are also two vaulted funerary monuments less than 2 m tall (both with looted tombs); very little jadeite production evidence was found in this area of the site. The majority of production debitage and associated production tools (chert drills), were found scattered around the smallest platform structures at the site. Their function is difficult to assess currently, but the southeastern group as a whole appears to have been a small patio group of four structures located 20 m away from the nearest structure group.

Magdalena I (Type V site) is the northernmost group of elite structures that form part of the site of Magdalena (Figure 5). It contains more than 25 structures on the bluffs above the Lato River and is bounded to the south by a small *quebrada*. We were unable to explore the entire site because we could not secure permission to access its entirety from local landowners. Evidence of jadeite artifact production was concentrated on the eastern and western peripheries of Magdalena I. The eastern portion consists of eight structures, some of which are situated on a large artificial platform built into the naturally sloping terrain. Jadeite debitage was found around structures 1 and 2, two low platform structures of uncertain function and Structure 3, a 2 m tall, rectangular, multi-roomed structure. Production evidence was also collected in association with cut-stone wall superstructures on the western edge of Magdalena I, located near a series of

low mounds and the large Structure 7. Although the vessel forms for many ceramics could not be identified, excavation units in both areas yielded fragments of *comals* and storage jars, further suggesting that domestic functions were carried out in or near these structures. Together, the association of production evidence at Magdalena I suggests the production of jadeite artifacts in association with elite (possibly residential) structures.

The most intensive test excavations were carried out at Guaytan 4 (Type II site), which consists of a small group of domestic structures laid out over a series of small platforms built into gently-sloping terrain (Figure 6). In 2004, archaeological reconnaissance identified a dense concentration of jadeite debitage on the southwestern portion of the structure group. Although the structure group is located within 100 m of the portion of the site that Walters (1982) identified as being a possible elite residential area, the structure group itself is of modest construction and size. Test excavations yielded over 2,500 jadeite artifacts and over 250 chert drills, including evidence of the entire range of jadeite artifact production techniques (e.g. percussion, sawing, drilling, grinding, and polishing), with the exception of incising. Additionally, we collected over 850 obsidian blades and blade fragments, and a cache of 245 exhausted obsidian polyhedral cores. Excavations also yielded evidence of other lapidary and shell artifact production. The majority of the excavated contexts date to the Magdalena Phase of the Late Classic Period (A.D. 700 – 900).

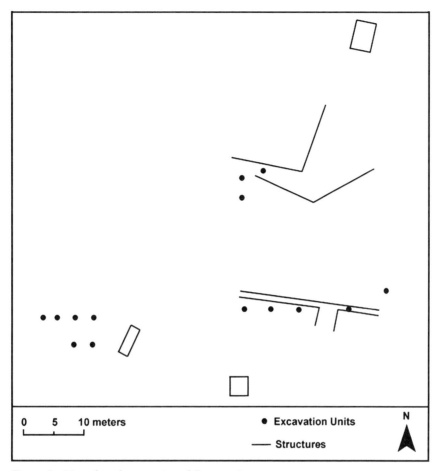

Figure 6. Map of southern portion of Guaytan 4.

Outside of the Lato River valley, the largest scatters of jade artifact production debitage are at KM 93-I (Type II site), which was first described as the "Terzuola site" by Feldman et al. (1975). With the exception of four low platform structures, the area has been leveled for aloe cultivation. Jadeite production evidence was concentrated on the southern and southwestern portions of the site. Descriptions by Feldman et al. (1975), Walters (1982) and local informants indicate that KM 93-I likely consisted of two domestic patio groups before its destruction. Further east, the site of KM 93-III (Type I site) contained no evidence of surface architecture (the area showed no evidence of modern destruction, an assessment that was confirmed by local informants), although jadeite production debitage and broken bead fragments were found in surface scatters with domestic refuse (e.g. bowl and jar fragments). Still further east, the site of Los Chaguites 01 (Type II site) consists of a series of three groups of low domestic structures (all less than 2 m tall; seven structures in all). Bead production evidence was

concentrated on the southern and eastern peripheries of the site.

Taken together, the survey data, surface collections and excavations indicate that jadeite artifact production on some scale was present at *all* levels of the hierarchy (Tables 2, 3). The evidence suggests that both elite and non-elite segments of the valley's population were involved in the production of jadeite artifacts. Non-elite production seems to have been geared primarily toward the production of jadeite beads and was situated within domestic household contexts. In total, over 9,900 jadeite artifacts were recovered from surface collections and excavations, representing almost all the steps involved in the production of jadeite artifacts such as globular, spherical and button beads, as well as fragments of polished plaques and possibly earflares and pendants.[5] In addition, we collected 37 unworked or partially-worked jadeite cobbles (Figure 7). Finally, we also recovered a large sample of tools related to jadeite artifact production, including 401 chert drills and eight jadeite hammerstones (Figure 8).

Table 2. Jadeite artifact production evidence from surface collections, hierarchical site type.

Site Type	Jadeite Flakes	Jadeite Beads	Broken Jadeite Beads	Jadeite Bead Preforms	Jadeite Bead Drill Cores	Cut Jadeite Fragments	Ground Jadeite Fragments	Jadeite Hammerstones	Chert Drills
I	71	–	2	–	–	–	–		2
II	1360	2	9	1	9	4	17	1	41
III	1547	2	10	10	1	2	12	3	25
IV	144	–	3	–	1	–	5		9
V	788	8	51	11	3	5	13	2	28
TOTALS	3910	12	75	22	14	11	47	6	105

Table 3. Jadeite production evidence from excavations by hierarchical site type.

Site Type	Jadeite Flakes	Jadeite Beads	Broken Jadeite Beads	Jadeite Bead Preforms	Jadeite Bead Drill Cores	Cut Jadeite Fragments	Ground Jadeite Fragments	Jadeite Hammerstones	Chert Drills
I	–	–	–	–	–	–	–	–	–
II	2649	6	34	9	47	9	44	1	235
III	72	–	–	1	–	–	–	–	1
IV	597	–	1	–	1	–	–	1	13
V	2267	–	1	2	–	–	6	–	47
TOTALS	5585	6	36	12	48	9	50	2	296

Figure 7. Jadeite cobbles recovered from Middle Motagua Valley sites.

Figure 8. Jadeite hammerstone (left) and chert drills (right) from Middle Motagua Valley sites.

Discussion

As Hirth discussed in Chapter 2 of this volume, the domestic economy refers to the ways households diversify production strategies to meet their physical and social needs. Because the household was the fundamental unit of adaptation in preindustrial agrarian society (Wilk 1989), the domestic economy perspective focuses attention on how households fit crafting within their overall production strategies. Although traditional models stress that elites seek to control the production of wealth goods to enhance their social position (Brumfiel and Earle 1987; Blanton et al. 1996),

Hirth (Chapter 2, this volume) notes that "there is nothing to keep non-elite households from making wealth goods if the resources are available to do so." Therefore, the domestic economy model directs interpretations of archaeological evidence of craft production toward the perspective of the household members doing the work, taking a "bottom-up", rather than "top-down" view of the household-level production of wealth goods.

The evidence for domestic craft production of wealth goods in the Middle Motagua Valley accords well with a domestic economy model, and suggests a more complex system of production than previously argued by many scholars for the Classic Maya, where production has been viewed as being done directly by elites or in close proximity to their residences (e.g. Inomata 2001; McAnany 1993; Potter and King 1995). The evidence presented in this paper supports recent models of Late Classic Maya craft production that recognize the diversity of production systems for both utilitarian and wealth goods (Aoyama 2007; Kovacevich 2006, 2007; McAnany et al. 2002) and that non-elites were likely involved in the production of some artifacts traditionally referred to as wealth or prestige goods. Although the data are too limited in scope for constructing a robust model of the organization of wealth goods production in the Middle Motagua Valley, the evidence does allow for some preliminary statements that will require testing and refinement.

Raw jadeite would have been difficult, if not impossible to control. Just as it is today, raw jadeite was an abundantly available local resource that could be easily obtained as river float in the many tributaries to the Motagua River flowing from the surrounding mountains, as well as from the diffuse outcrops that appear in pockets throughout the valley. This fact is borne out today by independent prospectors operating in the valley. Therefore, the procurement of raw material was likely out of the direct control of elites in the Middle Motagua Valley. This proposition is supported by evidence that prehispanic craftsmen in the region utilized river-worn cobbles in addition to block fragments that likely came from outcrops or quarries like the one at Manzonal. Therefore, the available data suggest that elite and non-elite households alike engaged in production of goods from abundantly-available raw materials.

The current evidence suggests that the production of jadeite artifacts took place on some scale at *every* site in the valley, regardless of its position within the local site hierarchy. The majority of production evidence was associated with domestic structures and structure groups, at both non-elite (Types I, II and III) and elite sites (Types IV and V). The great majority (96%) of jadeite artifacts were small percussion flakes measuring less than 5 cm in maximum length. The fact that these are the most abundant type of artifact found at Middle Motagua Valley sites suggests that percussion reduction of cobbles and larger fragments was the primary means by which small fragments suitable for the production of beads were obtained. This is congruent with jade production evidence at both Cancuen (Kovacevich 2007) and Nativitas (Hirth, Chapter 11, this volume), where such debitage was associated with bead production. In addition, almost all sites (n = 21, 75%) in the survey area contained evidence linked to jadeite bead production, either in the form of complete beads (along with the presence of jadeite debitage), beads broken or abandoned during drilling, preform beads or the presence of chert drills (Table 4).

Evidence of other production techniques, such as sawing, was present at only a few sites, although it was found at both low-ranked (Type II & III) and high-ranked (Types V)

sites. Because it was a laborious task, it is unlikely that craft producers sawed or cut jadeite in the process of producing beads. Instead, sawing was more frequently involved in the production of artifact forms such as plaques and earflares (Digby 1964; Proskouriakoff 1974). This suggests that artifact forms of higher "value" than beads were produced by both elites and non-elites. Similar evidence has been reported by Kovacevich (2007), who notes the use of sawing in the production of jadeite artifacts at a non-elite household at Cancuen.

Representing the final stages of jadeite bead and non-bead artifact production, evidence of grinding and polishing tasks (in the form of fragments with ground or polished facets) show a similarly widespread distribution among different site types. Again, this was not carried out solely in elite or non-elite site types, but seems to have been a crafting activity carried out at sites of varying status. Many of these fragments were likely from the production of non-bead artifacts as well, and thus add further support to the argument that non-elites in the Middle Motagua Valley were not just producing jadeite beads, but were producing other artifact forms as well.

The general redundancy of sawing, grinding, and possible non-bead production evidence across the local site hierarchy provide multiple lines of evidence to suggest that the types of goods being produced at lower-ranked (non-elite) sites were the same as those being produced at more highly-ranked (elite) sites. These data contradict assumptions about the organization of Classic Maya wealth goods production in two ways. First, contrary to the expectations of some models (e.g. Moholy-Nagy 1997; Walters 1982), non-elites were not simply performing the early stages of jade artifact production, but appear to have engaged in the same types of production activities as those carried out at elite sites. Second, non-elites were producing items that Mayanists would consider more valuable than small jade beads (e.g. Ball 1993), such as plaques, earflares or large beads, and were therefore more fully involved in the production of wealth goods than previously believed.

In a domestic economy model, the involvement of non-elite households in the production of jadeite wealth goods must be explained in terms of how it fit into overall household production strategies. There are three ways to explain this production in the Middle Motagua Valley from a domestic economy perspective. First, households may have produced jadeite artifacts for their own internal use, as well as for gifting to other households. Unfortunately, we cannot evaluate this proposition because no consumption contexts (i.e. burials or caches) were recovered during this field research. Thus, it is unclear how much jadeite artifact production was geared toward internal use and consumption by

Table 4. Evidence linked to jadeite bead production from excavations and surface collections.

Site Name	Hierarchy Type	Jadeite Beads	Broken/ Abandoned Jadeite Beads	Jadeite Bead Preforms	Hollow Drill Cores	Chert Drills
Guaytan 3	I	–	–	–	–	–
Guaytan 4	II	X	X	X	X	X
Guaytan 5	II	X	X	–	–	–
Guaytan 6	V	–	–	–	–	X
Guaytan 7	V	–	X	–	–	X
Guaytan 8	IV	–	X	–	X	X
Puente Hato	IV	–	–	–	–	X
Vargas I	V	–	–	–	–	–
Vargas IIA	V	X	X	X	X	X
Vargas IIB	III	X	X	X	–	X
Vargas III	III	–	X	X	–	X
Vargas IIIA	II	X	–	–	–	–
Vargas IV	IV	–	X	–	–	X
Magdalena I	V	X	–	X	X	X
Magdalena II	III	–	–	–	–	–
El Terron N.	V	–	–	–	–	–
El Terron S.	IV	–	–	–	–	–
KM 91–2	IV	–	X	–	–	X
KM 91–3	III	X	–	–	–	X
KM 91–4	III	–	X	–	–	X
KM 92–1	III	–	–	–	–	X
KM 92–2	II	–	–	–	–	X
KM 92–3	III	–	X	X	X	X
KM 93–1	II	–	X	X	X	X
KM 93–3	I	–	X	–	–	X
KM 93–4	III	–	–	–	–	–
Los Chaguites 01	II	–	X	–	X	X
Los Chaguites 02	III	–	–	X	–	–

elite and non-elite households. Obtaining information about overall consumption of jadeite artifacts by elites and non-elites from household assemblages and mortuary contexts is a primary goal of future research.

A second possibility is that wealth goods production may have been a way of mitigating subsistence risk, by providing households with a means to meet their needs through the exchange of valuable goods for subsistence products. Today, the Middle Motagua Valley receives an average annual rainfall of 550 mm, an amount at the margin of what is needed to support rainfall-based maize agriculture. This could have made it difficult for households with access to less productive agricultural land outside of the Lower Lato River Valley to consistently meet their subsistence needs. The exchange of wealth goods for subsistence products is one possible way that craft production may have complemented agricultural activity among non-elite households to meet the overall subsistence needs of the household. However, agricultural productivity and access to resources must be demonstrated, not assumed, and at this point, this

is a speculation that cannot be evaluated with the current evidence.

A final possibility is that Middle Motagua Valley households exchanged jadeite wealth goods for utilitarian goods (e.g. unworked obsidian, finished obsidian tools or utilitarian ceramics) or other wealth goods. During the Late Classic period, distribution mechanisms were certainly in place that moved goods over significant distances in the Maya area and throughout Mesoamerica. While the presence of a true "market economy" during the Late Classic period is a highly debated topic, it is likely that periodic markets existed where households could exchange goods that they produced with one another and for goods from outside of the local region. Obsidian is one possible material that households may have acquired in exchange for jadeite wealth goods. Although sourcing of obsidian artifacts recovered from surface collections and excavations was not undertaken, the closest large obsidian source is El Chayal, located over 50 km to the southwest. Unlike many parts of the Maya lowlands, obsidian was the predominant tool material used in the Middle Motagua Valley. I find it unlikely that individual households travelled to El Chayal to obtain their own obsidian, which leaves open the possibility that they may have acquired it in exchange for jadeite goods they produced in their own households. At Ceren, Sheets (2000) argues that most households were engaged in the production of various goods for extra-household exchange, including for the acquisition of exotic items such as obsidian tools and polychrome serving vessels. If this is indeed the case, it would be equally likely that Middle Motagua Valley households exchanged their wealth goods for exotic utilitarian goods imported from elsewhere.

A related issue for positioning the production of jade wealth goods within the domestic economy is how it fits with other household production activities. Although the production of jadeite beads and other artifacts would have been a difficult and time-consuming task given the technological constraints facing Classic Maya craft workers, it is not a task that requires a great deal of skill or technical expertise. As I have already noted, raw material for the production of jadeite artifacts was abundant and easily accessible. Additionally, abrasives of sufficient hardness were available in the form of local quartz sands and volcanic ash (Mohs 6–7). The critical element in the production of stylistically simple artifacts such as beads and blanks for plaques and pendants would have then been sufficient time to grind, drill and polish them, which were laborious tasks.

Within extended family households, sufficient labor for these tasks could have been harnessed within the household unit itself. During the agricultural season, children and household members too old to work in the fields could have helped produce beads and other artifact forms. Additionally, during the agricultural off-season, all household members could have devoted some time to these activities. It is in the context of these activities that Hirth's (this volume, Chapter 2) concept of *intermittent crafting* proves useful for characterizing the ways in which Motagua Valley domestic households could have fit jadeite artifact production into their agricultural cycles. If we view the production of jadeite artifacts in this manner, it provides a better explanation for the existing data than the traditional dichotomies of full/part-time and attached/independent specialization. Non-elite households could have fit craft activities within their normal production cycles by practicing these crafts when there was time available to do so. If they could exchange or otherwise transfer their finished or semi-finished products to elites or others for agricultural goods that they could not produce (domestic economy), the production of jadeite artifacts may have been one way to mitigate risk in the eventuality that their own agricultural production failed. This is a hypothesis that will require a great deal of further research, but provides intriguing possibilities for explaining

the unique system of wealth-goods production in the Middle Motagua Valley.

Although the current data is limited, evidence of *multicrafting* at Vargas IIA (Type V) and Guaytan 4 (Type II) fits well with what would be expected from a domestic economy model in which households used whatever resources were available to them. Excavations at Guaytan 4 yielded evidence of at least four craft activities: jadeite artifact production, obsidian blade production, shell ornament production and other stone bead production. Obsidian blade production is suggested by the recovery of 249 exhausted obsidian blade cores and 293 pieces of non-blade obsidian debitage, although it is unclear if their presence is the result of production for use in making craft items or tools needed for the production of craft goods (i.e. *contingent* production). In addition, Walters (1989:255) recovered 14 caches containing a total of 5,199 obsidian blade cores in a portion of the Guaytan 4 patio group that has since been destroyed by the construction of a school. Taken together, the evidence suggests that obsidian blade production was for both internal *and* external consumption.

The production of shell ornaments and stone beads involved the same technology as that of jade artifacts, and thus were craft activities that the lapidary artisans of Guaytan 4 and Vargas IIA (where shell and stone bead production evidence was recovered) could easily perform when raw materials were available, or when shell ornaments or stone beads were needed. This is similar to Hagstrum's (1992) concept of "intersecting technologies," because lapidary production techniques related to jade artifacts could be extended to shell and other stones. I find such multicrafting inconsistent with political economy models in which production activity was controlled by elites, because when found in non-elite households, it fits more readily within a domestic economy model in which households diversify by whatever means available to meet their needs. In fact, evidence of multicrafting of "non-utilitarian" goods has been found in an urban household compound at Teotihuacan (Widmer 1991) and in a household at a rural village site at Ejutla in Classic period Oaxaca (Feinman 1999; Feinman and Nichols 2000, 2004), neither of which appear to have been controlled by elites in any discernable way.

Recently, Wells (2006) and others (Wells and Davis-Salazar 2007a) have introduced the concept of "ritual economy" (c.f. Spielmann 2002) as an avenue to examine and understand the economic consequences of ritual activity in Mesoamerica. They argue that many craft activities in Mesoamerican societies were geared toward the production of goods needed for ritual and social purposes. In particular, they stress that the need for these items drove craft production, often in domestic households. I argue that framing the production of jadeite artifacts in the Middle Motagua

Valley in terms of ritual economy provides insight for understanding the structure of this production system. As I noted earlier, jadeite wealth goods served a variety of purposes for Classic Maya elites and non-elites alike. Goods that symbolically and ideologically legitimated the authority and status of elites, such as large necklaces, bracelets and skirts of jade beads, would have created an impetus for the production of these goods (see Foias 2007 for a similar argument regarding ceramic vessels). Additionally, the use of jadeite beads in non-elite, household level ritual activity (e.g. household termination rituals or the placement of jadeite beads in the mouths of buried individuals) would have further increased the demand for these goods. As archaeological research continues in the Middle Motagua Valley and elsewhere, understanding the structure of wealth goods production (not just of jadeite beads) in terms of the varied ritual and social purposes to which these goods were used will enable us to better capture the variety of craft production systems present among the Classic Maya. Additionally, this allows us to better recognize and understand the role that non-elites played in ancient Maya political economies.

Concluding Remarks

In this paper, I have presented data from recent archaeological research in the Middle Motagua Valley that is not easily explained within the framework of existing models of Classic Maya craft production. I feel that the difficulty in conceptualizing independent, domestic production of wealth goods stems from misconceptions that all wealth goods had the same "value" or meaning and end use. Elaborate, highly crafted and unique jadeite artifacts with iconographic imagery were certainly items that were restricted in their distribution to elites, and may even have been crafted as part of sponsored production arrangements by elites. Nevertheless, the types of jadeite artifacts (particularly beads) produced in the Middle Motagua Valley appear to have predominantly been "simple," "low-value" artifacts that were used in bulk by elites to signify their status, but which are also recovered in non-elite contexts in the Maya lowlands (e.g. Zeleznik 2002). Therefore, we should not assume that all jadeite artifacts would have been produced by elites or within elite contexts, but rather that their contexts of production may have varied in the same manner as their value. Our research has just begun to reconstruct the organization of craft production of jadeite and other wealth goods. Despite the preliminary nature of the present data and conclusions, the Middle Motagua Valley has the potential to offer a unique environment for understanding the variation in ancient Maya production systems.

Acknowledgements

This research project was accomplished thanks to the generous support of the Foundation for the Advancement of Mesoamerican Studies, Inc., (FAMSI) as well as a dissertation research grant from the Research and Grants Office (RGSO) of the Pennsylvania State University. The help of the Instituto de Antropología e Historia de Guatemala (IDAEH) was indispensable to the success of this research. I would also like to thank the following for insightful comments that have improved this paper: Kenneth Hirth, David Webster, Craig Goralski, Jason De Leon, J. Heath Anderson, Kirk Straight, Kirk French, and Scott Speal. Special thanks also to my co-director, Licenciada Mónica Pellecer Alecio, and to all who helped make this research a success, especially Karl Taube, Zacary Hruby, Erika Gomez, Elisa Mencos, Selket Callejas, Don Gustavo Guillen and Sergio Gonzalez Castro. Last, but certainly not least, I would like to thank my parents Harold and Kaarina, and especially my wife Sarah, for their steadfast support and understanding through the process of completing this project. Any errors or omissions are solely the responsibility of the author.

Notes

1. Distributional studies involving excavations at all levels of site hierarchies have not been carried out in sufficient numbers to address these issues fully, but others (e.g. Willey 1956) note that jade in at least small quantities is recovered in almost all excavations in the Maya area.

2. The term *jade* is a catchall typically used to refer to a number of distinct minerals. 'True' jades are *jadeite* and *nephrite*; only jadeite occurs in Mesoamerica. Other greenstones sometimes referred to as jade include *chloromelanite, diopside, bowenite, albitite, serpentine*, and various *quartzites* (Harlow 1993).

3. Much of the data from Walters' research in the Middle Motagua Valley were lost during the outbreak of violence as part of the Guatemalan civil war and in a subsequent fire that destroyed many of his records (Walters 2004, personal communication). Therefore, his dissertation and published work were unfortunately based on fragmentary data from his research and his own recollections.

4. Tombs in the Middle Motagua Valley are typically subsurface chambers centered below mounds, with walls of schist or waterworn stones that were capped with long slabs that spanned the chamber walls, or with a rough corbeled arch formed by two or three rows of large stone slabs (Smith and Kidder 1943: 129–130). Each tomb had a narrow entrance that permitted its continued use after interment of the

buried individual. This type of construction is unique in the Maya area and is easily visible and identified at MMV sites because of poor soil formation over structures and rampant looting of many of the tombs.

5. We found no evidence of the production of more elaborate forms of jade artifacts, such as tubular beads, diadems, figurines, or any evidence of incising or carving, which likely was in the hands of more skilled craftspersons at elite centers (c.f. Kovacevich 2007).

References

Aoyama, Kazuo
  1999 Ancient Maya State, Urbanism, Exchange and Craft Specialization: Chipped Stone Evidence of the Copan Valley and La Entrada Region, Honduras. Pittsburgh: University of Pittsburgh Memoirs of Latin American Archaeology, no. 12.
  2007 Elite Artists and Craft Producers in Classic Maya Society: Lithic Evidence from Aguateca, Guatemala. Latin American Antiquity 18(1):3–26.

Arnold, Jeanne, and Ann Munns
  1994 Independent or Attached Specialization: The Organization of Shell Bead Production in California. Journal of Field Archaeology 21:473–489.

Ball, Joseph W.
  1993 Pottery, Potters, Palaces, and Politics: Some Socioeconomic and Political Implications of Late Classic Maya Ceramic Industries. *In* Lowland Maya Civilization in the Eighth Century A.D. J.A. Sabloff and J.S. Henderson, eds. Pp. 243–272. Washington, DC: Dumbarton Oaks Research Library and Collection.

Ball, Joseph W., and Jennifer T. Taschek.
  1991 Late Classic Lowland Maya Political Organization and Central-Place Analysis: New Insights from the Upper Belize Valley. Ancient Mesoamerica 2(2):149–166.

Blanton, Richard E., Gary M. Feinman, Stephen A. Kowalewski, and Peter N. Peregrine
  1996 A Dual-Processual Theory for the Evolution of Mesoamerican Civilization. Current Anthropology 37(1):1–14.

Brumfiel, Elizabeth
  1987 Elite and utilitarian crafts in the Aztec State. *In* Specialization, Exchange, and Complex Societies. E. Brumfiel and T. Earle, eds. Pp. 102–118. Cambridge: Cambridge University Press.

Brumfiel, Elizabeth, and Timothy Earle
  1987 Specialization, exchange and complex societies: an introduction. *In* Specialization, Exchange, and Complex Societies. E. Brumfiel and T. Earle, eds. Pp. 1–9. Cambridge: Cambridge University Press.

Clark, John, and William Parry
  1990 Craft Specialization and Cultural Complexity. *In* Research in Economic Anthropology, Vol. 12. B. Isaac, ed. Pp. 289–346. Greenwich, CT: JAI Press.

Costin, Cathy
  1991 Craft Specialization: Issues in Defining, Documenting, and Explaining the Organization of Production. *In* Archaeological Method and Theory, Vol. 3. M. Schiffer, ed. Pp. 1–56. Tuscon: University of Arizona Press.
  1996 Craft Production and Mobilization Strategies in the Inka Empire. *In* Craft Specialization and Social Evolution: Studies in Memory of V. Gordon Childe. B. Wailes, ed. Pp. 211–225. Philadelphia: University of Pennsylvania Museum Publications.
  2001 Craft Production Systems. *In* Archaeology at the Millennium: A Sourcebook. G. Feinman and T.D. Price, eds. Pp. 273–328. New York: Kluwer Academic/Plenum Publishers.

Demarest, Arthur
  1992 Ideology in Ancient Maya Cultural Evolution: The Dynamics of Galactic Polities. *In* Ideology and Pre-Columbian Civilizations. A. Demarest and G. Conrad, eds. Pp. 137–157. Albuquerque: University of New Mexico Press.

Demarris, Elizabeth, Luis Jaime Castillo, and Timothy K. Earle
  1996 Ideology, Materialization and Power Strategies. Current Anthropology 37:15–31.

Digby, Adrian
  1964 Mayan Jades. London: British Museum.

Earle, Tmothy
  1981 Comment on P. Rice, Evolution of Specialized Pottery Production: A Trial Model. Current Anthropology 22(3):230–231.

Emery, Kitty, and Kazuo Aoyama
2007 Bone, Sell and Lithic Evidence for Crafting in Elite Maya Households at Aguateca, Guatemala. Ancient Mesoamerica 18:69–89.

Feinman, Gary
1999 Rethinking Our Assumptions: Economic Specialization at the Household Scale in Ancient Ejutla, Oaxaca, Mexico. *In* Pottery and People: Dynamic Interactions. J. M. Skibo and G. Feinman, eds. Pp. 81–98. Salt Lake City: University of Utah Press.

Feinman, Gary M., and Linda M. Nicholas
2000 High-Intensity Household-Scale Production in Ancient Mesoamerica: A Perspective from Ejutla, Oaxaca. *In* Cultural Evolution: Contemporary Viewpoints. G. Feinman and L. Manzanilla, eds. Pp. 119–142. New York: Kluwer Academic/Plenum Publishers.
2004 Unraveling the Prehispanic Highland Mesoamerican Economy: Production, Exchange, and Consumption in the Classic Period Valley of Oaxaca. *In* Archaeological Perspectives on Political Economies. Gary M. Feinman and Linda M. Nicholas, eds. Pp. 167–188. Salt Lake City: University of Utah Press.

Feldman, Lawrence
1971 A Tumpline Economy: Production and Distribution Systems in Early Central-East Guatemala. Ph.D. Dissertation, Department of Anthropology, Penn State University.

Feldman, Lawrence H., Robert Terzuola, Payson Sheets, and Constance Cameron
1975 Jade Workers in the Motagua Valley: The Late Classic Terzuola Site. Museum Brief 17. Columbia: Museum of Anthropology, University of Missouri.

Fields, Virginia
1991 The Iconographic Heritage of the Maya Jester God. *In* Sixth Palenque Round Table, 1986. M. G. Robertson and V. Fields, eds. Pp. 167–174. Norman: University of Oklahoma Press.

Foias, Antonia
2002 At the Crossroads: The Economic Basis of Political Power in the Petexbatún Region, Southwest Petén, Guatemala. *In* Ancient Maya Political Economies. M. Masson and D. Freidel, eds. Pp. 223–248. Walnut Creek, CA: Altamira Press.
2007 Ritual, Politics and Pottery Economies in the Classic Maya Southern Lowlands. *In* Mesoamerican Ritual Economy: Archaeological and Ethnological Perspectives. E.C. Wells and K.L. Davis-Salazar, eds. Pp. 167–194. Boulder: University of Colorado Press.

Foshag, William F., and Robert Leslie
1955 Jadeite from Manzanal, Guatemala. American Antiquity 21:81–83.

Fox, John, Garret Cool, Arlen Chase, and Diane Chase
1996 Questions of Political and Economic Integration: Segmentary Versus Centralized States Among the Ancient Maya. Cultural Anthropology 37(5):795–801.

Frankenstein, Susan, and Michael J. Rowlands
1978 The Internal Structure and Regional Context of Early Iron Age Society in Southwestern Germany. Institute of Archaeology Bulletin 15:73–112.

Freidel, David
1993 The Jade Ahau: Toward a Theory of Commodity Value in Maya Civilization. *In* Precolumbian Jade: New Geological and Cultural Interpretations. F. Lange, ed. Pp. 166–172. Salt Lake City: University of Utah Press.

Freidel, David, Kathryn Reese-Taylor, and David Mora-Martin
2002 The Origins of Maya Civilization: The Old Shell Game, Commodity Treasure, and Kingship. *In* Ancient Maya Political Economies. M. Masson and D. Freidel, eds. Pp. 41–86. Walnut Creek, CA: Alta Mira Press.

Garber, James
1983 Patterns of Jade Consumption and Disposal at Cerros, Northern Belize. American Antiquity 48(4):800–807.

Graham, Elizabeth
2002 Perspectives on economy and theory. *In* Ancient Maya Political Economies. M. Masson and D. Freidel, eds. Pp. 398–418. Walnut Creek, CA: Altamira Press.

Hagstrum, Melissa
1992 Intersecting Technologies: Ceramic Tools for Inka Metallurgy. Paper presented at the 28th Annual Symposium on Archaeometry, Los Angeles.

Hammond, Norman
1999 The Genesis of Hierarchy: Mortuary and Offertory Ritual in the Pre-Classic at Cuello, Belize. *In* Social Patterns in Pre-Classic Mesoamerica. D. Grove and R. Joyce, eds. Pp. 49–66. Washington, DC: Dumbarton Oaks.

Hammond, Norman, Arnold Aspinall, Stuart Feather, John Hazelden, Trevor Gazard, and Stuart Agrell
1977 Maya Jade: Source Location and Analysis. *In* Exchange Systems in Prehistory. T. Earle and J. Ericson, eds. Pp. 35–67. New York: Academic Press.

Harlow, George
1993 Middle American Jade: Geologic and Petrologic Perspectives on Variability and Source. *In* Precolumbian Jade: New Geological and Cultural Interpretations. F. Lange, ed. Pp. 9–29. Salt Lake City: University of Utah Press.

Healy, Paul F., John Lambert, J.T. Arnason, and Richard J. Hebda
1983 Caracol, Belize: Evidence of Ancient Maya Agricultural Terraces. Journal of Field Archaeology 10:397–410.

Hendon, Julia A.
1991 Status and Power in Classic Maya Society: An Archaeological Study. American Anthropologist 93(4):894–918.

Hester, Thomas, and Harry Shafer
1984 Exploitation of chert resources by the ancient Maya of northern Belize, Central America. World Archaeology 16(2):158–172.

Hirth, Kenneth
1992 Interregional Exchange as Elite Behavior: An Evolutionary Perspective. *In* Mesoamerican Elites: An Archaeological Assessment. D. Chase and A. Chase, eds. Pp. 18–29. Norman: University of Oklahoma Press.
1996 Politial Economy and Archaeology: Perspectives on Exchange and Production. Journal of Archaeological Research 4:203–239.

Inomata, Takeshi
2001 The Power and Ideology of Artistic Creation: Elite Craft Specialists in Classic Maya Society. Current Anthropology 42(3):321–349.
2007 Classic Maya elite competition, collaboration, and performance in multicraft production. *In* Craft production in complex societies: Multicraft and producer perspectives. I. Shimada, ed. Pp. 120–133. Salt Lake City: University of Utah Press.

Kidder, A.V.
1935 Notes on the ruins of San Agustin Acasaguastlan, Guatemala. Carnegie Institution of Washington, Publication no. 456, Contribution 15. Washington, DC.

Kovacevich, Brigitte
2006 Reconstructing Classic Maya Economic Systems: Production and Exchange at Cancuen, Guatemala. Unpublished Ph.D. Dissertation, Department of Anthropology, Vanderbilt University.
2007 Ritual, Crafting, and Agency at the Classic Maya Kingdom of Cancuen. *In* Mesoamerican Ritual Economy: Archaeological and Ethnological Perspectives. E.C. Wells and K.L. Davis-Salazar, eds. Pp. 67–114. Boulder: University of Colorado Press.

Lesure, Richard
1999 On the Genesis of Value in Early Hierarchical Societies. *In* Material Symbols: Culture and Economy in Prehistory. J. Robb, ed. Pp. 23–55. Carbondale: Center for Archaeological Investigations, Southern Illinois University at Carbondale.

Lewis, Brandon
1996 The Role of Attached and Independent Specialization in the Development of Sociopolitical Complexity. *In* Research in Economic Anthropology, Vol. 17. B. Isaac, ed. Pp. 289–346. Greenwich, CT: JAI Press.

Masson, Marilyn, and David Friedel (editors)
2002 Ancient Maya Political Economies. Walnut Creek, CA: Alta Mira Press.

McAnany, Patricia
1993 The Economics and Social Power of Wealth Among Eighth-Century Maya Households. *In* Lowland Maya Civilization in the Eighth Century A.D. J. Sabloff and J. Henderson, eds. Pp. 57–82. Washington, DC: Dumbarton Oaks.

McAnany, Patricia, Ben Thomas, Steven Morandi, Polly Peterson, and Eleanor Harrison
2002 Praise the Ajaw and Pass the Kakaw: Xibun Maya and the Political Economy of Cacao. *In* Ancient Maya Political Economies. M. Masson and D. Freidel, eds. Pp. 123–139. Walnut Creek, CA: Alta Mira Press.

Miller, Mary, and Marco Samayoa
1998 Where Maize Grows: Jade, Chacmools, and the Maize God. RES: Anthropology and Aesthetics 33:54–72.

Moholy-Nagy, Hattula
1997 Middens, Construction Fill, and Offerings: Evidence for the Organization of Classic Period Craft Production at Tikal, Guatemala. Journal of Field Archaeology 24(3):293–313.

Potter, Daniel, and Eleanor King
1995 A Heterarchical Approach to Lowland Maya Socioeconomics. *In* Heterarchy and the Analysis of Complex Societies [Anthropological Paper No. 6]. R. Ehrenreich, C. Crumley, and J. Levy, eds. Pp. 17–32. Washington, DC: American Anthropological Association.

Proskouriakoff, Tatiana
1974 Jades from the Cenote of Sacrifice, Chichen Itza, Yucatan. Cambridge, MA: Peabody Museum of Archaeology and Ethnology.

Rands, Robert L., and Ronald K. Bishop
1980 Resource Procurement Zones and Patterns of Ceramic Exchange in the Palenque Region, Mexico. *In* Models and Methods in Regional Exchange. R. Fry, ed. Pp. 19–46. Washington, DC: Society for American Archaeology Papers.

Rathje, William
1975 The Last Tango in Mayapán: A Tentative Trajectory of Production-Distribution Systems. *In* Ancient Civilization and Trade. J. Sabloff

and C.C. Lamberg-Karlovsky, eds. Pp. 409–448. Albuquerque: University of New Mexico Press.

Restall, Matthew
1997 *The Maya World: Yucatec Culture and Society, 1550–1850.* Palo Alto, CA: Stanford University Press.

Rice, Prudence M.
1987 Economic Change in the Lowland Maya Late Classic Period. *In* Specialization, Exchange, and Complex Societies. E. M. Brumfiel and T. K. Earle, eds. Pp. 76–85. Cambridge: Cambridge University Press.

Rochette, Erick
2009 The Late Classic Period Organization of Jade Artifact Production in the Middle Motagua Valley, Zacapa, Guatemala. Unpublished Ph.D. Dissertation. Department of Anthropology, The Pennsylvania State University.

Rochette, Erick, and Monica Pellecer-Alecio
2008 "¿A quién está asociado?: La producción artesanal doméstica de bienes de estatus en la cuenca media del río Motagua. *In* XXI Simposio de Investigaciones Arqueológicas en Guatemala, 2007. J.P. Laporte, B. Arroyo and H. Mejía, eds. Pp. 47–56. Guatemala: Museo Nacional de Arqueología y Etnología.

Sheets, Payson
2000 Provisioning the Ceren Household: The Vertical Economy, Village Economy, and Household Economy in the Southeastern Maya Periphery. Ancient Mesoamerica 11:217–230.

Simmons, C., J.M. Tarrano, and J.V. Pinto
1959 Clasificacion de Reconocimiento del los Suelos de la Republica de Guatemala. Guatemala: Editorial del Ministerio de Educacion Publica.

Sinopoli, Carla M.
1988 The Organization of Craft Production at Vijayanagara, South India. American Anthropologist 90(3):580–597.

Smith, Alfred L., and Alfred V. Kidder
1943 Explorations in the Motagua Valley, Guatemala. Carnegie Institution of Washington Publication

no. 546. Washington, DC: Carnegie Institution of Washington.

Smith, R. E., and J. Gifford
1965 Pottery of the Maya Lowlands. *In* Handbook of Middle American Indians, vol. 2, R. Wauchope and G. Willey, eds. Pp. 498–534. Austin: University of Texas Press.

Spielmann, Katherine A.
2002 Feasting, Craft Specialization, and the Ritual Mode of Production in Small-Scale Societies. *American Anthropologist* 104(1):195–207.

Taube, Karl
2000 Lightning Celts and Corn Fetishes: The Formative Olmec and the Development of Maize Symbolism in Mesoamerica and the American Southwest. *In* Olmec Art and Archaeology: Social Complexity in the Formative Period. J. Clark and M. Pye, eds. Pp. 296–337. Washington, DC: National Gallery of Art.
2005 The Symbolism of Jade in Classic Maya Religion. Ancient Mesoamerica 16:23–50.

Taube, Karl, Virginia Sisson, Russell Seitz, and George Harlow
2004 The Sourcing of Mesoamerican Jade: Expanded Geological Reconnaissance in the Motagua Region, Guatemala, Appendix to Olmec Art at Dumbarton Oaks. K. A. Taube, ed. Pp. 203–220. Washington, DC: Dumbarton Oaks.

Underhill, Anne
1991 Pottery Production in Chiefdoms: The Longshan Period of Northern China. World Archaeology 23:12–27.

Walters, Gary R.
1980 The San Agustin Acasaguastlan Archaeological Project: Report on the 1979 Field Season. University Museum Brief 25. Columbia, MO: University of Missouri.
1982 The Pre-Columbian Jade Processing Industry of the Middle Motagua Valley of East-Central Guatemala. Unpublished Ph.D. dissertation, Department of Anthropology, University of Missouri-Columbia.
1989 Un Taller de Jade en Guaytan, Guatemala. *In* La Obsidiana en Mesoamérica. M. Gaxiola

G and J. E. Clark, eds. Pp. 253–262. Colección Científica 176. Mexico: INAH.

Wattenmaker, Patricia
1998 Craft Production and Social Identity in Northwest Mesopotamia. *In* Craft and Social Identity. C. Costin and R. Wright, eds. Pp. 47–55. Anthropological Paper No. 8. Washington, DC: American Anthropological Association.

Webster, David
1998 Status Rivalry Warfare: Some Maya – Polynesian Comparisons. *In* Archaic States. G. Feinman and J. Marcus, eds. Pp. 311–352. Santa Fe: School of American Research.

Wells, E. Christian
2006 Recent Trends in Theorizing Prehispanic Mesoamerican Economies. Journal of Archaeological Research 14(4):265–312.

Wells, E. Christian Wells, and Karla L. Davis-Salazar
2007a Mesoamerican Ritual Economy: Archaeological and Ethnological Perspectives. Boulder: University of Colorado Press. (as editors).
2007b Mesoamerican Ritual Economy: Materialization as Ritual and Economic Process. *In* Mesoamerican Ritual Economy: Archaeological and Ethnological Perspectives. E.C. Wells and K. L. Davis-Salazar, eds. Pp. 1–26. Boulder: University of Colorado Press.

West, Georgia
2002 Ceramic Exchange in the Late Classic and Postclassic Maya Lowlands: A Diachronic Approach. *In* Ancient Maya Political Economies. M. Masson and D. Freidel, eds. Pp. 140–196. Walnut Creek, CA: Alta Mira Press.

Widmer, Randolph
1991 Lapidary craft specialization at Teotihuacan: implications for community structure at 33:S3W1 and economic organization in the city. *Ancient Mesoamerica* 2(1):131–141.

Wilk, Richard. R.
1989 The Household Economy: Reconsidering the Domestic Mode of Production. Boulder, CO: Westview Press.

Willey, Gordon R.
1956 The Structure of Ancient Maya Society: Evidence from the Southern Lowlands. American Anthropologist 58(5):777–782.

Wright, Rita
1998 Crafting Social Identity in Ur III Southern Mesopotamia. *In* Craft and Social Identity. C. Costin and R. Wright, eds. Pp. 57–70. Anthropological Paper No. 8. Washington, DC: American Anthropological Association.

Zeleznik, Scott
2002 The Varied Contexts of Social Distinction in Classic Maya Society from the Copan Valley, Honduras. Paper presented at the 67th Annual Meeting of the Society for American Archaeology, Denver, Colorado, March 22, 2002.

14

Metal for the Commoners: Tarascan Metallurgical Production in Domestic Contexts

Blanca Maldonado
Curt-Engelhorn-Zentrum
Archäometrie Mannheim and
El Colegio de Michoacan

At the time of the Spanish Conquest the main locus of metal production in Mesoamerica was the Tarascan region of western Mexico. Mining and metallurgy appears to have evolved to some extent into a state industry, as metal adornments used as insignia of social status and public ritual became closely associated with political control. Available archaeological and ethnohistorical data, however, indicate that implements used for subsistence activities, such as hoes and axes, were also produced and may have been traded through local market networks. Other copper tools, including needles, awls, punches, and fishhooks, appear to have been widely distributed as well. It seems clear from this evidence that some mining and smelting of copper and goods manufacturing were taking place outside the main system of the state and its centralized control, possibly in household contexts. The present paper explores possible ways in which metallurgical production was integrated into the domestic economy of prehispanic coppersmiths, within the context of the larger Tarascan metal production system.

A number of issues arise from the notion that metal items functioned as wealth finance in the economy of the Tarascan Empire of late Postclassic Michoacán (c. AD 1300 to AD 1530). Foremost among these is whether and how wealth was produced and controlled by the central power. Metallurgy, however, does not represent a single technological process. The transformation from ore to finished product involves many individual stages and numerous choices have to be made throughout the production sequence. The metallurgical *chaîne opératoire* (Leroi-Gourhan 1963) for Tarascan copper production requires a specific body of expertise and skills that includes: the procurement of minerals from which to extract metal (extractive metallurgy or smelting); the experimentation with, and use of alloys; the working of metal through some mechanical method (hot or cold hammering) or by fusion and molding (foundry); the application of polishing, and other finishing techniques; and the knowledge of the required forms and symbols.

The facts above raise several important questions regarding Tarascan metallurgy. How many different categories of producers participated in the manufacture of metal items in the Tarascan Empire? What was the degree of specialization of these producers in their particular craft? What was the level of involvement of the central state and the elites in each one of the stages of production of this craft? Although current data for both mining or extractive metallurgy in Mesoamerica are sparse and unclear, important aspects of the operational sequence for Tarascan copper production including ore deposit and mining, smelting, and final processing, can be inferred from a combination of ethnohistorical and archaeological data. Multiple lines of evidence are thus used to explore some dynamic levels of interaction between the production of copper and copper-based goods and the centralized power of the Tarascan Empire of late Postclassic Mesoamerica. Archaeological evidence and documentary sources provide a picture of organizational patterns in the prehispanic Tarascan copper industry.

The Study of Craft Production

The study of specialized craft production (its emergence, organization, and associated technologies) has a

ARCHEOLOGICAL PAPERS OF THE AMERICAN ANTHROPOLOGICAL ASSOCIATION, Vol. 19, Issue 1, pp. 225–238, ISSN 1551-823X,
online ISSN 1551-8248. DOI: 10.1111/j.1551-8248.2009.01022.x.

long history in archaeological research (see Hirth chapter 2, this volume; Wailes 1996; Patterson 2005). Because much craft production leaves distinctive material traces, archaeologists are able to address technologies, locations, and scales of production, and to examine their roles in the broader social, economic, and political contexts in which they occur. The concepts that different scholars use in defining and characterizing their findings may however vary. For the purposes of the present work, "political economy" is defined broadly as the relations between political structures and systems and the economic realms of production, consumption, and exchange (Stein 2001: 359). The term craft production entails "the investment of labor by (more or less) skilled practitioners who labor to transform potential into finished products that were in turn consumed by non-producers" (Sinopoli 2003: 1).

Archaeologists and social theorists have long been concerned with the relationship between craft production and political and institutional structures (see Hirth chapter 2, this volume, for a complete overview). Craft products can perform a number of functions in political economies: as exchange goods, sources of wealth, as tools that produce the material infrastructure of complex societies, and as prestige goods or symbols of power and status. The relations between craft producers and institutions tend to be both multiple and multidimensional, with varying degrees of autonomy and interdependence, and much production can occur outside the control of a centralized authority (Sinopoli 2003).

The distinction between attached and independent specialization has been taken up by many scholars seeking to explore the political dimensions of craft production activities (e.g. see contributions in Wailes 1996; Brumfiel and Earle 1987; Costin and Wright 1998; also Peregrine 1991). In an influential work, Brumfiel and Earle (1987) emphasized the difference between the production of wealth goods and staple products (see also D'Altroy and Earle 1985), and the divergent roles these played in political economies. Costin (1991, 2001) expanded on Brumfiel and Earle's perspective in an important study in which four parameters for documenting craft production are outlined: concentration, scale, intensity, and context. Costin's focus, however, was on the social, spatial, and political settings and structures of production, rather than the goods produced and their uses. She viewed each of the parameters as continua, which could vary independently of each other. Thus, rather than a limited set of types, craft production could be structured in a multitude of ways, within a single culture and cross-culturally.

Refining Models of Craft Production

The "attached" versus "independent" craft production paradigm has been heavily criticized by many who perceive it as a dichotomy, as opposed to the continuum of elite control that Costin and others conceptualize. There have been in recent years a number of attempts by archaeologists to refine the model, in order to apply it to specific research cases. Janusek (1999), for example, has adopted the term "embedded specialization" to define the organization of production at the level of corporate kin groups at Tiwanaku. Ames (1995) had earlier used this concept to refer to the production of craft items by elites. As employed by Janusek, however, embedded specialization entails relations of production, which are more centralized than independent specialization, but less constrained than attached specialization. In this context of production we may find a relatively high number of individuals who do not fully participate in subsistence activities because they can depend upon their kin ties. The access to raw materials also tends to be greater than that found among societies with a more "classic" system of attached specialization. The *calpulli* organization in the Aztec capital of Tenochtitlan may represent an example of this form of specialization.

The model of attached-independent craft production is further challenged by instances in which elites may have had control over the distribution networks or the means of transport, so independent specialists relied on them for the distribution of the produced goods (see Arnold and Munns 1994). This suggests that sometimes, autonomous production which reaches a level higher than that of the local consumption needs, has to depend on a ruling system for the distribution of the produced goods outside the community. The state-controlled merchant organization of the Aztec Pochteca (Hassig 1985) may represent an example for this form of semi-dependent specialization.

In some cases individual households can also display high levels of specialized production. Mesoamerica provides numerous examples where individual households could have access to raw materials and skills to produce goods at a relatively large scale. Feinman (1999) for instance, has argued that in early state periods in Oaxaca, many craft products were produced in household contexts. The evidence for such situations challenges our notion of the relationships between scale and intensity in craft manufacture (Feinman 1999; Feinman and Nicholas 2000). These examples should lead us to question the idea that large-scale production appears only among complex societies participating in trade networks, which foster independent or attached production away from the household context.

It is important to also recognize that even in formal workshop contexts, the kinds of relations that may have existed between producers and institutions can vary widely, can be multidimensional, and can change over time. Examples of multidimensional relations in production systems might include textile manufacturing by Aztec women, who devoted a portion of their efforts to meeting obligatory tribute demands, while also producing goods to meet the needs of their household and to distribute through market or other mechanisms. Whoever they produced for, production occurred in household settings using a consistent technology. Only the intended consumer varied (Brumfiel 1991). Aztec economy in this regard, seems to also exemplify what Stein (1996) has called a dual economy, in which certain specialists independently produced utilitarian items for the market, but were simultaneously attached to the elites and produced prestige and utilitarian goods for them (see Sahagún 1969–82 Bk.9, Ch. 20). This example challenges our notion of a dichotomized independent as opposed to attached specialization, since we may find attached specialists who, contrary to the expectations, were producing utilitarian goods along with (or instead of) wealth goods.

Craft Production and the Domestic Sphere

The overwhelming evidence of craft production taking place in domestic contexts has lead Hirth (chapter two, this volume) to approach craft production in terms of how it is integrated into the household economy as a whole. He sees craft production largely as a strategy for enhancing the well-being of the household and its members and buffering risk factors that might otherwise compromise it. Two major categories of craft production at the household level derive from this view: intermittent crafting and multi-crafting. The former relates to domestic craft production which takes place during the slack period of the agricultural season; the former describes the diversification of craft production within the same household. Both strategies are directed toward maximizing productivity and minimizing risk.

Within this framework, the importance of attached vs. independent production in the political economy of complex societies becomes a key issue, along with the question of how closely these forms corresponded to organizational strategies used in all households to intensify production. Hirth underscores the contrast between attached production and what he refers to as consigned production, which implies the existence of independent artisans who have the expertise to produce goods for elite consumption, yet can also continue to produce non-elite products. This kind of production was probably much more common in Mesoamerica than attached production. Evidence for the coexisting production of luxury and utilitarian metal goods, as well as other available data suggest that metallurgical production in the Tarascan state may have closely corresponded to a form of consigned production.

The Organization of Copper Production in the Tarascan Empire

Empires can be defined as large, multi-ethnic states ruled from a single center (Sinopoli 1995, 2003). By definition, empires incorporate cultural and economic diversity. In the sphere of production, such diversity is manifest in scale and organization, and the nature and degree of integration of different productive areas into an Imperial order (Sinopoli and Morrison 1995). The early Postclassic period in Mesoamerica (ca. A.D. 900–1200) fostered the development of what would become the most important state in West Mexico: the Tarascan Empire. According to Pollard (2003), during this period, important transformations took place among the populations of the central highlands of Michoacán. These included the political unification of formerly autonomous communities in the Lake Pátzcuaro basin, which became the geographical core of an expansionist polity, with its central power in Tzintzuntzan (Pollard 1993, 2003). By A.D. 1450, the Tarascan Empire (Figure 1) had also become the most important center of prehispanic metalworking in Mesoamerica.

Mesoamerican copper metallurgy first appeared in West México sometime between A.D. 600 and 800, and over the next 900 years a wide variety of artifacts was produced. At the time of the Spanish Conquest the main locus of metal production was the Tarascan region. Apparently the use of fine metal goods within the Tarascan territory was restricted to the social and political elite. Implements used for subsistence activities, such as hoes and axes, were also produced although not in quantity, and may have even been traded through local market networks within the Balsas Basin (Barrett 1987; Warren 1968; Pollard 1987). Other copper tools, including needles, awls, punches, and fishhooks, appear to have been widely distributed, but their procurement and use was probably limited to craft or occupational specialists (Hosler 1994:156; Pollard 1987: 744). Presumably, all other metal goods were limited to the central dynasty and the nobility.

Metallurgy played a significant role in the structure of political and economic power in the Tarascan Empire. The state government, according to Pollard (1987: 745–746; 1993: 119), acquired finished metal goods and/or smelted ingots through different mechanisms, including the following: (1) as gifts presented by foreign visitors and regional

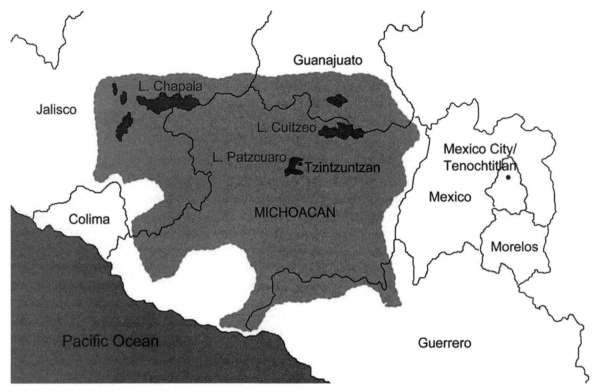

Figure 1. Maximum extension of the Tarascan territory, ca. 1500 A.D. (After Pollard 1993, p. 5).

elite to the king, (2) by government long distance merchants at the border of the Empire's territory, (3) as tribute paid to regional elites who in turn contributed part (or all) of the received goods to state storehouses in Tzintzuntzan, and (4) the direct movement of copper ingots from state controlled mines into the state storehouses.

The presence of craft producers with a considerable degree of specialization in the production of metal goods can be assumed from the relatively restricted spatial distribution of final products, the specific social and political context of their production and distribution, and the technological complexity of the industry behind their manufacture. Scattered references in documentary sources to craft specialists involved in the production of metal and metal goods support this assumption. Such sources include the *Legajo* 1204 (Warren 1968), which is an important 16th century manuscript dealing with copper mines, and the *Relación de Michoacán* (Alcalá 2000), written around 1540 by Fray Jeronimo de Alcalá and containing translated and transcribed narratives from Tarascan noblemen.

Ore Deposits and Mining

While the consumption of finished metal goods was highly concentrated within a limited social and spatial ter-

ritory, the production of metal from ore was naturally dispersed throughout the Tarascan territory (Pollard 1982: 258–259, 1987: 745). Ethnohistorical evidence suggests that production operations took place at a number of different locations within the domain of the Tarascan Empire (Pollard 1987: 748). Apparently, the bulk of the metal that moved into the Pátzcuaro Basin came in the form of regularly delivered tribute (see Paredes 1984; Pollard 1982, 1987). The primary supplier of copper was the central Balsas Basin, in the southern portion of the Tarascan territory.

Paredes (1984) and Pollard (1987) have suggested that during the last century of the Tarascan Empire the state took more direct control of the copper resources of central Balsas Basin than simply relying on tribute to supply its demands. This idea is based largely on accounts in the *Legajo* 1204 (Warren 1968), which suggest that the *Cazonci* (the paramount ruler of the Tarascan state) sent workers to extract copper from the mines of La Huacana (Figures 2, 3) to meet his needs (Pollard 1987: 748; Warren 1968: 47, 48). Some mines, however, continued to be exploited through the tribute system (Pollard 1987: 748).

According to the *Legajo* 1204 (in Pollard 1982: 258, 1987: 748; Warren 1968: 49) the schedule for payments of copper, of either every 40 days or on demand, substantially exceeds that of any other tributary item for the central

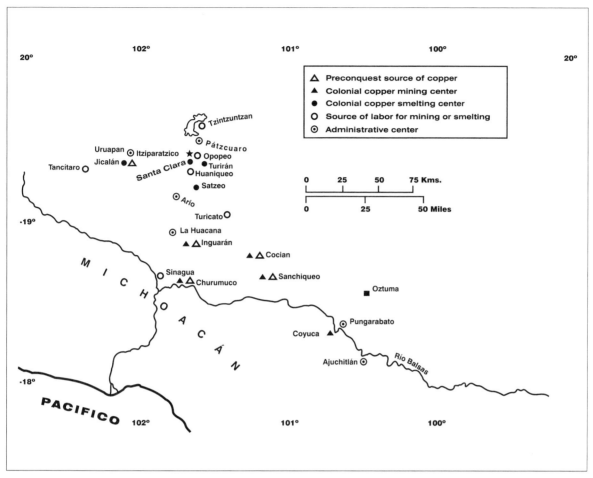

Figure 2. Pre-Hispanic and Colonial mining centers in the Central Balsas Basin (Adapted from Barrett 1987: Map 2).

authority. The *Legajo* indicates that mining activities and smelting operations often took place at separate locations within the central Balsas Basin. While mining centers were concentrated at Churumuco, Sinagua, Cutzian and La Huacana, among others, smelting operations were carried out at La Huacana, Cutzian, and Huetamo-Cutzio (Pollard 1987; Warren 1968) (see Figure 2). At the Cutzian mine alone, there were up to 50 miners and 40 other workers, some of whom were moving the dirt and mineral out of the mines and some who were processing the ore (Warren 1968: 49).

Accounts in the *Legajo* also declare that the metalworkers from La Huacana region owned and cultivated the fields at the foot of the hill where the copper veins were mined. This suggests that mining and metallurgy (at least at this particular location) represented part-time activities, undertaken mostly during the slack period in the agricultural season. The great climatic variation between the rainy and dry seasons in the region supports this assumption. During the rainy season the mines were probably flooded, while during the dry sea-

son, agricultural production must have fallen dramatically due the extreme dryness in the region. The miners/smelters most likely alternated between metalworking and farming, according to the seasons as well as to royal demands (Grinberg 1996: 433). This strategy seems to correspond with what Hirth (this volume) has termed *intermittent crafting*.

Smelting Operations

Considering the apparent involvement of the Tarascan state in the extraction of ore, it is possible that the smelting operations were also under some degree of supervision. Systematic research at the archaeological zone of Itziparátzico, in the Zirahuen Basin (Figure 3), has located potential production areas where concentrations of smelting slag were recorded. Surface survey carried out during the Itziparátzico Archaeological Research Project (IARP) in 2003–2004 identified and mapped three major sectors of

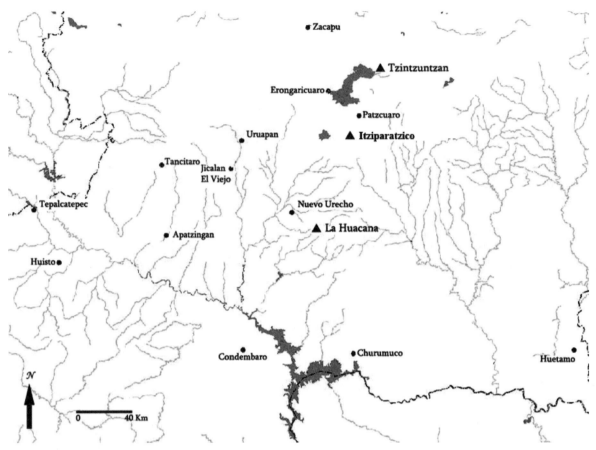

Figure 3. Location of Itziparátzico and other mining and smelting localities within the Tarascan territory (Modified from Roskamp et al. 2003: Figure 4).

the site, divided according to the variability of their archaeological materials and features (Figure 4) (see Maldonado 2006).

While ceramic and lithic artifacts were common throughout the research area, slag concentrations were located almost exclusively in one particular sector (Sector 1). The presence of smelting byproducts indicates that smelting activities took place in or around this zone, an indication possibly further supported by the proximity of this sector to water, indispensable for many metalworking processes. Other materials include moderate amounts of potsherds and lithics (mainly gray-black obsidian prismatic blades), as well as a set of stylistically diverse Tarascan pipes. These pipes and several polychrome ceramic fragments have been identified as corresponding to the late Postclassic period (c. AD 1350 to AD 1521).

Fieldwork at Itziparátzico also involved archaeological test excavations in the three major sectors of the area. The results of these excavations were consistent with the observations on the surface. No substantial evidence for occupation before or after the late Postclassic period was found;

all ceramic and lithic artifacts date to the late Postclassic Tarascan occupation. Although no identifiable metalworking structures (furnaces, hearths, and pits) were found at Itziparátzico during the test-pitting, large amounts of slag were recovered from the excavation, together with lithics and ceramics as found elsewhere on site. The absence of metallurgical materials other than slag (i.e. hearth structures, crucible fragments, mould fragments, stock metal, metal prills, failed castings, part-manufactured objects and spillages, etc.) around Itziparátzico indicates that only primary copper production (smelting) was being carried out at this location.

Analyses of slag samples corroborate that the production activities carried out at Itziparátzico involved primary smelting. Two major types of slag from Itziparátzico were identified macroscopically and labeled as either platy (Figure 5A) or lumpy (Figure 5B), according to their general morphology (see Maldonado et al. 2005 for detailed descriptions of these two types, as well as of a detailed report of the scientific analyses). Analyses slag formation phases such as fayalite and magnetite by SEM-EDS are consistent

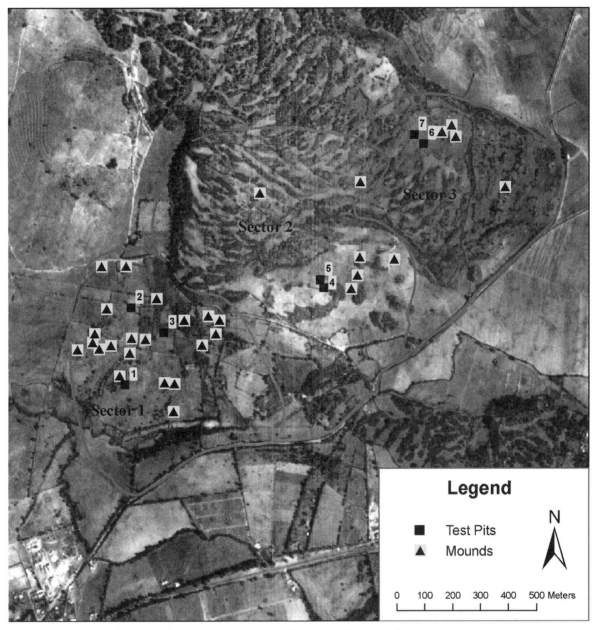

Figure 4. Three main sectors of the Itziparátzico area (Maldonado 2006: Map 4.6).

between the two types, indicating that the main difference between the lumpy and the platy slag is in the mechanical incorporation of residual quartz in the former. The two slag types thus likely represent sequential waste products of the same continuous smelting process (Maldonado et al. 2005).

Bulk analyses derived from XRF analyses of platy slag samples indicate that the mineral ore being processed at Itziparátzico was sulfidic ore, most likely chalcopyrite ($CuFeS_2$), in a silica-rich matrix. The dominance of well-crystallised fayalite and magnetite in a homogenous slag matrix, and the presence of copper prills indicate: 1) a consistent smelting temperature of around 1200 °C, and 2) the occurrence of smelting under strongly reducing conditions. The combination of temperature and reducing atmosphere necessary for consistent fayalite formation on a scale of several kilograms liquid slag at a time, as evidenced from the larger slag lumps from Itziparátzico (Maldonado et al. 2005), are very strong evidence for a specialized furnace technology. The furnaces themselves, however, may have

A

B

Figure 5. (A) Platy slag fragment from Itziparátzico (Maldonado 2006: Figure 4.19). (B) Lumpy slag fragment from Itziparátzico (Maldonado 2006: Figure 4.20).

been only semi-permanent structures. As indicated by the archaeological observations, slag disposal occurred in a relatively wide scatter around the smelting site, probably in order to keep the working space around the furnaces free, while the furnaces themselves were most likely left to decay in situ once copper production at the site had ceased. This, and the general fragility of furnace wall fragments in the archaeological record, may explain the absence of recognizable furnace wall material in the test pitting areas (Maldonado and Rehren 2009).

The most outstanding feature of Itziparátzico is its location about 125 kilometers away from the mines themselves.

It seems clear that copper ore (chalcopyrite) was brought a considerable distance (see Figure 3) to Itziparátzico for smelting, and copper ingots were probably transported elsewhere for their final processing (Maldonado et al. 2005). While this situation may not seem economically advantageous, the movement of ore from mine to settlement is well represented in the archaeological record. Several early examples from the Old World can be cited, including Chalcolithic sites such as Abu Matar (Gilead and Rosen 1992) and Shiqmim (Golden et al. 2001; Shalev and Northover 1987) in Israel, which lie some 150 kilometers from the nearest source of copper ore and yet present substantial evidence of smelting activities. The absence of any traces of further processing of the smelted copper and the near-absence of copper tools and objects from the site indicate that the copper production at Itziparátzico was embedded in a wider network, linking mining of chalcopyrite in the copper-rich regions around La Huacana with the administrative (and probably consumption) centre of the Tarascan state at Tzintzuntzan.

It is difficult to accurately assess the scale of metallurgical production at Itziparátzico based on the information currently available, since no smelting facilities were located during the survey or test-pitting. The highest slag concentrations, however, consist of some hundreds of kilograms and are located within a restricted area, away from the residential terraces. Systematic quantification of slag can therefore be used to obtain rough estimates of the copper production at Itziparátzico, based on the quantity of slag produced and an estimate of the ratio of slag to metal produced. Because the chemical composition of the slag reflects predominantly that of the ore, and since the chemical composition of the copper mineral is known, a good estimate of the copper yield may be obtained from the composition and total weight of the slag (see Maldonado and Rehren 2009 for detailed data on these estimates). These calculations, although preliminary, demonstrate that the scale of production for a single parcel of c. 30 by 40 m was of the order of ten tons of copper metal. Although we still do not know the chronological extent of the operations, or its spatial distribution and full scale within the region of Itziparátzico, even spreading this over a period of one century, the annual production would be of around 100 kg of metal. We assume that this amount of copper could have been produced by a small group of people within one or two months. The smelting activity at Itziparátzico would thus be part of a subsistence strategy of a farming community including part-time specialists, with the smelting set within the annual farming cycle, and fully integrated in a wider network of mining, long-distance transport of ore and metal, and tribute.

As mentioned before, the elemental raw materials (copper ores) were not locally available at Itziparátzico and had to be imported. The technology employed in the smelting process involved an efficient, highly reducing smelting environment, which suggests very skilled and experienced labor. Nevertheless, because extractive operations are best performed in dry conditions, it is plausible that smelting followed the same seasonal pattern as mining. In addition, the furnaces employed in and around Itziparátzico are likely to have been semi-permanent structures requiring only limited maintenance and repair during periods of use. The scale of production indicates that copper smelting was done by specialists embedded in a predominantly agricultural economy. These facts, once again, point toward a form of intermittent crafting, where smelters carried out copper production alongside other activities.

As the demands for copper of the central dynasty increased, the Tarascans appear to have established a production and distribution system planned to obtain metal from different locations, and divided the industry up into small components that could be easily managed: mining, transportation of copper (and probably tin) ores from different locations, smelting, alloying, finishing by casting and forging. The new system may have started with the smelting of ores away from the mines at sites like Itziparátzico, which had access to high quality charcoal (made of oak, which has far more efficient combustion than fuel made from scrub trees around the mines) for smelting, and was located strategically on the route connecting the central Balsas region and the Pátzcuaro Basin. The increasing demand of the state for copper may have favored the introduction of such technological innovation. Ore had to be carried some 125 km, which would also imply an increase in efficiency of the transport system to cope with high transportation costs. According to accounts in the *Relación de Michoacán* and the *Legajo* 1204, processed ingots were transported for final manufacture on the backs of *tamemes* (the Nahuatl term for human carriers), each load consisting of 20 to 30 ingots (Warren 1968: 47, 49) which weighed 32–72 kg (Pollard 1987: 748). Based on information found in the *Legajo*, Pollard (1987: 750) has estimated that the major smelting centers of La Huacana and Cutzian were a two days' journey from Tzintzuntzan. These estimates make the transport of ore to an intermediate point like Itziparátzico possible.

Final Processing and Manufacturing Activities

There is, at present, no direct archaeological evidence for workshops associated with the manufacture of metal objects in Mesoamerica. The types of metal artifacts and the manufacturing methods and materials (pure metals and alloys) that Tarascan metalworkers employed in their fabrication, however, have been relatively well documented through the analysis of metal artifacts (e.g. Grinberg 1990, 1996, 2004; Hosler 1988a, 1988b, 1988c, 1994; Pendergast 1962; Rubín de la Borbolla 1944). Copper was alloyed with tin and/or arsenic to produce bronzes or mixed with various concentrations of silver, gold, or both, to fashion bells, ornamental tweezers, rings and body ornaments. Although bronzes were also used to manufacture tools such as axes, hoes, and needles, the main focus of Tarascan metallurgy was on sumptuary objects that reflected fundamental religious and political agendas. Metals were directly associated with particular deities and the *Cazonci*, as the human representative on earth of the patron god Curicaueri, also shared this association (Hosler 1994; Pollard 1987). Given this piece of information, it is not surprising that the greater part of the metal items produced in the Tarascan territory were concentrated in the royal palace and associated quarters of the social and political elite in Tzintzuntzan, and in royal treasuries of the Lake Pátzcuaro Basin (Pollard 1987; 1993).

Outside the core of the empire, metal objects were found in relatively small quantities in elite contexts and, to a limited extent, as implements for basic production (Pollard 1987: 745). The Relación de Michoacán makes reference to a kind of 'guild' system in the crafts in the Tarascan core, each craft being under the authority and supervision of a subject of the *Cazonci* (Alcalá 2000: 171–178; Warren 1985: 20–21). While the presence of guilds is questionable (since no evidence of their existence has been reported anywhere else in Mesoamerica), apparently artisans who were in some way attached to the palace in Tzintzuntzan produced a wide range of goods for the royal household, including objects of gold, silver and copper. It is not clear whether these were royal retainers or individuals paying tribute in specialized activities (Pollard 1982: 259; Gorenstein and Pollard 1983: 103), the evidence however, points toward a category closer to the latter.

The Contexts of Copper Production in the Tarascan State

The diverse arenas of copper production in the Tarascan Empire suggest different pictures of the forms and degrees of craft specialization, as well as of the possible elite involvement and control of the manufacturing process. Here, like in other contexts of production and consumption of specialist craft products, individuals and groups would be linked in webs of interdependence and interaction. The Tarascan *chaîne opératoire* of copper production seems to indicate the involvement of social groups of various sizes, including raw material procurers or producers (who may include other specialists, e.g. miners, charcoal producers, and smelters who provided ores and smelted materials to forgers or casters), to people participating in various stages of production and distribution. Producers also interacted with those who acquired and used their products (e.g. elite patrons). The scale of production may have also varied accordingly. Considering the general nature of craft production in Mesoamerica, it is likely that some mining and smelting of copper ore and goods manufacturing were also taking place outside the state system of centralized control, possibly in household contexts. Although no hard evidence supports this assumption, the appearance of tools and items of daily use in non-elite contexts suggests this possibility. This additional dimension of production would open up a whole range of variation to the Tarascan copper industry.

The distinction between attached and independent specialization understood as a continuum of variability, as formulated by Costin (1991), can be used (although not without caution) to explore the nature of the relationship between the different categories of producers within the copper industry and the Tarascan state. In this context, such a scheme is perceived as particular relations of production with specific duration, rather than fixed and exclusive relations of production (see Smith 2004: 83; Sinopoli 2003: 32–33; Stein 1996: 25–26).

Copper production in the Tarascan Empire appears to have encompassed, for at least a period of time, variation in the different forms or units of production. Mining in the Tarascan territory was regulated mainly through the tribute system, although it also involved some direct exploitation by the Tzintzuntzan elite (see Paredes 1984; Pollard 1982, 1987). These varying state procurement strategies may have resulted in units of production roughly corresponding to at least two of the categories suggested by Costin (1991). One of these productive types is dispersed *corvée* production (e.g. labor in mines and smelters to produce tribute for the state) and the other one nucleated *corvée* (e.g. workers sent to state mines). Smelting operations are the least known and most problematic aspect of Tarascan copper production. It is likely that the degree of control from the state varied on basis of region, in a similar way as mining.

Finally, artifact manufacture is consistent with forms of retainer production (consigned or attached production, or both) in which metalworkers produced valued goods for the elite and the palace in supervised units. Metal ingots were presumably kept in state storage houses. This suggests that control of the final processing may have been exercised by restricting access to the raw materials for metalworking,

rather than controlling specialized labor. Casting, forging, and finishing, while labor intensive, are relatively easy tasks once the basic skills have been mastered.

If the scheme above applies, control by the elites and the central power in the Tarascan state was aimed at limiting access to both raw materials and finished products. By extension, the craft producers themselves may also have been under elite control. Sumptuary laws may have been used to regulate the display of metal objects. Two possible scenarios emerge. One scenario suggests that institutional representatives may have directly and forcefully imposed control, or exerted their "power over" the production process. In the alternative scenario control of informed actors may have been more subtle and indirect, involving inducements and rewards rather than coercion, that is, utilizing their "power to" control craft production (as did Aztec rulers who patronized certain crafts; see e.g. Blanton and Feinman 1984). The dialectic of control (or the relation between agency and power) is between these two scenarios.

It is obvious, however, that the model of metallurgical production and consumption presented above is incomplete. Implements used for subsistence activities, such as hoes and axes, were also produced and may have even been traded through local market networks. Other copper tools, including needles, awls, punches, and fishhooks, appear to have been widely distributed as well. This evidence suggests that some mining and smelting of copper and goods manufacturing were taking place in household contexts. While substantial evidence to discuss this possibility is currently unavailable, a combination of archaeological and ethnohistoric data may support this possibility.

Domestic Production of Metal Goods in the Tarascan Territory?

As pointed out above, *intermittent crafting* in the form of part-time mining and smelting activities was taking place within the Tarascan domain. The intermittent nature of both the mining and smelting activities suggests loose (if any) direct control of metal production. This also suggests that independent specialists already existed in the producing communities, which would indicate that consigned production may have been taking place at least in these two segments of the metallurgical *chaîne opératoire* in the Tarascan territory. The production of metal implements used for subsistence activities, tools for craft production, and woodworking suggests that metalworking may have involved similar strategies of independent production. Unfortunately, few copper tools with utilitarian functions come from secure archaeological contexts. In Huandacareo, Macías (1990) recovered 17 tools from burials and test pits. In the Apatzingan area, located in the Balsas region of Michoacan, Kelly (1947) recovered numerous metal artifacts from refuse mounds and test excavations. The presence of copper ore in the same contexts suggests that the metal objects were locally produced and used. Kelly, however, believes that there is no Tarascan presence in this region. The bulk of metal findings in domestic contexts are confined for the most part to areas outside the Tarascan territory. The most complete records come from Cuexcomate and Capilco, in western Morelos, where copper-based awls and needles have been recovered from household debris (Smith and Heath-Smith 1994). No convincing evidence for the production of metal has been found at either location, which suggests that the goods in question were imported (Hosler 1994; Smith and Heath-Smith 1994). According to Hosler (1994), during the late Postclassic period, West Mexican traders and/or metalworkers were transporting artifacts and ingots, as well as information on ore processing to adjacent areas. What were the contexts of production of such traded items? What were the patterns of distribution and consumption of these utilitarian items within the Tarascan state? Was their production marginal to the state production? At best, only partial answers are currently available to these questions.

Conclusion

The inferred existence of a domestic (and perhaps marginal) metal industry in the Tarascan territory suggests that the nature and degree of imperial elite involvement in and control over, production may have varied greatly across time and space and that in general, economic integration was predominantly local in character. Intermittent crafting appears to have remained a prime economic strategy, at least in some stages of the *chaîne opératoire* of copper production. We can argue that there was no single Tarascan economy. Instead, there existed a diversity of economic systems and strategies that varied with the nature of the goods being produced and its context of production: its political value, labor requirements, and role in long-distance exchange networks.

The present study, while focusing on a specific craft, metallurgy, could not isolate it completely from the larger Tarascan Imperial system, due to the multi-scalar and inter-related nature of the social units of production. The above discussion illustrates some of the political, social, economic and geographic variables that influenced the production of copper in the Tarascan state. The kinds of social and economic relations that developed among producers and between producers and consumers seem to have varied considerably throughout the empire (and probably through time).

The nature of these relations and the reasons for their patterning are also important questions to address in future research. The exploration of these relationships will enable us to consider both specific cases and broader cross-cultural patterns.

References

Alcalá, Jerónimo de, Fray
2000 Relación de las Ceremonias y Rictos y Población y Gobernación de los Indios de la Provincia de Mechuacan. Zamora: El Colegio de Michoacán.

Ames, Kenneth M.
1995 Chiefly power and household production on the Northwest Coast. *In* Foundations of Social Inequality. T. Douglas Price and Gary M. Feinman, eds. Pp. 155–87. New York: Plenum.

Arnold, Jeanne E., and Ann Munns
1994 Independent or Attached Specialization: The Organization of Shell Bead Production in California. Journal of Field Archaeology 21:473–489.

Barrett, Elinore M.
1987 The Mexican Colonial Copper Industry. Albuquerque: University of New Mexico Press.

Blanton, Richard E., and Gary M. Feinman
1984 The Mesoamerican World System. American Anthropologist 86:673–682.

Brumfiel, Elizabeth M.
1991 Weaving and Cooking: Women's Production in Aztec Mexico. *In* Engendering Archaeology: Women and Prehistory. Joan M. Gero and Margaret W. Conkey, eds. Pp. 224–254. Oxford: Basil Blackwell.

Brumfiel, Elizabeth M., and Timothy K. Earle
1987 Specialization, Exchange and Complex Societies: An Introduction. *In* Specialization, Exchange and Complex Societies. Elizabeth M. Brumfiel and Timothy K. Earle, eds. Pp. 1–9. Cambridge: Cambridge University Press.

Costin, Cathy L.
1991 Craft Specialization: Issues in Defining, Documenting, and Explaining the Organization of Production. *In* Archaeological Method and

Theory. Michael B. Schiffer, ed. Pp. 1–56. Tucson: University of Arizona Press.

2001 Craft Production Systems. *In* Archaeology at the Millennium: A Sourcebook. Gary M. Feinman and T. Douglas Price, eds. Pp. 273–327. New York: Kluwer Academic/Plenum Publishers.

Costin, Cathy L., and Rita P. Wright, eds.
1998 Craft and Social Identity. Archaeological Papers of the American Anthropological Association, 8: Washington: American Anthropological Association.

D'Altroy, Terrance N., and Timothy K. Earle
1985 Staple Finance, Wealth Finance, and Storage in the Inka Political Economy. Current Anthropology 26(2):187–206.

Feinman, Gary M.
1999 Rethinking Our Assumptions: Economic Specialization at the Household Scale in Ancient Ejutla, Oaxaca, Mexico. *In* Pottery and People: Dynamic Interactions. James M. Skibo and Gary Feinman, eds. Pp. 81–98. Salt Lake City: University of Utah Press.

Feinman, Gary M., and Linda M. Nicholas
2000 Household Craft Specialization and Shell Ornament Manufacture in Ejutla, Mexico. *In* Exploring the Past: Readings in Archaeology. James M. Bayman and Miriam T. Stark, eds. Pp. 303–314. Durham: Carolina Academic Press.

Gilead, Isaac, and Steve Rosen
1992 New Archaeo-Metallurgical Evidence for the Beginnings of Metallurgy in the Southern Levant: Excavations at Tell Abu Matar, Beersheba (Israel) 1990/1. Institute for Archaeo-Metallurgical Studies (IAMS) 18:11–14.

Golden, Jonathan, Thomas E. Levy, and Andreas Hauptmann
2001 Recent Discoveries Concerning Chalcolithic Metallurgy at Shiqmim, Israel. Journal of Archaeological Science 28:951–963.

Gorenstein, Shirley, and Helen. P. Pollard
1983 The Tarascan Civilization: A Late Prehispanic Cultural System. Publications in Anthropology 28, Nashville: Vanderbilt University.

Grinberg, Dora M.K. de
1990 Los Señores del Metal. Minería y Metalurgia en Mesoamérica. México: Dirección General de Publicaciones del CNCA/Pangea.
1996 Técnicas Minero-Metalúrgicas en Mesoamérica. *In* Mesoamérica y los Andes. Mayán Cervantes, ed. Pp. 427–471. México: Centro de Investigaciones y Estudios Superiores de Antropología Social.
2004 ¿Qué Sabían de Fundición los Antiguos Habitantes de Mesoamérica? Ingenierías VII(22):64–70.

Hassig, Ross
1985 Trade, Tribute, and Transportation: The Sixteenth-Century Political Economy of the Valley of Mexico. Norman: University of Oklahoma Press.

Hosler, Dorothy
1988a Ancient West Mexican Metallurgy: A Technological Chronology. Journal of Field Archaeology 15(2):191–217.
1988b Ancient West Mexican Metallurgy: South Central American Origins and West Mexican Transformations. American Anthropologist 90(4):832–855.
1988c The Metallurgy of Ancient West Mexico. *In* The Beginning of the Use of Metals and Alloys. Robert Maddin, ed. Pp. 328–343. Cambridge: MIT Press.
1994 The Sounds and Colors of Power. Cambridge: MIT Press.

Janusek, John W.
1999 Craft and Local Power: Embedded Specialization in Tiwanaku Cities. Latin American Antiquity 10(2):107–131.

Leroi-Gourhan, André G.
1964 Le Geste at la Parole. Paris: Albin Michelle.

Macías, G. Angelina
1990 Huandacareo: Lugar de Juicios, Tribunal. Serie Arqueología, Colección Científica Núm. 222. México: Instituto Nacional de Antropología e Historia.

Maldonado, Blanca E.
2006 Preindustrial Copper Production at the Archaeological Zone of Itziparatzico. Ph.D. Dissertation, Department of Anthropology, The Pennsylvania State University, University Park.

Maldonado, Blanca E., Thilo Rehren, and Paul R. Howell
2005 Archaeological Copper Smelting at Itziparátzico, Michoacan, Mexico. *In* Materials Issues in Art and Archaeology VII, MRS Proceedings Volume 852. Pamela B. Vandiver, Jennifer L. Mass, and Alison Murray, eds. Pp. 231–240. Warrendale: Materials Research Society.

Maldonado, Blanca, and Thilo Rehren
2009 Early copper smelting at Itziparátzico, Mexico. Journal of Archaeological Science 36(9):1998–2006.

Paredes M., Carlos S.
1984 El Tributo Indígena en la Región del Lago de Pátzcuaro. *In* Michoacán en el Siglo XVI. Carlos S. Paredes M., ed. Pp. 21–104. Colección Estudios Michoacanos VII. Morelia: FIMAX Publicistas.

Patterson, Thomas C.
2005 Craft Specialization, the Reorganization of Production Relations and State Formation. Journal of Social Archaeology 5(3):307–337.

Pendergast, David M.
1962 Metal Artifacts in Prehispanic Mesoamerica. American Antiquity 27(4):520–545.

Peregrine, Peter
1991 Some Political Aspects of Craft Specialization. World Archaeology 23:1–11.

Pollard, Helen P.
1982 Ecological Variation and Economic Exchange in the Tarascan State. American Ethnologist 9(2):250–268.
1987 The Political Economy of Prehispanic Tarascan Metallurgy. American Antiquity 52(4):741–752.
1993 Tariacuri's Legacy: The Prehispanic Tarascan State. Norman: University of Oklahoma Press.
2003 The Tarascan Empire. *In* The Postclassic Mesoamerican World. Michael E. Smith and Frances F. Berdan, eds. Pp. 78–86. Salt Lake City: University of Utah Press.

Roskamp, Hans, Mario Retiz, Anyul Cuellar, and Efraín Cárdenas
2003 Pre-Hispanic and Colonial Metallurgy in Jicalán, Michoacán, México: An Archaeological Survey. Reports Submitted to FAMSI: http://www.famsi.org/reports/02011/index.html

Rubín de la Borbolla, Daniel F.
1944 Orfebrería Tarasca. Cuadernos Americanos 3:125–138.

Sahagún, Fray Bernardino de
1969 Florentine Codex: General History of the Things of New Spain, 1590. 12 books.
1982 Arthur J.O. Anderson and Charles E. Dibble, translators and eds. Santa Fe: School of American Research and the University of Utah Press.

Shalev, Sariel, and Peter J. Northover
1987 Chalcolithic Metal and Metalworking from Shiqmim. *In* Shiqmim I: Studies Concerning Chalcolithic Societies in the Northern Negev Desert, Israel (1982–1984). Thomas E. Levy, ed. Pp. 357–371. Oxford: BAR International Series 356.

Sinopoli, Carla M.
1995 The Archaeology of Empires: A View from South Asia. Bulletin of the American Schools of Oriental Research 299/300:3–11.
2003 The Political Economy of Craft Production: Crafting Empire in South India, c. 1350–1650. Cambridge: Cambridge University Press.

Sinopoli, Carla M., and Kathleen D. Morrison
1995 Dimensions of Imperial Control: The Vijayanagara Capital. American Anthropologist 97(1):83–96.

Smith, Michael E.
2004 The Archaeology of Ancient State Economies. Annual Review of Anthropology 33:73–102.

Smith, Michael E., and Cynthia M. Heath-Smith
1994 Rural Economy in Late Postclassic Morelos: An Archaeological Study. *In* Economies and Polities in the Aztec Realm. Mary G. Hodge and Michael E. Smith, eds. Pp. 349–376. Albany: Institute for Mesoamerican Studies.

Stein, Gil J.
1996 Producers, Patrons, and Prestige: Craft Specialist and Emergent Elites in Mesopotamia from 5500–3100 B.C. *In* Craft Specialization and Social Evolution: In Memory of V. Gordon Childe.

Bernard Wailes, ed. Pp. 25–38. Philadelphia: The University of Pennsylvania Museum.

2001 Understanding Ancient State Societies in the Old World. *In* Archaeology at the Millennium. Gary M. Feinman and T. Douglas Price, eds. Pp. 353–379. New York: Kluwer Academic.

Wailes, Bernard, ed.

1996 Craft Specialization and Social Evolution. *In* Memory of V. Gordon Childe. University Museum Symposium Series, Volume 6. University Museum of Archaeology and Anthropology. Philadelphia: University of Pennsylvania.

Warren, J. Benedict

1968 Minas de Cobre de Michoacán, 1533. Anales del Museo Michoacano 6:35–52.

1985 The Conquest of Michoacán: The Spanish Domination of the Tarascan Kingdom in Western Mexico, 1521–1530. Norman: University of Oklahoma Pres.

15

Bitumen, Blades, and Beads: Prehispanic Craft Production and the Domestic Economy

Elizabeth M. Brumfiel
Northwestern University
and
Deborah L. Nichols
Dartmouth College

Housework launches a much-needed reexamination of craft production in prehispanic Mesoamerica. It offers important critiques of accepted ideas and lays out a long agenda for future research.

In chapters 1 and 2, Kenneth Hirth argues that although archaeologists have engaged in lengthy discussions of craft specialization, they have neglected the domestic economy as a topic of archaeological research and theory. He attributes this neglect to long-standing assumptions in archaeology regarding both households and the nature of part-time specialization.

According to Hirth, the study of households has been burdened by the faulty assumption that households are small-scale, self-sufficient, conservative, stable, and unchanging entities, a view which began to change only in the 1980's. We agree with Hirth that this stereotype was (and is) widespread, and that it has begun to change, but we disagree with Hirth as to why this stereotype has persisted for so long and why it is now being questioned.

In passing, Hirth suggests that the stereotype of the household as conservative and unchanging is the result of (1) ethnographers shifting away from household studies and (2) methodological problems making it difficult for archaeologists to study households in short-term temporal segments that can be correlated with episodes in the domestic life cycle. Without such tight temporal control, it is impossible to see households responding to new conditions as flexible adaptive units. But observing actual change in a single household is not the only way of delineating change and adaptation in domestic economies. The dynamic nature of households and household economies could be established by comparing households within and between broad periods or regions. Household studies and historical archaeology where temporal control is often tighter could be especially instructive (e.g. Allison 1999; Netting 1993; Wilk 1989, 1997).

We would attribute archaeological stereotypes of the household to the association of households with domestic life, the female sphere and low productivity. Western gender ideology has long associated households with the "domestic," "private," and "passive" lives of women in contrast to the extra-domestic institutions which are the settings for the "public" and "active" lives of men. As Luedke (2004) points out, even Engels' (1884) classic explanation of the origins of gender inequality attributed the decline in women's status to the development of dynamic extra-domestic spheres of wealth and power to which could not be accessed by women, confined by their biology to hearth and home and a uniform set of household tasks.

Relying on the accounts of Spanish chroniclers such as Bernardino de Sahagún who, on the basis of limited contact with Indian commoners, described Mesoamerican women as largely marginalized and confined to the domestic sphere, archaeologists have internalized assumptions of the uniformity of women's work and the unchanging character of the domestic economy. Under the sway of these assumptions, a

ARCHEOLOGICAL PAPERS OF THE AMERICAN ANTHROPOLOGICAL ASSOCIATION, Vol. 19, Issue 1, pp. 239–251, ISSN 1551-823X, online ISSN 1551-8248. © 2009 by the American Anthropological Association. All rights reserved. DOI: 10.1111/j.1551-8248.2009.01023.x.

Catch-22 has been in effect: archaeologists have not searched for examples of variability and change in domestic economies because they have assumed that domestic economies are static and uniform, and in the absence of case studies of variation and change in household economies, the assumption of static, uniform household economies has gone unchallenged (Brumfiel and Robin 2008). However feminist scholarship, emerging during the 1980's, revealed some of the biases coloring 16th-century sources on Mesoamerican women (e.g., Burkhart 2001), and feminist archaeology and household archaeology, developing during the 1990's, have demonstrated some of the flexibility, adaptability, and dynamism in the domestic economy and have provided some of our best case studies (Allison 1999; Brumfiel 1991; Costin 1993; Crown 2000; Gero and Scattolin 2002; Hastorf 1991; Hendon 1996; Robin 2002).

Hirth suggests that a second impediment to understanding domestic craft production is the emphasis placed upon part-time character of this production. Hirth argues that part-time specialization has been coded as small-scale, technologically unsophisticated, and inefficient—perhaps in implicit contrast to Adam Smith's (1937 [1776]) prototypic pin factory where mass production and a complex division of labor created efficiencies in acquisition of skills, the full use of tools, and reduced time lost in moving from one production task to another. The narrow focus on part-time specialization, and other dimensions of variation defined by Costin (1991), has led to a concern for classifying individual cases of domestic craft production, but not, as Costin (1991:44) had hoped, efforts to place domestic craft production in the context of social, political, and environmental conditions. As Hirth suggests, the study of domestic craft production in isolation, apart from the range of other activities in which households engaged, results in static, rather uninspiring studies.

What emerges as tremendously important about Hirth's twin emphasis on intermittent crafting and multicrafting is that both direct our attention to the integration of craft production with other household activities and to the attendant challenges of scheduling labor and reaching broader household goals, i.e., persistence and risk reduction.

Intermittent crafting refers to the discontinuous or periodic craft production that occurs within households. As it focuses on the temporal dimension of craft production, it necessarily directs us to inquire about the non-craft activities that absorb producers' time and how these complement or compete with craft production. That is, we are immediately encouraged to *think strategically* about the full range of household activities and how these might be *modified* to achieve higher efficiency or adjust to new internal and external circumstances. In other words, the concept of intermittent crafting generates a highly dynamic model of household craft production. Furthermore, intermittent crafting directs our attention to efficiencies other than Adam Smith's well known efficiencies of scale. Intermittent crafting might imply "just in time" inventory practices that save on storage facilities and minimize losses due to decay or pests. And, as Hirth and other contributors point out, intermittent crafting implies diversification, which is one strategy for minimizing risk.

Multicrafting refers to the practice of multiple crafts within a single household. Like intermittent crafting, multicrafting encourages us to think about one craft in relation to the others, that is to think strategically about how different forms of craft production might (or might not) complement with each other. Like intermittent crafting, multicrafting produces efficiencies other than efficiencies of scale. Multicrafting can enhance efficiency through the fuller use of production skills or facilities (Hagstrum 2001). For example, at Otumba, an Aztec regional center in the Basin of Mexico, ceramic specialists mass-produced a range of different ceramic artifacts: mold-made figurines, figurine molds, cotton and maguey spindle whorls, a local style of Red Ware pottery, marbles, stamps, whistles, censers and other pottery molds (Charlton et al. 1991, 2000). This range of products increases sales when customers are few in number or their purchases limited. Multicrafting can also enhance efficiency by recycling production by-products. For example, at Huaca Sialupe, on the northern coast of Peru, craftsmen took the charcoal produced in the course of pottery production and used it to smelt metal ore (Goldstein and Shimada 2007). At Postclassic Tula, Mexico, craftsmen took travertine cylinders removed during the process of making jars and used them go make beads or lip plugs (Diehl and Stroh 1978). And at Otumba, lapidary workers created ear spools and other forms of jewelry from exhausted obsidian cores (Otis Charlton 1993). Multicrafting makes fuller use of available household labor in the face of small consumer populations with limited demand. And like intermittent crafting, multicrafting implies diversification and risk minimization.

Both intermittent crafting and multicrafting must be as old as tool-making humans. After all, tool-making of any sort is a form of what Hirth calls contingent crafting, the manufacture of finished goods that are needed for other productive processes. Basic subsistence tasks like hunting and gathering employ tools, nets, baskets, and bags most of which are self-provisioned. In addition, foragers engage in the production of what Brookfield (1972) called "social surpluses," goods produced in excess of the household's subsistence needs for use in social exchanges that widen social networks and provide access to neighboring territories and non-local resources (e.g., Balikci 1970; Sharp 1952;

Wiessner 1982). With the shift to a sedentary agricultural way of life, domestic craft production must have expanded because sedentism (1) permits the accumulation of material goods and production facilities and (2) reduces mobility so that non-local goods have to be acquired through exchange.

It is also true, as Hirth suggests, that domestic craft production expanded after the adoption of agriculture because environmental fluctuations magnified uncertainties for early farmers. Early agriculturalists in Mesoamerica were vulnerable to unpredictable variations in rainfall, frosts, pests, and ash falls (Nichols and Frederick 1993). Social changes such as deaths, births, illnesses, disputes, and conflicts also created uncertainty. Agriculturalists responded with a range of buffering mechanisms including storage, intensification, diversification, expanded social networks, and perhaps raiding. In many cases, diversification via craft production reduced the household's vulnerability. But there are different kinds of threats to household survival. Some threats, such as spotty rainfall and accidental injuries, affect only some families and some agricultural fields. Other threats, such as epidemic disease and regional droughts, affect all households over a broad area. Still others, such as early frosts or volcanic ash falls, can be broadly catastrophic or highly localized.

In situations where damage is localized and some fields do well while others fail, the exchange of craft goods for food can see individual households through poor harvests, as Hirth observes. For example, Richard Ford (1992) documented for Pueblos of the American Southwest the importance of food exchanges among networks of kin groups embedded in annual ceremonial cycles, ceremonies that required the manufacture of ritual paraphernalia for their performance. However, craft production is virtually useless in countering the effects of regional crop failure. Ethnographic observation suggests that when crops fail, food-producers provision their own families first and provide little or no food to exchange partners (e.g., Sahlins 1972:129). Where marketplaces exist, peasants postpone their purchase of market goods, hoard their harvests, and refuse to bring food to markets for sale. Food prices skyrocket as supplies of marketed food dwindle, and craft producers are reduced to selling their wares at next to nothing (Mellor and Gavian 1987).

In fact, food shortages in times of regional crop failure are the principal reason why full-time craft specialization is rare in non-industrial societies. Since full-time craft specialists and wage workers suffer acutely in situations of regional crop failure, considerations of security dictate that crafting households also engage in food production in most non-industrial societies. Such part-time specialists retain the ability to fall back on subsistence agriculture when faced with adverse market conditions; full-time specialists

do not (Brumfiel 1986:271). This situation changes only when the territorial extent and the coercive ability of state institutions are great enough to force the movement of food supplies from peasant households to palace storerooms and urban markets even in bad years (Hicks 1987). This would normally require a political unit of imperial scale.

Thus, on theoretical grounds, diversified household craft production, characterized by intermittent crafting and multicrafting, should typify the vast majority of ancient societies from transegalitarian hunters and gatherers to well developed states such as the Classic Maya. And this is borne out by the very well documented case studies presented in this volume.

Rural Production and Commodity Chains: Organization and Goals of Production

The study of craft production in Mesoamerica has suffered from certain kinds of empirical biases. First, as Darras (this volume) points out, most well-documented examples of craft production in Mesoamerica come from urban and civic-ceremonial contexts occupied by social elites. This probably reflects a more general bias in archaeology towards the investigation of visually impressive political centers that yield striking remains able to bolster national pride and attract tourist development. It also reflects the implicit assumption that preindustrial urban centers were centers of manufacture and trade, like urban centers in the modern West (Brumfiel 1980). Second, as Pool (this volume) notes, the study of craft production has been biased in favor of locations where craft production is most visible archaeologically, that is, locations with greater production volumes, higher degrees of specialization, and/or more salient kinds of production facilities. Again, this most often prompts archaeologists to study craft production in urban centers and political capitals. With their large, wealthy consumer populations, these are the locations most likely to support craft production on a large scale (Costin 1991). While several previous studies have noted the presence of part-time specialization in rural areas (Brumfiel 1980, 1986, 1987, 1998; Charlton et al. 2000; Evans 1988; Feinman and Nicholas 2000; Hester and Shafer 1994; King and Potter 1994; Mason 1980; Masson 2002; Nichols 1994; Potter and King 1995; Sheets 2000; Smith and Heath-Smith 1994; Spence 1985; Stark 1992, 2007), most of these studies were based upon regional survey, rarely on excavated evidence of craft production. Thus, one of the great merits of this volume is the new methodologies it introduces to the study of craft production in rural, commoner contexts.

These studies make it possible for us to examine what Berdan et al. call the "interconnections of different levels of complex economic systems." One way of doing this is to trace commodity chains or material flows: reconstructing (1) the movement of raw materials from their sources to production locales, (2) the activities that create products and endow them with value, and (3) the channels and transactions that distribute the finished goods to their points of consumption (e.g. Bair 2009; Mintz 1985). This volume makes several contributions to the methodology of tracing these chains or flows in the prehistoric past. For example, production debris enables Hirth (this volume) to infer that imported obsidian reached Xochicalco in the form of already used obsidian cores. The representation of different obsidian source areas in different workshops suggest that the cores were distributed through the market rather than centralized procurement and redistribution. In contrast, Darras (this volume) finds that the obsidian was transported to the workshops at Zacapu in Michoacan in small unprepared blocks from a single source, which suggests that raw material was procured by the artisans, themselves, directly from its source. In a third case, Hirth et al. (this volume) conclude that jadeite from the Motagua Valley arrived at Nativitas, Tlaxcala, in the form of unworked nodules. The uniformity of the nodules suggests a single supplier, who could have been a merchant or a local ruler. Juxtaposed, these three cases might have something interesting to tell us about the implications of different forms of resource procurement. What are the costs, benefits, and/or limitations of depending on intermediaries such as merchants or rulers for raw materials rather than craftspeople procuring raw materials for themselves? How do these alternatives score in terms of cost, reliability, and control—variables that might influence subsequent stages of production and distribution?

Balkansky et al. (this volume) present technological analyses of ceramic materials that probably are capable of differentiating the products of individual ceramic workshops. Charting the distributions of ceramics from individual workshops might enable archaeologists to reconstruct the channels that artisans used to distribute of their products: direct exchange, marketing, or tribute payment. Again, this would enable archaeologists to assess the costs, benefits, and/or limitations of different distribution mechanisms. Are specific forms of resource procurement associated with specific forms of distributing finished products? Why or why not?

Tracking distribution might help archaeologists understand the goals of craft production. These goals can be sorted into economic and social/political advantages. Economic advantages included acquiring household supplies more efficiently through specialization and exchange with other households and/or raising household incomes through the sale of products in a market system. Social/political advan-

tages would include manufacture of status goods to enhance the appearance of household members, to express their social identities, and to participate in household consumption ceremonies (Clark and Blake 1994; Hayden 1990; Smith 1987). Domestic craft production might also have been required to meet the demands of ruling elites. Costin (1991) identifies this type of production as dispersed or nucleated corvée labor.

It is tempting to infer the goals of production from the type of good that is produced. That is, the production of "utilitarian goods" such as bitumen, salt, cooking/storage vessels, or obsidian blades (in central Mexico), might be regarded as meeting economic goals while the production of "prestige goods" such as obsidian jewelry, shell and jade beads might be seen as meeting social and political goals. However, the studies in this volume document two cases where jade beads and shell ornaments, normally regarded as "prestige goods," are produced in households that have no other indications of elite status such as stone architecture, elaborate pottery, or rich burials (see Hirth et al. and Rochette, this volume). The same is true of the shell-working workshop analyzed by Feinman and Nicholas (2000). In these cases, it appears that "prestige goods" were produced as commodities, geared toward economic gain rather than enhancing the status of craft workers and/or their household members.

Archaeologists might also infer the goals of production from the status of the producing households. That is, archaeologists might assume that elites were more actively engaged in craft production for social and political reasons and commoners more concerned with craft production to enhance their incomes. But household status is not a reliable guide to the goals of production. For example, the incomes of Yucatec Maya elites were greatly enhanced by participation in the commercial trade of salt and cacao (Kepecs 2003). And in Aztec society, even commoners had social status aspirations, relying upon feasting and gift-giving to establish inter-household alliances (Brumfiel 1987a, 1987b, 2004; Smith 1987).

The goals of production can be most reliably inferred from tracing the circuits of distribution. Goods that fed into the market system had economic goals; goods that were exchanged in ceremonial contexts had social/political goals. Since markets distribute goods in a wide, uniform pattern and reciprocal exchanges produce more heterogeneous distribution patterns (Hirth 1998), once the pattern of distribution is established through studies such as those carried out by Balkansky et al., it should be possible to define production goals.

In sum, using the innovative methodologies developed by the contributors of this volume to trace commodities chains and material flows in the prehistoric past, archaeologists will be able to learn much about the variability of domestic craft production: how different exchange mechanisms and different exchange goals determine the commodities produced and the volume of production. Comparative studies of the structure of commodity chains should constitute the next phase of research in the study of Mesoamerican craft production.

The Production of Value

As Hirth et al. (this volume) point out, studies of lapidary work in Tlaxcala and the Motagua Valley, of metallurgy in Michoacan, and of adhesives are of special interest because they raise questions about how some "prestige" goods move from their points of origin in commoner workshops to elite spheres of consumption, and how they acquire prestige or value along the way (Clark 2007). One possibility is that these goods have been misclassified as "prestige" goods. Some jade ornaments, for example, may have retained their attachment to commoners, meeting their needs for symbolic goods to establish their social relations, what Eric Wolf (1966) calls the peasant's "ceremonial fund." Lucero (2006:143) has documented the placement of jade beads in commoner burials. Another possibility is that jadeite or shell ornaments acquired elite connotations as they move through long-distance exchange to regions distant from their source areas. Transported by merchants to distant markets where supplies were limited and their commoner origins could be disguised, these goods lost their associations with commoners and moved into the realm of elite goods. A third possibility is that the materials worked by commoners were inputs to a final stage of manufacture performed by elites. For example, Berdan et al. (this volume) suggest that adhesives were not in themselves prestige goods, but they were used by elites or elite artisans to create valuable feather mosaics. Similarly, the paper produced by 70% of Postclassic rural households in Morelos (Smith and Heath-Smith 1994:359) may have flowed through market and tribute networks to elite scribes and painters who created valuable codices. Really elite jadeite pieces may have required the highly skilled craftsmanship that only elite producers could supply, such as the elite Maya producers studied by Widmer (this volume) or Inomata (2001).

A fourth possibility is that skilled rural artisans worked on consignment from elites, either on paid commissions from elite patrons or as unpaid tribute labor (i.e., *corvée*). Hirth et al. (this volume) suggest that the jadeite bead makers at Late Formative Nativitas were working on consignment for elites at Cerro Xochitécatl who procured the stone from

Guatemala and then controlled the product (however, this leaves unexplained how rural jadeite workers acquired their skills). Maldonado (this volume) suggests a tribute labor scenario to account for the mining and smelting of metals by rural workers under the Tarascan state, giving the state the ability to monopolize metals at their point of origin. Again, moving beyond individual case studies, a systematic comparison of different examples of craft production might enable archaeologists to unravel the circumstances or variables that determine when products will follow one or another of these paths.

A final possibility, and one not exclusive of any of the above, is that craft products acquired value not just through the technical skill of the artisans, or the social status of the producers and their patrons, but from "performances" that accompanied production and distribution. These performances might involve the deliberate display of manufacturing expertise in full view of the public (Inomata 2001, 2007a, 2007b), producing crafts in the course of a ritual (Carter 2007), or using the prayers, chants, sacrifices, gestures, or specific production locales to ensure the success of production efforts or to improve the performance of the craft products (Childs 1998; Hruby 2007). This is what Hruby (2007) refers to as "ritualized production." Widmer (this volume) demonstrates how archaeologists might identify such value-endowing performances in his contextual study of elite Maya production. In Widmer's case, production occurred in clandestine locations within elite residences, using inefficient methods, and in association with ritual paraphernalia, all of which seem oriented toward endowing the products with special efficacy and worth.

Such value-endowing performances are not confined to production by elite craftsmen. Non-elites also confer meaning and value upon their craft products through ritualized production. For example, some contemporary Huichol women undertake a five year program of spiritual training that involves prayer, fasting, vision quests, offerings and sacrifices in order to "complete themselves" in the arts of embroidery, beadwork and weaving (Schaefer 2002). The products of such master weavers are highly valued. Artisans who undertake such training acquire *technical* skill in their crafts, but it is the completion of their *spiritual* training which is of greater importance in endowing their products with special value. Similar practices seem to have been present among the Aztecs:

> Those women who were embroiderers and cotton thread workers first fasted for eighty days; some fasted for forty or twenty days, when penance was done. Thus, they requested of it that what they undertook might be well done; [that] their embroidery or design might be a work of art well fabricated and well painted. All therefore

offered incense and slew quail; and all bathed and sprinkled themselves with water, when [the fasting] had been lifted. Then the feast of the day sign, Seven Flower, was celebrated (Sahagún 1950–82 Bk. 4, Ch.2, p.7].

It seems that these activities would be carried out by any woman who sought to perfect the art of embroidery, both commoners and women of noble birth.

The household locations of many of the production sites reported in this volume provide opportunities to use Widmer's careful methods of contextual analysis to uncover "ritualized production" in commoner contexts. However, such efforts will require a conscious effort to recognize procedures which might not define as production steps in Western culture, but which be classified as such by non-Westerners.

Efforts to impart value to craft products beyond what Western analysts might recognize as technological efficacy might be observed not only in ritualized production but also in the decoration of tools used in craft production and in craft products. The Cree Indians of Canada believe that the decoration of a utilitarian object ensures that the object will perform its function properly. For example, the decorations on ammunition pouches, guns, and gun cases ensure that the guns will fire true (Tanner 1979:141–2). In a similar fashion, the sun and flower motives on spindle whorls from Postclassic Xaltocan, Mexico, may have been intended to endow thread and cloth with *tonalli*, a light-heat-energy source that is synonymous with divine energy and the heat of life (Brumfiel 2006). The bright orange color of serving dishes, together with their painted solar motifs, may have been meant to enrich food by endowing it with *tonalli* though the association with these designs (Brumfiel in press).

Using techniques of contextual analysis and iconography now applied only to cases of elite production, archaeologists could move beyond the analysis of commoner craft production as a purely technological activity to explore strategies for endowing "utilitarian" goods with greater or lesser value. Furthermore, the decorative motifs on objects such as spindle whorls and serving dishes might reveal new dimensions of expertise demanded from the producers of "utilitarian" goods, such as elements of cosmological and calendrical knowledge (Brumfiel 2008, in press).

Comparative Study

The contributors to this volume argue that domestic craft production, characterized by intermittent crafting and multicrafting, has been the most common form of craft production in Mesoamerica. But if, as Hirth argues, domestic craft production was a strategic response to the problems

and possibilities of household economies, it should exhibit a wide range of variation, given differing environmental, demographic, economic and political circumstances. Furthermore, the role of domestic craft production in the household economy should vary, given the economic and political goals of the household (or its members). This variation will be identified and understood only through comparative studies. Thus, future studies should devote more attention to (1) the non-craft activities of the household, (2) how households that engage in craft production compare to households that don't, (3) how households engaged in the same craft organize it differently under different circumstances, and (4) how households practicing some crafts compare to households practicing other crafts.

In sum, archaeologists could learn a lot about the organization of craft production by taking detailed case studies of craft production in rural, commoner contexts such as those presented in this volume and using them in systematic comparisons.

Craft Production and Agricultural Activity

Contributors to this volume present several kinds of evidence to support their argument that craft production was combined with agricultural production. Sometimes, agriculture is said to be present by default. For example, Hirth and Darras each use production debris to calculate the amount of raw material consumed and/or the quantity of goods produced by rural artisans. In both cases, they both conclude that craft production occupied only a small number of producers working on a very part time basis, and therefore, agriculture must have been the major activity in these households. Darras also uses an argument of proximity to assert the importance of agriculture to craft-producing households: the extensive agricultural terraces that surround craft-producing households in Michoacan suggest that they were involved in the practice of agriculture. Other authors provide more direct evidence of agriculture. Hirth argues that craft producing households at Xochicalco were also food producing households because the artifact assemblages of craft producing households did not differ from those of non-crafting agricultural households. Pool argues that craft producing households at Matacapan were also food producing households because bell shaped pits associated with craft producing households were storage facilities for harvested crops. At Bezuapan, low ratios of maize kernels to cupules suggest that maize was processed in houselots, rather than being brought there from markets in an already shelled state.

However, numerous forms of agriculture were present in Mesoamerica, and it would be interesting to see how craft production varied when combined with different agricultural regimes. For example, in many areas of Mesoamerica, agriculture is confined to the rainy season, which falls between May and October. During these months, the demands of planting, weeding, and harvesting reduce the amount of labor that is available for craft production. And these rainy months are precisely those least suited to making many products that rely upon the application of fire, including bitumen (Wendt), salt (De León), ceramics (Balkansky et al., Pool), lime plaster (Castanzo), and metals (Maldonado). As Pool (citing Arnold 1991) points out, rainfall prevents fuel from adequately drying, reduces firing temperatures, and can interrupt the firing process. Thus, dry season craft production nicely complements wet season rainfall agriculture.

But how is craft production organized when agricultural production is not so seasonal, for example, when irrigated agriculture makes multi-cropping is possible? Under these conditions, do farming households devote themselves more exclusively to farming and rely more on more on exchange with craft-producing households? By the Late Postclassic, farmers on the chinampas in the southern Basin of Mexico farmed year around, and we have no reports of their engaging in craft production (e.g., Avila López 1991). How is craft production organized when other uses are found for household labor during the dry season, such as the cultivation of specialized dry season crops such as maguey (e.g., Parsons and Parsons 1990) or when military service becomes an important dry season activity (e.g. Hassig 1988)? At Huexotla, the household production of thread (and presumably textiles) diminished as maguey cultivation or aguamiel byproducts intensified, is especially intriguing since Alva de Ixtlilxochitl (1975–77 I:346) mentions that women were involved in gathering sap from the mature plants (Brumfiel 1980). We should also consider that households may have specialized in particular crops and also raised animals for exchange. Manzanilla (1999) found evidence in the Oztoyzhualco apartment compound of Teotihuacan that some families bred turkeys, dogs, and rabbits for exchange. Parsons (1996:456) discusses a series of technological developments in the Postclassic related to resource specialization.

In a similar fashion, what is the relationship between agricultural production, craft production, and the organization of other domestic tasks, such as cooking? Are domestic tasks organized differently in households that combine agriculture and craft production and in those that only engage in agricultural production? Are domestic tasks organized differently in high status households where the demand for prestige goods is high? Are domestic tasks reorganized in households that produce goods that served as currencies such as cloth, cacao, or metals when demand for currencies increases? For example, in many parts of Mesoamerica,

spindle whorls and comals both become more frequent during the Postclassic era (Brumfiel 1991, 2005; Marcus 2004; Stark et al. 1998). Is the expansion of cloth production related in some direct or indirect way to changes in cooking? Do different organizations of domestic economy allot work to children in different ways (Crown 2001; Kamp 2002; Sofaer Derevenski 2000)?

Households that Engage in Craft Production and Households that Don't

In Chapter 2, Hirth mentions several "push" and "pull" factors that might induce households to engage in craft production. Arnold (1985) argues that households are pushed into craft production when their land holdings are insufficient to provide adequate subsistence to household members, and Rice (1987) suggests that increased political insecurity can push households into craft production. On the other hand, ethnographic accounts of peasant-artisans document cases where households enter craft production in response to falling farm incomes (García Canclini 1993; Nash 1993) or where households respond to expanding demand and marketing opportunities (Cohen 1998; Stolmaker 1996).

The comparison of the crafting households examined by many of the contributors to this volume with other households in the same communities that yield no evidence of craft production would contribute much to this discussion. Are households that engage in crafting generally poorer or more prosperous than households that do not? Crafting households that are poorer would suggest that crafting was a less attractive way of making a living perhaps requiring the "push" of land shortages. Crafting households that are wealthier than non-crafting households would suggest that crafting was indeed attractive and that households actively sought out new products and markets (the craft-producers at Otumba appear to have fallen into this category, see Charlton et al. 1991, 2000). Perhaps, the return on crafting varied by the craft practiced. Or, the return on crafting may have varied by proximity to urban markets. Or, a household's ability to engage in crafting might have depended on household size: large households could release members for commercial activities while the members of small households had to devote all of their efforts to securing their food supply. All of these statements are amenable to testing with archaeological data. Our knowledge would be greatly advanced if those who studied household craft production also studied households where craft production is absent, especially when both types of households belong to the same community.

Domestic Craft Production Under Different Circumstances: Responding to Increased Demand

As observed above, Hirth's twin emphasis on intermittent crafting and multicrafting emphasizes the strategic, maximizing behavior of domestic craft producers. Thus, it should be possible to define the relationship of particular modes of organizing production both to the organization of the households within which it is embedded and to the economic and political institutions that exist outside the household and impinge upon it.

The organization of craft production may be affected by the volume of demand. Demand for craft products can increase because of demographic growth, agricultural intensification (Blanton et al. 1993:22), or the weakening economic control of the state (Blanton 1983). However, as Sinopoli (2003:21) points out, craft producers can respond to heightened demand for craft products in a variety of ways. These might include increasing the complexity and scale of productive units, or just increasing the number of productive units. For example, Spence (1985) found indications of a 30–60% increase in obsidian workshop output in the Postclassic Teotihuacan Valley, just matching the growth of the local population. The expanded demand could have been accommodated by the movement of part-time specialists into full-time production, but in this case, it was not. Only the number of part-time specialists increased.

Holding the size and complexity of productive units constant, increased output can also be attained through a shift to mass production technologies. In Mesoamerica, several technological innovations appear to have met growing consumer demand. Ceramic molds, prismatic cores, and spindle whorls would be examples of technologies that increased the output of the household unit. For example, Sullivan (2006:32) reviews the use of ceramic molds at Teotihuacan. Stark et al. (1998) document the use of spindle whorls on coastal Veracruz during the Classic period, long before the common use of spindle whorls appears in the central highlands. They suggest that spindle whorls helped to increase thread production in response to demands for tribute in thread and/or cloth issued by the Teotihuacan state. However, increased production is only one consequence of ceramic molds; another is an increase in product standardization. Pasztory (1997) suggests that for Teotihuacanos, product standardization was an expression of cultural values: the uniformity of mold-made objects asserted the importance of the community over the importance of the individual.

Higher output can also be achieved through a finer division of production steps between craft-producing households. Distinctive biconical spindle whorls at Early Postclassic Río Viejo suggest that villagers specialized in the production of a distinctive cotton thread for inter-regional exchange (King 2003). High frequencies of copper needles at Copilco, Morelos, suggest that members of this community specialized in decorating already-woven cloth with embroidery or fringe or transforming cloth into garments (Fauman-Fichman 1999). Separate sellers of unspun cotton, dyes for dyeing cotton thread, cotton thread, cotton cloth, and finished items of clothing pedaled their wares in the Tlatelolco market, indicating production processes that included several types of specialists before the product arrived to the consumer (Sanders 2008).

As observed above, Hirth's twin emphasis on intermittent crafting and multicrafting is tremendously important because it embodies a dynamic and strategic approach to craft production which places the study of domestic craft production in the context of other activities and institutions with which the household is engaged. And Hirth explicitly calls for a more holistic perspective to the study of domestic craft production. The contributors to this volume certainly move away from studying craft production in isolation from other activities, but this trend will be carried still further in future studies.

Conclusion

This volume has brought together much new information on a range of household-based craft industries in Mesoamerica. Our ideas about prehispanic craft production have tended to over-generalize from a limited number of well-documented examples—for example, chronicler's descriptions of urban craft specialists in Tenochtitlan-Tlatelolco and depictions of scribes on Classic Maya vases. The documentation by archaeologists and ethnohistorians of more diversity and complexity in prehispanic craft production calls us to revisit our conceptual frameworks. In highland Mexico, more systematic surface collection, testing, and excavation programs, have tended to turn up more, not less, evidence of craft production than suggested by initial surveys. This also seems to be the case for Oaxaca and Mayapan. The residential context of most craft production highlights the importance of household archaeology, but major advances can also be expected from well thought out comparative studies that examine different classes of commodity flows and different types of household strategies. Prehispanic craft production encompassed a wide range of intensities and systems of organization that related to the broader social, economic, and political dynamics and contexts of households. In the future, our framework of study will expand to match the breadth of our subject matter, so deftly reconstructed by the contributors to this volume.

References

Allison, Penelope M., ed.
1999 The Archaeology of Household Activities. London: Routledge.

Alva Ixtlilxochitl, Fernando de
1975–77 Obras históricas. E. O'Gorman, ed. Mexico City: Universidad Nacional Autónoma de México.

Arnold, Dean
1985 Ceramic Theory and Cultural Process. Cambridge: Cambridge University Press.

Avila López, Raúl
1991 Chinampas de Iztapalapa, D.F. Mexico City: Instituto Nacional de Antropología e Historia.

Bair, Jennifer
2009 Frontiers of Commodity Chain Research. Stanford: Stanford University Press.

Balikci, Asen
1970 The Netsilik Eskimo. New York: Natural History Press.

Burkhart, Louise M.
2001 Gender in Nahuatl Texts of the Early Colonial Period: Native "Tradition" and the Dialogue with Christianity. *In* Gender in Pre-Hispanic America. C. Klein, ed. Pp. 87–107. Washington, DC: Dumbarton Oaks.

Blanton, Richard E.
1983 Factors Underlying the Origin and Evolution of Market Systems. *In* Economic Anthropology. S. Ortiz, ed. Pp. 51–66. Lanham: University Press of America.

Blanton, Richard E., Stephen A. Kowalewski, Gary M. Feinman, and Laura M. Finsten
1993 Ancient Mesoamerica. Cambridge: Cambridge University Press.

Brookfield, H. C.
1972 Intensification and Deintensification in Pacific Agriculture. Pacific Viewpoint 13:30–48.

Brumfiel, Elizabeth M.
1980 Specialization, Market Exchange, and the Aztec State: A View from Huexotla. Current Anthropology 21:459–478.

1986 The Division of Labor at Xico: The Chipped Stone Industry. *In* Economic Aspects of Pre-hispanic Highland Mexico. B.L. Isaac, ed. Pp. 245–279. Greenwich, CT: JAI Press.

1987a Elite and Utilitarian Crafts in the Aztec State. *In* Specialization, Exchange, and Complex Societies. E. Brumfiel and T. Earle, eds. Pp. 102–118. Cambridge: Cambridge University Press.

1987b Consumption and Politics at Aztec Huexotla. American Anthropologist 89:676–686.

1991 Weaving and Cooking: Women's Production in Aztec Mexico. *In* Engendering Archaeology. J. Gero and M. Conkey, eds. Pp. 254–251. Oxford: Blackwell.

1998 The Multiple Identities of Aztec Craft Specialists. *In* Craft and Social Identity. C. Costin and R.P. Wright, eds. Pp. 145–159. Arlington, VA: American Anthropological Association, Archaeological Papers, 8.

2004 Meaning by Design: Ceramics, Feasting, and Figured Worlds in Postclassic Mexico. *In* Mesoamerican Archaeology. J. Hendon and R. Joyce, eds. Pp. 239–264. Oxford: Blackwell.

2006 Presidential Address: Gender, Cloth, Continuity and Change: Fabricating Unity in Anthropology. American Anthropologist 108:861–877.

2008 Solar Disks and Solar Cycles: Spindle Whorls and the Dawn of Solar Art in Postclassic Mexico. *In* Engendering Social Dynamics: the Archaeology of Maintenance Activities. S. Montón-Subías, and M. Sánchez-Romero, eds. Pp. 33–40. Oxford: BAR International Series 1862.

in press Technologies of Time: Calendrics and Commoners in Postclassic Mexico. Ancient Mesoamerica.

Brumfiel, Elizabeth M., and Cynthia Robin
2008 Gender, Households, and Society: An Introduction. *In* Gender, Households, and Society: Unraveling the Threads of the Past and the Present. C. Robin and E. Brumfiel, eds. Pp. 1–16. Arlington, VA: Archaeological Papers of the American Anthropological Association, 18.

Carter, Tristand
2007 The Theatrics of Technology: Consuming Obsidian in the Early Cycladic Burial Arena. *In* Rethinking Craft Specialization in Complex Societies. Z. Hruby and R. Flad, eds. Pp. 88–107. Arlington, VA: American Anthropological Association, 17.

Charlton, Thomas H., Deborah L. Nichols, and Cynthia L. Otis Charlton
1991 Aztec Craft Production and Specialization: Archaeological Evidence from the City-State of Otumba, Mexico. World Archaeology 23:98–114.
2000 Otumba and its Neighbors: Ex Oriente Lux. Ancient Mesoamerica 11:247–265.

Clark, John E.
2007 In Craft Specialization's Penumbra: Things, Persons, Action, Value, and Surplus. *In* Rethinking Craft Specialization in Complex Societies. Z. Hruby and R. Flad, eds. Pp. 20–35. Arlington, VA: American Anthropological Association, 17.

Clark, John E., and Michael Blake
1994 The Power of Prestige: Competitive Generosity and the Emergence of Rank Societies in Lowland Mesoamerica. *In* Factional Competition and Political Development in the New World. E. Brumfiel and J. Fox, eds. Pp. 17–30. Cambridge: Cambridge University Press.

Cohen, Jeffrey
1998 Craft Production and the Challenge of the Global Market. Human Organization 57:74–82.

Costin, Cathy L.
1991 Craft Specialization: Issues in Defining, Documenting, and Explaining the Organization of Production. Archaeological Method and Theory 3:1–56. Textiles, Women, and Political Economy in Late Prehispanic Peru. Research in Economic Anthropology 14:3–28.

Crown, Patricia L.
2000 Women's Role in Changing Cuisine. *In* Women & Men in the Prehispanic Southwest. P. Crown, ed. Pp. 221–266. Santa Fe: School of American Research Press.
2001 Learning to make Pottery in the Prehispanic American Southwest. Journal of Anthropological Research 57:451–469.

Diehl, Richard A., and Edward G. Stroh, Jr.
1978 Tecali Vessel Manufacturing Debris at Tollan, Mexico. American Antiquity 43:73–79.

Engels, Friedrich
1972 [1884] Origin of the Family, Private Property, and the State. E. Leacock, ed. New York: International Publishers.

Evans, Susan T., ed.
1988 Excavations at Cihuatecpan: An Aztec village in the Teotihuacan Valley. Vanderbilt University Publications in Anthropology, 36, Nashville.

Fauman-Fichman, Ruth
1999 Postclassic Craft Production in Morelos, Mexico: The Cotton Thread Industry in the Provinces. Ph.D. dissertation, Department of Anthropology, University of Pittsburgh.

Feinman, Gary M., and Linda M. Nicholas
2000 High-Intensity Household-Scale Production in Ancient Mesoamerica: A Perspective from Ejutla, Oaxaca. *In* Cultural Evolution: Contemporary Viewpoints. G. Feinman and L. Nicholas, eds. Pp. 119–142. New York: Kluwer Academic/ Plenum.

Ford, Richard I.
1992 Ecological Analysis Involving the Population of San Juan Pueblo. New York: Garland Publishing.

García Canclini, Néstor
1993 Transforming Modernity: Popular Culture in Mexico. L. Lozano, transl. Austin: University of Texas Press.

Gero, Joan M., and M. Cristina Scattolin
2002 Beyond Complementarity and Hierarchy: New Definitions for Archaeological Gender Relations. *In* In Pursuit of Gender: Worldwide Archaeological Approaches. S. Nelson and M. Rosen-Ayalon, eds. Pp. 155–171. Walnut Creek, CA: Altamira.

Goldstein, David J., and Izumi Shimada
2007 Middle Sicán Multicraft Production: Resource Management and Labor Organization. *In* Craft Production in Complex Societies: Multicraft and Producer Perspectives. I. Shimada, eds. Pp. 44–67. Salt Lake City: University of Utah Press.

Hassig, Ross.
1988 Aztec warfare. Norman: University of Oklahoma Press.

Hayden, Brian
1990 Nimrods,Ppiscators, Pluckers, and Planters: The Emergence of Food Production. Journal of Anthropological Archaeology 9:31–69.

Hagstrum, Melissa
2001 Household Production in Chaco Canyon Society. American Antiquity 66:47–55.

Hastorf, Christine A.
1991 Gender, space, and food in prehistory. *In* Engendering Archaeology: Women and Prehistory. J. Gero and M. Conkey, eds. Pp.132–159. Oxford: Blackwell.

Hendon, Julia
1996 Archaeological Approaches to the Organization of Domestic Labor: Household Practice and Domestic Relations. Annual Review of Anthropology 25:45–61.

Hester, Thomas R., and Harry J. Shafer
1994 The Ancient Maya Craft Community at Colha, Belize, and its External Relationships. *In* Archaeological Views from the Countryside. G. Schwartz and S. Falconer, eds. Pp. 48–63. Washington, DC: Smithsonian Institution Press.

Hicks, Frederic
1987 First Steps Toward a Market-Integrated Economy in Aztec Mexico. *In* Early State Dynamics. H. Claessen and P. van de Velde, eds. Pp. 91–107. Leiden: E.J. Brill.

Hirth, Kenneth G.
1998 The Distributional Approach: A New Way to Identify Market-Place Exchange in the Archaeological Record. Current Anthropology 39:451–476.

Hruby, Zachary X.
2007 Ritualized Chipped-Stone Production at Piedras Negras, Guatemala. *In* Rethinking Craft Specialization in Complex Societies. Z. Hruby and R. Flad, eds. Pp. 68–87. Arlington, VA.: American Anthropological Association, 17.

Inomata, Takeshi
2001 The Power and Ideology of Artistic Creation: Elite Craft Specialists in Classic Maya Society. Current Anthropology 42:321–349.
2007a Knowledge and Belief in Artistic Production by Classic Maya Elites. *In* Rethinking Craft Specialization in Complex Societies. Z. Hruby and R. Flad, eds. Pp. 129–141. Arlington, VA.: American Anthropological Association, 17.

2007b Classic Maya Elite Competition, Collaboration, and Performance in Multicraft Production. *In* Craft Production in Complex Societies: Multicraft and Producer Perspectives. I. Shimada, ed. Pp. 120–133. Salt Lake City: University of Utah Press.

Kamp, Kathryn, ed.
2002 Children in the Prehistoric Puebloan Southwest. Salt Lake City: University of Utah Press.

Kepecs, Susan M.
2003 Chikinchel. *In* The Postclassic Mesoamerican World. M. Smith and F. Berdan, eds. Pp. 259–268. Salt Lake City: University of Utah Press.

King, Eleanor, and Daniel Potter
1994 Small Sites in Prehistoric Maya Socioeconomic Organization: A Perspective from Colha, Belize. *In* Archaeological Views from the Countryside. G. Schwartz and S. Falconer, eds. Pp. 64–90. Washington, DC.: Smithsonian Institution Press.

King, Stacie M.
2003 Social Practices and Social Organization in Ancient Coastal Oaxacan Households. Ph.D. dissertation, Department of Anthropology, University of California, Berkeley.

Luedke, Tracy
2004 Gendered States: Gender and Agency in Economic Models of Great Zimbabwe." *In* Ungendering Archaeology. K.A. Pyburn, ed. Pp. 47–70. New York: Routledge.

Luceo, Lisa
2006 *Water and Ritual: The Rise and Fall of Classic Maya Rulers.* Austin: University of Texas Press.

Manzanilla, Linda,
1999 The First Urban Development in the Central Highlands of Mexico. *In* The Archaeology of Mesoamerica: Mexican and European Perspectives. W. Bray and L. Manzanilla, eds. Pp. 13–31. London: British Museum Press.

Marcus, Joyce
2004 Maya Commoners: The Stereotype and the Reality. *In* Ancient Maya Commoners. J. Lohse and F. Valdez, eds. Pp. 255–283. Austin: University of Texas Press.

Mason, Roger
1980 *Economic and social organization of an Aztec provincial center: Archaeological research at Coatlan Viejo, Morelos, Mexico*. Ph..D. Dissertation, Department of Anthropology, University of Texas at Austin.

Masson, Marilyn A.
2002 Postclassic Maya community economy and the mercantile transformation in Northeastern Belize. *In* Ancient Maya political economies. M.A. Masson and D.A. Freidel, eds. Pp. 335–359. Walnut Creek, CA: Altamira.

Mellor, John W., and Sarah Gavian
1987 Famine: causes, prevention, and relief. Science 235:539–36.

Mintz, Sidney W.
1985 Sweetness and power. New York: Penguin.

Nash, June, ed.
1993 *Crafts in the world market*. Albany: State University of New York Press.

Netting, Robert
1993 Smallholders, Householders: Farm Families and the Ecology of Intensive, Sustainable Agriculture. Stanford: Stanford University Press.

Nichols, Deborah L.
1994 The organization of provincial craft production and the Aztec city-state of Otumba. *In* Economies and Polities in the Aztec Realm. M. Hodge and M. Smith, eds. Pp. 175–193. Albany: State University of New York, Institute for Mesoamerican Studies.

Nichols, Deborah L., and Charles D. Frederick
1993 Irrigation Canals and Chinampas: Recent Research in the Northern Basin of Mexico. Research in Economic Anthropology, Suppl. 7, pp. 123–150.

Otis Charlton, Cynthia
1993 Obsidian as Jewelry: Lapidary Production in Aztec Otumba, Mexico. Ancient Mesoamerica 4:231–243.

Parsons, Jeffrey R., and Mary H. Parsons
1990 Maguey Utilization in Highland Central Mexico. Ann Arbor: University of Michigan, Museum of Anthropology, Anthropological Papers, 82.
1996 Tequesquite and Ahuauhtle: Rethinking the Prehispanic Productivity of Lake Texcoco-Xaltocan-Zumpango. *In* Arqueología Mesoamericana: Homenaje a William T. Sanders. A. Mastache, J. Parsons, R. Santley, and M.C. Serra Puche, eds. Pp. 439–459. Mexico City: Instituto Nacional de Antropología e Historia.

Pasztory, Esther
1997 Teotihuacan: An Experiment in Living. Norman: University of Oklahoma Press.

Potter, David R., and Eleanor M. King
1995 A Heterarchical Approach to Lowland Maya Socioeconomics. *In* Heterarchy and the Analysis of Complex Societies. R. Ehrenreich, C. Crumley, and J. Levy, eds. Pp. 17–32. Arlington, VA: American Anthropological Association, Archaeological Papers, 6.

Rice, Prudence M.
1987 Economic Change in the Lowland Maya Late Classic Period. *In* Specialization, Exchange, and Complex Society. E. Brumfiel and T. Earle, eds. Pp. 76–85. Cambridge: Cambridge University Press.

Robin, Cynthia
2002 Gender and Maya Farming: Chan Nòohol, Belize. *In* Ancient Maya women. T. Ardren, ed. Pp. 12–30. Walnut Creek, CA.: Altamira.

Sahagún, Bernardino de
1950–82 Florentine Codex. A. Anderson and C. Dibble, trans. 13 vols. Santa Fe and Salt Lake City: School of American Research and The University of Utah.

Sahlins, Marshall
1972 Stone Age Economics. Chicago: Aldine.

Sanders, William T.
2008 Tenochtitlan in 1519: A Pre-Industrial Megalopolis. *In* The Aztec World. E. Brumfiel and G. Feinman, eds. Pp. 67–85. New York: Abrams.

Schaefer, Stacy B.
2002 To Think with a Tood Heart: Wixárida Women, Weavers, and Shamans. Salt Lake City: University of Utah Press.

Sharp, Richard L.
1952 Steel axes for stone-age Australians. Human Organization 11:17–22.

Sheehy, James J.
1992 Ceramic Production in Ancient Teotihuacan, Mexico: A Case Study of Tlajinga 33. Ph.D. dissertation, Department of Anthropology, Pennsylvania State University.

Sheets, Payson D.
2000 Provisioning the Ceren Household. Ancient Mesoamerica 11:217–230.

Smith, Adam
1937 [1776] The Wealth of Nations. New York: Modern Library.

Smith, Michael E.
1987 Household Possessions and Wealth in Agrarian States: Implications for Archaeology. Journal of Anthropological Archaeology 6:297–335.

Smith, Michael E., and Cynthia Heath-Smith
1994 Rural Economy in Late Postclassic Morelos. *In* Economies and Polities in the Aztec Realm. M. Hodge and M. Smith, eds. Pp. 349–376. Albany: State University of New York, Institute for Mesoamerican Studies.

Sofaer Derevenski, Joanna, ed.
2000 Children and Material Culture. London: Routledge.

Spence, Michael W.
1985 Specialized Production in Rural Aztec Society: Obsidian Workshops of the Teotihuacan Valley. *In* Contributions to the Archaeology and Ethnohistory of Greater Mesoamerica. W. Folan, ed. Pp. 76–125. Carbondale: Southern Illinois University Press.

Stark, Barbara L.
1992 Ceramic Production in La Mixtequilla, Ve-

racurz, Mexico. *In* Ceramic Production and Distribution. G. Bey and C. Pool, eds. Pp. 175–204. Boulder: Westview.
2007 Diachronic Change in Crafts and Centers in South-Central Veracruz, Mexico. *In* Craft Production in Complex Societies. I. Shimada, ed. Pp. 227–261. Salt Lake City: University of Utah Press.

Stark, Barbara L., Lynette Heller, and Michael A. Ohnersorgen
1998 People with Cloth: Mesoamerican Economic Change from the Perspective of Cotton in South-Central Veracruz. Latin American Antiquity 9:1–30.

Stolmaker, Charlotte
1996 Cultural, Social and Economic Change in Santa María Atzompa in the late 1960's. Nashville: Vanderbilt University Publications in Anthropology, No. 49.

Sullivan, Kristin S.
2005 Specialized Production of San Martín Orange Ceramics in the Tlajinga District of Classic Period Teotihuacan, Mexico. Latin American Antiquity 16:23–54.

Tanner, Adrian
1979 Bringing Home Animals. St. John's: Memorial University of Newfoundland, Institute of Social and Economic Research.

Wiessner, Polly
1982 Risk, Reciprocity and Social Influences in !Kung San Economics. *In* Politics and History in Band Society. E. Leacock and R. Lee, eds. Pp. 61–84. Cambridge: Cambridge University Press.

Wilk, Richard R.
1989 The Household Economy: Reconsidering the Domestic Mode of Production. Boulder, CO: Westview Press.
1997 Household Ecology: Economic Change and Domestic Life Among the Kekchi Maya in Belize. Dekalb, IL: Northern Illinois University Press.

Wolf, Eric R.
1966 Peasants. Englewood Cliffs, NJ: Prentice-Hall.

List of Contributors

About the Editor

Kenneth Hirth is a Professor of Anthropology at Penn State University. His primary research interest is in the development of socio-economic complexity, markets and craft production in ancient society. He has conducted long term field investigations at the site of Xochicalco, Mexico in addition to archaeological explorations in Honduras, Peru, and Turkey. He is currently investigating the structure of merchant commerce in prehispanic Mesoamerica.

The cover illustration is an original drawing by Eric Carlson entitled: A Reconstruction of Obsidian Blade Manufacture at Xochicalco, Mexico.

Andrew K. Balkansky
Department of Anthropology
Southern Illinois University Carbondale
Carbondale, Illinois 62901-4502
abalkan@siu.edu

Frances Berdan
Department of Anthropology
California State University San Bernardino
San Bernardino, California 92407
fberdan@csusb.edu

Elizabeth Brumfiel
Department of Anthropology
1810 Hinman Avenue
Northwestern University
Evanston, Illinois 60208-1310
ebrumfiel@northwestern.edu

Eric Carlson (Cover Artist)
232 N. 1st St. Missoula, Montana 59802
esccarlson@yahoo.com

Ronald Castanzo
Department of Anthropology
University of Baltimore
Baltimore, Maryland
castanzor@yahoo.com

Michelle M. Croissier
Department of Anthropology
Southern Illinois University Carbondale,
Carbondale, Illinois 62901-4502
mcroiss@siu.edu

Veronique, Darras
UMR 8096 Archeologie des Ameriques
CNRS Nanterre
Veronique.darras@mae.u-paris10.fr

Jason P. De León
Department of Anthropology
University of Washington
Seattle, Washington
jasonpatrickdeleon@gmail.com

Kenneth Hirth
Department of Anthropology
409 Carpenter Building
Penn State University
University Park, Pennsylvania 16802
kgh2@psu.edu

Jesus Carlos Lascanco Arce
Instituto de Investigaciones Antropologicas
Universidad Nacional Autonoma de Mexico
lascanoarce@excite.com

Blanca Maldonado
Centro de Estudios Arqueológicos
El Colegio de Michoacan, A.C., Extension La Piedad
Cerro de Nahuatzen 85, Fracc. Jardines del Cerro Grande
59379 La Piedad, Michoacan, Mexico
Tel./Fax (352) 525 8341 al 43, Ext. 2312
bem171@gmail.com

Deborah Nichols
Department of Anthropology
408 Silsby Hall HB 6047
Dartmouth College
Hanover, New Hampshire 03755-3547
Deborah.L.Nichols@Dartmouth.edu

Christopher Pool
Department of Anthropology
University of Kentucky
Lexington, Kentucky
cpool0@uky.edu

Erick Rochette
Department of Anthropology
409 Carpenter Building
Penn State University
University Park, Pennsylvania 16802
etr109@psu.edu

Jeffrey Sahagún
Department of Anthropology
California State University San Bernardino
San Bernardino, California 92407
92407.archaeojeff@hotmail.com

Mari Carmen Serra Puche
Instituto de Investigaciones Antropologicas
Universidad Nacional Autonoma de Mexico
mcserra@servidor.unam.mx

Edward Stark
Redlands East Valley High School
Redlands, California 92374
edstar_28@yahoo.com

Carl Wendt
Department of Anthropology
California State University Fullerton
Fullerton, California
cwendt@exchange.Fullerton.edu

Randolf Widmer
Department of Anthropology
University of Houston
Houston, Texas
rwidmer@uh.edu